6/05

THE LETTERS OF
EDGAR ALLAN POE

LONDON : GEOFFREY CUMBERLEGE

OXFORD UNIVERSITY PRESS

THE LETTERS OF
Edgar Allan Poe

EDITED BY
JOHN WARD OSTROM

II

HARVARD UNIVERSITY PRESS
CAMBRIDGE, MASSACHUSETTS
1948

MANUFACTURED BY NORWOOD PRESS
NORWOOD, MASSACHUSETTS, U.S.A.

CONTENTS

VOLUME TWO

ILLUSTRATIONS

VOLUME TWO

VIII

THE IMMEMORIAL YEAR

January 1846–January 1847

New-York: Jan^y — 3. 46.
85 Amity St.

Chas. G. Percival Esqr

Dr Sir,

A few moments of leisure leave me at liberty to look at the cypher which you have done me the honor of submitting to my inspection. It is an illegitimate cryptograph — that is to say, the chances are, that, even *with* the key, it would be insoluble by the authorized correspondent. Upon analysis, however, independent of the key-solution, I find the translation to be the 3 first verses of the 2d chapter of St John.

Very Resp^y
Yr. Ob. S^t

Edgar A Poe

I should be happy to hear from you in reply.

No further correspondence between Poe and Percival is known. Percival lived in Utica, New York. [CL 605]

[New York] Jan 8. 46

Dear Mr Duyckinck,

For "particular reasons" I am anxious to have another volume of my Tales published before the 1rst of March. Do you not think it possible to accomplish it for me? Would not Mr. Wiley give me, say $50, in full for the copyright of the collection I now send. It is a far better one than the first — containing, for instance, "Ligeia", which is undoubtedly the best story I have written — besides "Sheherazade", "The Spectacles", "Tarr and Fether," etc.

May I beg of you to give me an early answer, by note, addressed 85 Amity St.

Truly yours

E. A. Duyckinck Esqʳ Edgar A Poe

Poe's "reasons," besides financial, undoubtedly had to do with his re-newed interest in launching the *Stylus* (see Letter 225). Duyckinck had edited the *Tales* (1845) and omitted some of Poe's best stories, including "Ligeia" (see Letter 241; also Quinn, *Poe*, p. 466). No reply to this letter is known; and no second edition appeared. [CL 607]

224 ⤷ TO FITZ-GREENE HALLECK

My Dear Mr Halleck,

Miss Lynch desires me to say to you that she would be *very* much pleased to see you to-night. Miss Sedgwick, Cassius M. Clay, and some other notabilities will be present.

Truly yours

Saturday Jan. 10 [1846] Edgar A Poe

Catherine M. Sedgwick was a writer favorably reviewed by Poe in "The Literati," *Godey's*, September 1846 (reprinted in H, xv, 108–113). Cassius M. Clay was an abolitionist editor from Lexington, Kentucky. Anne C. Lynch, who lived at 116 Waverly Place, not far from Washington Square, was often hostess to literary meetings attended by the New York and visiting Blue Stockings. Poe was a frequent visitor (see Quinn, *Poe*, pp. 475–476). [CL 609]

224a ⤷ TO CHARLES EDWARDS LESTER

Saturday Jan. 10. [1846]

My Dear Sir,

Miss Lynch desires me to say to you that she would be especially pleased to see you at 116 Waverley Place, this evening. Miss Sedgwick, Cassius M. Clay, and some other notabilities will be present.

Very truly yours

C. Edwards Lester Esqr Edgar A Poe.

Charles Edwards Lester (1815–1890) was a Presbyterian minister and a staunch anti-slavery exponent. He was the author of numerous books and under President Polk served as Consul at Genoa and as Secretary of the Treasury (*Dictionary of American Biography*, XI, 189–190). For Anne C. Lynch, Miss Sedgwick, and Clay, see Letter 224 and note. [CL 610a]

225 ➤ TO SARAH J. HALE

New-York — Jan 16 — 46.

My Dear Madam,

I am afraid you have already found me guilty of gross discourtesy in failing to reply to your letter of Nov 14 — but I have postponed writing from day to day, and from week to week, in hope of being able to say something definite in regard to what you ask me concerning Wiley and Putnam — and I have, also, been in expectation of seeing you in New-York. I trust you have not quite abandoned the idea of paying us a visit.

Immediately upon receipt of "Ormond Grosvenor" I gave it a second careful reading — I had already seen it in "The Lady's Book" — and became confirmed in my first impression of its remarkable vigor and dramaticism. I not only think highly of this individual play, but I deduce from some passages of it — especially towards its *dénouement* — that, with earnest endeavor in this walk of Literature, you would succeed far better than any American in the composition of that rare work of art, an effective *acting* play. At the same time I must not forbear saying that a curtailment of some of the mere dialogue of [*page 2*] "Ormond Grosvenor" would, in my opinion, tend to its improvement.

In our literary circles here your "Alice Ray" is universally appreciated and admired.

For "Harry Guy" I should prefer the subtitle of "A Tale in Verse" to that of "A Tale in Rhyme" — although there is little choice. I think Clark & Austin or Paine & Burgess would be more willing to publish it, and afford you more liberal terms, than Wiley & Putnam — although, in point of caste, the latter are to be preferred, and their issues are sure of *some* notice in England.

I believe that, as yet, I have not even had the courtesy to thank you for your sweet lines from "The Sabbath and its Rest." Upon the principle of "better late than never" will you permit me to thank you, *very* sincerely, now?

Should I visit Philadelphia, at any time, I shall undoubtedly do myself the honor of calling on you.

> In the meantime I am With the Highest respect
> Your Ob. St.

Mrs S. J. Hale.   Edgar A Poe

[*page 3*] P.S. — I send the play, with this note, by Harden's express.

The B. Journal had fulfilled its destiny — which was a matter of no great moment. I have never regarded it as more than a temporary adjunct to other designs. I am now busy making arrangements for the establishment of a Magazine which offers a wide field for literary ambition. Professor Chas. Anthon has agreed to take charge for me of a Department of Criticism on Scholastic Letters. His name will be announced. I shall have, also, a Berlin and a Parisian correspondent — both of eminence. The first No. may not appear until Jan. 1847.

> *Ormond Grosvenor,* a tragedy, was published in 1838 (see *Appleton's Cyclopedia of American Biography* (1888), III, 35); *Alice Ray,* a romance in rhyme, was published in Philadelphia, 1845 (a copy is in the Library of Congress). Poe reviewed it in the *Broadway Journal,* November 1, 1845 (see H, XII, 259–262); and *Harry Guy* was published in 1848 (see *Appleton's, ibid.*). At the time of the present letter, Mrs. Hale was the editor of *Godey's.* In the *Broadway Journal,* January 3, 1846, Poe wrote: "Unexpected engagements demanding my whole attention, and the objects being fulfilled, so far as regards myself personally, for which 'The Broadway Journal' was established, I now, as its Editor, bid farewell — as cordially to foes as to friends" (see Quinn, *Poe,* p. 494). Poe's hope of establishing the *Stylus* was still but a hope, though his optimism was evidenced in various letters to friends at this time. No letters exist corroborating Poe's statements about Professor Anthon and the foreign correspondents. [CL 611]

226 ➤ TO [EVERT A. DUYCKINCK?]

[New York]

[. . . . .]

Have you any personal acquaintance with Carey (John Waters)? If so will you be kind enough to note me, in brief, a few memoranda resp^g his personal appearance, age, residence etc? — the same about W. A. Jones. Is Herbert living in N. Y? — if so, where? Where does Hoffman live? in what street I mean. Do you know where Hoyt & Hunt live? — or Inman — or Mancur — or Gen. Morris — or O'Sullivan — or Paulding — or Prof. Robinson of the Un^y or Verplanck — or Tuckerman. Do you know Stephens the traveller so as to describe him? Please describe Schoolcraft & tell me where he lives — and Cheever, if you can. A very few words ab^t each will suffice.

Have you seen Tupper's notice of my Tales yet? if so — how is it? long or short — sweet or sour? — if you have it, please lend it me.

I send this note by Mrs C. Should she not see you, can't you contrive to step in at 85 Amity St — some time to-day or to-morrow?

Truly Yours

Jan 30. [1846]   Poe.

Poe's present queries suggest preparation for his "Literati" papers, published in *Godey's*, May–October 1846. [CL 612]

227 ⇀ TO PHILIP P. COOKE

New-York — April 16 — 42. [1846]

My Dear Sir,

Your three last letters reached me day before yesterday, all at once. I have been living in the country for the last two months (haing been quite sick) and all letters addressed to 85 Amity St. were very sillily retained there, until their accumulation induced the people to send them to the P. Office. When you write again address me, at large, N. Y. I fully agree with you (and a little to boot) about Minor. He is the King of Donkey-dom. Your "Power of the Bards" is glorious. I have sent it to Colton, who will be delighted with it — I mean Colton of the "American Review." Not being yet able to leave my room I sent, also, your "Turkey-Hunter" to Porter, with a note, speaking of you as I have always spoken. I enclose you his reply. I retain the MSS. Tell me what I shall do with them. You ask for information about the usual pay of the Magazines. A definite

answer is impossible. They graduate their pay by mere whim —
apparent popularity — or *their own* opinion of merit. Real merit
is rather *no* recommendation. For my last two contributions to
"Graham" — 5 pp. of "Marginalia" and 4 pp "Philosophy of Composition" (have you seen this latter?) I received $50 — about 8 per
page. I furnish Godey regular papers (one each month) at $5 per
page. The $5 Magazines do not pay quite so well and are by no
means so prompt. Colton gives me $3 per page and the Dem.
Review $2 — but I seldom send anything to the latter. "Arthur's
Magazine" gave me, not long ago, $10 a page for a paper "The
Sphynx" — but the pay is no pay for the degradation. What others
get from the Magazines I can scarcely say — although I know that
Willis and Longfellow have been liberally paid — liberally as times
go & as publishers think. When your book comes out, I fancy that
it will make a stir in England — and enable you to do *well* in letters —
pecuniarily well. You will yet have Fame & get it easily. Money
follows at its heels, as a matter of course. Griswold is quite right
about the externals of your book. Never commit yourself as a
pamphleteer. — I am now writing for Godey a series of articles called
"The N. Y. City Literati". They will run through the year & include
personal descriptions, as well as frank opinions of literary merit.
Pending the issue of this series, I am getting ready similar papers
to include American littérateurs generally — and, by the beginning
of December, I hope to put to press (here and in England) a volume
embracing *all* the articles under the common head "The Living
Literati of the U S." — or something similar. Of course I wish to say
something [*page 2*] of yourself. What shall I quote? "Rosalie Lee"
I have not. Would it put you to much trouble to copy it for me?
Give me, also, (if you think it right) some account of your literary
projects — purposes etc. — The volume is to be prefaced by some
general remarks on our Literature and pre-prefaced by the Memoir
of myself, by Lowell, which appeared in Graham's Mag. for February
1845. This Memoir, however, is defective, inasmuch as it says nothing of my latest & I think my best things — "The Raven" (for
instance), "The Valdemar Case", etc. May I ask of you the great
favor to add a P.S. to Lowell's article — bringing up affairs as you
well know how. I ask this of you — what I would ask of no other
man — because I fancy that you appreciate me — estimate my
merits & demerits at a just value. If you are willing to oblige me —

speak frankly above all — speak of my *faults,* too, as forcibly as you can. The length of the P.S. I leave to yourself.

Very cordially yours

Edgar A Poe

P.S. I cannot lay my hand on Porter's note. The substance of it, however, was — that he had read the article with great pleasure but as the "present publisher of the Spirit of the T" could not *pay,* he was forced reluctantly to return the M.S.

> Poe seemingly left 85 Amity Street after January 30, 1846 (the last known letter citing that address) and moved to Turtle Bay, now the foot of 47th Street, then to Fordham (see Quinn, *Poe,* p. 506). William T. Porter was editor and publisher of the *Spirit of the Times* (New York), an "all-round sporting journal" (Mott, *History of American Magazines,* I, 480, 801). Poe's recital of payment for contributions should be compared with references in Letter 187 and elsewhere in the general correspondence; his figures here seem rather exaggerated. For the "Literati" articles, see Letter 241 and note. For Cooke's "Memoir" of Poe, herein asked for, see the note to Letter 240. [CL 621]

228 ⇥ TO GEORGE W. EVELETH

New-York — April 16. 46.

My Dear Sir,

You seem to take matters very easily and I really wonder at your patience under the circumstances. But the truth is I am in no degree to blame[.] Your letters, one and all, reached me in due course of mail — and I attended to them, *as far as I could.*

The business, in fact, was none of mine but of the person to whom I transferred the Journal and in whose hands it perished.

Of course, I feel no less in honor bound to refund you your money, and now do so, with many thanks for your promptness & courtesy.

Very cordially yours

G. W. Evelett Esqr   Edgar A Poe

> Eveleth's first letters concerned a subscription fee sent for the *Broadway Journal.* Poe sold a one-half interest in the magazine to Thomas H. Lane, December 3, 1845, Poe retaining editorial charge (see Quinn, *Poe,* p. 492). Poe wrote his valedictory in the issue dated January 3, 1846. [CL 622]

229 ✣ TO EVERT A. DUYCKINCK

[New York] April 28. [1846]

Dear Duyckinck,

Mrs C. tells me that you had some conversation with her about Keese and myself — and I have thought it best to enclose you my letter to him. May I ask of you the favor to look it over and then seal it and send it to him? — unless you have anything to suggest — in which case please do not send it until you can communicate with me.

I enclose, also, a letter from the Lit. Societies of the Vermont University. My object is to ask you to get inserted, editorially, in the "Morning News", or some other paper, a paragraph to this effect: — or something similar.

EDGAR A. POE. — By a concurrent vote of the Literary Societies of the University of Vermont. Mr Poe has been elected Poet for their ensuing Anniversary in August next — but we are sorry to hear that continued ill health, with a pressure of engagements, will force him to decline the office.

Please preserve the letter of the Societies.

It strikes me that, some time ago, Wiley & Putnam advertised for autographs of distinguished Amer. statesmen. Is it so? I have well-preserved letters from John Randolph, Chief Justice Marshall, Madison, Adams, Wirt, Duane, E. Everett, Clay, Cass, Calhoun and some others — and I would exchange them for books.

Truly Yours

E A Poe (over[ ])

[*page 2*] Can either you or Mathews furnish me with autographs of any of the following persons? Cheever — Cary — Cranch — Francis — Mrs Stephens — Clark — Verplanck — Aldrich — Maroncelli — Wetmore — Fay — Greeley — Godwin — J. Willis — Maturin — Deming — Mrs Smith — Raymond — Headley — Brownlee — Kent — Ward — Tellkampf — S. Smith — Mrs Child — G. Spring — Jno. Stephens — Cooley — Mancur — King — T. Irving — Inman — Jones — Tuckerman — Mrs Godwin — Gallatin — Harring — J. Sargent — Prof. Robinso[n] — Channing — Lewis — Schoolcraft — Dewey — Brisbane — Tasistro.

What Duyckinck told Mrs. Clemm probably inspired Poe's letter to John Keese (unlocated), which, if sent, probably bore the date of April 28, 1846. The letter from the "Literary Societies" (unlocated) possibly belongs to April 1846, also, and would suggest a reply from Poe, though he may have felt that the newspaper paragraph would suffice. Poe possessed the autographs of some, if not all, of the statesmen named: those of John Marshall, John Quincy Adams, William Wirt, Edward Everett, and Lewis Cass appeared in his "*Autography*"; for the signature of William Duane, he had Duane's letter of October 15, 1844 (see Letter 184). Poe's request for autographs was undoubtedly in connection with his preparation of the "Literati" papers, which appeared in *Godey's*, May–October 1846; the first ten in the list given in the letter and Mrs. Child were discussed in the series. Though autographs were not printed in the articles, Poe apparently used them for character-reading. Whether Duyckinck or Cornelius Mathews supplied any of the requested autographs is unknown. [CL 628]

230 ⊁ TO JEROME A: MAUBEY

New-York   April 28.   46.

Dear Sir,

You have, evidently, supposed me editor of "Godey's Magazine" and sent me the poem (a very beautiful one) under that supposition. It has been returned to me from Phil^d I am not connected, at present, with any journal in which I could avail myself of your talents —

Truly your

E A Poe

The poem referred to here is "The Toilette," by Jerome Maubey (see Note 230). [CL 629]

231 ⊁ TO T. HONLAND

New York, May 25, 1846

Dr Sir,

It gives me great pleasure to comply with your very flattering request for an autograph.

Respy Yr Mo Ob St

Edgar Allan Poe

The identity of Honland is unknown. [CL 632]

232 ⇀ TO VIRGINIA POE

June. 12th — 1846   [New York]

My Dear Heart, My dear Virginia! our Mother will explain to you why I stay away from you this night. I trust the interview I am promised, will result in some *substantial good* for me, for your dear sake, and hers — Keep up your heart in all hopefulness, and trust yet a little longer — In my last great disappontment, I should have lost my courage *but for you* — my little darling wife you are my *greatest* and *only* stimulus now. to battle with this uncongenial, unsatisfactory and ungrateful life — I shall be with you tomorrow P.M. and be assured until I see you, I will keep in *loving remembrance* your *last words* and your fervant prayer!

Sleep well and may God grant you a peaceful summer, with your devoted

Edgar

This is the only letter Poe is known to have written to his wife (but see Letter 48, and Letter 141). Mrs. Houghton, however, wrote Ingram, January 23, 1875 (original in Ingram collection), that Poe wrote numerous "notes" to Virginia; she says that she does not have them, but she knows they were written. The circumstances surrounding the "interview" mentioned by Poe are unknown. [CL 635]

233 ⇀ TO JOSEPH M. FIELD

(Confidential)

New-York : June 15. 46.

Dear Field,

I have frequently seen in "The Reveillé" notices of myself, evincing a kindly feeling on your part which, believe me, I reciprocate in the most cordial manner. This conviction of your friendship induces me now to beg a favor of you. I enclose an article from "The New-York Mirror" of May 26 th. headed "Mr Poe and the N. Y. Literati". The attack is editorial & the editor is Hiram Fuller. He was a schoolmaster, about 3 years ago, in Providence, and was forced to leave that city on account of several swindling transactions in which he was found out. As soon as Willis & Morris discovered the facts, they abandoned "The Mirror", perferring to leave it in his hands rather than keep up so disreputable a connexion. This Fuller ran off with the daughter of a respectable gentleman in this city & was married. The father met the couple in the Park theatre (the Park, I think) and was so carried away by indignation at the disgrace inflicted upon his family by the marriage, that he actually struck Mrs Fuller repeated blows in the face with his clenched fist — the husband looking calmly on, and not even attempting to interfere. I pledge you the honor of a gentleman that I have not exaggerated these facts in the slightest degree. They are here notorious.

All that I venture to ask of you in the case of this attack, however, is to say a few words in condemnation of it, and to do away with the false impression of my personal appearance* it *may* convey, in those parts of the country where I am not individually known. You have seen me and can describe me as I am. Will you do me this act of justice, and influence one or two of your editorial friends to do the same? *I know you will.*

[*] I am 33 years of age — height 5 ft. 8.   (over)

[*page 2*] I think the "N. O. Picayune", which has always been friendly to me, will act in concert with you.

There is, also, an incidental service of great importance, just now, which you have it in your power to render me. That is, to put the following, editorially, in your paper:

<The British literary journals are admitting Mr Poe's merits, in the most unequivocal manner>. A long and highly laudatory review of his Tales, written by *Martin Farquhar Tupper,* author of "Proverbial Philosophy", "The Crock of Gold" etc., appeared in a late number of "The London Literary Gazette". "The Athenaeum," "The British Critic,["] "The Spectator", "The Popular Record" "Churton's Literary Register", and various other journals, scientific as well as literary, have united in approbation of Tales & Poems. "The Raven" is copied in full in the "British Critic" and "The Athenaeum". "The Times" — the matter of fact *"Times!"* — copies the "Valdemar Case". The world's greatest poetess, *Elizabeth Barrett Barrett,* says of Mr Poe: — "This *vivid* writing! — this power *which is felt!* 'The Raven' has produced a *sensation* — a 'fit horror' — here in England. Some of my friends are taken by the yias of it and some by the music — but all are taken. I hear of persons absolutely *haunted* by the 'Nevermore', and one acquaintance of mine who has the misfortune of possessing a 'bust of Pallas' never can bear to look at it in the twi-

light. Our great poet, Mr Browning, the author of 'Paracelsus', 'The Pomegranates' etc. is enthusiastic in his admiration of the rhythm."

After all this, Mr Poe may possibly make up his mind to endure the disapprobation of <one Hiram Fuller> the editor of the *Mirror*. <and other>.

Miss Barrett continues: — "Then there is a tale of his which I do not find in this volume, but which is going the rounds of the newspapers, about Mesmerism (The Valde- [*page 3*] mar case) throwing us all into 'most admired disorder', or dreadful doubts as to 'whether it can be true'. . . . The *certain* thing in the tale in question is the *power* of the writer and the faculty he has of making horrible improbabilities seem near & familiar."

If you can oblige me in this case, you may depend on my most earnest reciprocation when where & how you please.

Cordially yours

Edgar A Poe.

P.S. Please *cut out* anything you may say and en[close i]t to me in a letter. A newspaper wil[l] not be [li]kely to reach me.

I have been very seriously ill for some months * and, being thus utterly unable to defend myself, must rely upon the chivalry of my friends. Fuller knows of my illness & <reli> depends upon it for his security. I have never said a word about the vagabond in my life. Some person, I presume, has hired him to abuse me.

* — am now scarcely able to write even this letter —

When Wiley and Putnam, probably in February 1846, published as a compound book Poe's *Raven and Other Poems* (first published in November 1845) and his *Tales* (first published in June 1845), Poe sent his dedication copy to Elizabeth Barrett Barrett; she received it on March 20, 1846 (see Mabbott's edition of *The Raven and Other Poems*, xvi–xviii). This compound book was made from sheets from the earlier printings, and did not include "The Facts in the Case of M. Valdemar," which was first published in the *American Review*, II (December 1845), 561–565 (see Wyllie, *Poe's Tales*, p. 326). Poe quotes to Field passages from Miss Barrett's letter, dated April 1846 (original in New York Public Library), but he takes certain liberties with her original passage, though he does not materially change her meaning. Regarding Poe's statement, . . . seriously ill for some months," one should note his remark to Eveleth, December 15, 1846, "For more than six months, I have been ill — for the greater part of that time, dangerously so, and quite unable to write even an ordinary letter." Neither statement, of course, should be taken literally. To be noticed, also, is Poe's reiteration of his age as four years younger than it was, and, therefore, his adherence to his birth date as 1813, as given to Griswold in Letter 317. [CL 636]

234 ⇥ TO ——————

[New York] June 16, 1846

My Dear Sir,

Can you oblige me by getting the following in "The Tribune" or some other daily?

Mr. Poe has been invited by the Literary Societies of Dickinson College, Carlisle, Pa. to deliver a poem at their approaching anniversary, but this invitation, as well as that of the University of Vermont, he is forced to decline through continued illness and a press of other engagements.

Who is the "great writer of small things in Ann St" referred to by Briggs in the article about me in the Mirror, of the 26? Has anything concerning me appeared lately in Morris' "National Press"?

Truly yours,

Poe

Poe's request is similar to that expressed in Letter 229 to Duyckinck, and the present letter may have been addressed to Duyckinck, who probably could have provided the answers to the questions; but it seems incredible that Poe himself would not have known the "great writer of . . . Ann Street," probably Willis, former editor of the *Evening Mirror* and author of such inconsequentials as "Trifles" and "Slipshoddities." In the present letter Poe identifies Charles F. Briggs as the writer of the article in the *Mirror* (see also Letter 233). Both N. P. Willis and George P. Morris, former editors of the *Mirror*, were friendly toward Poe. Morris' *National Press*, begun in 1846, later became the *Home Journal* (see Mott, *History of American Magazines*, I, 330). [CL 638]

235 ⇥ TO HENRY B. HIRST

New : York — June 27. 46.

My Dear Hirst,

I presume you have seen what I said about you in "The New-York Literati" and an attack made on me by English, in consequence. *Vive la Bagatelle!*

I write now, to ask you if you can oblige me by a fair account of your duel with English. I would take it as a great favor, also, if you would get from Sandy Harris a statement of the fracas with *him*. See Du Solle, also, if you can & ask him if he is willing to give me, for publication, an account of his kicking E. out of his office.

I gave E. a flogging which he will remember to the day of his death — and, luckily, in the presence of witnesses. He thinks to avenge himself by lies — by I shall be a match for him by means of simple truth.

Is it possible to procure me a copy of E's attack on H. A. Wise?

Truly yours,

Poe.

Henry Beck Hirst was a young poet of Philadelphia and had written, probably with Poe's aid, the biographical sketch of Poe that appeared in the Philadelphia Saturday Museum, March 4, 1843; he also wrote a defense of Poe in McMakin's *Model American Courier*, XIX (Saturday, October 20, 1849), 2 (see Quinn, *Poe*, p. 653). In his "Literati" article in *Godey's*, XXXIII (July 1846), 17–18, out soon after June 15, Poe attacked Thomas Dunn English, who replied in the *Evening Mirror*, June 23, 1846 (see Quinn, *Poe*, pp. 503–504). In the fall of 1845 Poe and English had been on friendly terms (see Mabbott, *The Raven and Other Poems*, p. xxviii). For references to names in this letter, see Poe's "Reply to English" in the *Spirit of the Times*, July 10, 1846 (reprinted in H, XVII, 239–247). The nature and outcome of the "flogging" mentioned by Poe cannot at present be determined, both Poe and English having their defenders; the evidence for either side is still too tenuous. Though Poe letters "found in trunks and pillow-cases" are frequently forgeries, the above letter (found in a pillowcase, according to a comment in the *Current Opinion*, cited in Note 235) is genuine. At the sale of the present letter an auctioneer told Thomas O. Mabbott that the various MSS. came from a relative of Hirst; moreover, the MSS. themselves were of such nature as to exclude the possibility of forgery. There is no extant reply by Hirst to Poe's queries; however, Poe's published "Reply to English," in the *Spirit of the Times*, suggests either that Hirst sent data or that Poe wrote the article, which is also dated June 27, using details as he knew them with the expectation of later corroboration. If Hirst replied and sent the information Poe probably incorporated it, but did not change the date at the head of the "Reply to English," which in that case must have been begun on June 27 (see Letter 237). [CL 640]

236 ➤ TO EVERT A. DUYCKINCK

[New York] Monday 29. [June, 1846]

My Dear Mr Duyckinck,

I am about to send the "Reply to English" (accompanying this note) to Mr Godey — but feel anxious that some friend should read it before it goes. Will you be kind enough to look it over & show it to Mathews? Mrs C. will then take it to Harden. The *particulars* of the reply I would not wish mentioned to *any* one — of course you see the necessity of this.

The no of Littell's Age cont^g the notice, is 106 — so he writes me.

Most truly yours

Poe

Cornelius Mathews was a friend of both Duyckinck and Poe. Mrs. Clemm often carried notes for Poe. Harnden's Express was a public carrier. Reference to the notice of Poe's *Tales* (1845) in Littell's *Living Age* indicates a letter from Littell (unlocated) and suggests one from Poe (also unlocated), since Littell edited the magazine in Boston. [CL 643]

237 ➤ TO LOUIS A. GODEY

New-York: July 16. 46.

My Dear Sir,

I regret that you published my Reply in "The Times". I should have found no difficulty in getting it printed here, in a *respectable* paper, and gratis. However — as I have the game in my own hands, I shall not stop to complain about trifles.

I am rather ashamed that, knowing me to be as poor as I am, you should have thought it advisable to make the demand *on me* of the $10. I confess that I thought better of you — but let it go — it is the way of the world.

The man, or men, who told you that there was anything wrong in *the tone* of my reply, were either my enemies, or your enemies, or asses. When you see them, tell them so from me. I have never written an article upon which I more confidently depend for *literary* reputation than that Reply. Its merit lay in being *precisely* adapted to its purpose. In this city I have had, upon it, the favorable judgments of the best men. All the error about it was yours. You should have done as I requested — published it in the "Book". It is of no use to conceive a plan if you have to depend upon another for its execution.

Please distribute 20 or 30 copies of the Reply [*page 2*] in Phil. and send me the balance through Harnden.

What paper, or papers, have copied E's attack?

I have put this matter in the hands of a competent attorney, and you shall see the result. Your charge, $10, will of course be brought before the court, as an item, when I speak of damages.

> In perfect good feeling
> Yours truly
>
> Poe.

It *would* be as well to address your letters to West Farms.

Please put *Miss Lynch* in the next number.

I enclose the Reveillé article. I presume that, ere this, you have seen the highly flattering notices of the "Picayune" and the "Charleston Courier".

The contents of Poe's letter to Duyckinck (Letter 236) suggest that Poe wrote to Godey, June 29, 1846, requesting that Godey print the "Reply to English," editorially dated June 27 (see H, XVII, 239), in the *Lady's Book*. Instead, Godey had it published in the Philadelphia *Spirit of the Times,* July 10, a sportsman's periodical, at a cost of ten dollars, and then wrote to Poe, *ca.* July 14, submitting the bill. The "competent attorney" was E. L. Fancher (see Letter 238); concerning the "damages," see the note to Letter 238. "Miss Lynch" appeared in *Godey's,* September 1846 (reprinted in H, xv, 116–118), as one of the "Literati." For identification of Miss Anne C. Lynch, see the note to Letter 224. Joseph M. Field printed in his *Daily Reveillé* (St. Louis), June 30, 1846, and in his weekly *Reveillé,* July 6, 1846, an article made up largely from Poe's letter to him of June 15 (Letter 233); the articles in the New Orleans *Picayune* and the *Charleston* (South Carolina) *Daily Courier* (at present inaccessible) may have been of a similar nature. [CL 646]

238 ⊁ TO JOHN BISCO

New-York July 17. 1846.

My Dear Mr Bisco,

You will confer a *very* great favor on me by stepping in, when you have leisure, at the office of E. L. Fancher, Attorney-at-Law, 33 John Sᵗ. Please mention to him that I requested you to call in relation to Mr English. He will, also, show you my Reply to some attacks lately made upon me by this gentleman.

Cordially yours.

Mr John Bisco.   Poe

> John Bisco, publisher of the *Broadway Journal,* had sold his interest
> to Poe in October 1845 (see several contracts between Bisco and Poe
> printed in Quinn, *Poe,* pp. 751–753). Fancher, as Poe's lawyer, prob-
> ably prosecuted the case against Fuller and Clason, editor and proprietor,
> of the *Evening Mirror* in the Superior Court of New York City, insti-
> tuted on July 23, 1846, and closed on February 17, 1847, with a ver-
> dict of $225 damages in Poe's favor (Quinn, *Poe,* p. 505). For the
> Poe–English controversy, see the note to Letter 235; also H, XVII, 233–
> 255. [CL 647]

239 ⊁ TO DR. THOMAS H. CHIVERS

New-York, July 22 / 46.

My Dear Friend,

I had long given you up (thinking that, after the fashion of numerous other *friends,* you had made up your mind to desert me at the first breath of what seemed to be trouble) when this morning I received no less than 6 letters from you, all of them addressed 195 East Broadway. Did you not know that I merely boarded at this house? It is a very long while since I left it, and as I did not leave it on very good terms with the landlady, she has given herself no concern about my letters — not one of which I should ever have received but for the circumstance of new tenants coming in to the house. I am living out of town about 13 miles, at a village called Fordham, on the rail-road leading north. We are in a snug little cot-tage, keeping house, and would be very comfortable, but that I have been for a long time dreadfully ill. I am getting better, however, although slowly, and shall get *well.* In the meantime the flocks of little birds of prey that always take the opportunity of illness to peck at a sick fowl of larger dimensions, have been endeavoring with all their power to effect my ruin. My dreadful poverty, also, has given them every advantage. In fact, my dear friend, I have been driven to the very gates of death and a despair more dreadful than death, and I had not even *one* friend, out of my family, with whom to advise. What would I not have given for the kind pressure of your hand! It is only a few days since that I requested my mother in law, Mrs Clemm, to write to you — but she put it off from day to day.

I send you, as you request, the last sheet of the "Luciferian Revelation". There are several other requests in your letters [*page 2*] which I know you would pardon me for not attending to if you only were aware of my illness, and how impossible it is for me to put my foot out of the house or indeed to help myself in any way. It is with the greatest difficulty that I write you this letter — as you may perceive, indeed, by the M.S. I have not been able to write *one line* for the Magazines for more than 5 months — you can then form some idea of the dreadful extremity to which I have been reduced. The articles lately published in "Godey's Book" were written and paid for a long while ago.

Your professions of friendship I reciprocate from the inmost depths of my heart. Except yourself I have never met the man for whom I felt that intimate *sympathy* (of intellect as well as soul) which is the sole basis of friendship. Believe me that never, for one moment, have I doubted the sincerity of your *wish* to assist me. There is not one word you say that I do not *see* coming up from the depths of your heart.

There is one thing you will be glad to learn: — It has been a long while since any artificial stimulus has passed my lips. When I see you — should that day ever come — this is a topic on which I desire to have a long talk with you. I am done forever with drink — depend upon that — but there is much more in this matter than meets the eye.

Do not let anything in this letter impress you with the belief that I *despair* even of worldly prosperity. On the contrary although I feel ill, and am ground into the very dust with poverty, there is a sweet *hope* in the bottom of my soul.

I need not say to you that I rejoice in your success with the silk. I have always conceived it to be a speculation [*page 3*] full of promise if prudently conducted. The revulsion consequent upon the silk mania has, of course, induced the great majority of mankind to look unfavorably upon the business — but such feelings should have no influence with the philosophic. Be cautious and industrious — that is all.

I enclose you a slip from the "Reveilée". You will be pleased to see how they appreciate me in England.

When you write, address simply "New-York-City". There is no Post Office at Fordham.

God Bless You.
Ever Your friend,

Edgar A Poe

P.S. I have been looking over your "Luciferian Revelation" again. There are some points at which I might dissent with you — but there a 1000 glorious thoughts in [it.]

By October 1, 1845, Poe had left 195 East Broadway and gone to 85 Amity Street (see Letter 215). According to Quinn, *Poe,* p. 506, Poe later moved to Turtle Bay, now the foot of 47th Street, and then to Fordham, by May or June; thus Chivers' letters may well have been delayed. Poe's statement that he had not written *"one line"* for the magazines is hardly true; though a number of his compositions, printed in the first half of 1846, were probably written in 1845, it would seem that the "Literati" papers were prepared in 1846 (see Letter 227; see also Letter 241 where he says, regarding the "Godey series," "I thought too little of the series myself to guard sufficiently against haste, inaccuracy, or prejudice"; also, see the "Editor's Book Table," *Godey's,* June 1846, reprinted in H, xv, viii-ix: "Mr. Poe has been ill, but we have letters from him of very recent dates; also a new batch of the *Literati"* — a statement that, despite its obvious "editorial" purpose, does suggest the recency of the papers); of course, Poe may mean that he has not written any truly literary pieces. Chivers, besides being a poet, invented "a machine for unwinding the fibre from silk cocoons" (see W, ii, 380). [CL 649]

240 ＞ TO PHILIP P. COOKE

New-York — August 9. 1846.

My Dear Sir,

Never think of excusing yourself (to me) for dilatoriness in answering letters — I know too well the unconquerable procrastination which besets the poet. I will place it all to the accounts of the turkeys. Were I to be seized by a rambling fit — one of my customary *passions* (nothing less) for vagabondizing through the woods for a week or a month together — I would not — in fact I *could* not be put out of my mood, were it even to answer a letter from the Grand Mogul, informing me that I had fallen heir to his possessions.

Thank you for the compliments. Were I in a serious humor just now, I would tell you[,] frankly, how your words of appreciation make my nerves thrill — not because you praise me (for others have praised me more lavishly) but because I feel that you comprehend and discriminate. You are right about the hair-splitting of my French friend: — that is all done for effect. These tales of ratiocination owe most of their popularity to being something in a new key. I do not mean to say that they are not ingenious — but people think them more ingenious than they are — on account of their method and *air* of method. In the "Murders in the Rue Morgue", for instance, where is the ingenuity of unravelling a web which you yourself (the author) have woven for the express purpose of unravelling? The reader is made to confound the ingenuity of the sup- [*page 2*] posititious Dupin with that of the writer of the story.

Not for the world would I have had any one else to continue Lowell's Memoir until I had heard from you. I wish *you* to do it (if you will be so kind) and nobody else. By the time the book appears you will be famous, (or all my prophecy goes for nothing) and I shall have the éclât of your name to aid my sales. But, seriously, I do not think that any one so well enters into the poetical portion of my mind as yourself — and I deduce this idea from my intense appreciation of those points of your own poetry which seem lost upon others.

Should you undertake the work for me, there is one topic — there is one particular in which I have had wrong done me — and it may not be indecorous in me to call your attention to it. The last selection of my Tales was made from about 70, by Wiley & Putnam's reader, Duyckinck. He has what he thinks a taste for ratiocination, and has accordingly made up the book mostly of analytic stories. But this is not *representing* my mind in its various phases — it is not giving me fair play. In writing these Tales one by one, at long intervals, I have kept the book-unity always in mind — that is, each has been composed with reference to its effect as part of *a whole*. In this view, one of my chief aims has been the widest diversity of subject, thought, & especially *tone* & manner of handling. Were all my tales now before me in a large volume and as the composition of another — the merit which would principally arrest my attention would be the wide *diversity and* variety. You will be surprised to hear me say that (omitting one or two of my first efforts) I do not consider any one of [*page 3*] my stories *better* than another. There is a vast variety of kinds and, in degree of value, these kinds vary — but each tale is equally good *of its kind*. The loftiest kind is that of the highest imagination — and, for this reason only, "Ligeia" may be called my *best* tale. I have much improved this last since you saw it and I mail you a copy, as well as a copy of my best specimen of analysis — "The Philosophy of Composition."

Do you ever see the British papers? Martin F. Tupper, author of "Proverbial Philosophy" has been paying me some high compliments — and indeed I have been treated more than well. There is one "British opinion", however, which I value highly — Miss Barrett's. She says: — "This vivid writing! — this power *which is felt!* The Raven has produced a sensation — 'a fit horror' here in England. Some of my friends are taken by the fear of it and some by the music. I hear of persons *haunted* by the 'Nevermore', and one acquaintance of mine who has the misfortune of possessing a 'bust of Pallas' never can bear to look at it in the twilight. . . . Our great poet Mr Browning, author of Paracelsus etc is enthusiastic in his admiration of the rhythm. . . . . Then there is a tale of his which I do not find in this volume, but which is going the rounds of the newspapers, about Mesmerism [The Valdemar Case] throwing us all into most admired disorder or dreadful doubts as to whether it can be true, as the children say of ghost stories. The certain thing in the tale in question is the power of the writer & the faculty he has of making horrible improbabilities seem near and familiar." Would it be in bad taste to quote these words of Miss B. in your notice?

Forgive these egotisms (which are rendered in [*page 4*] some measure necessary by the topic) and believe me that I will let slip *no* opportunity of reciprocating your kindness.

Griswolds new edition I have not yet seen (is it out?) but I will manage to find "Rosalie Lee". Do not forget to send me a few personal details of yourself — such as I give in "The N. Y. Literati". When your book appears I propose to review it fully in Colton's "American Review." If you ever write to him, please suggest to him that I wish to do so. I hope to get your volume before mine goes to press — so that I may speak more fully.

I will forward the papers to which I refer, *in a day or two* — not by to-day's mail.

Touching "The Stylus": — this is the one great purpose of my literary life. Undoubtedly (unless I die) I will accomplish it — but I can afford to lose nothing by precipitancy. I cannot yet say when or how I shall get to work — but when the time comes I will write to you. I wish to establish a journal in which the men of genius may fight their battles; upon some terms of equality, with those dunces the men of talent. But, apart from this, I have *magnificent* objects in view — may I but live to accomplish them!

Most cordially Your friend

Edgar A. Poe.

The first sentence alludes to Cooke's delay in answering Poe's letter of April 16, 1846. Lowell's critical "Memoir" appeared in *Graham's*, February 1845; Cooke's was published in the SLM, January 1848, and incorporated the comments of Elizabeth Barrett (reprinted in H, 1, 383–392). "By the time the book appears . . ." must refer to Poe's projected but uncompleted "Literary America" (the MS. of the title page and of three articles is now in the Huntington Library, for which, see Quinn, *Poe*, pp. 560–561). Evert A. Duyckinck chose the twelve tales that made up the *Tales* (1845), published by Wiley and Putnam; the selection omitted several of Poe's best works, including "Ligeia," which Cooke admired and criticized with understanding in his letter to Poe, September 16, 1839 (see H, xvii, 49–51). In writing his Memoir of Poe, Griswold lifted the fourth paragraph of the present letter, stated that it was to himself, and in printing it made the second sentence read: "The last selection of my tales was made from about seventy by one of our great little cliquists and claqueurs, Wiley and Putnam's reader, Duyckinck" (see H, xvii, 228). For more on Tupper, see Letter 233. Elizabeth Barrett's "opinion" came not from a British paper but from her letter to Poe, April 1846 (see H, xvii, 229); Poe "edits" the passage to suit his purpose. Griswold's *Poets and Poetry of America* was first published in 1842 and went through many editions. Cooke's *Froissart Ballads and Other Poems* was published in 1847, three years before his death (see the *Dictionary of American Biography*, iv, 388–389). Apparently Poe did not review it. [CL 654]

241 ➤ TO GEORGE W. EVELETH

New-York : Dec. 15 / 46.

My Dear Sir,

By way of beginning this letter let me say a word or two of apology for not having sooner replied to your letters of June 9 and Oct. 13. For more than six months I have been ill — for the greater part of that time dangerously so, and quite unable to write even an ordinary letter. My Magazine papers appearing in this interval were all in the publishers' hands before I was taken sick. Since getting better, I have been, as a matter of course, overwhelmed with the business accumulating during my illness.

It always gives me true pleasure to hear from you, and I wish you could spare time to write me more frequently. I am gratified by your good opinion of my writings, because what you say evinces the keenest discrimination. Ten times the praise you bestow on me would not please me half so much, were it not for the intermingled scraps of censure, or [of] objection, which show me that you well know what you are talking about.

Let me now advert to the points of your two last letters:

What you say about the blundering criticism of "the Hartford Review man" is just. For the purposes of poetry it is quite sufficient that a thing is possible — or at least that the improbability be not offensively glaring. It is true that in several ways, as you say, the lamp might have thrown the bird's shadow on the floor. *My* conception was that of the bracket candelabrum affixed against the wall, high up above the door and bust — as is often seen in the English palaces, and even in some of the better houses in New-York.

Your objection to the *tinkling* of the footfalls is far more pointed, and in the course of composition occurred so forcibly to myself that I hesitated to use the term. I finally used it because I saw that it had, in its first conception, been suggested to my mind by the sense of the *supernatural* with which it was, at the moment, filled. No human or physical foot could tinkle on a soft carpet — therefore the tinkling of feet would vividly convey the supernatural impression. This was the idea, and it is good within it- [*page 2*] self: — but if it fails (as I fear it does) to make itself immediately and generally *felt* according to my intention — then in so much is it badly con[v]eyed, or expressed. Your appreciation of "The Sleeper" delights me. In the higher qualities of poetry, it is better than "The Raven" — but there is not one man in a million who could be brought to agree with me in this opinion. The Raven, of course, is far the better as a work of art — but in the true basis of all art The Sleeper is the superior. I wrote the latter when quite a boy.

You quote, I think, the 2 *best* lines in "The Valley of Unrest" — those about the palpitating trees. There *is* no more of "Politian". It may be some years before I publish the rest of my Tales, essays &c. The publishers cheat — and I must wait till I can be my own publisher. The collection of tales issued by W. & P. were selected by a gentleman whose taste does not coincide with my own, from 72, written by me at various times — and those chosen are *not* my best — nor do they fairly represent me in any respect.

The critique on Rogers is *not* mine — although, when it appeared, I observed a similarity to my ordinary manner. The notice of Lowell's "Brittany" *is* mine. You will see that it was merely a preparatory notice — I had designed speaking in full — but something prevented me. The criticism on Shelley is *not* mine; it is the work of Parke Godwin. I never saw it. The critic alluded to by Willis as connected with the Mirror, and as having found a parallel between Hood & Aldrich *is* myself. See my reply to "Outis" in the early numbers of the Broadway Journal. My reference to L. G. Clark, in spirit but not in letter, is what you suppose. He *abused* me in his criticism — but so feebly — with such a parade of intention & effort, but with so little effect or power, that I — forgave him: — that is to say, I had little difficulty in pardoning him. His strong point was that I ought to write well because I had asserted that others wrote ill — and that I *didn't* write well because, although there had been a great deal of fuss made about me, I had written so little — only a small volume of 100 pages. Why he had written more himself!

You will see that I have discontinued the "Literati" in Godey's Mag. I was forced to do so, because I found that people insisted on considering them elaborate criticisms when I had no other design than critical *gossip*. The unexpected circulation of the series, also, suggested to me that I might make a hit and some profit, as well as proper fame, by extending [*page 3*] the plan into that of *a book* on American Letters generally, and keeping the publication in my own hands. I am now *at* this — body & soul. I intend to be thorough — as far as I can — to examine analytically, without reference to previous opinions by *anybody* — all the salient points of Literature in general — e.g Poetry, The Drama, Criticism, Historical Writing — Versification etc. etc. You may get an idea of the manner in which I propose to write the whole book, by reading the notice of Hawthorne which will appear in the January "Godey", as well as the article on "The Rationale of Verse" which will be out in the March or April no: of Colton's Am. Magazine, or Review.

Do not trust, in making up your library, to the "opinions" in the Godey series. I *meant* "honest" — but my meaning is not as fully made out as I could wish. I thought too little of the series myself to guard sufficiently against haste, inaccuracy, or prejudice. The book will be *true* — according to the best of my abilities. As regards Dana — it *is* more than possible that I may be doing him wrong. I have [not] read him since I was a boy, & must read him carefully again. The Frogpondians (Bostonians) have badgered me so much that I fear I am apt to fall into prejudices about them. I have used some of their Pundits up, at all events, in "The Rationale of Verse". I will mail you the number as soon as it appears — for I really wish you to tell me what you think of it.

As regards the Stylus — that is the grand purpose of my life, from which I have never swerved for a moment. But I cannot afford to risk anything by precipitancy — and I *can* afford to wait — at least until I finish *the book*. When that is out, I will start the Mag. — and then I will pay you a visit at Phillips. In the meantime let me thank you, heartily, for your name as a subscriber.

Please write — and *do not* pay the postage.

Truly Your Friend

Edgar A Poe

Concerning Poe's inactivity owing to his illness, see Letter 239 and note; see also the letters he wrote during the same period. In connection with the second paragraph, see H, xvii, 347, and in the present edition Letter 317. "The Hartford Review man" refers to Rufus White Griswold (not Poe's biographer, Rufus Wilmot Griswold), who reviewed "The Raven" (see *American Literature*, vi (March 1934), 69–72). "The Sleeper" first appeared in *Poems* (1831), as "Irene." Poe's poetic drama, "Politian," was never acted professionally, but parts were printed in the *Southern Literary Messenger*, December 1835, and January 1836 (see PE (reprint), p. 9; Quinn, *Poe*, pp. 231–234; and Thomas Ollive

Mabbott's edition of "Politian"). Evert Duyckinck selected the *Tales,* published by Wiley and Putnam (1845). Poe reviewed Lowell's *Poems* (including "Brittany") in *Graham's,* March 1844 (reprinted in H, xi, 243–249). Poe's "Reply to Outis" appeared in the *Broadway Journal,* March 8, 15, 22, 29, and April 5, 1845 (reprinted in H, xii, 41–106). For Lewis Gaylord Clark, see "Literati," *Godey's,* September 1846 (reprinted in H, xv, 114–116). The "Literati" series ran from May through October 1846. For Poe's "book," see the note to Letter 240. For the "Hawthorne" and "The Rationale of Verse," see Letter 259. For Richard H. Dana, see Poe's "Autography" (H, xv, 224). [CL 660]

242 ➤ TO EVERT A. DUYCKINCK

Fordham — Dec. 24. 46.

Dear Duyckinck,

You remember showing me about a year ago, at your house, some English stanzas — by a lady I think — from the rhythm of which Longfellow had imitated the rhythm of the Proem to his "Waif." I wish very much to see the poem — do you think you could loan me the book, or (which will answer as well) give me the title of the book in full, and copy me the 2 first stanzas? I will be greatly obliged if you can.

I am much in need, also, of Gilfillan's "Sketches of Modern Literature" — 2 vols — published by Appleton. If you could loan me the work (or the vol. containing the sketch of Emerson) I would take it as a great favor.

I am taking great care of your Irving & Arcturus — but, unless you need them, I should like to keep them some time longer — as I have to make constant reference to them.

Truly yours

E A Poe

This is the first of Poe's known letters to be headed "Fordham." Apparently Poe made no specific use of the stanzas "Longfellow had imitated," if Duyckinck supplied them. Poe had reviewed George Gilfillan's *Sketches of Modern Literature and Eminent Literary Men* (Appleton's Literary Miscellany, Nos. 6 and 7) in the *Broadway Journal,* December 27, 1845 (see P, ii, 1197). Poe was possibly gathering material for his projected "Literary America" when he asked for the volumes (see Letter 240 and note). For *Arcturus,* see the note to Letter 201. [CL 662]

243 ➤ TO WILLIAM D. TICKNOR

New-York : Dec. 24, 46.

Wm. D. Ticknor Esqr

Dr Sir,

I am engaged on a work which I will probably call "Literary America," and in which I propose to make a general and yet a minute survey of our Letters. I wish, of course, to speak of Oliver Wendell Holmes, and as I can say nothing of him to which you, as his publisher, could object, I venture to ask you for a copy of his Poems, and any memoranda, literary or personal, which may serve my purpose, and which you may have it in your power to supply. If you could procure me his autograph, also, I would be greatly obliged to you.

You will of course understand that I should not feel justified in asking these favors, unless I thought, as all men do, *very* highly of Mr Holmes.

Please send anything for me, to the care of Freeman Hunt Esq, Merchants' Magazine Office, N. York.

Very truly and respectfully Yours

Edgar A Poe.

"Literary America," never completed or published, exists today in MS. in the Huntington Library, and consists of three articles, of the "Literati" variety, on Richard Adams Locke, Christopher Pearse Cranch, and "Thomas Dunn Brown [English]." Griswold in publishing the "Literati" substituted the article on "Thomas Dunn Brown" for Poe's earlier article on English in *Godey's*, XXXIII (July 1846), 17–18. Harrison (XVII, 389–390) prints a letter from Holmes to J[ames] T[homas] Fields, which implies a letter from Poe to Fields; Poe's letter to Ticknor is probably the one meant. The firm of William D. Ticknor & Company, publishers, was located at 135 Washington Street, Boston, and was known as the Old Corner Bookstore (*Dictionary of American Biography*, XVIII, 528–529); the company was known as Ticknor, Reed, and Fields from 1849–1854. Poe, therefore, probably wrote his request to the senior partner, and Fields wrote to Holmes. (The MS. letter of Holmes to Fields, once in the Griswold collection, according to Harrison, is not now in the Boston Public Library with the present Griswold items.) [CL 663]

244 ≻ TO EVERT A. DUYCKINCK

[New York] Dec. 30. 46.

Dear Duyckinck,

Mrs Clemm mentioned to me, this morning, that some of the Parisian papers had been speaking about my "Murders in the Rue Morgue". She could not give me the details — merely saying that you had told her. The "Murders in the R. M." was spoken of in the Paris "Charivari", soon after the first issue of the tale in Graham's Mag: — April 1841. By the enclosed letter from Stonehaven Scotland, you will see that the "Valdemar Case" still makes a talk, and that a pamphlet edition of it has been published by Short & co. of London under the title of "Mesmerism in Articulo Mortis." It has fairly gone the rounds of the London Press, commencing with "The Morning Post". The "Monthly Record of Science" &c gives it with the title "The Last Days of M. Valdemar. By the author of the Last Conversation of a Somnambule" — (Mesmeric Revelation).

My object in enclosing the Scotch letter and the one from Miss Barrett, is to ask you to do me a favor which (*just at this moment*) may be of great importance. It is, to make a paragraph or two for some one of the city papers, stating the facts here given, in connexion with what you know about the "Murders in the Rue Morgue". If this will not give you too much trouble, I will be deeply obliged. If you think it advisable, there is no objection to your copying any portion of Miss B's letter. Willis or Morris will put in anything you may be kind enough to write; but as "The Home Journal" has already said a good deal about me, some other paper would be preferable.

Truly yours

Poe.

Poe was probably wrong in his reference to the *Charivari* (see Quinn, *Poe,* pp. 516–517). The letter from Stonehaven was from Arch Ramsay, November 30, 1846 (see Letter 245). "Facts in the Case of M. Valdemar" (titles varied in subsequent printings) was first published in December 1845 (see Letter 245); it was reprinted in the London *Morning Post,* January 5, 1846, and in the *Popular Record of Modern Science,* January 10 (see Thomas O. Mabbott, *Notes and Queries,* CLXXXIII (November 21, 1942), 311–312). Miss Elizabeth Barrett's letter was that of April 1846 (see H, XVII, 229–230). Nathaniel Parker Willis and George Pope Morris had edited the New York *Evening Mirror;* Willis left it to found the *Home Journal,* in February 1846 (see Mott, *History of American Magazines,* I, 366, 808), Morris later joining him, when the *Mirror* died in the same year. If Duyckinck wrote the paragraph, it is unlocated. [CL 664]

245 ⋟ TO ARCH RAMSAY

'New York December 30. 46.

Dr Sir,

"Hoax" *is* precisely the word suited to M. Valdemar's case. The story appeared originally in "The American Review", a Monthly Magazine, published in this city. The London papers, commencing with the "Morning Post" and the "Popular Record of Science", took up the theme. The article was generally copied in England and is now circulating in France. Some few persons believe it — but *I* do not — and don't you.

Very Resp^y

Yr Ob. S^t

Edgar A Poe

P.S, I have some relations, I think, in Stonehaven, of the name of Allan, who again are connected with the Allans and Galts of Kilmarnock. My name is Edgar *Allan* Poe. Do you know any of them. If so, and it would not put you to too much trouble, I would take it as a favor if you could give me some account of the family.

To A. Ramsay Esqr

"The Facts in the Case of M. Valdemar" first appeared as "Facts of M. Valdemar's Case" in the *American Review,* II (December 1845), 561–565; in 1846 it appeared in London as "Case of M. Valdemar" in the *Popular Record of Modern Science,* also in a 16-page pamphlet entitled "Mesmerism 'In Articulo Mortis' " (see Wyllie, *Poe's Tales,* p. 326; also the letter of Ramsay to Poe, April 14, 1847, in H, XVII, 284–285). Ramsay was a druggist, according to his own signature in the April letter just cited; he also tells Poe he has not been able to learn anything concerning the particular Allan family mentioned in the post-script, above. [CL 665]

246 ➤ TO NATHANIEL P. WILLIS

[New York] December 30th, 1846.

My Dear Willis: —

The paragraph which has been put in circulation respecting my wife's illness, my own, my poverty etc., is now lying before me; together with the beautiful lines by Mrs. Locke and those by Mrs. ——, to which the paragraph has given rise, as well as your kind and manly comments in "The Home Journal."

The motive of the paragraph I leave to the conscience of him or her who wrote it or suggested it. Since the thing is done, however, and since the concerns of my family are thus pitilessly thrust before the public, I perceive no mode of escape from a public statement of what is true and what erroneous in the report alluded to.

That my wife is ill, then, is true; and you may imagine with what feeling I add that this illness, hopeless from the first, has been heightened and precipitated by her reception, at two different periods, of anonymous letters — one enclosing the paragraph now in question; the other, those published calumnies of Messrs ——, for which I yet hope to find redress in a court of justice.

Of the facts, that I myself have been long and dangerously ill, and that my illness has been a well understood thing among my brethren of the press, the best evidence is afforded by the innumerable paragraphs of personal and literary abuse with which I have been latterly assailed. This matter, however, will remedy itself. At the very first blush of my new prosperity, the gentlemen who toadied me in the old, will recollect themselves and toady me again. You, who know me, will comprehend that I speak of these things only as having served, in a measure, to lighten the gloom of unhappiness, by a gentle and not unpleasant sentiment of mingled pity, merriment and contempt.

That, as the inevitable consequence of so long an illness, I have been in want of money, it would be folly in me to deny — but that I have ever materially suffered from privation, beyond the extent of my capacity for suffering, is not altogether true. That I am "without friends" is a gross calumny, which I am sure *you* never could have believed, and which a thousand noble-hearted men would have good right never to forgive me for permitting to pass unnoticed and undenied. Even in the city of New York I could have no difficulty in naming a hundred persons, to each of whom — when the hour for speaking had arrived — I could and would have applied for aid and with unbounded confidence, and with absolutely *no* sense of humiliation.

I do not think, my dear Willis, that there is any need of my saying more. I am getting better, and may add — if it be any comfort to my enemies — that I have little fear of getting worse. The truth is, I have a great deal to do; and I have made up my mind not to die till it is done.

Sincerely yours,

Edgar A. Poe.

The "paragraph" that Poe refers to appeared in the *New York Morning Express,* December 15, 1846 (page 2, col. 1):

ILLNESS OF EDGAR A. POE. — We regret to learn that this gentleman and his wife are both dangerously ill with the consumption, and that the hand of misfortune lies heavy upon their temporal affairs. We are sorry to mention the fact that they are so far reduced as to be barely able to obtain the necessaries of life. That is, indeed, a hard lot, and we do hope that the friends and admirers of Mr. Poe will come promptly to his assistance in his bitterest hour of need. Mr. Poe is the author of several tales and poems, of which Messrs. Wiley & Putnam are the publishers, and, as it is believed, the profitable publishers. At least, his friends say that the publishers ought to start a movement in his behalf.

For the "beautiful lines" by Mrs. Jane Locke, see Letter 251 and note. "Mrs. ——" is unidentified, but probably does not refer to Mrs. Hewitt (see H, XVII, 272–273, n.). "Messrs ——" probably refers to Thomas Dunn English and Hiram Fuller (see the note to Letter 238). [CL 666]

247 ⊁ TO CHARLES A. BRISTED

Fordham — Jan. 17 — 47.

Dear Sir,

Permit me to thank you, from the bottom of my heart, for the ten dollars which you were so considerate and generous as so send me through Mr. Colton. I shall now cease to regard my difficulties as misfortune, since they have shown me that I possessed such friends.

With the most sincere gratitude and esteem,

Yr Ob. S^t

To Charles A Bristed Esqr Edgar A. Poe.

Concerning Bristed, see the note to Letter 269. The gift of ten dollars may have been prompted by the general publicity in the press and among Poe's friends concerning the poor health of both Poe and Virginia (see Letter 246 and note). George H. Colton was the editor of *The American Review*. [CL 667]

248 ➤ TO MARIE L. SHEW

Kindest — dearest friend — My poor Virginia still lives, although failing fast and now suffering much pain. May God grant her life until she sees you and thanks you once again! Her bosom is full to overflowing — like my own — with a boundless — inexpressible gratitude to you. Lest she may never see you more — she bids me say that she sends you her sweetest kiss of love and will die blessing you[.] But come — oh come to-morrow! Yes, I *will* be calm — everything you so nobly wish to see me. My mother sends you, also, her "warmest love and thanks"[.] She begs me to ask you, if possible, to make arrangements at home so that you may stay with us tomorrow night. I enclose the order to the Postmaster.

Heaven bless you and farewell

Fordham,   Edgar A Poe.
Jan. 29. 47.

Concerning this letter, Mrs. Shew wrote to Ingram, February 16 [1875] (original MS. in the Ingram collection, University of Virginia): "I had told him in all candor that nothing would or could save him from a sudden death, but a prudent life, of calm, with a woman fond enough — and strong enough to manage his work . . ." However, only the part about being calm would have been written before Virginia's death. This is the first known letter in the Poe–Shew correspondence. Mrs. Shew later became Mrs. Roland Houghton and corresponded extensively with Ingram while he was preparing his biography of Poe. Virginia died January 30, 1847. [CL 670]

IX

FORDHAM

GRASPING AT STRAWS

February 1847–July 1848

New-York: Feb. 16. 47.

My Dear Sir,

Some weeks ago I mailed you two newspapers which, from what you say in your last letter I see you have not received. I now enclose some slips which will save me the necessity of writing on painful topics. By and bye I will write you more at length.

Please re-inclose me the slips, when read.

What you tell me about the accusation of plagiarism made by the "Phil. Sat. Ev. Post" surprises me. It is the first I heard of it — with the exception of a hint made in one of your previous letters — but which I did not then comprehend. Please let me know as many *particulars* as you can remember — for I must see into the charge — Who edits the paper? — who publishes it? etc etc. etc. — about what time was the accusation made? I assure you that it is *totally* false. In 1840 I published a book with this title — "The Conchologist's First-Book — A System of Testaceous Malacology, arranged expressly for the use of Schools, in which the animals, *according to Cuvier,* are given with the shells, a great number of new species added, and the whole brought up, as accurately as possible, to the present condition of the science. By Edgar A. Poe. With Illustrations of 215 shells, presenting a correct type of each [*page 2*] genus." This, I presume, is the work referred to. I wrote it, in conjunction with Professor Thomas Wyatt, and Professor Mc Murtrie of Phª — my name being put to the work, as best known and most likely to aid its circulation. I wrote the Preface and Introduction, and translated from Cuvier, the accounts of the animals etc. *All* school-books are necessarily made in a similar way. The very title-page acknowledges that the animals are given "according to Cuvier".

This charge is infamous and I shall prosecute for it, as soon as I settle my accounts with the "Mirror."

Truly your friend,

E A Poe

On July 9, 1848, Eveleth returned certain "slips" — perhaps those requested by Poe in the present letter and in that of January 4, 1848
(Letter 259). *The Conchologist's First Book* (1839) was published
under Poe's name for the benefit of Thomas Wyatt; the body of the
work is largely a paraphrase of Wyatt's *A Manual of Conchology*
(1838), and Poe's own contribution is a close paraphrase of Thomas
Brown's *The Conchologist's Text-Book* (1837) and, as he says, a
translation from Cuvier (see W, I, 194–198; for the title page, see
Quinn, *Poe*, p. 276). Poe never carried out his threat to prosecute
the *Post* for charges of plagiarism. In this connection, see also Letter
252. [CL 671]

250 ≻ TO HORACE GREELEY

New-York: Feb. 21 — 47.

My Dear Mr Greeley,

Enclosed is an editorial article which I cut from "The Tribune" of
the 19th ult. When I first saw it I did not know you were in Washington and yet I said to myself — "this misrepresentation is *not* the work
of Horace Greeley".

The facts of my case are these: — In "Godey's Magazine" I wrote
a *literary criticism* having reference to T. D. English. The only thing
in it which resembled a "personality," was contained in these words —
"I have no acquaintance, personally, with Mr English" — meaning, of
course, as every body understood, that I wished to decline his acquaintance for the future. This, English retaliates by asserting under his
own name, in the Mirror, that he *holds my acknowledgment for a
sum of money obtained under false pretences,* and by creating the impression on the public mind that I have been *guilty of forgery.* These
charges (being false and, if false, easily shown to be so) could have
been ventured upon by English only in the hope that on account of
my illness and expected death, it would be impossible for me to reply
to them at all. Their baseness is thus trebly aggravated by their
cowardice. I sue; to redeem my character from these foul accusations.
Of the obtaining money under false pretences from E. not a shadow of
proof is shown: — the "acknowledgment" is *not forthcoming.* The
"forgery," by reference to the very man who originated the charge, is
shown to be *totally, radically baseless.* The jury returned a verdict in
my favor — and the paragraphs enclosed are the comments of *the
"Tribune"!*

You are a man, Mr Greeley — an honest and a generous man — or
I should not venture to tell you so, and to your face; and *as* a man you

must imagine what I feel at finding those paragraphs to my discredit going the rounds of the country, *as the opinions of Horace Greeley*. Every body supposes that *you* have said these things. The weight of your character — the general sense of your truth and love of justice — cause those few sentences (which in almost any other paper in America I would treat with contempt) to do me a vital injury — to wound and oppress me beyond measure. I therefore ask you to do me what justice you can find it in your heart to do under the circumstances. (over[ )]

[*page 2*] In the printed matter I have underscored two passages. As regards the first: — it alone would have sufficed to assure me that *you* did not write the article. I owe you money — I have been ill, unfortunate, no doubt weak, and as yet unable to refund the money — but on this ground *you*, Mr Greeley, could *never* have accused me of being habitually "unscrupulous in the fulfillment of my pecuniary engagements." The charge is *horribly false* — I have a hundred times left myself destitute of bread for myself and family that I might discharge debts which the very writer of this infamous accusation (Fuller) would have left undischarged to the day of his death.

The 2^d passage underscored embodies a falsehood — and *therefore* *you* did not write it. I did *not* "throw away the quill". I arose from a sick-bed (although scarcely able to stand or see) and wrote a reply which was published in the Phil. "Sp. of the Times", and a copy of which reply I enclose you. The "columns of the Mirror" were tendered to me — with a proviso that I should forego a suit and omit this passage and that passage, to suit the purposes of Mr Fuller.

I have now placed the matter before you — I should not hope or ask for justice from any other man (except perhaps one) in America — but from you I demand and expect it. You will see, at once, that so gross a wrong, done in your name, dishonors yourself and me. If you do differ then, as I know you do, from these editorial opinions supposed to be yours — I beg of you to do by me as you would have me do by you in a similar case — disavow them.

> With high respect Yours [tr]
>
> Edgar A. Poe

Poe's "19th ult." certainly refers to the *Tribune* article of February 19, 1847, "ult." meaning "last," not "last month." Poe's case against Fuller and Clason was settled February 17, 1847. On October 24, 1845, Greeley signed a 60-day promissory note made out to Edgar A.

Poe to the value of $50 (see P, ii, 1063), which, endorsed by Poe, was
turned over to John Bisco on the same day as the down-payment on
Poe's purchase of the *Broadway Journal* (see W, ii, 151–152, and
Quinn, *Poe*, pp. 489–490). Greeley never collected the loan. [CL 672]

251 ﹩ TO JANE ERMINA LOCKE

New-York, March 10. 1847

My Dear Madam,

<Your kind letter of Feb. 21>.

In <replying to> ans[w]eri[n]g your kind letter <of Feb. 21>.
permit me in the very first place to <say> absolve myself from
<any> a suspicion <of discourtesy to yourself> — <in not hav>
ing sooner <replied to yo>u. which, under the circumstances you
could scarcely have failed to entertain — <a suspicion of in regard
to> [*Interlineated:* in regard to m] me — and <suspicio> one
<which it gives me the deepest regr>et a suspicion of my <my>
very g[r]oss discourtesy towards yourself in not having more promptly
replied <to the> to you. I assure you, madam, that your letter
dated Feb. 21 — has only this moment reached me <, and through a
channel and> A[l]though postmarked <in> Lowell &c in the ordinary manner, it was handed to <me> a friend of mine, for me, by Mr
Freeman Hunt of the Merchants' Magazine, without any explanation of the mode in which it came into his hands or of the cause of
its detention. Being <too> still too unwell to leave my room I have
been prevented as yet from <making inquiry respecting> satisfy-
i[ng] myself on these points, and of course cannot now delay replying
to your <kind> noble and generous words even until I shall shall
have an opportunity of <doing so.> making <the inv the investiga-
tion>. inquiry.

Your beautiful lines <were written> appeared at a time when
[*Interlineated:* be[c]] [*page 2*] I was indeed very ill, and <I> might
never have seen them but f[or th]e kindness of Mr Willis who enclosed them to me — and who knew me too well to suppose <that>
as some of my friends did that I I would be pained by so sweet an
evidence of interest on the part of one of whose <writings spirit>
[*Interlineated:* with] writings — <of> [*Interlineated:* with esp[*illegible*]] whose <glowing> fervid and generous spirit which they
evince he had so often heard me express sympathy.

At the same time I could not help <seeing and> fearing that

should you see my letter to Mr Willis <published> (in "The Home Journal" in which a natural pride which I feel you could not blame impelled me to <disavow my necessities> shrink from public charity even at the cost of <disavowing> [*Interlineated*: expense of truth at denying] those necessities which were but too real — and an illness which I t[h]en expectede would <a> soon terminate in death — I could not help fearing that <when you saw> should you see this letter you would yourself feel pained at having caused me pain — at having been the means of giving farther publicity to a <poverty> [*Interlineated*: n unfounded] report <which was unfounded> — at all events to <a> the report <of a poverty and a wretchedness> which <at all even>ts (since the world regards <it [*illegible*]> wretchedness as a crime) I had thought it prudent so publicly to disavow. In a word <judging> venturing to judge your noble nature by my own, I felt grieved lest my <denial lette> published <letter> denial <of> my cause you to regret what you had <written,> done and my first impulse was to write you and assure [*Interlineated*: yo[u]] you even at the risk of <speaking too war> doing so too warmly of the sweet <emotion of> emotion made up of respect and gratitude alone with which, <your poem [had]> my heart was filled to overflowing. <But> While I was hesitating, however, in regard [*page 3*] to the propriety of this step — I w[as o]verwhelmed by a <trial> sorrow so poignant as to deprive me for several weeks of all power of thought or action.

Your letter now lying before me, <assur assures me> tells me that I had not been mistaken in your nature and that I should not have hesitated to address you — but believe me, dear Mrs Locke, that I <shall> am alreading <begin[n]ing to> ceasing to regard those difficulties as misfortune which have led me to even this partial correspondence. with yourself.

[*Here follow some scribblings by Poe:*]

Ind   Inde
Indeed In   Indeed
                       Indee

          Tri

               I Inde
          Ind
          with

                    [*No signature*]

If corrected and sent, this is Poe's first known letter to Jane E. Locke. Mrs. Ermina Starkweather Locke, a relative of Mrs. Frances Sargent Osgood, lived at Wamesit Cottage, Lowell, Massachusetts. At her invitation Poe delivered his lecture on the "Poets and Poetry of America" in Lowell, July 10, 1848 (see Quinn, *Poe*, pp. 565–566). Concerning Mrs. Locke, see the notes to Poe's other letters to her, and also Letters 306 and 309. It is quite possible that Hunt gave Mrs. Locke's letter to Willis, who transmitted it to Poe. Mrs. Locke's "beautiful lines" seem to have been enclosed in Willis' letter to Poe, [December 23, 1846] (see H, XVII, 272), which included also, apparently, a letter from her to Willis, and Willis' editorial on Poe's health and character printed in the *Home Journal,* December 26, 1846, available in advance of date (see the note to Letter 310); thus Poe's letter to Willis (December 30, 1846), printed in the *Home Journal,* January 9, 1847, alludes to these matters in its attempt to deny the seeming hopelessness of his situation. His "sorrow so poignant" refers to the death of Virginia, January 30, 1847. [CL 677]

252 ➤ TO GEORGE W. EVELETH

New-York March 11. 47.

My Dear Sir,

I am still quite sick and overwhelmed with business — but I snatch a few moments to reply to yours of the 21rst ult.

I really forget whether I did mail you one or two papers — but presume that the slips enclosed in my letter, covered all.

The "scholar and gentleman" referred to, is Evert A. Duyckinck, of this city, formerly editor of "Arcturus" now of "The Literary World".

I fear that according to the law technicalities there is nothing "actionable" in the Post's paragraphs — but I shall make them retract by *some* means.

My suit against "The Mirror" has terminated, by a verdict of $225, in my favor. The costs and all will make them a bill of $492. Pretty well — considering that there was *no* actual "damage" done to me.

I enclose you my reply to English — which will enable you to comprehend his accusations. The vagabond, at the period of the suit's coming on, ran off to Washington for fear of being criminally prosecuted. The "acknowledgment" referred to was not forthcoming, and "the Mirror" could not get *a single witness* to testify *one word* against my character.

[*page 2*] Thank you for your promise about "The Stylus". I depend upon you implicitly.

You were *perfectly* right in what you said to Godey.

I cannot tell why the review of Hawthorne does not appear — but I presume we shall have it by and bye. He paid me for it when I sent it — so I have no business to ask about it. <When>

Most truly your friend

Edgar A Poe

P. S. "The Valdemar Case" was a hoax, of course.

> For the papers and slips, see Letter 249. *Arcturus,* edited by Evert A. Duyckinck and Cornelius Mathews, was founded in New York, December 1840, and merged with the *Boston Miscellany,* June 1842 (Mott, *History of American Magazines,* I, 713–714); Duyckinck edited the *Literary World* for its first three issues, February–April 1847 (see also, the note to Letter 320). For Poe's reference to the *Post,* see Letter 249. Concerning the suit against the *Mirror,* see the Poe–English controversy, H, XVII, 233–255. For Eveleth's "promise" regarding the *Stylus* and what he wrote to Godey, see Eveleth to Poe, February 21, 1847 (EP (reprint), pp. 13–14). Poe's article on Hawthorne appeared in *Godey's,* November 1847 (reprinted in H, XIII, 141–155). For the "Valdemar Case," see also Letter 245. [CL 679]

253 ➤ TO J. F. REINMAN & J. H. WALKER

New-York March 11. 1847

Gentlemen,

Very serious illness has hitherto prevented me from replying to your most flattering letter of the 24th ult.

May I now beg you to express to your society my grateful acceptance and appreciation of the honor they have conferred on me?

With respect & esteem I am, Gentlemen, Yr. mo. ob. S^t

To Mess J. F. Reinman   Edgar A Poe
& J. H. Walker

In various letters Poe speaks of his serious illness before and after Virginia's death, January 30, 1847. [CL 680]

254 ≻ TO MARIE LOUISE SHEW

[Fordham] Sunday night [May 1847]

My dear Friend Louise

Nothing for months, has given me so much real pleasure, as your note of last night. I have been engaged all day on some promised work — otherwise I should have replyed immediately as my heart inclined. I sincerely hope you may not drift out of my sight before I can thank you. How kind of you to let me do even *this small service* for you, in return for the great debt I owe you. Louise — my brightest — most unselfish of all who ever loved me, I should return the money, if I did not know it would grieve you, as I shall have so much pleasure in thinking of you & yours, in that Music Room & Library. Louise — I give you great credit for taste in these things, & I know I can please you in the purchases. During my first call at your house after my Virginia's death, I noticed with so much pleasure the large painting over the Piano which is a masterpiece indeed deserving a place in a palace or church & I noticed the size of all your paintings[.] The scrolls, instead of set figures — of the drawing room carpet — the soft effect of the window shades also the crimson & gold &c & I was charmed to see the Harp & Piano uncovered. The pictures of Raphael & the Cavelier I shall never forget — their softness & beauty. The Guitar with the blue ribbon, music stand & antique jars. I wondered that a little country maiden like you had developed so classic a taste & atmosphere. Please present my kind regards to your uncle & say that I am at his service any or every day this week & ask him please, to specify time & place[.]

Yours sincerely

Edgar A Poe

According to Ingram (II, 154), Mrs. Shew invited Poe to help her uncle select furnishings for a new house and "gave him *carte blanche* to furnish the music-room and library as he pleased." Mrs. Shew (letter to Ingram, February 16, 1875(?), in the Ingram collection) identified her uncle as Hiram Barney, senior member of the New York law firm of Barney, Butler, and Parsons. [CL 683]

254a ➤ TO G. P. BRONSON

[Fordham, June 1847]

I wish to ascertain if the poem which, at your suggestion, I have written is of the lenth, the character &c. you desire: — if not, I will write another . . .

[Edgar A. Poe]

According to the Dodd, Mead catalogue (see Note 254a), Bronson was an elocutionist. The poem referred to is unidentified. [CL 685a]

255 ➤ TO ROBERT T. CONRAD

New-York August 10. 1847.

Dear Sir,

Permit me to thank you, in the first place, very sincerely, for your considerate kindness to me while in Philadelphia. Without your aid, at the precise moment and in the precise manner in which you rendered it, it is more than probable that I should not now be alive to write you this letter. Finding myself exceedingly ill — so much so that I had no hope except in getting home immediately — I made several attempts to see Mr Graham and at last saw him for a few minutes just as he was about returning to Cape May. He was very friendly — more so than I have ever known him, and requested me to write continuously for the Mag. As you were not present, however, and it was uncertain when I could see you, I obtained an advance of $10 from Mr G. in order that I might return home at once — and thinking it, also, more proper to leave you time in which to look over the articles.

I would be deeply obliged if you could now give me an answer respecting them. Should you take both, it will render me, just now, the most important service. I owe Mr G. about $50. The articles, at the old price ($4 per page) will come to $90 — so [*page 2*] that, if you write me that they are accepted, I propose to draw on Mr G. for $40 — thus squaring our account.

P.S. I settled my bill with Arbuckle before leaving Phil. but am not sure <whether it included> how much I owe yourself for the previous bill etc. Please let me know.

Very gratefully your friend

Edgar A. Poe

No articles by Poe of such length as Poe indicates appeared in *Graham's* after the date of this letter. Judge Robert T. Conrad was an editor of the *North American* and was assisting in the editing of *Graham's* (see Quinn, *Poe*, p. 531). [CL 687]

256 ⤐ TO ROBERT T. CONRAD

New-York Aug. 31 — 1847

My Dear Sir,

It is now a month since I wrote you about the two articles I left with you — but, as I have heard nothing from you, I can only suppose that my letter has not reached you — or, at all events, that, in the press of other business, you have forgotten it and me.

In it, after thanking you (as I do again most sincerely) for your late kindness to me in Phil*, I begged an answer in respect to the articles — mentioning $40 as the sum in which the Magazine would be indebted to me in case of their acceptance, and asking permission to draw for that amount. — I owed Mr Graham $50 (as nearly as I can remember) and the papers, at the old price, would come to 90.

May I beg of you to reply, as soon as convenient, and oblige

Yours very cordially

Hon R. T. Conrad.   Edgar A. Poe

No letter is known from Conrad to Poe, though Poe wrote three to him. In connection with the above letter, see Letter 255. [CL 688]

257 ⤐ TO SARAH ANNA LEWIS

[New York] Nov. 27. [1847]

Dear Mrs Lewis —

A thousand thanks for your repeated kindness, and, above all, for the comforting and cheering words of your note. Your advice I feel as a command which neither my heart nor my reason would venture to disobey. May Heaven forever bless you and yours!

A day or two ago I sent to one of the Magazines the sonnet enclosed. Its tone is somewhat too light; but it embodies a riddle which I wish to put you to the trouble of expounding. Will you try?

My best regards, with those of Mrs Clemm, <to Mr Lewis,> and believe me, with all the affection of a brother,

Yours always,

Edgar A Poe.

Sarah Anna Lewis, whose pen name was Estelle Anna Lewis, was the wife of Sylvanus D. Lewis, a lawyer, and lived at 125 Dean Street, Brooklyn. According to Mr. Lewis, he and Poe became personal friends in 1845 (see P, II, 1374). For Poe's favorable reviews of Mrs. Lewis' poems, "for a consideration," see the note to Letter 321; and for Poe's comments in such reviews, see H, XIII, 155–165, 215–226. In connection with Mrs. Shew's report to Ingram in a letter of April 3, 1875 (University of Virginia), that Poe avoided such persons as Mrs. Lewis (quoted by Quinn, *Poe*, p. 563), must be kept in mind the apparent gratitude he felt toward her for her care of Mrs. Clemm during his absence from New York in the summer of 1849 (see letters to Mrs. Clemm and to Mrs. Lewis at this time). According to Mrs. Lewis (see Ingram, II, 219), "My girlish poem — 'The Forsaken' — made us acquainted. He had seen it floating the rounds of the press, and wrote to tell me how much he liked it: '*It is inexpressibly beautiful,*' he said, 'and I should like much to know the young author.'" Though the italicized clause can be found in Poe's review of Mrs. S. Anna Lewis' *Child of the Sea and Other Poems,* which appeared in the SLM, September 1848 (reprinted in H, XIII, 155–165), the rest of the sentence suggests a letter from Poe, which is unlocated. "The sonnet enclosed" refers to Poe's "An Enigma" (see Note 257); the "riddle" consists of reading out of the poem Mrs. Lewis' name by juxtaposing the first letter of the first line, with the second letter of the second line, the third of the third line, and so on. [CL 691]

258 ⋟ TO NATHANIEL P. WILLIS

Fordham, December 8 [1847]

My dear Mr. Willis,

Many thanks for the kind expressions in your note of three or four weeks ago.

I send you an "American Review" — the number just issued — in which is a ballad by myself, but published anonymously. It is called

"Ulalume" — the page is turned down. I do not care to be known as its author just now; but I would take it as a great favor if you would copy it in the H. J., with a word of *inquiry* as to who wrote it: — provided always that you think the poem worth the room it would occupy in your paper — a matter about which I am by no means sure. Always yours gratefully,

Edgar A. Poe.

Willis reprinted "Ulalume" in the *Home Journal*, January 1, 1848 (see Campbell, *Poems*, p. 265), anonymously, with an introductory paragraph in which he spoke of the poem as an "exquisitely piquant and skilful exercise of rarity and niceness of language . . . Who is the author?" (*ibid.*, p. 268). Subsequently, the poem was reprinted and commented upon by various publications, and finally Poe saw to it that he was identified as its author (for a full discussion, see Campbell, *Poems*). [CL 693]

259 ➤ TO GEORGE W. EVELETH

New-York — Jan. 4, 1848.

My Dear Sir —

Your last, dated July 26, ends with — "Write will you not"? I have been living ever since in a constant state of intention to write, and finally concluded not to write at all until I could say something definite about The Stylus and other matters. You perceive that I now send you a Prospectus — but before I speak farther on this topic, let me succinctly reply to various points in your letter. 1. — "Hawthorne" is out — how do you like it? 2 — "The Rationale of Verse" was found to come down too heavily (as I forewarned you it did) upon some of poor Colton's personal friends in Frogpondium — the "pundits" you know; so I gave him "a song" for it & took it back. The song was "Ulalume a Ballad" published in the December number of the Am. Rev. I enclose it as copied by the Home Journal (Willis's paper) with the Editor's remarks — please let me know how you like "Ulalume". As for the "Rat. of Verse" I sold it to "Graham" at a round advance on Colton's price, and in Grahams hands it is still — but not to remain even there; for I mean to get it back, revise or re-write it (since "Evangeline has been published) and deliver it as a lecture when I go South & West on my Magazine expedition. 3 — I have been "so still" on account of preparation for the magazine cam-

paign — also have been working at my book — nevertheless I have
written some trifles not yet published — some which have been. 4 —
My health is better — best. I have never been so well. 5 — I do not
well see how I could have otherwise replied to English. You must
know him, (English) before you can well estimate my reply. He is so
thorough a "blatherskite" that [to] have replied to him with *dignity*
would have been the extreme of the ludicrous. The only true plan —
not to have replied to him at all — was precluded on account of the
nature of some of his accusations — forgery for instance. To such
charges, even from the Auto[crat] of all the Asses — a man is *compelled* to answer. There he had me. Answer him I must[.] But how?
Believe me there exists no such dilemma as that in which a gentleman
[is] placed when he is forced to reply to a blackguard. If he have any
genius then is the time for its display. I confess to you that I rather
like that reply of mine in a literary sense — and so do a great many
of my friends. It fully answered its purpose beyond a doubt — would
to Heaven every work of art did as much! You err in supposing me
to have been "peevish" when I wrote the reply: — the peevishness was
all "put on" as a part of my argument — of my plan: — so was the
"indignation" with which I wound up. *How* could I be either
[peev-]ish or indignant about a matter so well adapted to further my
purposes? Were I able to afford so expensive a luxury as personal and
especially as *refutable* abuse, I would [w]illingly pay any man $2000
per annum, to hammer away at me all the year round. I suppose you
know that I sued the Mirror & got a verdict. English eloped. 5 — The
"common friend" referred to is Mrs Frances S. Osgood, the poetess. —
6 — I agree with you only in part as regards Miss Fuller. She has some
general but no particular critical powers. She belongs to a *school* of
criticism — the Göthean, asthetic, eulogistic. The creed of this school
is that, in criti[-] [*page 2*] cizing an author you must imitate him,
ape him, out-Herod Herod. She is grossly dishonest. She abuses
Lowell, for example, (the best of our poets, perhaps) on account of a
personal quarrel with him. She has omitted all mention of me for
the same reason — although, a short time before the issue of her book,
she praised me highly in the Tribune. I enclose you her criticism
that you may judge for yourself. She praised "Witchcraft" because
Mathews (who toadies her) wrote it. In a word, she is an ill-tempered
and very inconsistent old maid — avoid her. 7 — Nothing was omitted in "Marie Roget" but what I omitted myself: — all *that* is mys-

tification. The story was originally published in Snowden's "Lady's Companion". The "naval officer" who committed the murder (or rather the accidental death arising from an attempt at abortion) *confessed* it; and the whole matter is now well understood — but, for the sake of relatives, his is a topic on which I must not speak further. 8 — "The Gold Bug" was originally sent to Graham, but he not liking it, I got him to take some critical papers instead, and sent [i]t to The Dollar Newspaper which had offered $100 for the best story. It obtained the premi[u]m and made a great noise. 9 — The "necessities" were pecuniary ones. I referred to a [s]neer at my poverty on the part of the Mirror. 10 — You say — "Can you *hint* to me what was the terrible evil" which caused the irregularities so profoundly lamented?" Yes; I can do more than hint. This "evil" was the greatest which can befall a man. Six years ago, a wife, whom I loved as no man ever loved before, ruptured a blood-vessel in singing. Her life was despaired of. I took leave of her forever & underwent all the agonies of her death. She recovered partially and I again hoped. At the end of a year the vessel broke again — I went through precisely the same scene. Again in about a year afterward. Then again — again — again & even once again at varying intervals. Each time I felt all the agonies of her death — and at each accession of the disorder I loved her more dearly & clung to her life with more desperate pertinacity. But I am constitutionally sensitive — nervous in a very unusual degree. I became insane, with long intervals of horrible sanity. During these fits of absolute unconsciousness I drank, God only knows how often or how much. As a matter of course, my enemies referred the insanity to the drink rather than the drink to the insanity. I had indeed, nearly abandoned all hope of a permanent cure when I found one in the *death* of my wife. This I can & do endure as becomes a man — it was the horrible never-ending oscillation between hope & despair which I could *not* longer have endured without the total loss of reason. In the death of what was my life, then, I receive a new but — oh God! how melancholy an existence.

And now, having replied to all your queries let me refer to The Stylus. I am resolved to be my own publisher. To be controlled is to be ruined. My ambition is great. If I succeed, I put myself (within 2 years) in possession of a fortune & infinitely more. My plan is to go through the South & West & endeavor to interest my friends so as *to commence with a list of at least 500 subscribers.* With this list I can take the matter into my own hands. There are some few of my friends who have sufficient confidence in me to advance their sub-scriptions — but at all events succeed *I will*. Can you or will you help me? I have room to say no more.

Truly Yours —

E A Poe.

[Please re-enclose the printed slips when you have done with them. Have you seen the article on "The American Library" in the Novem-ber No. of Blackwood, and if so, what do you think of it? E. A. Poe.]

> Poe's long review of Hawthorne appeared in *Godey's*, November 1847 (reprinted in H, xiii, 141–155). "Ulalume" was first published in Colton's *American Whig Review*, December 1847 (see Campbell, *Poems*, p. 265). "Frogpondium" refers especially to Boston, center of the transcendentalists. The *Home Journal* printed "Ulalume" in the issue of January 1, 1848 (Campbell, *ibid.*). The "Rationale of Verse," in its earlier title, "Notes on English Verse," appeared in Lowell's *Pioneer*, March 1843; then, elaborated, was published in the SLM, October–November 1848 (see head-note and reprinting in H, xiv, 209–265). For Poe's "book," see the note to Letter 240. The Poe–English con-troversy is reprinted in H, xvii, 233–255; see also Letter 252. Margaret Fuller's criticism of Poe appeared in the *New York Tribune*, Novem-ber 26, 1845 (see Quinn, *Poe*, p. 538, n.), prior to her *Papers on Litera-ture and Art*, 1846 (see *Cambridge History of American Literature*, 1, 343). "Marie Rogêt" was published in Snowden's *Ladies' Companion* in the issues of November and December 1842, and February 1843 (see Wyllie, *Poe's Tales*, p. 332). Contrary to Poe's statement, Graham bought *The Gold Bug* for $52 (see George R. Graham's "defense of Poe," "The Late Edgar Allan Poe," *Graham's*, March 1850, reprinted in H, 1, 399–410); then, apparently, at Poe's request returned it so that Poe could enter it in the *Dollar Magazine* contest, in which news-paper it was published, June 21 and 28, 1843. "The American Library" appeared in *Blackwood's Magazine*, lxii (November 1847), 574–592; it discussed Poe's *Tales* (1845) and praised it. [cl 694]

260 ⊁ TO H. D. CHAPIN

Fordham — Jan. 17 — 48.

My dear Sir,

Mrs. Shew intimated to me, not long ago, that you would, perhaps, lend me your aid in my endeavour to re-establish myself in the literary world; and I now venture to ask your assistance. When I last spoke with you, I mentioned my design of going to see Mr. Neal at Portland, and there, with his influence, deliver a Lecture — the proceeds of which might enable me to take the first steps towards my proposed Magazine: — that is to say, put, perhaps, $100 in my pocket; which would give me the necessary outfit and start me on my tour. But, since our conversation, I have been thinking that a better course would be to make interest among my friends here — in N. Y. city — and deliver a Lecture, in the first instance, at the Society Library. With this object in view, may I beg of you so far to assist me as to procure for me the use of the Lecture Room? The difficulty with me is that payment for the Room is demanded *in advance* and I have no money. I believe the price is $15. I think that, without being too sanguine, I may count upon an audience of some 3 or 4 hundreds — and if even 300 are present, I shall be enabled to proceed with my plans.

Should you be so kind as to grant me the aid I request, I should like to engage the Room for the *first Thursday in February.*

Gratefully yours,

Edgar A. Poe.

I am deeply obliged to you for your note of introduction to Col. Webb. As yet I have not found an opportunity of presenting it — thinking it best to do so when I speak to him about the Lecture.

Mr. Chapin seems to have been a friend of the Poe family in New York. He is probably the Mr. C—— spoken of by Mrs. Clemm in her letter to Mrs. Shew, Friday Evening [1847], printed in H, xvii, 390–391. "Mr. Neal of Portland" was John Neal, former editor of the *Yankee*, with whom Poe had some correspondence, *q.v.* Early in 1848 Poe was planning a trip through the South in the interests of launching his *Stylus*. Poe's lecture on the universe was delivered before the small audience that gathered in the Library of the New York Historical Society, February 3, Thursday. [CL 696]

261 ➤ TO LOUIS A. GODEY

[New York] Jan. 17, 1848

Dr Sir

What do you say to an article? I have one which I think may please you. Shall I send it and draw as usual? . . . Please reply. . . . The article is imaginative — not critical.

[*Signature missing*]

The article was probably "Mellonta Tauta," Poe's last contribution to *Godey's,* and appeared February 1849. The article or tale is dated April 2848, as if Poe in sending it in January 1848 expected it to be published in the April number, 1848, of *Godey's,* but being an imaginative article it is dated ahead a thousand years. If this supposition be true, Godey probably replied to the present letter. [CL 697]

262 ⥲ TO NATHANIEL P. WILLIS

Fordham, January 22, 1848.

My dear Mr. Willis: —

I am about to make an effort at re-establishing myself in the literary world, and *feel* that I may depend upon your aid.

My general aim is to start a Magazine, to be called "The Stylus;" but it would be useless to me, even when established, if not entirely out of the control of a publisher. I mean, therefore, to get up a Journal which shall be *my own,* at all points. With this end in view, I must get a list of, at least, five hundred subscribers to begin with: — nearly two hundred I have already. I propose, however, to go South and West, among my personal and literary friends — old college and West Point acquaintances — and see what I can do. In order to get the means of taking the first step, I propose to lecture at the Society Library, on Thursday, the 3d of February — and, that there may be no cause of *squabbling,* my subject shall *not be literary* at all. I have chosen a broad text — "The Universe."

Having thus given you *the facts* of the case, I leave all the rest to the suggestions of your own tact and generosity. Gratefully — *most* gratefully —

Your friend always,

Edgar A. Poe.

For similar remarks on the *Stylus,* see the last paragraph of Letter 259. Poe delivered the lecture on "The Universe," on February 3, at the Society Library in New York before a small audience; he read *Eureka,* on which he had been working for some time (see Quinn, *Poe,* p. 539). Willis wrote a very complimentary notice of the forthcoming lecture in the *Home Journal, ante* February 11, 1848 (see Quinn, *Poe,* pp. 539–540. [CL 698]

263 ✈ TO GEORGE W. EVELETH

New-York — Feb. 29 — 48.

My Dear Sir,

I mean to start for Richmond on the 10th March. Every thing
has gone as I wished it, and my final success is certain, or I abandon
all claims to the title of Vates. The only contretemps of any moment,
lately, has been Willis's somewhat premature announcement of my
project: — but this will only force me into action a little sooner
than I had proposed. Let me now answer the points of your last
letter.

Colton acted pretty much as all mere men of the world act. I think
very little the worse of him for his endeavor to succeed with you at
my expense. I always liked him and I believe he liked me. His intellect was o. His "I understand the matter perfectly," amuses me.
Certainly, then, it was the only matter he *did* understand. "The
Rationale of Verse" will appear in "Graham" after all: — I will stop
in Phil: to see the proofs. As for Godey, he is a good little man and
means as well as he knows how. The editor of the "Weekly Universe"
speaks kindly and I find no fault with his representing my habits as
"shockingly irregular". He could not have had the "personal acquaintance" with me of which he writes; but has fallen into a very
natural error. The fact is thus: — My *habits* are rigorously abstemious
and I omit nothing of the natural regimen requisite for health: —
i,e — I rise early, eat moderately, drink nothing but water, and take
abundant and regular exercise in the open air. But this is my private
life — my studious and literary life — and of course escapes the eye
of the world. The desire for society comes upon me only when I have
become excited by drink. Then *only* I go — that is, at these times only
I *have been* in the practice of going among my friends: who seldom,
or in fact never, having seen me unless excited, take it for granted
that I am always so. Those who *really* know me, know better. In the
meantime I shall turn the general error to account. But enough of
this: the causes which maddened me to the drinking point are no
more, and I am done drinking, forever. — I do *not* know the "editors
& contributors" of the "Weekly Universe" and was not aware of the
existence of such a paper. Who are they? or is it a secret? The "most

distinguished of American scholars" is Prof. Chas. Anthon, author of the "Classical Dictionary".

I presume you have seen some newspaper notices of my late lecture on [*page 2*] the Universe. You could have gleaned, however, no idea of what the lecture was, from what the papers said it was. All praised it — as far as I have yet seen — and all absurdly misrepresented it. The only report of it which approaches the truth, is the one I enclose — from the "Express" — written by E. A. Hopkins — a gentleman of much scientific acquirement — son of Bishop Hopkins of Vermont — but he conveys only my general idea, and his digest is full of inaccuracies. I enclose also a slip from the "Courier & Enquirer": — *please return them*. To eke out a chance of your understanding what I really *did* say, I add a loose summary of my propositions & results:

The General Proposition is this: — Because Nothing was, *therefore* All Things are.

1 — An inspection of the *universality* of Gravitation — i.e, of the fact that each particle tends, *not* to any one common point, but to *every other* particle — suggests *perfect* totality, or *absolute* unity, as the source of the phaenomenon.

2 — Gravity is but the mode in which is manifested the tendency of all things to return into their original unity; is but the reaction of the first Divine Act.

3 — The *law* regulating the return — i.e, the *law* of Gravitation — is but a necessary result of the necessary & sole possible mode of equable *irradiation* of matter through space: — this *equable* irradiation is necessary as a basis for the Nebular Theory of Laplace.

4 — The Universe of Stars (contradistinguished from the Universe of Space) is limited.

5 — Mind is cognizant of Matter *only* through its two properties, attraction and repulsion: therefore Matter *is* only attraction & repulsion: a finally consolidated globe of globes, being but *one* particle, would be without attraction, i e, gravitation; the existence of such a globe presupposes the expulsion of the separative ether which we know to exist between the particles as at present diffused: — thus the final globe would be matter without attraction & repulsion: — but these *are* matter: — then the final globe would be matter without matter: — i,e, no matter at all: — it must disappear. Thus Unity is *Nothingness*.

6. Matter, springing from Unity, sprang from Nothingness: — i,e, was *created*.

7. All will return to Nothingness, in returning to Unity. Read these items *after* the Report. As to the Lecture, I am very quiet about it — but, if you have ever dealt with such topics, you will recognize the novelty & *moment* of my views. What I have propounded will (in good time) revolutionize the world of Physical & Metaphysical Science. I say this calmly — but I say it.

I shall not go till I hear from you.

Truly Yours,

E A Poe

[By the bye, lest you infer that my views, in detail, are the same with those advanced in the *Nebular Hypothesis,* I venture to offer a few addenda, the substance of which was penned, though never printed, several years ago, under the head of — A Prediction.[. . .] How will *that* do for a postscript?]

> Apparently Poe did not leave for Richmond until July, probably on the 17th (see Letters 274 and 278). George H. Colton, first editor of the *American Whig Review,* was sketched by Poe in "Literati," May 1846 (see H, xv, 7–9). "The Rationale of Verse" did not appear in *Graham's* (see the note to Letter 259). Louis A. Godey was the owner and publisher of *Godey's Lady's Book.* The editors of the New York *Weekly Universe* wrote Eveleth, August 17, 1847, praising Poe as a writer, critic, and gentleman, and adding that any magazine conducted by him "could hardly fail of success"; they also said that "his habits have been shockingly irregular" (see P, II, 1236–1237). Poe's identification of E. A. Hopkins is incorrect; see Letter 265 and note. [CL 700]

264 ⊁ TO GEORGE E. ISBELL

New-York: Feb. 29 — 48.

Geo. E. Irbey Esqr

Dear Sir,

A press of business has hitherto prevented me from replying to your letter of the 10th.

"The Vestiges of Creation" I have not yet seen; and it is always unsafe and unwise to form opinions of books from reviews of them. The extracts of the work which have fallen in my way, abound in inaccuracies of fact: — still these may not materially affect the general argument. One thing is certain; that the objections of *merely* scientific men — men, I mean, who cultivate the physical sciences to the exclusion, in a greater or less degree, of the mathematics, of metaphysics and of logic — are generally invalid except in respect to scientific *details*. Of all persons in the world, they are at the same time the most bigoted and the least capable of using, generalizing, or deciding upon the facts which they bring to light in the course of their experiments. And these are the men who chiefly write the criticisms *against* all efforts at generalization — denouncing these efforts as "speculative" and "theoretical".

The notice of my Lecture, which appeared in the "New-World", was written by some one grossly incompetent to the task which he undertook. No idea of what I said can [*page 2*] be gleaned from either that or any other of the newspaper notices — with the exception, perhaps, of the "Express" — where the critique was written by a gentleman of much scientific acquirement — Mr E. A. Hopkins, of Vermont. I enclose you his Report — which, however, is inaccurate in numerous particulars. He gives my *general* conception so, at least, as not to caricature it.

I have not yet published the "Lecture["], but, when I do so, will have the pleasure of mailing you a copy. In the meantime, permit me to state, succinctly, my principal *results*.

GENERAL PROPOSITION. Because Nothing was, therefore All Things are.

1 — An inspection of the *universality* of Gravitation — of the fact that each particle tends not to any one common point — but to every other particle — suggests perfect totality, or *absolute unity*, as the source of the [p]haenomenon.

2. Gravity is but the mode in which is manifested the tendency of all things to return into their original unity.

3. I show that the law of the return — i.e the law of gravity — is but a necessary result of the necessary and sole possible mode of equable irradiation of matter through a *limited* space.

4. Were the Universe of stars — (contradistinguished from the universe of space) unlimited, no worlds could exist.

5. I show that Unity is Nothingness.

6. All matter, springing from Unity, sprang from Nothingness. i e, was *created*.

7. All will return to Unity; i e — to Nothingness.

I would be obliged to you if you would let me know how far these ideas are coincident with those of the "Vestiges".

Very Resp^y Yr. Ob. S^t

Edgar A Poe

P.S. Please return the printed slip when you have done with it.

The present prospectus was printed prior to January 4, 1848 (see Letter 259). For Poe's lecture, see Letter 262 and note; and for his mistake in identifying John H. Hopkins as "E. A. Hopkins," see Letter 265. For the publication of the lecture as *Eureka,* see the note to Letter 269. No letter from Isbell returning the "printed slip" is known. In the present prospectus Poe implies that he will have correspondents in "London, Paris, Rome and Vienna"; he does not say when the magazine will be first published. [CL 701]

265 ≻ TO MARIE LOUISE SHEW

[New York]
Thursday, March 30. [1848]

Dearest Louise, —

You see that I am not yet off to Richmond as I proposed. I have been detained by some very unexpected and very important matters which I will explain to you when I see you. What *is* the reason that you have not been out? I believe the *only* reason is that you suspect I am really anxious to see you.

When you see Mr. H.—— I wish you would say to him that I would take it as an especial favor if he would pay me a visit at Fordham next Sunday. I have something to communicate to him *of the highest importance,* and about which I need his advice. Won't you get him to come — and come with him to show him the way?

Sincerely yours,

Edgar A. Poe

For his trip to Richmond, see Letters 259 and 269. The "important matters" referred to his preparation of *Eureka* for publication by George P. Putnam (June 1848). "Mr. H.——" was John Henry Hopkins, Jr., son of Bishop Hopkins; at the time of the present letter, he was a student of the General Theological Seminary in New York. He had reviewed for the *Express* Poe's lecture on "the Universe" at the Society Library, February 3 (see Letter 263). According to an unpublished letter in the Ingram collection, University of Virginia, dated February 9, 1875, Hopkins wrote to Mrs. Shew (then Mrs. Roland Houghton) that he visited Fordham, at Poe's request, in 1848, at the time Poe was planning to publish *Eureka,* and that they argued about its pantheism. But an unpublished letter from Hopkins to Poe, dated May 15, 1848 (MS. in the Boston Public Library), speaks of having seen, a few days before, the MS. of *Eureka* in Putnam's office, and protests against a "new developement" (probably concerning the pantheistic views against which he had argued at Fordham), which, if left in, he will be forced to attack. Thus Hopkins visited Poe at Fordham, perhaps alone, prior to May 15, and possibly on the Sunday suggested in the present letter. [CL 703]

266 ➤ TO HENRY B. HIRST

New-York: May 3, 48.

My Dear Hirst,

Your letter came to hand but not your Prospectus — so that I am still in the dark as to what you mean to do. Send me a Prospectus in a letter-envelope. It is more than possible, however, that I will be in Philadelphia before the week is out: — but at all events send the Prospectus.

I am glad to hear that you are getting out "Endymion", of which you *must* know that I think highly — very highly — if I *did* fall asleep while hearing it read.

I live at Fordham, Westchester Co: — 14 miles from the city by rail-road. The cars leave from the City Hall. Should you have any trouble about finding me, inquire at the office of the "Home Journal" — or "Union Magazine."

Truly your friend

Edgar A Poe.

There is no evidence that Hirst visited Poe at Fordham, and Poe's correspondence of this period does not indicate that Poe went to Philadelphia. *Endymion, a Tale of Greece,* a poem in four cantos, was published in 1848 (*Dictionary of American Biography,* IX, 68–69). N. P. Willis was editing the *Home Journal,* and Bayard Taylor, the *Union Magazine* (see Letter 271). [CL 705]

267 ≻ TO JANE E. LOCKE

Fordham May 19 48

My Dear Friend,

Several times since the day on which your last kind and noble letter reached me I have been on the point of replying to it — but as often have been deterred through a consideration which you would not be likely to surmise, and which, most assuredly, had never influenced me in the slightest degree at any previous period of my life — at the very least since the epoch at which I attained "years of discretion": — it was simpy that *I knew not what to say* — that, in spite of your generous assurances, I feared to offend you, or at least to grieve you, by saying too much, while I could not reconcile myself to a possibility of saying too little. I felt, and still do feel, an embarrassment in writing to you that surprises me even more than it will surprise yourself. But for duties that, just now, *will not* be neglected or even postponed — the proof-reading of a [*page 2*] work of scientific detail, in which a trivial error would involve me in very serious embarrassment — I would, ere this, have been in Lowell — to clasp you by the hand — and to thank you personally for all that I owe you: — and oh, I feel that this is *very — very* much.

There are some passages in your letter which fill me with a pleasure inexpressible — but there are others which would wound me to the heart were it possible for me, even for a single moment, to suppose you in earnest — "They attach to the brief page of my own history an importance — an 'all' that while it surprises, grieves me". And again — "But what it can be? again I ask. Is it Glyndon's 'great fear' — a fear of the world? Can it be that because you absolutely know 'nothing' of me — because of what seems to you my obscurity there may be something wrong that makes you secretly hesitate to call me friend." Sweet friend, dear friend, these are *your* words but are they not *very* cruel? You have spoken of me, too, as "a poet" and yet you would accuse me — if even only impliedly, — of "a fear of the world". You can*not* mean this in your heart, or *you* can know nothing of *my* "personal history". Alas, my whole existence has been the merest Romance — in the sense of the most utter [*page 3*] unworldliness. I have never regretted this before, but there is something which whispers to me that an hour has come, or may speedily come, in which I shall most bitterly regret it.

You will not suspect me of affectation, dear friend, or of any un-worthy passion for being mysterious, merely because I find it impossible to tell you *now* — in a letter — what that one question was which I 'dare not even ask' of you. It is your own kindness — you own manifestation of a chivalrous nature — your own generous sentiment about which I am not and cannot be mistaken — it is all this, of good and loveable, existing in yourself, which have insensibly brought about in me this "fear". *Will* you not remember that the hermit life which for the last three years I have led, buried in the woods of Fordham, has necessarily prevented me from learning *anything* of you, and will you still refuse to tell me at least *one* particular of your personal history? I feel that you cannot misunderstand me. Tell me nothing — I ask nothing — which has any reference to 'worldliness' or the 'fear of the world'. Tell me only of the ties — if any exist — that bind you to the world: — and yet I perceive that I may have done very wrong in asking you this: — now that I have asked it, it seems to me the maddest of questions, involving, possibly, the most visionary of hopes. (over[ ])

[*page 4*] I have seen much that you have written, but "now that I know you" I have a deep curiosity to see all. Can I procure in N. York the volume of poems to which you refer in your second letter? [*space for address*]

A Critical and Biographical Memoir of myself appeared in "Graham's Mag:" for Feb. 45 — also one in the "Phil. Sat^y Museum" the year previous: — one also in the "Boston Notion" I forget exactly when: — and one also in the last January number of the "South. Liter^y Messenger". The only portrait, I believe, was in "Graham". I have no copy & have made several ineffectual efforts to get one. I do not think the portrait would be recognized.

Truly — *most* truly yours *always*.

E A P.

For Jane E. Locke, see the note to Letter 251. Poe's indiscretion in this letter, together with his going to Lowell, at Mrs. Locke's invitation (see Quinn, *Poe,* p. 565), to lecture in July, and his later interest in Annie L. Richmond, led to unfortunate circumstances, about which he wrote to Annie (see Letter 306). Poe's book of "scientific detail" was *Eureka,* published by Putnam, probably in June 1848 (see the note to Letter 269). Poe's statement that he has been buried "for the last three years" in Fordham is incorrect (see the note to Letter 239). The critical article on Poe in *Graham's* was by James R. Lowell (reprinted in H,

1, 367–383); the one in the *Saturday Museum,* undoubtedly by both
Henry B. Hirst and Poe, appeared with a portrait, February 25, 1843
(see Letter 153; and Quinn, *Poe,* p. 370); the one in the Boston *Times
and Notion,* an abridgment by Robert Carter of the sketch in the
Saturday Museum, appeared April 29, 1843 (see Carter to Poe, June 19,
1843, in H, XVII, 146–148); and the one in the *Southern Literary Messenger* for January 1848, was by P. P. Cooke (see H, I, 383–392).
[CL 708]

268 ➤ TO CHARLES H. MARSHALL

Fordham N. Y. May 48
Dr Sir,

Learning from Doctor Freeman that he is an applicant for the post
of Surgeon on board the Steam-Packet "United States," I have great
pleasure in mentioning that he has attended my family for the last
two years, and that I believe him in *all* respects qualified for the office
which he seeks.

Very Resp^y
Yr. Ob. S^t

To Chas. H. Marshall Esqr   Edgar A. Poe.

Charles Henry Marshall (1792–1865), a sea captain and later owner
of the Black Ball Line, mentioned in the *Dictionary of American Biography,* XII, 305–306, may have been Poe's present correspondent. The
letter is interesting for the only reference in Poe's correspondence of
the name of his family physician during his New York period. [CL 710]

269 ➤ TO CHARLES ASTOR BRISTED

Fordham — June 7 — 48.
Dr Sir,

I fear that, on reading this note, you will think me (what God
knows I am not) most ungrateful for your former kindness — and
that I presume upon it more than I should, in asking you to aid me
again. My only excuse is, that I am desperately circumstanced — in
very bitter distress of mind and body — and that I looked around me
in vain to find any friend who both can and will aid me, unless it be
yourself. My last hope of extricating myself from the difficulties
which are pressing me to death, is in going personally to a distant
connexion near Richmond, Va, and endeavoring to interest him in

my behalf. With a very little help all would go well with me — but
even that little I cannot obtain; the effort to overcome one trouble
only serving to plunge me in another. Will you forgive me, then, if
I ask you to loan me the means of getting to Richmond? My mother
in law, Mr⁵ Clemm, who will hand you this, will explain to you the
particulars of my situation.

Truly & gratefully yours

C. A. Bristed Esqre   Edgar A Poe

Mr Putnam has my book in press, but he could make me no advance,
beyond $14 — some weeks ago[.]

> Charles Astor Bristed, grandson of John Jacob Astor and one of the
> trustees of the Astor library, was a writer of some prominence, though
> his chief publications came at a date later than this letter. Poe in "Mar-
> ginalia" (*Graham's*, January 1848) spoke somewhat favorably of Bris-
> ted's article, "The Scotch School of Philosophy and Criticism," in
> *Colton's Review*, October 1845 (see also Quinn, *Poe*, pp. 566–567).
> Accompanying the letter in the sale, cited in Note 269, was one of
> Poe's calling cards with black mourning border (reproduced in Quinn,
> *Poe*, p. 567); below his name Poe wrote: "Will Mr Bristed honor Mr
> Poe with a few minutes of private conversation?" Perhaps the card
> was used at the time of Bristed's "former kindness" (see also, Letter
> 247). The Koester collection, which has the original letter, also includes
> the original MS. of a receipt that explains the postscript of the above let-
> ter: "Received of George P. Putnam Fourteen Dollars money loaned,
> to be repaid out of the proceeds of the Copyright of my work entitled
> "Eureka, a Prose Poem"; and I hereby engage, in case the sales of said
> work do not cover the expenses, according to the account rendered by
> said Putnam in January 1849, to repay the said amount of Fourteen
> Dollars; and I also engage not to ask or apply for any other loans or
> advances from said Putnam in any way, and to wait until January 1849
> for the statement of account as above, before making any demand
> whatever. Edgar A. Poe. New York, May 23, 1848. Witness, Maria
> Clemm, Marie Louise Shew." [CL 711]

270 ⇥ TO ANNA BLACKWELL

Fordham — June 14 — 48

My Dear Miss Blackwell

I fear you have been thinking every thing ill of me, and especially
that I lack common courtesy — since your letter of three weeks ago
remains unanswered.

The truth is, I have been absent from home rather more than that time. Yours came a day or two after my departure and I have only this moment received it.

And now how am I to answer it? You could not have applied for advice to any one more utterly incompetent to give it. Think, for a moment, how long I have been out of the literary world altogether. I have *no* influence — none. Your poems are, in my honest opinion, admirable — infinitely superior to many — to most of those which have succeeded in America: — but you will find difficulty in getting them published — for Copyright-Law [*page 2*] reasons, needless to specify. The Appletons will publish them, leaving you the eventual copyright, but binding you to supply all loss resulting from the publication: — and they will allow you ten per cent on all values effected after all expences are paid — so long as they continue to publish the book. No publisher will make better terms with you than these — and even these will be more advantageous to you than printing on your own account.

If there is any service I can render you, critically or otherwise, after issue of your book or before, command me without scruple[.]

I would be gratified if you would reply to this note. How happens it that you have flown away to Providence? or is this a Providential escape? Do you know Mrs Whitman? I feel deep interest in her poetry and character. I have never seen her — but once. Anne Lynch, however, told me many things about the romance [*page 3*] of her character which singularly interested me and excited my curiosity. Her poetry is, beyond question, *poetry* — instinct with genius. Can you not tell me something about her — any thing — every thing you know — and *keep my secret* — that is to say let no one know that I have asked you to do so? *May* I trust you? I can — and will.

Believe me truly your friend

Miss Anna Blackwell   Edgar A. Poe

P.S. Perhaps it would be advisable for you to defer your volume until after issue of "The Painters of America" — so as to take advantage of any impressions which may be made by your "Legend of the Waterfall" — but I am talking nonsense — you will do this *of course*.

I have no doubt whatever of the literary success of your book.

Anna Blackwell and her sister Elizabeth were English. During their visit to America in 1847–1848, Poe had met them in New York. Poe had no correspondence with Elizabeth (see her letter to Ingram, February 12, 1877, Ingram collection, University of Virginia). Poe's known letters during May and June belie his absence from Fordham. (The uncertain movements of Poe during May–June 1847 suggest that the present letter might belong to that year; however, available evidence, none of it conclusive, to be sure, tends to support the 1848 dating.) No reply by Miss Blackwell is known. Poe saw but did not meet Mrs. Whitman during his visit to Providence with Mrs. Osgood in 1845 (Quinn, *Poe*, pp. 572–573); and in the first half of 1848, Mrs. Whitman sent Poe, indirectly, some valentine verses, and Poe replied with his two poems entitled "To Helen." [CL 712]

271 ➤ TO BAYARD TAYLOR

[New York] June 15 — 48

Bayard Taylor Esq.

Dʳ Sir,

I would feel greatly indebted to you if you could spare time to look over the lines enclosed and let me know whether they will be accepted for "The Union" — if so, what you can afford to pay for them, and when they can appear.

Truly Yours,

Edgar A. Poe.

P.S. I feel that I have been guilty of discourtesy in not sooner thanking you for your picturesque and vigorous "Views A-Foot" — but when they reached me, and long afterwards, I was too ill to write — and latterly I have been every day hoping to have an opportunity of making your acquaintance and thanking you in person.

Post's *Union Magazine of Literature and Art* was sold to James L. DeGraw in 1848, and was edited by Caroline Kirkland (see Mott, *History of American Magazines*, I, 769); but P, II, 1288, and Quinn, *Poe*, p. 573, show Taylor as the editor; Poe's present letter suggests that Taylor was at least a co-editor. According to Quinn (*ibid.*), the "lines" referred to above were the second version of "To Helen," in blank verse, and appeared as "To ——" in the *Union*, November 1848. The acceptance of the poem implies a letter, perhaps from Taylor, though it is unlocated. Taylor's "Views A-Foot" was published in 1846 (see Walter C. Bronson, *American Literature*, p. 262); for Poe's comment on Taylor, see "Marginalia" in SLM, April 1849 (reprinted in H, XVI, 145–148). [CL 713]

272 ⤳ TO SARAH ANNA LEWIS

[New York] June 21 [1848]

[Dear Mrs. Lewis]

I have been spending a couple of hours most pleasantly . . . in reading and re-reading your "Child of the Sea." When it appears in print — less enticing to the eye, perhaps, than your own graceful MS. — I shall endeavor to do it critical justice in full; but in the meantime permit me to say, briefly, that I think it well conducted as a whole — abounding in narrative passages of unusual force — but especially remarkable for the boldness and poetic fervor of its sentimental portions, where a very striking *originality* is manifested. The descriptions, throughout, are warmly imaginative. The versification could scarcely be improved. The conception of Zamen is unique — a *creation* in the best poetic understanding of the term. I most heartily congratulate you upon having accomplished a work which will *live*.

Yours most sincerely,

Edgar A. Poe.

In connection with Poe's favorable comment upon Mrs. Lewis' work, see the note to Letter 321. [CL 714]

273 ⤳ TO MARIE LOUISE SHEW

[Fordham, June, 1848]

Can it be true Louise that you have the idea [fixed] in your mind to desert your unhappy and unfortunate friend and patient. You did not say so, I know, but for months I have known you was deserting me, not willingly but none the less surely — my destiny —

Disaster following fast, following faster &c.

I have had promonitions of this for months I [say] my good spirit, my loyal heart! must this follow as a sequel to all the benefits and blessings you have so generously bestowed?, are you to vanish like all I love, or desire, from my darkened and "lost Soul" — I have read over your letter again, and again, and can not make it possible with any degree of certainty, that you wrote it in your right mind (*I know you did not without tears of anguish and regret*), Is it possible your influence is lost to me? Such tender and true natures are ever loyal until death, but you are not dead, you are full of life and beauty! Louise you came in with the parson, in your floating white robe "Good morning Edgar" There was a [touch] of conventional coldness in your hurried manner and your attitude as you opened the kitchen door to find Muddie is *my last remembrance of you of you,* There was *love,* hope, and *sorrow* in your smile, instead of, love, hope & *courage,* as ever before, Oh Louise how many sorrows are before you, your ingenuous and sympathetic nature, will be constantly wounded in contact with the hollow heartless world, and for me alas! unless some true and tender and pure womanly love saves me, I shall hardly last a year longer, alone! a few short months, will tell, how far my strength — (physical, and moral) will carry me in life here, How can I believe in Providence when *you* look coldly upon me, was it not you who renewed my hopes and faith in God? . . . & in humanity Louise I heard your voice as you passed out of my sight leaving me with the Parson, "The man of God, The servant of the most High." He stood smiling and bowing at the madman Poe! *But, that* I had invited him to my house, I would have rushed out into Gods light and freedom! but I still listened to your voice! I heard you say with a sob "dear Muddie,' I heard you greet *my Caterina,* but it was only as a memory of . . . . nothing escaped *my* ear, and I was convinced it was not your generous self that was repeating words so foreign to your nature, to your tender heart! . . I heard you sob out your sense of duty to my mother, and I heard her reply — "yes Loui "yes, *"it was the mother of Alma,* that child with the madonna eyes! she is good and pure, and passably loving, but she is of her fathers type, she has not your nature, Why sacrifise your angelic perogative for a common place nature?, Why turn your soul from its true work for the desolate, to the thankless and miserly world! Why I was not a priest is a mystery, for I feel I am now a prophet and I did then, and *toward* in mind, and body, over my invited guest in spite of the duties of hospitality and regard for your feelings, Louise when he said grace and you said a low "amen," I felt my heart stop, and I was sure I was then to die before your eyes. Louise it is well, it is fortunate you looked up, with a tear in your dear eyes, and raised the window and talked of the [guava] you "had "brought for my sore thoat" your *instincts* are better than a strong mans reason — *for me,* I trust they may be for *your self!* Louse I feel I shall not prevail a shadow has already fallen upon your soul and is reflected in your eyes. It is *too late* you are floating away with the [cruel] tide. I am a coward to write this to you, but it is not a common trial, it is a fearful one to me. Such rare souls as yours, so beautify this earth! So releave it of all that is repulsive and sordid. so brighten its toils, and cares, it is hard to loose sight of them even for a short time, Again I say I am a coward, to wound your loyal unselfish and womanly heart, but you must know *and be assured,* of my *regret,* my *sorrow,* if aught I have ever written has hurt you! My *heart* never *wronged you.* I place you in *my esteem* in all *solemnity* beside the friend of my boyhood, the mother of my school fellow, of whom I told you, and as I have repeated in the poem the "Beloved Physician," as the truest, tenderest, of this worlds most womanly souls, and an angel to my forlorn and darkened nature, I will not say "lost soul" again, for your sake. I will try to overcome my grief for the sake of your unselfish care of me in the past, and in life or death, I am ever yours gratefully & devotedly

June, 1849 [1848]   Edgar A. Poe

According to her letter to Ingram (cited in Note 273), Mrs. Shew, "a mere country-girl," became alarmed at Poe's eccentricities and decided to define her position. Thus, she added, the letter was written "after my visit with Mr. Hopkins, the last time." The clarification of her position was due not so much, as the biographies imply, to Poe's "romantic" tendencies, but to the insistence on the part of the Reverend John H. Hopkins, Jr., who objected vigorously to Poe's ideas expressed in *Eureka* (see the note to Letter 265) and who felt that Mrs. Shew's duty to family and church was endangered by a continued association with Poe (see the Shew—Houghton—Ingram correspondence in the University of Virginia). In the same letter to Ingram, Mrs. Shew said, "Mr. Poe always treated me with respect and I was to him a friend in need and a friend indeed . . . and after he was dead I deeply regretted my letter to him." Poe's "Muddie" was, of course, Mrs. Clemm, and "Catarina" was the cat. The "Parson" was the Reverend John H. Hopkins, Jr. According to Mrs. Shew's letter to Ingram, April 3, 1875 (?), Hopkins "went twice to see Poe" (for the first visit, see the note to Letter 265). Poe's composition that "hurt" Mrs. Shew must refer to *Eureka.* Poe's unpublished poem to Mrs. Shew, the "Beloved Physician" ("The Beautiful Physician," see Campbell, *Poems,* p. 264), is lost. [CL 716]

274 ⊁ TO DR. THOMAS H. CHIVERS

Fordham — Westchester Co —
July 13. [14] 48.

My Dear Friend,

I have just returned from an excursion to Lowell: — this is the reason why I have not been to see you. My mother will leave this note at your hotel in the event of your not being in when she calls. I am *very* anxious to see you — as I propose going on to Richmond on Monday. Can you not come out to Fordham & spend tomorrow & Sunday with me? We can talk over matters, then, at leisure. The cars for Fordham leave the dépôt at the City Hall almost every hour — distance 14 miles[.]

Truly Yours

Poe.

Poe's "excursion to Lowell" was the occasion of his lecture on "The Poets and Poetry of America," July 10, 1848 (see Quinn, *Poe,* p. 565). Poe's trip to Richmond was for the purpose of furthering his interest in establishing the *Stylus;* he hoped by his trip through the South and West to secure a subscription list of 500 (see Letter 259). [CL 718]

275 ⊁ TO MARY OSBORNE

Fordham — July 15 — 48.

I return, dear Madam, with many thanks, the volumes you were so kind as to lend me, and which have increased even the respect and admiration I have been so long entertaining for the unknown author of "Praise and Principle". "Charms and Countercharms" — "as it is last so is it best". May I beg of you to make my acknowledgments as warmly as possible — or as admissible — to Miss McIntosh, for the favor she has done me in sending me the book — rendered doubly valuable by her autograph? Will you request for me, also, her acceptance of a late work of my own — "Eureka" — which accompanies this note? I have ventured to send with it, too, a duplicate copy, in the hope that Mrs Osborne will honor me by receiving it as an expression of my very sincere esteem and friendship.

Most truly and respectfully

Mrs Mary Osborne.   Edgar A. Poe.

Mrs. Mary Osborne lived in Fordham, and at her house Poe met Maria J. McIntosh, of Providence (see P, II, 1287). Miss McIntosh was a friend of Sarah Helen Whitman and Anna Blackwell, to whom Poe wrote, June 14, 1848; she was also the author of *Two Lives* (see P, II, 1287). Poe's *Eureka* had just been published (see Letter 269). [CL 719]

X

THE SARAH HELEN WHITMAN INTERLUDE

September 1848–January 1849

New-York — Sep. 5. 48.

Dear Madam —

Being engaged in making a collection of autographs of the most distinguished American authors, I am, of course, anxious to procure your own, and if you would so far honor me as to reply, however briefly, to this note, I would take it as a *very especial* favor.

Res^y Yr mo. ob. s^t

Mrs Sarah Helen Whitman   Edward S. T. Grey.

> "Edward S. T. Grey" was a pseudonym of Poe's (used again in Letter 332 to Mrs. Clemm). On the envelope, Mrs. Whitman wrote: "Sent by E. A. P. under an assumed name in order to ascertain if [I was] in Providence." [CL 720]

277 ➤ TO CHARLES F. HOFFMAN

Dear Sir: —

In your paper of July 29, I find some comments on "Eureka," a late book of my own; and I know you too well to suppose, for a moment, that you will refuse me the privilege of a few words in reply. I feel, even, that I might safely claim, from Mr. Hoffman, the right, which every author has, of replying to his critic *tone for tone* — that is to say, of answering your correspondent, flippancy by flippancy and sneer by sneer — but, in the first place, I do not wish to disgrace the "World;" and, in the second, I feel that I never should be done sneering, in the present instance, were I once to begin. Lamartine blames Voltaire for the use which he made of (*ruse*) misrepresentation, in his attacks on the priesthood; but our young students of Theology do not seem to be aware that in defence, or what they fancy to be defence, of Christianity, there is anything wrong in such gentlemanly peccadillos as the deliberate perversion of an author's text — to say nothing of the minor *indecora* of reviewing a book without reading it and without having the faintest suspicion of what it is about.

You will understand that it is merely the *misrepresentations* of the *critique* in question to which I claim the privilege of reply: — the mere *opinions* of the writer can be of no consequence to me — and I should imagine of very little to himself — that is to say if he knows himself, personally, as well as *I* have the honor of knowing him. The first misrepresentation is contained in this sentence: — "This letter is a keen burlesque on the Aristotelian or Baconian methods of ascertaining Truth, both of which the writer ridicules and despises, and pours forth his rhapsodical ecstasies in a glorification of the third mode — the noble art of *guessing*." What I *really* say is this: — That there is no absolute *certainty* either in the Aristotelian or Baconian process — that, for this reason, neither Philosophy is so profound as it fancies itself — and that neither has a right to sneer at that seemingly imaginative process called Intuition (by which the great Kepler attained his laws;) since "Intuition," after all, "is but the conviction arising from those *in*ductions or *de*ductions of which the processes are so shadowy as to escape our consciousness, elude our reason or defy our capacity of expression." The second misrepresentation runs thus: — "The developments of electricity and the formation of stars and suns, luminous and non-luminous, moons and planets, with their rings, &c., is deduced, very much according to the nebular theory of Laplace, from the principle propounded above." Now the impression intended to be made here upon the reader's mind, by the "Student of Theology," is, evidently, that my theory may all be very well in its way, but that it is nothing but Laplace over again, with some modifications that he (the Student of Theology) cannot regard as at all important. I have only to say that no gentleman can accuse me of the disingenuousness here implied; inasmuch as, having proceeded with my theory up to that point at which Laplace's theory *meets* it, I then *give Laplace's theory in full*, with the expression of my firm conviction of its absolute truth *at all points*. The *ground* covered by the great French astronomer compares with that covered by my theory, as a bubble compares with the ocean on which it floats; nor has he the slightest allusion to the "principle propounded above," the principle of Unity being the source of all things — the principle of Gravity being merely the Reaction of the Divine Act which irradiated all things from Unity. In fact, *no* point of *my* theory has been even so much as alluded to by Laplace.

I have not considered it necessary, here, to speak of the astronomical knowledge displayed in the "stars *and* suns" of the Student of Theology, nor to hint that it would be better grammar to say that "development and formation" *are,* than that development and formation *is.* The third misrepresentation lies in a foot-note, where the critic says: — "Further than this, Mr. Poe's claim that he can account for the existence of all organized beings — man included — merely from those principles on which the origin and present appearance of suns and worlds are explained, must be set down as mere bald assertion, without a particle of evidence. In other words we should term it *arrant fudge.*" The perversion at this point is involved in a wilful misapplication of the word "principles." I say "wilful;" because, at page 63, I am *particularly* careful to distinguish between the principles proper, Attraction and Repulsion, and those merely resultant, *sub*-principles which control the universe in detail. To these sub-principles, swayed by the immediate spiritual influence of Deity, I leave, without examination, *all that* which the Student of Theology so roundly asserts I account for on the *principles* which account for the constitution of suns, &c.

In the third column of his "review" the critic says: — "He asserts that each soul is its own God — its own Creator." What I *do* assert is, that "each soul is, *in part,* its own God — its own Creator." Just below, the critic says: — "After all these contradictory propoundings concerning God we would remind him of what he lays down on page 28 — "Of this Godhead in itself he alone is not imbecile — he alone is not impious who propounds *nothing.* A man who thus conclusively convicts himself of imbecility and impiety needs no further refutation." Now the sentence, *as I wrote it,* and as *I find it* printed on that very page which the critic refers to and which *must have been lying before him* while he quoted my words, runs thus: — "Of this Godhead, *in itself,* he alone is not imbecile, &c., who propounds nothing." By the italics, as the critic well knew, I design to distinguish between the two possibilities — that of a knowledge of God through his works and that of a knowledge of Him in his *essential nature.* The Godhead, *in itself,* is distinguished from the Godhead observed in *its effects.* But our critic is zealous. Moreover, being a divine, he is honest — ingenuous. It is his *duty* to pervert my meaning by omitting my italics — just as, in the sentence previously quoted, it was his Christian duty to falsify my argument by leaving out the two words, "in part," upon which turns the whole force — indeed the whole intelligibility of my proposition.

Were these "misrepresentations" (*is* that the name for them?) made for any less serious a purpose than that of branding my book as "impious" and myself as a "pantheist," a "polytheist," a Pagan, or a God knows what (and indeed I care very little so it be not a "Student of Theology,") I would have permitted their dishonesty to pass unnoticed, through pure contempt for the boyishness — for the *turn-down-shirt-collar-ness* of their tone: — but, as it is, you will pardon me, Mr. Editor, that I have been compelled to expose a "critic" who, courageously preserving his own *anonymosity,* takes advantage of my absence from the city to misrepresent, and thus villify me, *by name.*

Fordham, September 20, 1848   Edgar A. Poe.

> Charles Fenno Hoffman edited the *Literary World,* a weekly published in New York, from May 1847–September 1848 (see the note to Letter 201); Hoffman had "praised Poe's cosmographical lecture on hearing it, but was less friendly to *Eureka* when published" (see Mott, *History of American Magazines,* 1, 766–767). Poe seems to have identified the "Student of Theology" with John Henry Hopkins, Jr., who was attending the General Theological Seminary in New York City at the time *Eureka* was published and who seems to have exerted his influence in alienating Mrs. Shew's affection for Poe (see the note to Letter 265 and Letter 273 and note). Ingram thought he had discovered the real identity of the "Student of Theology," for on May 16, 1875, Mrs. Shew-Houghton wrote him: "I am glad Mr. Hopkins did not write the article on the Eureka, but I fear Mr. Poe thought he did, as the description of the 'turn down shirt collar' was so like the artistic habit of dress of Mr. Hopkins when he was a theological student" (MS. in the Ingram collection, University of Virginia). In all probability, however, Hopkins wrote the article. [CL 721]

278 ⇥ TO SARAH HELEN WHITMAN

[Fordham]
Sunday Night — Oct. 1 — 48.

I have pressed your letter again and again to my lips, sweetest Helen — bathing it in tears of joy, or of a "divine despair". But I — who so lately, in your presence, vaunted the "power of words" — of what avail are mere words to me now? *Could* I believe in the efficiency of prayers to the God of Heaven, I would indeed kneel —

humbly kneel — at this the most earnest epoch of my life — kneel in entreaty for words — *but* for words that should disclose to you — that might enable me to lay bare to you my whole heart. All thoughts — all passions seem now merged in that one consuming desire — the mere wish to make you comprehend — to make you see *that* for which there is no human voice — the unutterable fervor of my love for you: — for so well do I know your poet-nature, oh Helen, Helen! that I feel sure if you could but look down *now* into the depths of my soul with your pure spiritual eyes you *could* not refuse to speak to me what, alas! you still resolutely have unspoken — you would *love* me if only for the greatness of my love. Is it not something in this cold, dreary world, *to be loved?* — Oh, if I could but burn into your spirit the deep — the *true* meaning which *I* attach to those three syllables underlined! — but, alas: the effort is all in vain and "I live and die unheard".

When I spoke to you of what I felt, saying that I loved now for the *first* time, I did not hope you would believe or even understand me; nor can I hope to convince you now — but if, throughout some long, dark summer night, I could but have held you close, close to my heart and whispered to you the strange secrets of its passionate history, then indeed you would have seen that I have been far from attempting to deceive you in this respect. I could have shown you that it was not and could never have been in the power of any other than yourself to move me as I am now moved — to oppress me with this in[-] [*page 2*] effable emotion — to surround and bathe me in this electric light, illumining and enkindling my whole nature — filling my soul with glory, with wonder, and with awe. During our walk in the cemetery I said to you, while the bitter, bitter tears sprang into my eyes — "Helen, I love now — now — for the first and only time." I said this, I repeat, in no hope that you could believe me, but because I could not help feeling how unequal were the heart-riches we might offer each to each: — I, for the first time, giving my all at once, and forever, even while the words of your poem were yet ringing in my ears: —

> Oh then, beloved, I think on thee
> And on that life so strangely fair
> Ere yet one cloud of Memory
> Had gathered in Hope's golden air.

I think on thee and thy lone grave
On the green hill-side far away —
I see the wilding flowers that wave
Around thee as the night-winds sway;

And still, though only clouds remain
On Life's horizon, cold and drear,
The dream of Youth returns again
With the sweet promise of the year.

Ah Helen, these lines are indeed beautiful, beautiful — but their very beauty was cruelty *to me*. Why — *why* did you show them to me? There seemed, too, so very especial a purpose in what you did.

I have already told you that some few casual words spoken of you — [not very kindly] — by Miss Lynch, were the first in which I had ever heard your name mentioned. She described you, in some [m]easure, personally. She alluded [*page 3*] to what she called your "eccentricities" and hinted at your sorrows. Her description of the former strangely arrested — her [half sneers at] the latter enchained and riveted, my attention. She had referred to thoughts, sentiments, traits, *moods* which I knew to be my own, but which, until that moment, I had believed to be my own solely — unshared by any human being. A profound sympathy took immediate possession of my soul. I cannot better explain to you what I felt than by saying that your unknown heart seemed to pass into my bosom — there to dwell forever — while mine, I thought, was translated into your own. From that hour I loved you. Yes, I *now* feel that it was then — on that evening of sweet dreams — that the very first dawn of human love burst upon the icy Night of my spirit. Since that period I have never seen nor heard your name without a shiver half of delight, half of anxiety. The impression left, however, upon my mind, by Miss Lynch ([wh]ether through my own fault or her design I know not) was that you were a wife *now* and a most happy one; — and it is only within the last few months that I have been undeceived in this respect. For this reason I shunned your presence and even the city in which you lived. — You may remember that once, when I passed through Providence with Mrs Osgood, I positively refused to accompany her to your house, and even provoked her into a quarrel by the obstinacy and seeming unreasonableness of my refusal. I *dared* neither go nor say why I could not. I *dared* not speak of you — much less see you. For years your name never passed my lips, while my soul drank in, with a delirious thirst, all that was uttered in my presence respecting you. The merest whisper that concerned you awoke in me a shuddering sixth sense, vaguely compounded of fear, ecstatic happiness, and a wild, inexplicable [*page 4*] sentiment that resembled nothing so nearly as the consciousness of guilt. — Judge, then, with what wondering, unbelieving joy I received in your well-known MS., the Valentine which first gave me to see that you knew me to exist. The idea of what men call Fate lost then for the first time, in my eyes, its character of futility. I felt that nothing hereafter was to be doubted, and lost myself, for many weeks, in one continuous, delicious dream, where all was a vivid yet indistinct bliss. — Immediately after reading the Valentine, I wished to contrive some mode of acknowledging — without wounding *you* by seeming directly to acknowledge — my sense — oh, my keen — my profound — my exulting — my ecstatic sense of the honor you had conferred on me. To accomplish, *as* I wished it, precisely *what* I wished, seemed impossible, however; and I was on the point of abandoning the idea, when my eyes fell upon a volume of my own poems; and then the lines I had written, in my passionate boyhood, to the first, purely ideal love of my soul — to the Helen Stannard of whom I told you — flashed upon my recollection. I turned to them. They expressed all — *all* that I would have said to you — so fully — so accurately and so exclusively, that a thrill of intense superstition ran at once throughout my frame. Read the verses and then take into consideration the peculiar need I had, at the moment, for just so seemingly unattainable a mode of communicating with you as they afforded. Think of the absolute appositeness with which they fulfilled that need — expressing not only all that I would have said of your person, but all that of which I most wished to assure you, in the lines commencing "On desperate seas long wont to roam." Think, too, of the rare agreement of name — Helen and not the far more usual Ellen [—] [*page 5*] think of all these coincidences, and you will no longer wonder that, to one accustomed as I am to the Calculus of Probabilities, they wore an air of positive miracle. There was but one difficulty. — I did not wish to copy the lines in my own MS — nor did I wish you to trace them to my volume of poems. I hoped to leave at least something of doubt on your mind as to how, why, and especially whence they came. And now, when, on accidentally turning the leaf, I found even this difficulty obviated, by the

poem *happening* to be the last in the book, thus having no letter-press
on its reverse — I yielded at once to an overwhelming sense of Fatal-
ity. From that hour I have never been able to shake from my soul the
belief that my Destiny, for good or for evil, either here or hereafter,
is in some measure interwoven with your own. — Of course, I did not
expect on your part any acknowledgment of the printed lines "To
Helen"; and yet, without confessing it even to myself, I experienced
an undefinable sorrow in your silence. At length, when I thought you
had time fully to forget me (if indeed you had ever really remembered) I sent you the anonymous lines in MS. I wrote them, first,
through a pining, burning desire to communicate with you in *some*
way — even if you remained in ignorance of your correspondent. The
mere thought that *your* dear fingers would press — *your* sweet eyes
dwell upon characters which *I* had penned — characters which had
welled out upon the paper from the depths of so devout a love —
filled my soul with a rapture which seemed *then* all sufficient for my
human nature. It *then* appeared to me that merely this one thought
involved so much of bliss that here on Earth I could have no right ever
to repine — [*page 6*] no room for discontent. — If ever, *then*, I dared
to picture for myself a richer happiness, it was always connected with
your image in Heaven. But there was yet another idea which impelled
me to send you those lines: — I said to myself — The sentiment — the
holy passion which glows within my spirit *for her,* is of Heaven,
heavenly, and has no taint of the Earth. Thus there *must* lie, in the
recesses of her own pure bosom, at least the germ of a reciprocal love;
and if this be indeed so, she will need no earthly clew — she will indistinctly feel who is her correspondent. — In this case, then, I may
hope for some faint token, at least, giving me to understand that the
source of the poem is known and its sentiment comprehended even if
disapproved. Oh God! how long — *how long* I waited *in vain* —
hoping against Hope — until at length I became possessed with a
spirit far sterner — far more reckless than Despair. — I explained to
you — but without detailing the vital influence they wrought upon
my fortune — those singular additional yet seemingly trivial fatalities
by which you *happened* to address your lines to Fordham in place of
New-York — by which my aunt *happened* to get notice of their being
in the West-Farms Post Office — and by which it *happened* that, of
all my set of the "Home Journal", I failed in receiving only that individual number which contained your published verses; but I have

not yet told you that your MS. lines reached me in Richmond *on the very day* in which I was about to depart on a tour and an enterprize which would have changed my very nature — fearfully altered my very [*page 7*] soul — steeped me in a stern, cold and debasing, although brilliant and gigantic ambition — and borne me "far, far away" and forever, from *you*, sweet, sweet Helen, and from this divine dream of your Love.

And now, in the most simple words at my command, let me paint to you the impression made upon me by your personal presence. — As you entered the room, pale, timid, hesitating, and evidently oppressed at heart; as your eyes rested appealingly, for one brief moment, upon mine, I felt, for the first time in my life, and tremblingly acknowledged, the existence of spiritual influences altogether out of the reach of the reason. I saw that you were *Helen* — *my* Helen — the Helen of a thousand dreams — she whose visionary lips had so often lingered upon my own in the divine trance of passion — she whom the great Giver of all Good had prëordained to be mine — mine only — if not now, alas! then at least hereafter and *forever*, in the Heavens. — You spoke falteringly and seemed scarcely conscious of what you said. I heard no words — only the soft voice, more familiar to me than my own, and more melodious than the songs of the angels. Your hand rested within mine, and my whole soul shook with a tremulous ecstasy. And then but for very shame — but for the fear of grieving or oppressing you — I would have fallen at your feet in as pure — in as real a *worship* as was ever offered to Idol or to God. And when, afterwards, on those two successive evenings of all-Heavenly delight, you passed to and fro about the room — now sitting by my side, now far away, now standing with your hand resting on the back of my chair, while the praeternatural thrill of your touch vibrated even through the senseless wood into my heart — while you [*page 8*] moved thus restlessly about the room — as if a deep Sorrow or a more profound Joy haunted your bosom — my brain reeled beneath the intoxicating spell of your presence, and it was with no merely human senses that I either saw or heard you. It was my soul only that distinguished you there. I grew faint with the luxury of your voice and blind with the voluptuous lustre of your eyes.

Let me quote to you a passage from your letter: — "You will, perhaps, attempt to convince me that my person is agreeable to you — that my countenance interests you: — but in this respect I am so variable that I should inevitably disappoint you if you hoped to find in me to-morrow the same aspect which won you to-day. And, again, although my reverence for your intellect and my admiration of your genius make me feel like a *child* in your presence, you are not, perhaps, aware that I am many years older than yourself. I *fear* you do not know it, and that if you *had* known it you would not have felt for me as you do." — To all this what shall I — what *can* I say — except that the heavenly candor with which you speak oppresses my heart with so rich a burden of love that my eyes overflow with sweet tears. You are mistaken, Helen, very far mistaken about this matter of age. I am older than you; and if illness and sorrow have made you seem older than you are — is not all this the best of reason for my loving you the more? Cannot my patient cares — my watchful, earnest attention — cannot the magic which lies in such devotion as I feel for you, win [*page 9*] back for you much — oh, very much of the freshness of your youth? But grant that what you urge were even true. Do you not feel in your inmost heart of hearts that the "soul-love" of which the world speaks so often and so idly is, in this instance at least, but the veriest, the most absolute of realities? Do you not — I ask it of your reason, *darling*, not less than of your heart — do you not perceive that it is my diviner nature — my spiritual being — which burns and pants to commingle with your own? Has the soul *age*, Helen? Can Immortality regard Time? Can that which began *never* and shall never end, consider a few wretched years of its incarnate life? Ah, I could weep — I could *almost* be angry with you for the unwarranted wrong you offer to the purity — to the sacred reality of my affection. — And how *am* I to answer what you say of your personal appearance? Have I not *seen* you, Helen? Have I not heard the more than melody of your voice? Has not my heart ceased to throb beneath the magic of your smile? Have I not held your hand in mine and looked steadily into your soul through the crystal Heaven of your eyes? Have I not done all these things? — or do I dream? — or am I mad? Were you *indeed* all that your fancy, enfeebled and perverted by illness, tempts you to suppose that you are, still, life of my life! I would but love you — but worship you the more: — it would be so glorious a happiness to be able to *prove* to you what I feel! But as it is, what can I — what *am* I to say? *Who* ever spoke of you without emotion — without praise? Who *ever* saw you and did not love?

[*page 10*] But now a deadly terror oppresses me; for I too clearly see that these objections — so groundless — so futile when urged to one whose nature must be so well known to you as mine is — can scarcely be meant earnestly; and I tremble lest they but serve to mask others, more real, and which you hesitate — perhaps in pity — to confide to me. Alas! I too distinctly perceive, also, that in no instance you have ever permitted yourself to say that you *love me.* You are aware, sweet Helen, that on my part there are insuperable reasons forbidding me to *urge* upon you my love. Were I not poor — had not my late errors and reckless excesses justly lowered me in the esteem of the good — were I wealthy, or could I offer you worldly honors — ah then — then — how proud would I be to persevere — to sue — to plead — to kneel — to pray — to beseech you for your love — in the deepest humility — at your feet — at your feet, Helen, and with floods of passionate tears.

And now let me copy here one other passage from your letter: — "I find that I cannot now tell you all that I promised. I can only say to you [that had I youth and health and beauty, I would live for you and die with you. *Now,* were I to allow myself to love you, I could only enjoy a bright, brief hour of rapture and die — perhaps [***********]." — The last five words have been [***************] Ah, beloved, beloved Helen the darling of my heart — my first and my real love]! — may God forever shield *you* from the agony which these your words occasion *me!* [How *selfish* — how despicably selfish seems [*page 11*] now all — *all* that I have written! Have I not, indeed, been demanding at your hands a love which might endanger your life?] You will never, *never* know — you can *never* picture to yourself the hopeless, rayless despair with which I now trace these words. Alas Helen! my soul! — what is it that I have been saying to you? — to what madness have I been urging you? — *I* who am *nothing* to you — *you* who have a dear mother and sister to be blessed by your life and love. But ah, darling! if I *seem* selfish, yet believe that I truly, *truly* love you, and that it is the most spiritual of love that I speak, even if I speak it from the depths of the most passionate of hearts. Think — oh, think for *me,* Helen, and for yourself! *Is* there *no* hope? — is there *none?* May not this terrible [disease] be conquered? Frequently it *has* been overcome. And more frequently are we deceived in respect to its actual existence. Long-continued nervous disorder — espe-

cially when exasperated by ether or [*excision*] — will give rise to *all*
the symptoms of heart-dis[ease an]d so deceive the most skillful
physicians — as even in [my o]wn case they were deceived. But admit
that this fearful evil *has* indeed assailed you. Do you not all the more
really need the devotionate care which only one who loves you as *I* do,
could or would bestow? On my bosom could I not still the throbbings
of your own? Do not mistake me, Helen! Look, with your search-
ing — your seraphic eyes, into the soul of my soul, and see if you can
discover there one taint of an ignoble nature! At your feet — if you
so willed it — I would cast from me, forever, all merely human
desire, and clothe myself in the glory of a pure, calm, and *unexacting*
affection. I would [*page 12*] comfort you — soothe you — tranquil-
lize you. My love — my faith — should instil into your bosom a
praeternatural calm. You would rest from care — from all worldly
agitation. You would get better, and finally well. And if *not*,
Helen, — if not — if you *died* — then at least would I clasp your
dear hand in death, and willingly — *oh, joyfully — joyfully — joyfully* — go down *with* you into the night of the Grave.

Write soon — soon — oh, *soon!* — but not *much.* Do not weary or
agitate yourself for *my* sake. Say to me those coveted words which
would turn Earth into Heaven. If Hope is forbidden, I will *not*
murmur if you comfort me with Love. — The papers of which you
[speak] I will procure and forward immediately. They will cost me
nothing, *dear* Helen, an[d] I therefore re-enclose you what you so
thoughtfully s[ent.] Think that, in doing so, my lips are pressed
ferv[ently] and lingeringly upon your own. And now, in closing this
long, long letter, let me speak last of that which lies nearest my heart —
of that precious gift which I would not exchange for the surest hope of
Paradise. It seems to me too sacred that I should even whisper *to you*,
the dear giver, what it is. My soul, this night, shall come to you in
dreams and speak to you those fervid thanks which my pen is all
powerless to utter.

                                                            Edgar

P. S. Tuesday Morning. — I beg you to believe, dear Helen, that I
replied to your letter *immediately* upon its receipt; but a most unusual
storm, up to this moment, precludes all access to the City.

    Anna C. Lynch, New York poetess and Blue Stocking, held soirées
    which were attended by Poe and other literary figures (for correspond-

ence between her and Poe, see the notes to Letter 237). She and Frances
Sargent Osgood, with whom Poe visited Providence in the summer of
1845 and saw but did not meet Mrs. Whitman, were instrumental in
starting the "affair" between Poe and the Seeress of Providence (see
Quinn, *Poe*, pp. 572–573). For Poe's reference to the valentine, see
Quinn, *ibid*. Poe had planned to tour the South to get subscriptions
for his *Stylus*. [CL 723]

279 ⊁ TO T. L. DUNNELL

New York October 18, 1848

Dear Sir,

I accept with pleasure your very flattering invitation to lecture in
Providence, and will be at the Earl-House on the 13th of December.

Respectfully Yr. Ob. St.

Edgar A. Poe

Dunnell wrote again (location of original unknown) about November
23–24, apparently asking Poe to lecture on December 6 instead of on
the 13th, and Poe answered (location of original unknown) about
November 25–26 (see Letter 291). This correspondence suggests another exchange of letters between Dunnell and Poe, setting December 20
as the lecture date, but no evidence exists, except the actual delivery
of the lecture at the Earl House, Providence, on the night of December 20, that such an exchange took place. Mrs. Whitman wrote Stoddard, September 30, 1872 (see Quinn, *Poe*, p. 579), that the lecture
date [of December 13] had to be postponed owing to the excitement
created by the presidential election of 1848. [CL 726]

280 ⊁ TO SARAH HELEN WHITMAN

[Fordham, Oct. 18, 48]

In pressing my last letter between your dear hands, there passed into
your spirit a sense of the *Love* that glowed within those pages: — you
say this, and I feel that indeed it *must* have been so: — but, in receiving the paper upon which your eyes now rest, did no shadow steal over
you from the *Sorrow* within? — Oh God! how I now curse the im-
potence of the pen — the inexorable *distance* between us! I am
pining to speak to *you*, Helen, — to you in person — to be near you
while I speak — gently to press your hand in mine — to look into

your soul through your eyes — and thus to *be sure* that my voice passes into your heart. Only thus could I hope to make you understand what I feel; and even thus I *should* not hope to make you do so; for it is only Love, which can comprehend Love — and alas! you do *not* love me. — Bear with me! have patience with me! — for indeed *my heart is broken*; and, let me struggle as I will, I cannot *write* to you the calm, cold language of a world which I loathe — of a world in which I have no interest — of a world which is *not mine*. I repeat to you that my heart is broken — that I have no farther object in life — that I have absolutely no wish but to die. These are hackneyed phrases; but they will not now impress you as such — for you must and *do* know the passionate agony with which I write them. *"You do not love me"*: — in this brief sentence lies all I can conceive of despair. I have no resource — no hope: — Pride itself fails me now. You do not love me; or you could not have imposed upon me the torture of eight days' silence — of eight days' terrible suspense. You do not love me — or, responding [*page 2*] to my prayers, you would have cried to me — *"Edgar, I do."* Ah, Helen, the emotion which now consumes me teaches me too well the nature of the impulses of Love! Of what avail to me, in my deadly grief, are your enthusiastic words of mere *admiration?* Alas; — alas! — I *have been* loved, and a relentless Memory contrasts what *you* say with the unheeded, unvalued language of others. — But ah, — again, and most especially — you do *not* love me, or you would have felt too thorough a sympathy with the sensitiveness of my nature, to have so wounded me as you have done with this terrible passage of your letter: — "How often I have heard men and even women say of you — 'He has great intellectual power, but *no* principle — *no* moral sense.'" Is it possible that such expressions as these could have been *repeated* to me — to me — by one whom I loved — ah, whom I *love* — by one at whose feet I knelt — I *still* kneel — in deeper worship than ever man offered to God? — And you proceed to ask me *why* such opinions exist. You will feel remorse for the question, Helen, when I say to you that, until the moment when those horrible words first met my eye, I would not have believed it *possible* that any such opinions could have existed at all: — but that they *do* exist *breaks my heart* in separating us forever. I love you too truly ever to have offered you my hand — ever to have sought your love — had I known my name to be *so* stained as your expressions imply. — Oh God! what *shall* I say to you Helen, *dear* Helen? — let me call you *now* by that sweet name, if I may never so call you again. — It is altogether in vain that I tax my Memory or my Conscience. There is no oath which seems [*page 3*] to me so sacred as that sworn by the all-divine love I bear you. — By this love, then, and by the God who reigns in Heaven, I swear to you that my soul is incapable of dishonor — that, with the exception of occasional follies and excesses which I bitterly lament, but to which I have been driven by intolerable sorrow, and which are hourly committed by others without attracting any notice whatever — I can call to mind no act of my life which would bring a blush to my cheek — or to yours. If I have erred at all, in this regard, it has been on the side of what the world would call a Quixotic sense of the honorable — of the chivalrous. The indulgence of this sense has been the true voluptuousness of my life. It was for this species of luxury that, in early youth, I deliberately threw away from me a large fortune, rather than endure a trivial wrong. It was for this that, at a later period, I did violence to my own heart, and married, for another's happiness, where I knew that no possibility of my own existed. — Ah, how profound is my love for you, since it forces me into these egotisms for which you will inevitably despise me! Nevertheless, I *must* now speak to you the truth or nothing. It was in mere indulgence, then, of the sense to which I refer, that, at one dark epoch of my late life, for the sake of one who, deceiving and betraying, still loved me much, I sacrificed what seemed in the eyes of men my honor, rather than abandon what *was* honor in hers and in my own. — But, alas! for nearly three years I have been ill, poor, living out of the world; and thus, as I now painfully see, have afforded opportunity to my enemies — and especially to one, the most malignant and pertinacious of all fiends — [a woman whose loathsome love I could do nothing but repel with scorn —] [*page 4*] to slander me, in private society, without my knowledge and thus with impunity. Although much, however, may (and I now see must) have been said to my discredit, during my retirement, those few who, knowing me well, have been steadfastly my friends, permitted nothing to reach my ears — unless in one instance, where the malignity of the accuser hurried her beyond her usual caution, and thus the accusation was of such character that I could appeal to a court of justice for redress. The tools employed in this instance were Mr Hiram Fuller and Mr T. D. English. I replied to the charge fully, in a public newspaper — afterwards suing the

"Mirror" (in which the scandal appeared) obtaining a verdict and recovering such an amount of damages as, for the time, completely to break up that journal. — And you ask me *why* men so *mis*judge me — *why* I have enemies. If your knowledge of my character and of my career does not afford you an answer to the query, at least it does not become *me* to suggest the answer. Let it suffice that I have had the audacity to remain poor that I might preserve my independence — that, nevertheless, in letters, to a certain extent and in certain regards, I have been "successful" — that I have been a critic — and unscrupulously honest and no doubt in many cases a bitter one — that I have uniformly attacked — where I attacked at all — those who stood highest in power and influence — and that, whether in literature or in society, I have seldom refrained from expressing, either directly or indirectly, the pure contempt with which the pretensions of ignorance, arrogance, or imbecility inspire me. — And you who know all this — *you* ask me *why* [*page 5*] I have enemies. Ah, Helen, I have a hundred friends for every individual enemy — but has it never occurred to you that you do not live *among* my friends? Miss Lynch, Miss Fuller, Miss Blackwell, Mrs Ellet — neither these nor any within their influence, are my friends. Had you read my criticisms generally, you would see, too, how and why it is that the Channings — the Emerson and Hudson coterie — the Longfellow clique, one and all — the cabal of the "N. American Review" — you would see why all these, whom *you* know best, know *me* least and are my enemies. Do you not remember with how deep a sigh I said to you in Providence — "My heart is heavy, Helen, for I see that *your* friends are not my own."? — But the cruel sentence in your letter would not — *could* not so deeply have wounded me, had my soul been first strengthened by those assurances of your love which I so wildly — so vainly — and, I now feel, so presumptuously entreated. That our souls are one, every line which you have ever written asserts — but our hearts do *not* beat in unison. Tell me, *darling!* to *your* heart has any angel ever whispered that the very noblest lines in all human poetry are these — hackneyed though they be?

> I know not — I ask not if guilt's in thy heart: —
> I but know that *I love thee* whatever thou art.

When I first read your letter I could do nothing but shed tears, while I repeated, again and again, those glorious, those all-compre-

175

Fordham N.Y.

May 48

Dr Sir,

Learning from Doctor Freeman that he is an applicant for the post of Surgeon on board the Steam-Packet "United States," I have great pleasure in mentioning that he has attended my family for the last two years, and that I believe him in _all_ respects qualified for the office which he seeks.

Very Resp.ʸ

Yr. Ob. Sᵗ

Edgar A. Poe.

To Chas. H. Marshall Esqᵉ

POE TO CHARLES H. MARSHALL, MAY 1848
(Letter 268)

POE'S FORDHAM COTTAGE

hensive verses, till I could scarcely hear my own voice for the passionate throbbings of my heart.

Forgive me, best and only beloved Helen, if there be bitterness in
my tone. Towards *you* there is no room in my soul [*page 6*] for any
other sentiment than devotion: — it is Fate only which I accuse: —
it is my own unhappy nature which wins me the true *love* of no
woman whom by <by> any possibility *I* could love.

I heard something, a day or two ago, which, had your last letter
never reached me, *might* not irreparably have disturbed the relations
between us, but which, as it is, withers forever all the dear hopes up-
springing in my bosom. — A few words will explain to you what I
mean. Not long after the receipt of your Valentine I learned, for the
first time, that you were free — unmarried. I will not pretend to
express to you what is absolutely inexpressible — that wild — long-
enduring thrill of joy which pervaded my whole being on hearing that
it was not *impossible* I might one day call you by the sacred title, wife:
— but there was one alloy to this happiness: — I *dreaded* to find you
in worldly circumstances superior to my own. Let me speak freely to
you *now*, Helen, for perhaps I may never thus be permitted to speak
to you again — Let me speak openly — fearlessly — trusting to the
generosity of your own spirit for a *true* interpretation of my own.
I repeat, then, that I *dreaded* to find you in worldly circumstances
superior to mine. So great was my *fear* that you were rich, or at least
possessed some property which might cause you to *seem* rich in the
eyes of one so poor as I had always permitted myself to be — that, on
the day I refer to, I had not the courage to ask my informant any
questions concerning you. — I feel that you will have difficulty in
comprehending me; but the horror with which, during my sojourn
[*page 7*] in the world, I have seen affection made a subject of barter,
had, long since, — long before my marriage — inspired me with the
resolution that, under *no* circumstances, would I marry where "interest," as the world terms it, could be suspected as, on my part, the
object of the marriage. As far as this point concerned yourself, however, I was relieved, the next day, by an assurance that you were
wholly dependent upon your mother. May I — dare I add — can you
believe me when I say that this assurance was rendered doubly *grateful*
to me by the additional one that you were in ill health and had suffered more from domestic sorrow than falls usually to the lot of
woman? — and even if your faith in my nature is *not* too greatly

tasked by such an assertion, *can* you forbear thinking me unkind, selfish or ungenerous? You can*not*: — but oh! the sweet dreams which absorbed me at once: — dear dreams of a devotional care for you that should end only with life — of a tender, cherishing, patient solicitude which should bring you back, at length, to health and to happiness — a care — a solicitude — which should find its glorious reward in winning me, after long years, that which I could *feel* to be your *love!* Without well understanding *why,* I had been led to fancy you ambitious: — perhaps the fancy arose from your lines:

> Not a bird that roams the forest
> Shall our lofty eyrie share! —

but my very soul glowed with ambition for *your* sake, although I have always contemned it for my own. It was then only — then when I thought of *you* — that I dwelt exultingly upon what I felt that I could accomplish in Letters and in Literary Influence — in the widest and noblest field of human ambition. [*page 8*] "I will erect", I said, "a prouder throne than any on which mere monarch ever sat; and on this throne she — *she* shall be my queen". When I saw you, however — when I touched your gentle hand — when I heard your soft voice, and perceived how greatly I had misinterpreted your womanly nature — these triumphant visions melted sweetly away in the sunshine of a *love* ineffable; and I suffered my imagination to stray with you, and with the few who love us both, to the banks of some quiet river, in some lovely valley of our land. Here, not *too* far secluded from the world, we exercised a taste controlled by no conventionalities, but the sworn slave of a Natural Art, in the building for ourselves a cottage which no human being could ever pass without an ejaculation of wonder at its strange, wierd, and incomprehensible yet most simple beauty. Oh, the sweet and gorgeous, but not often rare flowers in which we half buried it! — the grandeur of the little-distant mag-nolias and tulip-trees which stood guarding it — the luxurious velvet of its lawn — the lustre of the rivulet that ran by the very door — the tasteful yet quiet comfort of the interior — the music — the books — the unostentatious pictures — and, above all, the love — the *love* that threw an unfading *glory* over the whole! — Ah Helen! my heart is, *indeed, breaking* and I must now put an end to these divine dreams. Alas! *all* is now a dream; for I have lately heard that of you which, (taken in connexion with your letter and with that of which your letter does *not* assure me) puts it forever out of my power to ask you — *again* to ask you — to become my wife. That [*page 9*] *many* persons, in your presence, have declared me wanting in honor, appeals irresistibly to an instinct of my nature — an instinct which *I feel* to be honor, let the dishonorable say what they may, and forbids me, under such circumstances, to insult you with my love: — but that you are quite independent in your worldly position (as I have just heard) — in a word that *you are comparatively rich while I am poor,* opens between us *a gulf* — a gulf, alas! which the sorrow and the slander of the World have rendered forever impassable — by *me.*

I have not yet been able to procure all the criticisms &c. of which you spoke, but will forward them, by express, in a day or two. Meantime I enclose the lines by Miss Fuller; and "The Domain of Arnheim" which happens to be at hand, and which, moreover, expresses *much of my soul.* — It was about the 10th of Sep., I think, that your sweet MS. verses reached me in Richmond. I lectured in Lowell on the 10th of July. Your first letter was received by me, at Fordham, on the evening of Saturday, Sep. 30. I *was* in Providence, or its neighborhood, during the Monday you mention. In the morning I re-visited the cemetery: — at 6 P.M. I left the city in the Stonington train for N. Y. I cannot explain to you — since I cannot myself comprehend — the feeling which urged me not to see you again before going — not to bid you a second time *farewell.* I had a sad foreboding at heart. In the seclusion of the cemetery you sat by my side — on the very spot where my arm first tremblingly encircled your waist.

Edgar

Mrs. Whitman omitted numerous passages in transcribing this letter for J. H. Ingram. The "fiend" referred to is the same Mrs. Elizabeth Frieze Ellet mentioned at the beginning of page 5 in connection with Anna C. Lynch, Margaret Fuller, and probably Elizabeth Blackwell, sister of Anna Blackwell to whom Poe wrote on June 14, 1848; Elizabeth Blackwell wrote Ingram, February 12, 1877 (Ingram collection, University of Virginia), that she had seen Poe but twice, once on a visit with another lady during his convalescence in 1847, and later when he returned the call, that she had never corresponded with him. William Henry Channing and William Ellery Channing, the younger, were transcendentalists, "Frogpondians" as Poe termed the whole group. Henry Norman Hudson, a New England Shakespearean, was belittled by Poe in the *Broadway Journal,* December 13, 1845 (see P, II, 1070). Poe's charges of plagiarism against Longfellow are well known. In the left margin of page 9, opposite "10th of Sep.," Mrs. Whitman wrote: "It was earlier"; Poe is wrong in his date of September 10, for he was back in Fordham by September 5, the date of his first letter to her. Poe's lecture of July 10, 1848, was on "The Poets and Poetry of America" (see Quinn, *Poe*, p. 565). Quinn (*ibid.*, p. 575) says Poe visited Mrs. Whitman on September 21; if true, then Poe's reference to "Monday" is probably to September 25. [CL 727]

281 ⋟ TO JANE E. LOCKE

My dear Mrs Locke,

Permit me, by this note, to make you personally acquainted with my friend, Mrs S. Anna Lewis: — through her works I am aware that she is already well known to you. I feel that I need not ask you to show her every attention: — You will do it for her own sake, for *your* own and for mine.

Faithfully Yours ever,

Fordham — October — 1848.   Edgar A. Poe.
To Mrs Jane Ermina Locke

In connection with this letter, see Letter 282 and Letter 267. [CL 728]

282 ⋟ TO ANNIE L. RICHMOND

Fordham — Oct — 48.

My *very dear* friend —

This note will be handed you by Mrs Stella Anna Lewis, of whose poetic genius you will remember I spoke so much at length in my late lecture at Lowell. But I need scarcely have alluded to this: — she is, no doubt, well known to you through her works; and I feel assured that you have but to know her personally to be as proud of her friendship as, unquestionably, she must and will be of your own[.]

Forever the most sincere of your friends

Mrs N. L. Richmond.   Edgar A. Poe.

This is the first known letter from Poe to Annie (Nancy Locke Heywood) Richmond, wife of Charles B. Richmond, of Lowell, Massachusetts. Westford was the home of the Heywoods, and was not far from

Lowell; Poe visited in Westford at least once (see Letter 309). Poe met Annie through Mrs. Jane (Ermina Starkweather) Locke, at the time of his Lowell lecture on "The Poets and Poetry of America," July 10, 1848. The friendship became a lasting one. No letters from Mrs. Richmond to Poe are extant, but Poe's reveal a sincere, even passionate affection. Mrs. Richmond exerted a good influence on Poe, inspiring his genius, and fortifying him against many weaknesses; in fact, in Letter 330, he wrote: "I *must* be somewhere where I can see Annie." Mrs. Richmond copied for J. H. Ingram many of Poe's letters to her, but never intended that they should be printed. When his *Appleton's Journal* article appeared, she expressed her displeasure and regret. Subsequently, in his *Life* of Poe, Ingram made further editings of the letters. Therefore, in order to arrive at the fullest known text of what Poe wrote to Mrs. Richmond, it has been necessary in several instances to formulate a composite text from the different printings made by Ingram (see Letters 298, 301, 303, 309, 311). Mrs. Sarah Anna Lewis was an unimportant New York poetess (see Letter 257). [CL 729]

283 ≻ TO [SARAH HELEN WHITMAN]

[November 3, 1848?]

[. . . . .]

Oh how powerless is the pen to express such feelings as now consume me! May the God of Heaven protect you until I clasp you to my heart —

Your own

Edgar.

In connection with this fragment, see Letter 284 and note. [CL 731]

284 ≻ TO SARAH HELEN WHITMAN

[Providence, November 7, 1848]

Dearest Helen —

I have *no* engagements, but am *very* ill — so much so that I must go home, if possible — but if you say "stay", I will try & do so. If you cannot see me — write me *one word* to say that you *do* love me and that, *under all circumstances,* you will be mine. Remember that these coveted words you have never yet spoken — and, nevertheless, I have not reproached you. It was not in my power to be here on

Saturday as I proposed, or I would undoubtedly have kept my promise.
If you can see me, even for a few moments do so — but if not write —
or send some message which will comfort me.

[Signature missing]

Poe's inability to come to Providence on Saturday is treated in Letter
286. [CL 733]

285 ➤ TO SARAH HELEN WHITMAN

[New York] Steamboat Nov 14 1848

My own dearest Helen, *so* kind so true, so generous — so unmoved
by all that would have moved one who had been less than angel: — beloved of my heart of my imagination of my intellect — life of my
life — soul of my soul — dear, dearest Helen, how shall I ever thank
you as I ought.

I am calm & tranquil & but for a strange shadow of coming evil
which haunts me I should be happy. That I am not supremely happy,
even when I feel your dear love at my heart, terrifies me. What can
this mean?

Perhaps however it is only the necessary reaction after such terrible
excitements.

It is 5 o'clock & the boat is just being made fast to the wharf. I
shall start in the train that leaves New York at 7 for Fordham. I write
this to show you that I have not *dared* to break my promise to you.
And now dear *dearest* Helen be true to me[. . . . .]

[Signature missing]

Poe is returning from Providence. Probably he "promised" not to
drink. [CL 736]

286 ➤ TO ANNIE L. RICHMOND

Fordham Nov. 16ᵗʰ 1848 —

Ah, Annie Annie! *my* Annie! what cruel thoughts about your Eddy
must have been torturing your heart during the last terrible fortnight,
in which you have heard *nothing* from me — not even one little word
to say that I still lived & loved you. But Annie I know that you *felt*

too deeply the nature of my love for you, to doubt *that*, even for one moment, & this thought has comforted me in my bitter sorrow — I could bear that you should imagine *every other evil except that one* — that my soul had been untrue to yours. Why am I not *with* you now *darling* that I might sit by your side, press your dear hand in mine, & look deep down into the clear Heaven of your eyes — so that the words which I now can only *write*, might sink into your heart, and make you comprehend what it is that I would say — And yet Annie, *all* that I wish to say — all that my soul pines to express at this instant, is included in the one word, *love* — To be with you now — so that I might whisper in your ear the divine emotion[s], which agitate me — I would willingly — oh *joyfully* abandon this world with all my hopes of another: — but you *believe* this, Annie — you do believe it, & will always believe it — So long as I think that you *know* I love you, as no man ever loved woman — so long as I think you comprehend in some measure, the fervor with which I adore you, *so* long, no worldly trouble can ever render me absolutely wretched. But oh, *my darling, my* Annie, my own sweet *sister* Annie, my *pure* beautiful angel — *wife* of my soul — to be mine hereafter & *forever in the Heavens* — how shall I explain to you the *bitter, bitter* anguish which has tortured me since I left you? You saw, you *felt* the agony of grief with which I bade you farewell — You remember my expressions of gloom — of a dreadful horrible foreboding of ill — Indeed — *indeed* it seemed to me that death approached me even then, & that I was involved in the shadow which went before him — As I clasped you to my heart, I said to myself — "it is for the last time, until we meet in Heaven" — I remember nothing distinctly, from that moment until I found myself in Providence — I went to bed & wept through a long, long, hideous night of despair — When the day broke, I arose & endeavored to quiet my mind by a rapid walk in the cold, keen air — but all *would* not do — the demon tormented me still. Finally I procured two ounces of laudnum & without returning to my Hotel, took the cars back to Boston. When I arrived, I wrote you a letter, in which I opened my whole heart to you — to *you* — my Annie, whom I so madly, so distractedly love — I told you how my struggles were more than I could bear — how my soul revolted from saying the words which were to be said — and that not even for your dear sake, could I bring myself to say them. I then reminded you of that holy promise, which was the last I exacted from you in parting — the promise that,

under all circumstances, you would come to me on my bed of death —
I implored you to come *then* — mentioning the place where I should
be found in Boston — Having written this letter, I swallowed about
half the laudnum & hurried to the Post-Office — intending not to take
the rest until I saw you — for, I did not doubt for one moment, that
my own Annie would keep her sacred promise — But I had not cal-
culated on the strength of the laudanum, for, before I reached the
Post Office my reason was entirely gone, & the letter was never put in.
Let me pass over, my darling *sister,* the awful horrors which succeeded
— A friend was at hand, who aided & (if it can be called saving)
saved me — but it is only within the last three days that I have been
able to remember what occurred in that dreary interval — It appears
that, after the laudanum was rejected from the stomach, I became
calm, & to a casual observer, sane — so that I was suffered to go back
to Providence — Here I saw *her,* & spoke, for *your* sake, the words
which you urged me to speak — Ah Annie Annie! *my* Annie! — *is*
your heart *so* strong? — is there *no* hope! — is there *none?* — I feel
that I *must* die if I persist, & yet, how can I now retract with honor? —
Ah *beloved,* think — think for *me* & for yourself — do I not *love* you
Annie? do you not *love me?* Is not this *all?* Beyond this blissful
thought, what other consideration *can* there be in this dreary world!
It is not *much* that I ask, *sweet sister Annie* — my mother & myself
would take a small cottage at Westford — oh *so* small — so *very*
humble — I should be far away from the tumult[s] of the world —
from the ambition which I loathe — I would labor day & night, and
with industry, I could accomplish *so* much — Annie! it would be a
Paradise beyond my wildest hopes — I could see some of your beloved family *every* day, & you often — oh VERY often — I would hear
from you continually — regularly & *our* dear mother would be with
us & love us both — ah *darling* — do not these pictures touch your
inmost heart? Think — oh *think* for me — before the words — the
vows are spoken, which put yet another terrible *bar* between us —
before the time goes by, beyond which there must be *no* thinking —
I call upon you in the name of God — in the name of the holy love
I bear you, to be *sincere* with me — *Can* you, *my* Annie, *bear* to think
I am another's? *It would give me supreme — infinite bliss* to hear you
say that you could *not* bear it — I am at home now with my dear
muddie who is endeavoring to comfort me — but the sole words which
soothe me, are those in which she speaks of "*my Annie*" — she tells

me that she has written you, begging you to come on to Fordham — ah beloved Annie, IS IT NOT POSSIBLE? I am so *ill* — so terribly, hopelessly ILL in body and mind, that I feel I CANNOT live, unless I can feel your sweet, gentle, loving hand pressed upon my forehead — oh my *pure, virtuous, generous, beautiful, beautiful sister* Annie! — is it not POSSIBLE for you to come — if only for one little week? — until I subdue this fearful agitation, which if continued, will either destroy my life or, drive me hopelessly mad — Farewell — here & hereafter —

forever your own

Eddy —

In connection with this letter, see Letter 284 and notes. The present letter is of the utmost importance. It reveals Poe's sincere feeling for Mrs. Richmond, a feeling that did not decrease in its passion during the rest of his life. The contrast between the intense emotion expressed in the present letter and the rather formal objectivity of the note of October 1848 (Letter 282) is difficult both to explain and to accept. Still, Poe would not reveal to Mrs. Lewis his feelings for Mrs. Richmond, and since July 1848, when he first met Mrs. Richmond, Poe's love for her may have grown through contacts and even letters, not now supported by available evidence. When Poe says, ". . . how my soul revolted from saying the words which were to be said," he alludes to his proposed engagement to Mrs. Whitman. The letter Poe wrote to Mrs. Richmond in Boston has never come to light. Biographers of Poe have stated that he went to Lowell late in October to deliver a lecture, which was postponed owing to the excitement of the national election, and that at this time he visited Mrs. Richmond. Direct evidence points not to an October but to a December lecture, which was postponed (see Letters 279 and 291); thus Poe was in Lowell probably to see Mrs. Richmond before going to Providence. This letter also clears away, to some extent, Poe's movements at this time. Whether Poe gained Mrs. Whitman's promise to write to him, either during a visit to Providence prior to his arrival in Lowell, or by a letter (unlocated), she seems to have complied, and the letter (see Mrs. Whitman to Ingram, October 25, 1875, in the Ingram collection) reached him about November 1–2. It "perplexed and agitated him," but he answered that he would reach Providence on November 4. Thus the present letter shows Poe setting out for Providence on November 4, buying laudanum there and returning to Boston on November 5, writing the unsent letter to Mrs. Richmond and swallowing the laudanum on November 5, recuperating and proceeding to Providence sometime before the morning of November 7, when he wrote his note of Tuesday, November 7, to

Mrs. Whitman (Letter 284). Poe continued to dream of a home for himself and Mrs. Clemm in Westford or Lowell, in order to be near Mrs. Richmond (see Letters 303 and 330). [CL 737]

287 ⤝ TO EDWARD VALENTINE

New-York, — Nov. 20ᵗʰ 1848:

Dear Sir,

After a long & bitter struggle with illness, poverty, and the thousand evils which attend them, I find myself at length in a position to establish myself permanently, and to triumph over all difficulties, if I could but obtain, from some friend, a very little pecuniary aid. In looking around me for such a friend, I can think of no one, with the exception of yourself, whom I see the least prospect of interesting in my behalf — and even as regards yourself, I confess that my hope is feeble. In fact I have been *so long* depressed that it will be a most difficult thing for me to rise — and rise I never can without such aid as I now entreat at your hands. I call to mind, however, that, during my childhood, you were very kind to me, and, I believe, very fond of me. For this reason and because I really do *not* know where else to turn for the assistance I so *much* need at this moment, I venture to throw myself upon your generosity & ask you to lend me $200. With this sum I should be able to take the first steps in an enterprise where there could be no doubt of my success, and which, if successful, would, in one or two years ensure me fortune and very great influence. I refer to the establishment of a Magazine for which I have already a good list of subscribers, and of which I need a Prospectus — If for the sake of "auld lang syne" you will advance me the sum needed, there are no words which can express my gratitude.

                                        Most sincerely yours,

Edward Valentine Esq   Edgar A. Poe

Ingram's printing of the letter, followed by Harrison's (XVII, 315–316), reads "of which I send a Prospectus" (see the next to last sentence, above), a very different matter from Poe's real statement. The above letter to Mr. Valentine, a brother of the first Mrs. Allan (see W, II, 282), was sent by Poe with a letter to Miss Susan Talley, probably of the same date (unlocated), requesting that she forward the enclosed letter (see Miss Talley's letter to Poe, November 29, 1848, in H, XVII, 324). [CL 741]

288 ➤ TO SARAH HELEN WHITMAN

[New York]
Wednesday Morning — the 22 d. [November 1848]

My dearest Helen —

Last Monday I received your note, dated Friday, and promising that on Tuesday I should get a long letter from you. It has not yet reached me, but I presume will be at the P.O. when I send this in. In the meantime, I write these few words to thank you, from the depths of my heart, for the dear expressions of your note — expressions of tenderness so wholly undeserved by me — and to assure you of my safety and health. The terrible excitement under which I suffered, has subsided, and I am as calm as I well could be, remembering what has past. *Still* the Shadow of Evil *haunts* me, and, although tranquil, I am unhappy. I dread the Future. — and you alone can rëassure me. I have *so* much to say to you, but must wait until I hear from you. My mother was delighted with your wish to be remembered and begs me to express the pleasure it gave her.

Forever your own

Edgar

Remember me to Mr Pabodie.

> William J. Pabodie was a friend of the Whitman family. Following Poe's death, he wrote letters to the *New York Tribune* (June 2, 1852, reprinted in H, XVII, 408–410) and to Rufus W. Griswold, June 11, 1852 (*ibid.*, pp. 412–415), discounting certain allegations made against Poe's character. Poe seems to have thought well of him (see also Note 295). [CL 742]

289 ➤ TO SARAH H. HEYWOOD

Fordham Nov. 23ᵈ 1848 —

Dear Sarah — my own dear *sister* Sarah —

If there is any pity in your heart reply immediately to this letter, & let me know *why* it is, I do not hear from Annie — If I do not hear from her soon, I shall surely die — I fancy everything evil — sometimes I even think that I have offended her, & that she no longer loves or cares for me — I wrote her a long letter eight days ago, enclosing one from my mother who wrote again on the 19th[.] Not one word has reached us in reply[;] oh Sarah, if I did not love your sister, with the *purest* & most unexacting love, I would not dare confide in you — but you do know, how truly — how *purely* I love her, & you will forgive me, for you know also, how impossible it is to see & not to love her — In my wildest dreams, I have never fancied any being so totally lovely — so *good* — so *true* — so *noble* so *pure* — so *virtuous* — her silence fills my whole soul with terror — *Can* she have recieved my letter? If she is angry with me dear Sarah, say to her, that on my knees, I beseech her to pardon me — tell her that I am her *slave* in all things — that whatever she bids me do, I will do — if even she says, I must never see her again or write to her — Let me but hear from her *once more*, & I can bear whatever happens. oh Sarah you would pity me, if you knew the agony of my heart, as I write these words — *do not fail to answer me at once*[.]

God bless you my sweet sister —

Miss S. H. Heywood.   Edgar —
Westford — Mass.

Sarah Heywood, younger sister of Annie Richmond, lived in Westford, Massachusetts. Poe's letter to Mrs. Richmond of "eight days ago" was that of November 16 (Letter 286). No letter from Annie or Sarah is known between the present date and December 28, 1848, when Poe again wrote to Annie; his December letter may imply one received from Mrs. Richmond. [CL 743]

290 ➤ TO SARAH HELEN WHITMAN

[Fordham]

Friday the 24th. [November, 1848]

In a little more than a fortnight, dearest Helen, I shall, once again, clasp you to my heart: — until then I forbear to agitate you by speaking of my wishes — of my hopes, and especially of my fears. You say that all depends on my own firmness. If this be so, all is safe — for the terrible agony which I have so lately endured — an agony known only to my God and to myself — seems to have passed my soul through fire and purified it from all that is weak. Henceforward I am strong:

— this those who love me shall see — as well as those who have so relentlessly endeavored to ruin me. It needed only some such trials as I have just undergone, to make me what I was born to be, by making me conscious of my own strength. — But all does *not* depend, dear Helen, upon my firmness — all depends upon the sincerity of your love.

You allude to your having been "tortured by reports which have all since been explained to your entire satisfaction". On this point my mind is fully made up. I will rest neither by night nor day until I bring those who have slandered me into the light of day — until I expose them, *and their motives,* to the public eye. I *have* the means and I will ruthlessly employ them. On [*page 2*] one point let me caution you, *dear* Helen. No sooner will Mrs E. hear of my proposals to yourself, than she will set in operation every conceivable chicanery to frustrate me: — and, if you are not prepared for her arts, she will *infallibly* succeed — for her whole study, throughout life, has been the gratification of her malignity by such means as any other human being would die rather than adopt. You will be sure to receive anonymous letters so skillfully contrived as to deceive the most sagacious. You will be called on, possibly, by persons whom you never heard of, but whom she has instigated to call & villify me — without even *their* being aware of the influence she has exercised. I do not know *any* one with a more *acute* intellect about such matters than Mrs Osgood — yet even she was for a long time completely blinded by the arts of this fiend & simply because her generous heart could not conceive how any woman could stoop to machinations at which the most degraded of the fiends would shudder. I will give you here but one instance of her baseness & I feel that it will suffice. When, in the heat of passion — stung to madness by her inconceivable perfidy & by the grossness of the injury which her jealousy prompted her to inflict upon *all of us* — upon both families — I permitted myself to say what I should not have said — I had no sooner uttered the words, than I *felt* their dishonor. I felt, too, that, although *she* must be damningly conscious of her own baseness, she would still have a right to reproach me for having betrayed, under *any* circumstances, her confidence.

[*page 3*] Full of these thoughts, and terrified almost to death lest I should again, in a moment of madness, be similarly tempted, I went immediately to my secretary — (when these two ladies went away —) made a package of her letters, addressed them to her, and with my own hands left them at her door. Now, Helen, you *can*not be prepared for the diabolical malignity which followed. Instead of feeling that I had done all I could to repair an unpremeditated wrong — instead of feeling that almost any other person would have retained the letters to make good (if occasion required) the assertion that I possessed them — instead of this, she urged her brothers & brother in law to *demand of me the letters.* The position in which she thus placed me you may imagine. Is it any wonder that I was driven *mad* by the intolerable sense of wrong? — If you value your happiness, Helen, beware of this woman! She did not cease her persecutions here. My poor Virginia was continually tortured (although not deceived) by her anonymous letters, and on her death-bed declared that Mrs. E. had been her murderer. Have I not a right to hate this fiend & to caution you against her? You will now comprehend what I mean in saying that the *only* thing for which I found it impossible to forgive Mrs O. was her reception of Mrs E.

Be *careful of your health, dearest Helen,* and perhaps all will yet go well. Forgive me that I let these wrongs prey upon me — I did not so bitterly feel them until they threatened to deprive me of you. I confess, too, that the [intolerable insults of your mother & sister still rankle at] my heart — but for your dear sake I will endeavor to be calm.

Your lines "To Arcturus" are truly beautiful. I would retain the Virgilian words — omitting the translation. The first note leave out: — [*page 4*] 61 Cygni has been proved *nearer* than Arcturus & Alpha Lyrae is presumably so. — Bessel, also, has shown 6 other stars to be *nearer* than the brighter ones of this hemisphere. — There is an obvious tautology in "pale candescent"[.] To be *candescent* is to become *white* with heat. Why not read — "To blend with thine its incandescent fire?" Forgive me, *sweet* Helen, for these *very* stupid & captious criticisms. Take vengeance on my next poem. — When "Ulalume" appears, cut it out & enclose it: — newspapers seldom reach me. — In last Saturday's "Home Journal" is a letter from M. C. (who is it?). I enclose a passage which seems to refer to my lines:

> — the very roses' odors
> Died in the arms of the adoring airs.

The accusation will enable you to see how groundless such accusations *may* be, even when seemingly best founded. Mrs H's book

was published 3 months ago. You had my poem about the first of
June — was it not?

> *Forever Your own,*
>
> Edgar.

Remember me to Mr Pabodie — Mrs Burgess & Mrs Newcomb.

"Mrs. E" refers to Mrs. Elizabeth Frieze Ellet, mentioned in Letter 280
(see also Letter 306). Though there is no letter from Poe to Mrs. Ellet,
two unpublished items from her are in the Boston Public Library. One,
postmarked December 16 [1845], is addressed to the *Broadway Journal*:
"Do not use in any way the memorandum about the So. Ca.[rolina]
College. Excuse the repeated injunction — but as you would not de-
cipher my German Manuscript — I am fearful of some other mistake."
This one-page letter is unsigned, but is identified by an earlier note,
undated, signed "E," which tells of the dismissal of Dr. [Robert] Henry
from the Presidency of South Carolina College; on the verso appears,
"Ich habe einen Brief fur Sie — wollen Sie gefalligst heute abend nach
Uhr den sebben bei mir entnehmen oder abholen lassen" (the particular
"letter" cited is unknown). The letters alluded to by Poe in the
present letter to Mrs. Whitman are unlocated. For the Osgood-Ellet
relationship to the incident that Poe describes, see W, II, 183–184, and
Quinn, *Poe*, pp. 497–498. The "two ladies" mentioned in sentence 1,
page 3, are identified in the right margin of the original MS. by Mrs.
Whitman as "Miss L[ynch] & Margaret F[uller]," though Miss Lynch
apparently disowned her part in the affair (see Quinn, *Poe*, p. 498).
"Ulalume" was first published in Colton's *American Review*, December 1847 (see Quinn, *Poe*, p. 532). The identity of "M. C." is unknown. Mrs. H[ewitt]'s *The Songs of Our Land and Other Poems*
was reviewed by Poe in the *Broadway Journal*, October 25, 1845 (reprinted in H, XII, 254–259). For William J. Pabodie, see the note to
Letter 288. Mrs. Burgess and Mrs. Newcomb were friends of Mrs.
Whitman. [CL 745]

291 ⇒ TO SARAH HELEN WHITMAN

[Fordham]

Sunday Evening. 26 [November, 1848]

I wrote you yesterday, sweet Helen, but, through fear of being
too late for the mail, omitted some things I wished to say. I fear,
too, that my letter must have seemed cold — perhaps even harsh or
selfish — for I spoke nearly altogether of my own griefs. Pardon
me, *my* Helen, if not for the love I bear you, at least for the sor-

rows I have endured — more, I believe, than have often fallen to the lot of man. How much have they been aggravated by my consciousness that, in too many instances, they have arisen from my own culpable weakness or childish folly! — My sole hope, now, is *in you,* Helen. As you are true to me or fail me, so do I live or die.

I forgot to rëenclose your poem & do so now. Why have you omitted the two forcible lines —

> While in its depths withdrawn, far, far away,
> I see the dawn of a diviner day.?

— is that dawn no longer perceptible? "Who wrote the verses signed "Mary" I am unable to say.

Can you solve me the riddle of the poem [*page 2*] enclosed? It is from last Saturday's "Home Journal." Somebody sent it to me in M.S.

Was I right, dearest Helen, in my first impression of you? — you know I have implicit faith in first impressions. Was I right in the idea I had adopted before seeing you — in the idea that you are ambitious? If so and *if you will have faith in me,* I can & will satisfy your wildest desires. It would be a glorious triumph, Helen, for *us* — for *you & me.* I dare not trust my schemes to a letter — nor, indeed, have I room even to hint at them here. When I see you I will explain all — as far, at least, as I dare explain *all* my hopes even to you.

Would it *not* be "glorious", *darling,* to establish, in America, the sole unquestionable aristocracy — that of intellect — to secure its supremacy — to lead & to control it? All this I *can* do, Helen, & will — if you bid me — and aid me.

I received yesterday a letter from Mr Dunnell. He says that they have "lost" their lect- [*page 3*] urer for the 6th prox. & offers me that night instead of the 13th. I have written him, however, that I cannot be in Providence before the 13th.

My kindest regards to Mr Pabodie.

> Devotedly Your own
>
> Edgar

Preserve the printed lines. I send the M S. — perhaps you may recognise it.

As one of the "signs of the times" I notice that Griswold has lately

June 15 — 48

Bayard Taylor Esq
        Dr Sir,

                I would feel greatly
indebted to you if you could spare
time to look over the lines enclosed
and let me know whether they will be
accepted for "The Union" — if so, what
you can afford to pay for them, and
when they can appear.
                        Truly Yours,
                        Edgar A. Poe.

        P.S. I feel that I have been guilty
of discourtesy in not sooner thanking you
for your picturesque and vigorous "Views
A-Foot" —— but when they reached me,
and long afterwards, I was too ill to
write — and latterly I have been every day
hoping to have an opportunity of making
your acquaintance and thanking you
in person.

POE TO B. TAYLOR, 15 JUNE 1848
(Letter 271)

FRANCES SARGENT OSGOOD

copied my "Raven" in his "Hartford Weekly Gazette" — I enclose his editorial comments — so that you have quite a budget of enclosures.

P. S — I open this letter, *dearest love,* to ask you to mail me, *as soon as possible,* three articles of mine which you will find among the *critical papers* I gave you, viz: "The Philosophy of Composition" — Tale-Writing — Nath¹ Hawthorne" — and a review of "Longfellow's Poems." I wish to refer to them in writing my Lecture & can find no other copies. Do not fail to send them *dear dear* Helen, as soon as you get this. Enclose them *in a letter* — so that I may be sure to get them in season.

Mrs O's "Ida Grey" is in "Graham" for August — 45.

> Poe's "yesterday" probably refers to his letter of November 24. For more about Mr. T. L. Dunnell, see the note to Letter 293. For William J. Pabodie, see the note to Letter 288. For Rufus White Griswold (not Poe's editor and biographer), see *American Literature,* VI (March 1934), 69–72. "Mrs. O" was Mrs. Frances Sargent Osgood. [CL 747]

292 ⇢ TO WILLIAM J. PABODIE

Fordham — Dec. 4 — 48.

My dear Mr. Pabodie —

On the principle of "better late than never" I seize the first opportunity afforded me, in the midst of cares and vexations of all kinds, to write you a few words of cordial thanks for your considerate and gentlemanly attentions to me while in Providence. I do hope that you will always think of me as one of the most obliged and most devoted of your friends. — Please say to Mrs. W., when you next see her, that I thank her for the "papers" and for her promptitude. Say, also, that perhaps Mrs. Wright is right, but that I believe her wrong, and desire to be kindly remembered. The commands, about Post, have been attended to. — Present my respects to Mrs. Allen and to your father.

Truly yours always.

W. J. Pabodie Esqr   Edgar Allan Poe

> William J. Pabodie was a friend of both Mrs. Whitman and of Poe, but was opposed to their marriage (see Quinn, *Poe,* pp. 585–586). For

his defense of Poe in the *New York Tribune*, June 2, 1852, see Quinn, *Poe*, pp. 679–681; see also the note to Letter 288. Poe returned from Providence, November 14 (see Letter 285). In that postscript of Letter 291, Poe asked that three critical articles be returned to him. "Mrs. Wright" was probably Mrs. Paulina Wright, of Providence (see Varner, "Sarah Helen Whitman, Seeress of Providence," I, 350). [CL 750]

293 ➤ TO SARAH HELEN WHITMAN

New-York City —
Saturday, 2 P. M. [December 16, 1848]

My *own dearest* Helen —

Your letters — to my mother & myself — have just been received, & I hasten to reply, in season for this afternoons [mail . . .] I cannot be in Providence until Wednesday morning; and, as I must try and get some sleep after I arrive, it is more than probable that I shall not see you until about 2 P. M. Keep up heart — *for all will go well.* My mother sends her dearest love and says she will return good for evil & treat you *much* better than *your* mother has treated me. Remember me to Mr. P. & believe me

Ever Your own

Edgar.

Poe was going to Providence to deliver his lecture on "The Poetic Principle," December 20 (see Letters 279 and 291). "Mr. P." is William J. Pabodie. [CL 753]

294 ➤ TO MARIA CLEMM

[Providence, December 23, 1848]

My own dear Mother —

We shall be married on Monday, and will be at Fordham on Tuesday. on the first train.

[*Unsigned*]

The marriage between Poe and Mrs. Whitman never took place. Poe was back in Fordham by December 28 (see Letter 296). In connection with this letter, see Letter 302. [CL 757]

295 ⇥ TO THE REVEREND DR. CROCKER

[Providence, December 23, 1848]

Will Dr. Crocker have the kindness to publish the banns of matrimony between Mrs. Sarah Helen Whitman and myself, on Sunday and on Monday. When we have decided on the day of the marriage we will inform you, and will thank you to perform the ceremony.

Resp^y yr. Ob. S^t

Edgar A. Poe.

Pabodie's letter to Griswold and Mrs. Whitman's letter to Mrs. Hewitt, both cited in Note 295, indicate that Poe's letter to Dr. Crocker was never delivered. [CL 758]

296 ⇥ TO ANNIE L. RICHMOND

[New York] Thursday Morning — 28.
[December, 1848]

Annie, —

My own dear Mother will explain to you how it is that I cannot write to you in full — but I *must* write only a few words to let you *see* that I am well, lest you suspect me to be ill. *All* is right! . . . . I *hope* that I distinguished myself at the Lecture — I *tried* to do so, for your sake. There were 1800 people present, and such applause! I did so much better than I did at Lowell. If *you* had only been there. . . . Give my dearest love to all.

Eddy.

Poe lectured in Providence on the "Poetic Principle," December 20, 1848 (see the note to Letter 279; also W, II, 284). The Lowell lecture was delivered July 10, 1848; its subject was "The Poets and Poetry of America." This is Poe's first known letter to Annie since that of November 16; no letter from her is known for the same period, though the present letter may imply one recently received. [CL 759]

297 ⇥ TO SARAH ANNA LEWIS

[New York, Late 1848 (?)]

Dear Mrs Lewis —

Upon the whole I think this the most spirited poem you have written. If I were you, I would retain *all* the prose prefix.

You will observe that I have taken the liberty of making some *suggestions* in the body of the poem — the force of which, I think, would be *much* increased by the introduction of an occasional *short* line.

For example [*here Poe lists certain lines of the poem and suggests that*] These short lines should be "indented" — as for instance

> So, to cheer thy desolation,
> Will I cling to thee.

[*Unsigned*]

Mrs. Lewis incorporated, without acknowledgment, all but one or two of Poe's corrections of the poem ("The Prisoner of Peroté"; see Note 297). Ingram printed a portion of the poem with Poe's corrections in the *Albany Review*, cited in Note 297. [CL 761]

298 ⤝ TO ANNIE L. RICHMOND

[New York, January 11, 1849]

†. . . Annie! . . .†[1]

It seems to me *so* long since I have written you that I feel condemned, and almost tremble lest you should have evil thoughts of †. . .† Eddy. . . . But no, you will never doubt me under *any* circumstances — will you †. . .† ? †. . .† It seems to me that Fate is against our meeting †again† *soon* — †but oh, we *will not* let distance diminish our affection, and by-and-by all will go right.† Oh, Annie, in spite of so many worldly sorrows — in spite of all the trouble and *misrepresentation* (so hard to bear) that Poverty has entailed on me for so long a time — in spite of *all* this I am *so* — *so* happy †to think that you *really* love me. If you had lived as long as I, you would understand *fully* what I mean. Indeed, indeed, Annie, there is *nothing* in this world worth living for except love — love *not* such as I once thought I felt for Mrs. —— but such as burns in my very soul for *you* — so pure — so unworldly — a love which would make *all* sacrifices for your sake.† [I need not tell you, Annie, how great a burden is taken off my heart by my rupture with Mrs. W.; for I have fully made up my mind to break the engagement. . . .][2]

[1] Matter between daggers appears in *Appleton's* but not in *Life*.
[2] Bracketed matter, except for place and date, is inserted from *Life*.

†Could I have accomplished what I wished, *no* sacrifice would have seemed to me too great, I felt so burning — so *intensely passionate* a longing to show you that I loved you. . . .† [Nothing would have deterred me from the match but — what I tell you. . . .]

Write to me †. . .† whenever you can spare time, if it be only a line. . . . I am beginning to do very well about money as my spirits improve, and soon — *very* soon, I hope, I shall be *quite* out of difficulty. You can't think how industrious I am. I am resolved to *get rich* — to triumph — †for your sweet sake. . . . Kiss dear Sarah for me — tell her I will write to her soon — we talk *so much* about her.† When you write tell me something about B[ardwell]. Has he gone to Richmond? or what is he doing? Oh, if I could only be of service to him in any way! Remember me to *all* — to your father and mother and dear little Caddy, and Mr. R. and Mr. C. And now good-by, my own dear sister Annie!

[*Signature missing*]

For an opposite attitude toward Fate, see Letter 138. "Mrs. ——" was Mrs. Sarah Helen Whitman. What Annie wished Poe to accomplish was probably a settled married life. A. Bardwell Heywood was Annie's brother and a school teacher. "Caddy" (later Mrs. Edward Coffin) was the daughter of Charles B. Richmond and Annie, and though called "Caddy" in Poe's correspondence with Annie, was always known to her family and friends as "Carrie" (this information was provided through the courtesy of James Southall Wilson). "Mr. R." was Mr. Richmond, Annie's husband, and "Mr. C." was the Reverend Warren H. Cudworth, of Lowell. [CL 763]

299 ➤ TO JOHN R. THOMPSON

New-York — Jan. 13. — 49.

My Dear Sir,

Accept my thanks for the two Messengers containing Miss Talley's "Genius." — I am glad to see that Griswold, although imperfectly, has done her justice in his late "Female Poets of America."

Enclosed, I send you the opening chapter of an article, called "Marginalia", published, about three years ago, in "The Democratic Review". I send it that, by glancing it over — especially the prefatory remarks — you may perceive the general *design* — which I think well adapted to the purposes of such a Magazine as yours: — affording great scope for variety of critical or other comment. I may add that "Marginalia", continued for five or six chapters, proved as *popular* as any papers written by me. — My object in writing you now, is to propose that I continue the papers in "The Messenger" — running them through the year, at the rate of 5 pages each month — commencing with the March number. You might afford me, as before, I presume, $2 per page.

One great advantage will be that, at a hint from yourself, I can touch, briefly, any topic you might suggest; and there are many points affecting the interests of Southern Letters — especially in reference to Northern neglect or misrepresentation of them — which stand sorely in need of *touching*. — If you think well of my proposal, I will send you the two first numbers [*page 2*] (10 pp.) immediately on receipt of a letter from you. You can pay me at your convenience — as the papers are published — or otherwise.

Please re-enclose me the printed papers, when you have done with them.

Very truly yours,

Jno: R. Thompson Esq.   Edgar Allan Poe

P.S — I am about to bestir myself in the world of Letters rather more busily than I have done for three or four years past — and a connexion which I have established with 2 weekly papers may enable me, now & then, to serve you in respect to "The Messenger".

> Susan Archer Talley (see her letter to Poe, November 29, 1848, in H, XVII, 324) was a Richmond poetess and later the author of "The Last Days of Edgar A. Poe." Griswold's *Female Poets of America* was "off the press" by December 30, 1848 (see the note to Letter 321). The "Marginalia" here cited appeared in J. L. O'Sullivan's *Democratic Review*, November and December 1844 (reprinted in H, XVI, 1–66). Poe wrote during his career a total of fifteen "Marginalia" papers (see H, XVI, 1–178), the last five being printed in the SLM, April, May, June, July, and September 1849. In this connection, see also Letter 313. The present letter, above, the May 10 letter, just cited, and the appearance of the "Marginalia" in the SLM suggest at least one letter to Poe from Thompson, of which there is no known MS. or printing; in all likelihood there was an answer to Poe's letter, above, and a later one to which Poe's May 10 letter is an answer. Regarding Poe's request for "$2 per page," see Letter 301. Poe's connections with "2 weekly papers" may refer to the *Metropolitan* (see the note to Letter 309) and

to the *Flag of Our Union* (see Letter 303 and note). John Reuben
Thompson edited the SLM, November 1847–May 1860 (Mott, *History
of American Magazines,* I, 629). [CL 764]

300 ⋟ TO JOHN PRIESTLEY

Fordham, Saturday, January 20 [1849]

[My Dear Sir]

May I trouble you to hand the accompanying brief article to
Mr. Whelpley and see if he can give me $10 for it? About four years
ago, I think, I wrote a paper on "The American Drama" for your
review. It was printed anonymously — my name was not given in
the index. The criticism referred chiefly to Willis's "Tortesa" and
Longfellow's "Spanish Student." Could you procure me the number containing it?

[Truly your friend,

Edgar Allan Poe]

James D. Whelpley was editor of the *American Whig Review* (1848–
1849), having succeeded George H. Colton, who had founded it in
January 1845 (see Mott, *History of American Magazines,* I, 752). The
article, "Critics and Criticism," was not purchased by Whelpley; it
appeared in *Graham's,* January 1850, after Poe's death. Poe's "American
Drama" had appeared in the *American Whig Review,* August 1845
(reprinted in H, XIII, 33–73). [CL 766]

301 ⋟ TO ANNIE L. RICHMOND

†New York† [1]

[January 21 (?), 1849]

†My own† *faithful* Annie!

How shall I ever be grateful enough to God for giving me, in all
my adversity, so true, so beautiful a friend! I felt *deeply* wounded
by the cruel statements of your letter — and yet I had anticipated
nearly all. . . . [From the bottom of my heart I forgive her all, and
would forgive her even more.] [2] Some portions of your letter I do

[1] Matter between daggers appears in *Appleton's* but not in *Life.*
[2] Bracketed matter, except for the date, is inserted from *Life.*

not fully understand. If the reference is to my having violated my
promise *to you*, I simply say, Annie, that I have not, and by God's
blessing never will. Oh, if you *but* knew how happy I am in keeping it for *your* sake, you *could* never believe that I would violate it.
The reports, if any such there be — may have arisen, however, from
what I did in Providence on that terrible day — you know what I
mean: — Oh — I shudder even to think of it. That . . . [her
friends] will speak ill of me is an inevitable evil — I must bear it.
In fact, Annie, I am beginning to grow wiser, and do not care so
much as I did for the opinions of a world in which I see, with my
own eyes, that to act generously is to be considered as designing, and
that to be poor is to be a villain. I must get rich — rich. Then all
will go well — but *until* then I must submit to be abused. I deeply
regret that Mr. R—— should think ill of me. If you can, disabuse
him — and at all times act for me as *you* think best; I put my honor,
as I would my life and soul, implicitly in your hands; but I would
rather not confide my purposes, *in that one regard,* to any one but
your dear sister.

[I enclose you a letter for Mrs. Whitman. Read it — show it only
to those in whom you have faith, and then *seal* it with wax and mail
it from Boston. . . . When her answer comes I will send it to you:
that will convince you of the truth. If she refuse to answer I will
write to Mr. Crocker. By the by, if you know his exact name and
address send it to me. . . . But] as long as you and yours love me,
†my true and beautiful Annie,† what need *I* care for this cruel, un-
just, calculating world? †Oh, Annie, there are *no* human words that
can express my devotion to you and yours. My love for you has
given me renewed life.† In all my present anxieties and embarrass-
ments, I still feel in my inmost soul *a divine joy* — a happiness inexpressible — that nothing seems to disturb. †For hours at a time
I sit and think of you — of your lovely character — your true faith
and *unworldliness*. I do not believe *that any one in this whole world
fully understands me except your own dear self.* . . . How glad I
am to hear about Sarah's living with you, and about the school. Tell
her that she is my own *dear sister*, whom I shall always love. Do
not let *her* think ill of me;† I hope Mr. C—— is well. Remember
me to him, and ask him if he has seen my "Rationale of Verse" in the
last October and November numbers of the *Southern Literary Messenger*. . . . I am *so* busy now, and feel so full of energy. Engage-

ments to write are pouring in upon me every day. I had two proposals within the last week *from Boston.* I sent yesterday an article
to the *American Review* about "Critics and Criticism." Not long
ago I sent one to the *Metropolitan* called "Landor's Cottage:" it has
something about Annie in it, and will appear, I suppose, in the March
number. To the *S. L. Messenger* I have sent fifty pages of "Marginalia" — five pages to appear each month of the current year. I have
also made permanent engagements with every magazine in America
(except *Peterson's National*), including a Cincinnati magazine called
The Gentlemen's. So you see that I have only to keep up my spirits
to get out of all my pecuniary troubles. [The *least* price I get is $5
per "Graham page," and I can easily average 1½ per day — that is
$7½. As soon as "returns" come in I shall be out of difficulty. I see
Godey advertises an article by me, but I am at a loss to know what
it is.] You ask me, Annie, to tell you about some book to read. Have
you seen "Percy Ranthorpe," by Mrs. Gore? You can get it at any
of the agencies. I have lately read it with deep interest, and derived
great *consolation* from it also. It relates to the career of a literary
man, and gives a just view of the true aims and the true dignity of
the literary character. Read it for my sake. . . .

But of one thing rest assured, Annie — from this day forth I shun
the pestilential society of *literary women.* They are a heartless, un-
natural, venomous, dishonorable *set,* with no guiding principle but
inordinate self-esteem. Mrs [Osgood] is the *only* exception I know.
†Our dear mother sends you a hundred kisses (fifty for Sarah). She
will write very soon.† Kiss little Caddy for me, and remember me to
Mr. R—— and to *all.*

[I have had a most distressing headache for the last two weeks. . . .]

[Signature missing]

Poe's reference to "that terrible day" in Providence is not clear: it may
be to his purchasing laudanum, and his "promise" to Mrs. Richmond
may have been never again to attempt suicide. "Mr. R——" was
Annie's husband, and Mrs. Richmond's letters to Ingram picture him
as exceedingly deferential toward Poe. Mrs. Richmond's sister was
Sarah Heywood, then living with the Richmonds, in Lowell. "Mr.
C——" refers to the Reverend Warren H. Cudworth, of Lowell, author
of "Mr. Poe as a Cryptographer," in the Lowell *Journal,* April 19, 1850
(see Mrs. Richmond to Ingram, January 14, 1877, Ingram collection,
University of Virginia). There are no known letters to support Poe's

claim of *many* "engagements to write"; indeed Poe seems to have urged editors to accept his MSS. (see Letters 299 and 300). For one possible "proposal . . . *from Boston,*" see the note to Letter 303. According to letters from Sarah H. Whitman to Ingram, February 20 and April 2, 1874 (Ingram collection, University of Virginia), the *Metropolitan* ran for only two issues (see also Letter 309). Poe's "*least* price" is belied by his letter to John R. Thompson, already cited (Letter 299). No article by Poe is advertised in any issue of *Godey's* prior to this letter to which Poe could have had reference. *Percy Ranthorpe,* a novel printed in London, 1847, was by George Henry Lewes, and not Mrs. Gore. "Caddy" was Annie's daughter (see Letter 298). [CL 768]

302 ➤ TO SARAH HELEN WHITMAN

Fordham Jany. 25th / 49
[January 21 (?), 1849]

Dear Madam,

In commencing this letter, need I say to you, *after what has passed between us,* that no amount of provocation on your part, or on the part of your friends, shall induce me to speak ill of you even in my own defence? If to shield myself from calumny however undeserved, or however unendurable, I find a need of resorting to explanations that might condemn or pain you, most solemnly do I assure you, that I will patiently endure such calumny, rather than avail myself of any such means of refuting it — You will see then, that so far I am at your mercy — but in making you such assurances, have I not a right to ask of you some forbearance in return? My object in now writing you is to place before you an extract from a letter recently addressed to myself — "I will not repeat *all* her vile & slanderous words — you have doubtless heard them — but one thing she says that I cannot *deny* though I do not believe it — viz — that you had been *published to her once,* & that on the Sat. preceding the Sabbath on which you were to have been published for the *second time,* she went herself to the Rev Mr Crocker's, & *after stating her reasons for so doing,* requested him to stop all further proceedings" — That *you* Mrs W- have uttered, promulgated or in any way countenanced this pitiable falsehood, I do not & cannot believe — some person equally your enemy & mine has been its author — but what I beg of you is, to write me at once a few lines in explanation — you know of course that by reference either to Mr Pabodie (who at my request forbore

to speak to the minister about publishing the *first banns* on the day
I left) or, to the Rev. Mr Crocker himself, I can disprove the facts
stated in the most satisfactory manner — but there can be no need
of disproving what I feel confident was never asserted *by you* — Your
simple disavowal is all that I wish — You will of course write me immediately on receipt of this — only in the event of my not hearing
from you within a few days, will I proceed to take more definite
steps — Heaven knows that I would shrink from wounding or grieving you! I blame no one but your Mother — Mr Pabodie will tell you
the words which passed between us, while from the effects of those
terrible stimulants you lay prostrate without even the power to bid
me farewell — Alas! I bitterly lament my own weaknesses, & nothing
is farther from my heart than to blame you for yours — May Heaven
shield you from all ill! So far I have assigned no reason for my de-
clining to fulfil our engagement — I had none but the suspicious &
grossly insulting parsimony of the arrangements into which you suffered yourself to be forced by your Mother — Let my letters & acts
speak for themselves — It has been my intention to say simply, that
our marriage was postponed on account of your ill health — Have you
really said or done anything which can preclude our placing the rupture on such footing? If not, I shall persist in the statement & thus
this unhappy matter will die quietly away —

E. A. Poe

Regarding the quotation in this letter, Mrs. Richmond wrote Ingram,
January 14, 1877 (Ingram collection): "The quotation in this letter
of course was written by me — not on my own account but to satisfy
my friends." Her "friends" included Mr. Richmond's family, who lived
in Providence, and who, apparently, sided with Mrs. Whitman. She
continued: "Of course I had no other alternative, but to . . . ask
some explanation — Mrs. W.'s reply exonerated him completely, yet I
think they were inclined to discredit it and believe him still a very
unprincipled man to say the least — ." (This note was written by
Mrs. Richmond on her transcript of Poe's letter to Mrs. Whitman,
above, sent with her own letter to Ingram, January 14, 1877.) Regarding the "banns," see Letter 295. Whether Mrs. Whitman answered
Poe's request for a disavowal, is uncertain. Mrs. Richmond's note,
quoted above, implies that she did, though whether made in writing
to Poe or orally in Providence is open to question. In his letter to
Mrs. Richmond, February 8, 1849, Poe says: "I have got no answer yet
from Mrs W. . . ." (Letter 303 and note); Mrs. Whitman told In-

gram: "His letter I did not dare to answer" (Ingram, II, 186). For her remarks to Griswold, see notes to Letter 303. The evidence most difficult to explain away is Mrs. Richmond's; perhaps Mrs. Whitman did make some oral disavowal to certain persons in Providence, yet did not dare write to Poe. This is the last known letter from Poe to Mrs. Whitman. [CL 769]

XI

FORDHAM—LOWELL—RICHMOND

THE VEIN RUNS OUT

February 1849–October 1849

[New York]
Thursday, — 8th. [February, 1849]

Dear, dear Annie —

Our darling mother is just going to town, where, I hope, she will find a sweet letter from you, or from Sarah, but, as it is so long since I have written, I *must* send a few words to let you see and *feel* that your Eddy, even when silent, keeps you always in his mind and heart — in his *inmost* heart. I have been *so* busy, dear Annie, ever since I returned from Providence — six weeks ago. I have not suffered a day to pass without writing from a page to three pages. Yesterday, I wrote five, and the day before a poem considerably longer than "The Raven." I call it "The Bells." †How I wish my Annie could see it! Her opinion is so dear to me on such topics. On *all* it is everything to me — but on poetry in especial. And Sarah, too. — I told her, when we were at Westford, that I hardly ever knew any one with a keener discrimination in regard to what is *really* poetical. The 5 prose pages I finished yesterday are called — what do you think? — I am sure you will never guess — "*Hop-Frog!*" Only think of *your* Eddy writing a story with *such* a name as "Hop-Frog"! You would never guess the subject (which is a terrible one) from the title, I am sure. It will be published in a weekly paper, of Boston, called "The Flag of Our Union" — not a *very* respectable journal, perhaps, in a literary point of view, but one that pays as high prices as most of the Magazines. The proprietor wrote to me, offering about 5$ a "Graham page" and as I was anxious to get out of my pecuniary diffi-culties, I accepted the offer. He gives $5 for a Sonnet, also. Mrs Osgood, Park Benjamin, & Mrs Sigourney are engaged. I think "The Bells" will appear in the "Am. Review". — I have got no answer yet from Mrs W. who, I understand, has left Providence (*for the first time in her life*) and gone to New Bedford. My opinion is, that her mother (who is an old devil) has intercepted the†¹ [*page 2*] letter and will never give it to her. . . .

¹ Matter between daggers comes from the Morgan Library fragment.

†Dear Muddy says she w[ill write you a *long* letter in a day][2] or two & tell you *how good* I am. She is in high spirits [at my] prospects and at our hopes of soon seeing Annie. We have told our landlord that we will not take the house next year. Do not let Mr. R., however, make any arrangements for us in Lowell, or Westford — for, being poor, we are so much the slaves of circumstances. At all events, we will both come & see you & spend a week with you in the early spring, or before — but we will let you know some time before we come. Muddy sends her dearest — dearest love to you & Sarah & to *all*. And now good bye, my *dear, darling, beautiful Annie.*

Your own Eddy.†

The Flag of Our Union was established in 1846 by Frederick Gleason, and by 1850 it had an estimated circulation of 100,000, netting Gleason $25,000 yearly (see Mott, *History of American Magazines*, II, 10, 35). Mrs. Whitman wrote Griswold, December 12, 1849: "With a heavy heart, & after the most dispassionate reflection, I resolved, for his sake rather than my own, not to reply to this letter, but to defer all painful reminiscences & explanations to a future day" (Quinn, *Poe*, p. 650; see also the note to Letter 302). "The Bells" was published in *Sartain's Magazine*, November 1849 (Quinn, *Poe*, p. 563). "Mr. R." is Charles Richmond, Annie's husband; Sarah is Sarah Heywood, Annie's sister (see Letter 289); "Muddy," of course, was Mrs. Clemm. [CL 772]

304 ➤ TO FREDERICK W. THOMAS

Fordham, near New-York
Feb. 14 — 49.

My dear friend Thomas,

Your letter, dated Nov. 27, has reached me at a little village of the Empire State, after having taken, at its leisure, a very considerable tour among the P. Offices — occasioned, I presume, by your endorsement "to forward" wherever I might be — and the fact is, where I might *not* have been, for the last three months, is the legitimate question. At all events, now that I have your well-known M.S. before me, it is most cordially welcome. Indeed, it seems an age since I heard from you and a decade of ages since I shook you by the hand — although I hear *of* you now and then. Right glad am I to find you once more in a true position — in the field of Letters." Depend upon it,

[2] Matter in brackets, except for the address, date, and pagination, comes from the *Life* text.

after all, Thomas, Literature is the most noble of professions. In fact, it is about the only one fit for a man. For my own part, there is no seducing me from the path. I shall be a *littérateur,* at least, all my life; nor would I abandon the hopes which still lead me on for all the gold in California. Talking of gold, and of the temptations at present held out to "poor-devil authors", did it ever strike you that all which is really valuable to a man of letters — to a poet in especial — is absolutely unpurchaseable? Love, fame, the dominion of intellect, the consciousness of power, the thrilling sense of beauty, the free air of Heaven, exercise of body & mind, with the physical and moral health which result — these and such as these are really all that a poet cares for: — then answer me this — *why* should he go to California? Like Brutus, "I pause for a reply" — which, like F. W. Thomas, I take it for granted you have no intention of giving me. — [I have read the Prospectus of the "Chronicle" and like it much especially the part where you talk about "letting go the finger" of that conceited body, the East — which is by no means the East out of which came the wise men mentioned in Scripture!] I wish you would come down on the Frogpondians. They are getting worse and worse, and pretend not to be aware that there *are* any literary people out of Boston. The worst and most disgusting part of the matter is, that the Bostonians are really, as a race, far inferior in point of *anything beyond mere talent*, to any other *set* upon the continent of N. A. They are decidedly the most servile imitators of the English it is possible to conceive. I always get into a passion when I think about. It would be the easiest thing in the world to use them up *en masse*. One really well-written satire would accomplish the business: — but it must not be such a dish of skimmed milk-and-water as Lowell's.

[*page 2*] I suppose you have seen that affair — the "Fable for Critics" I mean. Miss Fuller, that detestable old maid — told him, once, that he was "so wretched a poet as to be disgusting even to his best friends". This set him off at a tangent and he has never been quite right since: — so he took to writing satire against mankind in general, with Margaret Fuller and her *protégé*, Cornelius Matthews, in particular. It is miserably weak upon the whole, but has one or two good, but by no means *original*, things — Oh, there is *"nothing new under the sun"* & Solomon is right — for once. I sent a review of the "Fable" to the "S. L. Messenger" a day or two ago, and I only hope Thompson will print it. Lowell is a ranting abolitionist and *deserves* a good using up. It is a pity that he is a poet. — I have not seen your paper yet, and hope you will mail me one — regularly if you can spare it. I will send you something whenever I get a chance. — [With your co-editor, Mr [*illegible*]] I am not acquainted personally but he is well known to me by reputation. Eames, I think, was talking to me about him in Washington once, and spoke very highly of him in many respects — so upon the whole you are in luck] — The rock on which most new enterprizes, in the paper way, split, is namby-pamby-ism. It never did do & never will. No yea-nay journal *ever* succeeded. — but I know there is little danger of your making the Chronicle a yea-nay one. I have been quite out of the literary world for the last three years, and have *said* little or nothing, but, like the owl, I have "taken it out in thinking". By and bye I mean to come out of the bush, and then I have *some* old scores to settle. I fancy I see some of my *friends* already stepping up to the Captain's office. The fact is, Thomas, living buried in the country makes a man savage — wolfish. I am just in the humor for a fight. You will be pleased to hear that I am in better health than I ever knew myself to be — full of energy and bent upon success. You shall hear of me again shortly — and it is not improbable that I may soon pay you a visit in Louisville. — If I can do anything for you in New-York, let me know. — Mrs Clemm sends her best respects & begs to be remembered to your mother's family, if they are with you. — You would oblige me very especially if you could squeeze in what follows, editorially. The lady spoken of is a most particular friend of mine, and deserves *all* I have said of her. I will reciprocate the favor I ask, whenever you say the word and show me how. Address me at *N. York City*, as usual and if you insert the following, please cut it out & enclose it in your letter.

Truly your friend,

Edgar A Poe.

Little is known of Poe's movements and activities between August 9 (letter to Cooke) and December 15, 1846 (letter to Eveleth), except that he told Eveleth he had been ill for "more than six months." In this connection, Thomas' letters of August 14 and 24, 1846 (cited in Note 304), are interesting. In the former, directed to New York, he tells Poe to give a manuscript to his friend Heape, who will bring it to Washington; and in the latter, addressed to Philadelphia, he says Heape has informed him that Poe is living in Philadelphia. Poe seems to have moved to Fordham about May or June 1846 (see Quinn, *Poe*, p. 506); Heape's information may have arisen from a visit Poe may have made to Philadelphia. In the "last three months" Poe had been in and out of Providence, Lowell, and Boston. Thomas seems to have left Washington and returned to Louisville to edit a newspaper. Poe's review of Lowell's *A Fable for Critics* (1848) appeared in the SLM, March 1849, anonymously, under "Notices of New Works" (reprinted in H, XIII, 165–175). For Mrs. Lewis, see the note to Letter 257. [CL 773]

305 ⊁ TO EVERT A. DUYCKINCK

Fordham — Feb. 16 — 49

Dear Duyckinck,

Perhaps, in the conversation I had with you, in your office, about "Ulalume", I did not make you comprehend precisely what *was* the request I made: — so, to save trouble, I send now the enclosed from the "Providence Daily Journal". If you will oblige me by copying the slip as it stands, prefacing it by the words "From the Providence Journal" it will make every thing straight.

Sincerely Yours

Edgar A Poe.

"Ulalume," first published in the *American Whig Review*, December 1847, was printed in the *Providence Daily Journal*, November 22, 1848, and in Duyckinck's *Literary World*, March 3, 1849 (see Campbell, *The Poems of Edgar Allan Poe*, p. 265). Duyckinck did not follow the prefatory remarks of the Providence *Journal*, but supplied his own puff, including, however, Poe's identity as the author of the poem, which in the *Whig Review* had appeared anonymously (see Campbell, *Poems*, pp. 268–269). [CL 774]

306 ⊁ TO ANNIE L. RICHMOND

Fordham Feb. 19. [18] Sunday 1849

Dear — dearest Annie — my sweet friend & sister —

I fear that in this letter, which I write with a heavy heart, you will find much to disappoint & grieve you — for I must abandon my proposed visit to Lowell & God only knows when I shall see & clasp you by the hand. I have come to this determination to-day, after looking over some of your letters to me & my mother, written since

I left you. You have not *said* it to me, but I have been enabled to glean from what you *have* said, that Mr Richmond has permitted himself (perhaps without knowing it) to be influenced against me, by the malignant misrepresentations of Mr & Mrs Locke. Now I frankly own to you dear Annie, that *I am proud,* although I have never shown myself proud to you or yours & never will — You know that I quarrelled with the Lockes *solely* on your account & Mr R's — It was obviously my interest to keep in with them, & moreover they had rendered me some services which entitled them to my gratitude up to the time when I discovered they had been blazoning their favors to the world — Gratitude then, as well as interest, would have led me not to offend them; and the insults offered to *me* individually by Mrs Locke were not sufficient to make me break with them. It was only when I heard them declare that through their patronage alone, you were admitted into society — that your husband was everything despicable — that it would ruin my mother even to enter your doors — it was only when such insults were offered *to you,* whom I sincerely & most purely loved, & to Mr R. whom I had every reason to like & respect, that I arose & left their house & incurred the unrelenting vengeance of that worst of all fiends, "a woman scorned" — Now feeling all this, I cannot help thinking it unkind in Mr R. when I am absent & unable to defend myself, that he *will* persist in listening to what these people say to my discredit — I cannot help thinking it, moreover, the most unaccountable instance of weakness — of obtuseness — that ever I knew a *man* to be guilty of: — women are more easily misled in such matters. In the name of God, what else had I to anticipate, in return for the offence which I offered to Mrs Locke's insane vanity & self-esteem, than that she would spend the rest of her days in ransacking the world for scandal against me, (& the falser the better for her purpose,) & in fabricating accusations where she could not find them ready made? *I* certainly anticipated no other line of conduct on her part — but, on the other hand, I certainly did not anticipate that any man *in his senses,* would ever *listen* to accusations, from so suspicious a source. That any man could be really *influenced* by them surpasses my belief, & the fact is, Annie, to come at once to the point — I cannot & *do* not believe it — The obvious prejudices of Mr R. *cannot* be on this ground. I much fear that he has mistaken the nature — the purity of that affection which I feel for you, & have not scrupled to avow — an affection which first

entered my heart I believe, through a natural revulsion of feeling, at
discovering you — *you,* the subject of the debased Mrs L's vile
calumnies — to be not only purer than Mrs. L. but purer & nobler,
at all points, than any woman I had ever known, *or could have imagined to exist upon the earth.* God knows dear *dear* Annie, with what
horror I would have shrunk from insulting a nature so *divine* as
yours, with any impure or earthly love — But since it is clear that
Mr R. cannot enter into my feelings on this topic, & that he even
suspects *what is not,* it only remains for me beloved Annie to consult
your happiness — which under all circumstances, will be & must be
mine — Not only must I *not* visit you [at] Lowell, but I must dis-
continue my letters & you yours — I cannot & *will* not have it on
my conscience that I have interfered with the domestic happiness of
the only being in the whole world, whom I have loved, at the same
time with truth & with *purity* — I do not *merely* love you Annie —
I admire & respect you even more — & Heaven knows there is no
particle of selfishness in my devotion — I ask nothing for myself, but
your *own* happiness — with a charitable interpretation of those calumnies which for your sake, I am now enduring from this vile
woman — & which, for your dear *dear* sake, I would most willingly
endure if multiplied a hundred fold — The calumnies indeed, Annie,
do not materially wound me, except in depriving me of your society —
for of your affection & respect, I *feel* that they never can. As for any
injury the falsehoods of these people can do *me,* make your mind
darling, easy about that — It is true, that "Hell has no fury like a
woman scorned," but I have encountered such vengeance before, on
far lighter grounds — that is to say, for a far less holy purpose, than
I feel the defence of your good name to be. I scorned Mrs Ellet,
simply because she revolted me — & to this day, she has never ceased
her *anonymous* persecutions. But in what have they resulted? She has
not deprived me of one friend who ever knew me & once trusted me —
nor has she lowered me one inch in the public opinion. When she
ventured too far, I sued her at once (through her miserable tools)
& recovered exemplary damages — as I will unquestionably do, forth-
with, in the case of Mr L. if ever he shall muster courage to utter a
single *actionable* word — It is true I shrink with a nameless horror
from connecting my name in the public prints, with such unmention-
able nobodies & blackguards as L. & his *lady* — but they may provoke
me a little too far — You will now have seen dear Annie, how & why

it is that my mother & myself cannot visit you as we proposed — In the first place my presence might injure you, in your husband's opinion — & in the second, I could not feel at ease in *his* house, so long as he permits himself to be prejudiced against me, or so long as he associates with such persons as the Lockes. It had been my design to ask you & Mr R. (or perhaps your parents) to *board* my mother while I was absent at the South, & I intended to start after remaining with you a week — but my whole plans are now disarranged — I have taken the cottage at Fordham for another year — *Time* dear *dea1* Annie, will show all things. Be of good heart, I shall never cease to think of you — & bear in mind the *two* solemn promises I have made you — The one I am now religiously keeping, — & the other (so help me Heaven!) shall sooner or later be kept —

> Always your dear friend & brother
>
> Edgar —

For Poe's comments concerning the Lockes, see Letter 309. For Poe's indebtedness to Mrs. Locke, see Letter 251. Concerning Mrs. Elizabeth F. Ellet, see Letter 280. For Poe's "*two* solemn promises," see Letters 298 and 301, and notes. [CL 777]

307 ➤ TO SARAH HEYWOOD

[New York]

For Sarah —

My dear sweet sister — why have you not kept your promise & written me. Do not *you* be influenced against me by *anybody* — at least in my absence when I have it not in my power either to deny or to explain. Present my warmest regards to your father, mother & brother — & *kiss dear Carrie* [Annie?] *for me.*

> Your own friend & brother

March 1. — 1849   Edgar

Sarah Heywood was the sister of Annie Richmond; Carrie was the Richmonds' daughter (see the note to Letter 298). In connection with the injunction of this letter, see Letters 306 and 309. Though Sarah's home was in Westford, Massachusetts, she frequently visited her sister in Lowell. [CL 778]

308 ► TO EVERT A. DUYCKINCK

Fordham March 8. [1849]

Dear Sir,

If you have looked over the Von Kempelen article which I left with your brother, you will have fully perceived its drift. I mean it as a kind of "exercise", or experiment, in the plausible or verisimilar style. Of course, there is *not one* word of truth in it from beginning to end. I thought that such a style, applied to the gold-excitement, could not fail of effect. My sincere opinion is that nine persons out of ten (even among the best-informed) will *believe* the quiz (provided the design does not leak out before publication) and that thus, acting as a sudden, although of course a very temporary, *check* to the gold-fever, it will create a *stir* to some purpose.

I had prepared the hoax for a Boston weekly called "The Flag" — where it will be quite thrown away. The proprietor will give me $15 for it on presentation to his agent here; and [*page 2*] my object in referring the article to you is simply to see if you could not venture to take it for the "World". If so, I am willing to take for it $10 — or, in fact, whatever you think you can afford.

I believe the quiz is the first deliberate literary attempt of the kind on record. In the story of Mrs Veal, we are permitted, now & then, to perceive a tone of *banter*. In "Robinson Crusoe" the design was far more to please, or excite, than to deceive by verisimilitude, in which particular merely, Sir Ed. Seaward's narrative is the more skilful book. In my "Valdemar Case" (which *was* credited by many) I had not the slightest idea that any person should credit it as any thing more than a "Magazine-paper" — but here the whole strength is laid out in verisimilitude.

I am *very* much obliged to you for your reprint of "Ulalume".

Truly Yours,

Edgar A Poe.

[*page 3*] P.S. If you feel the least *shy* about the article, make no hesitation in returning it, of course: — for I willingly admit that it is not a paper which every editor would like to "take the responsibility" of printing — although merely as a contribution with a known name: — but if you decline the quiz, please *do not let out the secret*.

Evert A. Duyckinck Esqr

> Duyckinck and his brother George (see the note to Letter 201) edited
> the *Literary World;* Duyckinck apparently refused the tale, for it was
> published in the *Flag of Our Union* as "Von Kempelen and His Dis-
> covery," April 14, 1849 (see Wyllie, *Poe's Tales*, p. 337). Poe is re-
> ferring to Defoe's *A True Relation of the Apparition of One Mrs. Veal*
> and *Robinson Crusoe*, the latter of which he reviewed in the SLM,
> January 1836 (reprinted in H, VIII, 169–173). Sir Edward Seaward's
> diary was edited by Jane Porter and published in London, 1831; see
> Allibone's *Dictionary of Authors* (Philadelphia: J. B. Lippincott,
> 1890), II, 1646. For the "Valdemar Case," see Letter 245 and note.
> [CL 779]

309 ≯ TO ANNIE L. RICHMOND

† New York † [1]
March 23, 1849

† . . . † Will not Annie confide † . . . † the secret[s] [2] about
W[estford]? Was it anything *I* did which caused you to "give up
hope?" Dear†est† Annie, I am so happy in being able to afford Mr. R.
proof of something in which he seems to doubt me. You remember
that Mr. and Mrs. [L—] strenuously denied having spoken ill of you
to me, and I said "then it must remain a simple question of veracity
between us, as I had no witness" — but I observed afterward[s] —
"Unfortunately I have returned Mrs. [L——] her letters (which were
filled with abuse of you both), but, if I am not mistaken, my mother
has some in her possession that will prove the truth of what I say."
Now, Annie, when we came to look over these last, I found, to my
extreme sorrow, that *they* would not corroborate me. I say "to my
extreme sorrow," for oh, it is so painful to be doubted when we *know*
our own integrity. Not that I fancied, even for one moment, that *you*
doubted me — but then I saw that Mr. R. and Mr. C. *did,* and perhaps
even your brother. Well! what *do* you think? Mrs. [L——] has again
written my mother, and I enclose her letter. Read it! You will find it
thoroughly *corroborative of all I said*. The verses to *me* which she
alludes to I have not seen. You will see that she [admits having cau-
tioned me against you, as I said, and] in fact admits all that I accused
her of. Now, you distinctly remember that they both loudly denied

[1] Matter between daggers appears in *Appleton's* but not in *Life*.
[2] Bracketed matter is inserted from *Life*.

having spoken against you! — this, in fact, was the sole point at issue. I have marked the passage alluded to. I wish that you would write to your relation in Providence and ascertain for me *who* slandered me as you say. I wish to prove the falsity of what has been said (for I find that it will not do to permit such reports to go unpunished), and, especially, obtain for me some *details* upon which I can act. . . . Will you do this? [. . .]I enclose also some other lines "For Annie" — and will you let me know in what manner they impress you? I have sent them to the [*Flag of our Union.*] By the way, did you get "Hop-Frog?" I sent it to you by mail, not knowing whether you ever see the paper in ——. I am sorry to say that the *Metropolitan* has stopped, and "Landor's Cottage" is returned upon my hands unprinted. I think the lines "For Annie" (those I now send) much the *best* I have ever written — but an author can seldom depend on his own estimate of his own works — so I wish to know what my Annie *truly* thinks of them — also your dear sister and Mr. C.

Do not let these verses go *out of your possession* until you see them in print — as I have sold them to the publisher of the [*Flag*] . . . [Remember me to all.]

[*Signature missing*]

For "Westford," see the note to Letter 282. "Mr. R." was Annie's husband. "Mr. and Mrs. L——" were Jane Ermina Locke and her husband, of Lowell. Though Mrs. Locke seems to have written several letters to Poe, none is extant, but there is in the Ingram collection (University of Virginia) a MS. of her poem, "Ermina's Gale," sent by her presumably to Poe, though there is no such identification other than its appearance in the Ingram collection, and carrying, in part, the note: "I hope you will acknowledge the *receipt* of this *immediately,* tho' more than this I shall not entreat of you . . ."; it is signed, "Yours as ever, Jane E. Locke." The only possible dating is that heading the poem: "August/ 48." "Mr. C." was the Reverend Warren H. Cudworth, of Lowell. Perhaps the verses concerning Poe, alluded to by Mrs. Locke, were from Mrs. Osgood's poem, "Love's Reply" (see P, II, 1410; see also Letter 319, for further identification. Annie's brother was A. Bardwell Heywood. In connection with Poe's remarks about Mrs. Locke, see Letter 306. The "relation in Providence" were Mr. Richmond's parents. "For Annie" appeared in the *Flag of Our Union,* April 28, 1849 (see Letter 310 and note). "Hop-Frog" appeared in the *Flag of Our Union,* March 17, 1849, and Poe's reference to "the paper in ——" concerns Mrs. Richmond's seeing the *Flag* in Westford or Lowell. According to Mrs. Whitman's letters to Ingram, February 20,

1874, and April 2, 1874, Poe had a regular engagement with the *Metropolitan,* which ran for only two issues (the magazine is not listed in Mott's *History of American Magazines*). "Landor's Cottage" was first printed in the *Flag of Our Union,* June 9, 1849 (Wyllie, *Poe's Tales,* p. 329). [CL 781]

310 ⤳ TO NATHANIEL P. WILLIS

Fordham, April 20, 1849.

My dear Willis: —

The poem which I enclose, and which I am so vain as to hope you will like, in some respects, has been just published in a paper for which sheer necessity compels me to write, now and then. It pays well as times go — but unquestionably it ought to pay ten prices; for whatever I send it I feel I am consigning to the tomb of the Capulets. The verses accompanying this, may I beg you to take out of the tomb, and bring them to light in the Home Journal? If you can oblige me so far as to copy them, I do not think it will be necessary to say "From the ——" that would be too bad; — and, perhaps, "From a late —— paper," would do.

I have not forgotten how a "good word in season" from you made "The Raven," and made "Ulalume," (which, by-the-way, people have done me the honor of attributing to you) — therefore I *would* ask you (if I dared,) to say something of these lines — if they please you.

Truly yours ever,

Edgar A. Poe.

Poe was sending "For Annie" to the *Home Journal* for a "true copy" (see Letters 309 and 311). "For Annie" appeared in the *Home Journal,* April 28, 1849. It had appeared in the *Flag of Our Union* (Boston), April 28, 1849, vol. 4, no. 17, p. 2, col. 6, as follows: For Annie [Written for The Flag of Our Union] (this datum was supplied through the courtesy of Clarence S. Brigham). Poe's letter is evidence that the *Flag* appeared in advance of date, a procedure characteristic especially of weeklies of those days; the printing of the poem in the *Home Journal* of the same date as the *Flag* shows that the *Home Journal,* for that issue at least, followed the *Flag* on the stands. Of course, the date of Poe's letter may have been misprinted in Willis' article, or Poe's original "6" may have been read as a "0"; but an April "26" dating would probably have prevented the appearance of the poem in the issue of April 28, if the magazine emerged on time. Moreover, the May 5 issue of the *Flag* appeared or went to press too late for it to carry a complaint against the *Home Journal's* printing of the poem, the complaint appearing in the May 12 issue (see Campbell, *Poems*, note on "For Annie"). Thus it would seem that the poem appeared first in the *Flag* of April 28, but in advance of date; Poe's letter to Willis, correctly dated, enclosed a corrected version; and the true copy was printed in the *Home Journal* of April 28, on schedule or somewhat in advance of date. There is one other matter that does not, however, change the dating of the letter but might lessen the number of days by which the *Flag* was issued in advance of date: Poe's statement "has just been published" might mean "will be published before the *Home Journal* can appear." For Willis' remark concerning "The Raven," see the note to Letter 317. For Willis' prefatory comment on "Ulalume," in the January 1 number, 1848, ". . . a poem . . . full of beauty and oddity in sentiment and versification, but a curiosity . . . in philologic flavor. Who is the author?" see P, II, 1247. Willis did "say something" about "For Annie" in the *Home Journal,* calling it, in part, an "exquisite specimen of *private property*" (see P, II, 1396). [CL 782]

311 ⊁ TO ANNIE L. RICHMOND

[New York]
[April 28 (?)–May 23 (?), 1849]

† . . . †[1] Annie, —

You will see by this note that I am nearly, if not quite, well — so be no longer uneasy on my account. I was not so ill as my mother supposed, and she is so anxious about me that she takes alarm often without cause. It is not so much *ill* that I have been as depressed in spirits — I cannot express to you how terribly I have been suffering from gloom. . . . † I begin to have a secret terror lest I may *never* behold you again. . . . Abandon all hope of seeing me soon. . . .† You know how cheerfully I wrote to you not long ago — about my prospects — hopes — how I anticipated being soon out of difficulty. Well! all seems to be frustrated — at least for the present. As usual, misfortunes never come single, and I have met one disappointment after another. The *Columbian Magazine,* in the first place, failed — then Post's *Union* (taking with it my principal dependence); then the *Whig Review* was forced to stop paying for contributions — then the *Democratic* — then (on account of his oppression and insolence) I was obliged to quarrel, finally, with ——; and then, to crown all, the

---

[1] Matter between daggers is found in *Appleton's* but not in *Life*.

"—— ——" (from which I anticipated so much and with which I had made a regular engagement for $10 a week throughout the year) has written a circular to correspondents, pleading poverty and declining to receive any more articles. More than this, the S. *L. Messenger*, which owes me a good deal, cannot pay just yet, and, altogether, I am reduced to Sartain and Graham — both very precarious. No doubt, Annie, you attribute my *"gloom"* to these events — but you would be wrong. It is not in the power of any mere *worldly* considerations, such as these, to depress me. . . . No, my sadness is *unaccountable,* and this makes me the more sad. I am full of dark forebodings. *Nothing* cheers or comforts me. My life seems wasted — the future looks a dreary blank: but I will struggle on and "hope against hope." . . . What do you think? *I* have received a letter from Mrs. [L——] [2], and such a letter! She says she is about to publish a detailed account of *all* that occurred between us, under guise of romance, with fictitious names, &c., — that she will make me appear noble, generous, &c. &c. — nothing bad — that she will "do justice to my motives," &c. &c. She writes to know if "I have any suggestions to make." If I do not answer it in a fortnight, the book will go to press as it is — and, more than all this — she is coming on immediately *to see me at Fordham.* I have not replied — shall I? and what? The "friend" who sent the lines to the "H. J." was the friend who loves *you* best — was myself. The [*Flag*] so misprinted them that I was resolved to have a true copy. The [*Flag*] has two of my articles yet — "A Sonnet to my Mother," and "Landor's Cottage." . . . I have written a ballad called "Annabel Lee," which I will send you soon. *Why* do you not send the tale of which you spoke?

[Signature missing]

Concerning Poe's illness, see Mrs. Clemm's note appended to the above letter: ". . . he has been very ill . . . I thought he would *die* several times. God knows I wish we were both in our graves — it would, I am sure, be far better" (Ingram, II, 215). The *Columbian* [Lady's and Gentleman's] *Magazine*, a monthly, had its first issue, January 1844, and its last, February 1849 (see Mott, *History of American Magazines*, I, 743-744). Post's *Union* was first issued July 1847, and following the issue for December 1848, was bought by Sartain to become *Sartain's Union* (Mott, *ibid.*, p. 769). For the *Whig Review*, see the note to Letter 300. The *United States Magazine and Democratic Review* was

[2] Bracketed matter, except for the date, place, and note on the signature, is inserted from *Life.*

first issued, October 1837, and was known by that title through 1851
(Mott, *ibid.*, p. 677). With whom Poe quarreled is not known. The
magazine with which Poe had made a "regular engagement" may have
been *The Gentlemen's* (see Letter 301). Whether Mrs. L[ocke] published her "romance," though she seems to have written it (see Letter
319), or whether she visited Poe at Fordham is not known. The *Flag
of Our Union* printed "For Annie," April 28, 1849, and the *Home
Journal* printed a revised version of the poem in its issue of the same
date (see the note to Letter 310). Poe's sonnet "To My Mother" appeared in the *Flag*, July 7, 1849 (Quinn, *Poe*, p. 605), and "Landor's
Cottage" in the same magazine, June 9, 1849 (Quinn, *Poe*, p. 597).
"Annabel Lee" appeared posthumously in the *New York Tribune*,
October 9, 1849 (Quinn, *Poe*, p. 606). [CL 785]

312 ⇥ TO EDWARD H. N. PATTERSON

New York: April [30 (?)] 1849

Dear Sir,

No doubt you will be surpri[s]ed to learn that your letter dated
Dec. 18. has only this moment reached me. I live at the village of
Fordham; about 14 miles from New-York on the Harlam Rail-Road
— but as there is no Post-Office at the place, I date always from New-
York and get all my letters from the city Post-Office. When, by acci-
dent or misapprehension, letters are especially directed to me at Fordham, the clerks — some of them who do not know my arrangements
— forward them to West-Farms, the nearest Post-Office town, and
one which I rarely visit. Thus it happened with *your* letter — on account of the request which you made Mr. Putnam, I presume, "to
forward it to my residence". I have thought it proper to make you
this explanation, lest you may have been all this time fancying me
discourteous in not replying to your very flattering proposition.

I deeply regret that I did not sooner receive it; and had it reached
me in due season, I would have agreed to it unhesitatingly. In assuming "originality" as the "keystone of success" in such enterprises, you
are right; and not only right, but, in yourself, almost "original" —
for there are none of our publishers who have the wit to perceive this
vital truth. What the public seek in a Magazine is *what they cannot
elsewhere procure.*

Should you not have changed your mind on the subject, I should
be pleased to hear from you again. I do not think — (in fact I am
perfectly sure of the contrary) — that a [*page 2*] Magazine could

succeed, to any great extent, under the precise form, title, and general plan which (no doubt hurriedly) you have suggested; but your idea of the duplicate publication, East & West, strikes me forcibly.

Experience, not less than the most mature reflection on the topic, assures me that no *cheap* Magazine can ever again prosper in America. We must aim high — address the intellect — the higher classes — of the country (with reference, also, to a certain amount of foreign circulation) and put the work at $5: — giving about 112 pp. (or perhaps 128) with occasional wood-engravings in the first style of art, but only in obvious illustration of the text. Such a Mag. would begin to pay after 1000 subscribers; and with 5000 would be a fortune worth talking about: — but there is no earthly reason why, under proper management, and with energy and talent, the work might not be made to circulate, at the end of a few years — (say 5) 20,000 copies — in which case it would give a clear income of 70 or 80,000 dollars — even if conducted in the most expensive manner, paying the highest European prices for contributions & designs. I need not add that such a Mag. would exercise a literary and other influence never yet exercised in America. — I presume you know that during the second year of its existence, the "S. L. Messenger" rose from less than 1000 to 5000 subs., and that "Graham", in 18 months after my joining it, went up from 5000 to 52,000. I do not imagine that a $5 Mag. could ever be forced into so great a circulation as this latter; but, under certain circumstances, I would answer for 20,000. The whole income from Graham's 52,000 [*page 3*] never went beyond 15,000 $: — the proportional expenses of the $3 Mags. being so very much greater than those of the $5 ones.

My plan, in getting up such a work as I propose, would be to take a tour through the principal States — especially West & South — visiting the small towns more particularly than the large ones — lecturing as I went, to pay expenses — and staying sufficiently long in each place to interest my personal friends (old College & West Point acquaintances scattered all over the land) in the success of the enterprize. By these means, I would guarantee, in 3 months (or 4) to get 1000 subs. in advance, with their signatures — nearly all pledged to pay on the issue of the first number. Under such circumstances, success would be certain. I have now about 200 names pledged to support me whenever I venture on the undertaking — which perhaps you are aware I have long had in contemplation — only awaiting a *secure* opportunity.

If you will write me your views on the subject — as much in detail as possible — and if they accord in any degree with mine — I will endeavor to pay you a visit at Oquawka, or meet you at any place you suggest, where we can talk the matter over with deliberation. Please direct your reply simply to New-York City.

Very Resp[y]
YrOb. S[t]

E. H. N. Patterson Esq.   Edgar A Poe.

Edward Howard Norton Patterson came of age on January 27, 1849, and received from his father the Oquawka *Spectator*. A passage from the extant memoranda of Patterson's May 7 letter to Poe (see SLP, p. 16) will serve here better than later to show his reason for asking Putnam, the publisher, to forward the letter to Poe: ". . . my principal object [he writes Poe] being to enlist your sympathies and interests in a periodical (*to be published by me*), the literary contents of which should be *exclusively* under your control, believing that such an enterprise would prove successful, not doubting that even a cheap Magazine, under *your* editorial control, could be made to pay well, and at the same time exert a beneficial influence upon American Literature." For Poe's estimates for the proposed *Stylus*, see his parallel figures in Letter 186. Certainly Poe's "old College & West Point acquaintances were not as legion as he implies; but he did have numerous persons in mind who had signified their approval of his magazine plans and who had promised their aid. [CL 786]

313 ⇒ TO JOHN R. THOMPSON

New-York: May 10. 49.

My Dear Sir —

I forward some more of the "Marginalia" — rather more piquant, I hope, and altogether more to my own liking, than what I sent before. I shall probably be in Richmond about the 1[rst] of June & will bring the MS "Raven", in obedience to your flattering request.

Truly yours.

John R. Thompson Esq[r]   Edgar A Poe

Concerning "Marginalia," see Letter 299. For the visit to Richmond, see Letters 316, 318, and 319. [CL 789]

314 ⤳ TO SARAH ANNA LEWIS

Fordham — May 17 — [1849]

My *dear* friend,

I have not been well enough, lately, to copy the lines "For Annie" but will copy them to-day[.] In regard to the other matter, depend upon me — as in *all* respects you may, with implicit confidence[.] Please make a memorandum as explicit as possible — so that I may know precisely what you wish.

Believe me Yours ever,

Mrs Stella Anna Lewis   Edgar A Poe.

> The "other matter" suggests two interpretations. On May 18, 1849, Poe wrote to George Putnam (Letter 315) and suggested that he publish a new edition of Mrs. Lewis' *Child of the Sea and Other Poems.* Also, on June 28, 1849, Poe wrote to Griswold (Letter 321) and suggested that he use for a second edition of *Female Poets* a longer critical notice of Mrs. Lewis to be prepared by Poe. If Mrs. Lewis replied to the present letter without delay, the first note may have concerned a second edition of her poems; if she answered after May 18, she probably sought a more flattering critical notice. For Poe's services to Mrs. Lewis in such matters, see the note to Letter 321. [CL 791]

315 ⤳ TO GEORGE P. PUTNAM

Fordham — May 18 — 49.

Geo. P. Putnam Esqre,

Dr Sir,

It has been suggested to Mrs. S. Anna Lewis, by several of her friends, that she should publish a new edition of her "Child of the Sea" &c including some compositions lately written — the whole in a handsome volume, with illustrations by Darley.

My object, in this note, is to submit the idea to your consideration. — Mrs Lewis has an unusually large circle of personal friends, has been highly praised by the critics, is very popular as an authoress and daily growing more so: — no doubt, therefore, she will exercise, before long, a very extensive literary influence.

If the volume suggested were prepared in season for the next Holi-
[*page 2*] days, I think you will agree with me that it could not fail
of success.

> Most Resp^y
> Yr. Ob. S^t
>
> Edgar A Poe.

Mrs. Lewis' *Child of the Sea and Other Poems* was published first in
1848, and reviewed by Poe in the SLM, September 1848, with a few
biographical facts about the author (reprinted in H, XIII, 155–165);
Poe's present attempt to have Putnam publish a second edition failed.
Poe's "object, in this note," was the result, not of a belief in Mrs. Lewis's
"very extensive literary influence," but rather of a sense of obligation in
certain personal matters affecting him and Mrs. Clemm. [CL 792]

316 ⇥ TO EDWARD H. N. PATTERSON

> New-York — May 23 — 49.

My Dear Sir,

Your letter of the 7th. came to hand in due course of mail; but I
have delayed my reply for a week, that I might deliberate well upon
your proposition. You will comprehend the caution with which I
feel it necessary to act, when you refer to my former letter, in which
I endeavored to explain to you the ambition of my views and the
importance I assign to *success* in the Magazine enterprize. If we
attempt it we *must* succeed — for, so far as concerns myself individually, all my prospects, pecuniary as well as literary, are involved in the project — but I shrink from making any attempt which
may fail. For these reasons, I have thought long and carefully on
what you propose; and I confess that some serious difficulties present
themselves. They are not insuperable, however; and, if we bring a
proper energy to the task, they may be even readily overcome. Your
residence at Okquawka is certainly one of the most serious of these
difficulties; and I submit to you whether it be not possible to put
on our title-page "Published simultaneously at New-York & St *Louis*"
— or something equivalent.

However, these are points to be discussed when we meet — for,
upon the whole, I say *Yes* to your proposition. Enclosed, you will
find a title-page designed by myself about a year ago: — your join-

ing me will, of course, necessitate some modifications — but the *title* &c should, for many reasons (to be explained hereafter) be adhered to.

We will find the 7 months between now and January brief enough for our preparations. It will be absolutely necessary that we begin at once. To-day I am going *to* Boston & Lowell, to remain a week; and immediately afterwards I will start for Richmond, where I will await your answer to this letter. Please direct to me *there,* under cover, or to the care of John R. Thompson, Ed^r of the "South. Lit. Messenger." On receipt of your letter (should you still be in the mind you now are) I will proceed to St Louis & there meet you. We can then visit N. York together, or I can continue the tour, as may be agreed on. In the mean- [*page 2*] time I will do what I can in Boston & Virginia — without involving your name in the enterprise until I hear from you.

I fancy that I shall be able to meet the current expenses of the tour by lecturing as I proceed; but there is something required in the way of outfit; and as I am not overstocked with money (what poor-devil author *is?*) I must ask you to advance half of the sum I need to begin with — about $100. Please, therefore, enclose $50 in your reply, which I will get at Richmond.

If these arrangements suit you, you can announce the agreement &c to your friends & proceed as if all was signed & sealed.

I enclose a poem from Willis's "Home Journal" & would be obliged to you if you could have it copied (with Willis's editorial prefix) in some paper either in St Louis or Oquawka: — enclosing me the copy when you write.

Cordially yours,

E. H. N. Patterson Esq^{r}e.   Edgar A Poe.

The title page sent by Poe was his own hand-drawing of the contemplated design for the *Stylus,* made with black ink on pink paper; it is reproduced in facsimile in SLP, facing p. 16. Poe went to visit Annie Richmond, but just when he returned to New York is not certain (see Letter 319). Concerning Poe's plan to get the $50 "at Richmond," see Letter 318. Patterson sent the money to Richmond (see Letter 329). Poe's poem was "For Annie," which Willis had printed in the *Home Journal,* April 28, 1849 (see Letter 310). Apparently Patterson had the poem reprinted (see Letter 328). [CL 794]

317 ➤ TO RUFUS W. GRISWOLD

[New York, May (?), 1849]

Dear Griswold —

I enclose perfect copies of the lines "For Annie" and "Annabel Lee" — in hope that you may make room for them. As regards "Lenore" (which you were kind enough to say you would insert) I would prefer the concluding stanza to run thus: —

Avaunt! avaunt! to friends from fiends the indignant ghost is riven —
From Hell unto a high estate far up within the Heaven —
From grief and moan to a golden throne beside the King of Heaven: —
Let *no* bell toll, then, lest her soul, amid its hallowed mirth,
Should catch the note, as it doth float up from the damnèd Earth;
And I! — to-night my heart is light! — no dirge will I upraise
But waft the angel on her flight with a Paean of old days.

It is a point of no great importance — but, in one of your editions, you have given my sister's age instead of mine. I was born Dec. 1813 — my sister Jan 1811.

Willis (whose opinion I highly value & of whose good word I have a right to be proud) has done me the honor to speak very pointedly in praise of "The Raven" — I enclose what he said — & if you could contrive to introduce it, you would render me an essential favor & greatly further my literary interests at a point where I am most anxious they should be advanced: — but I fear I am asking too much.

Truly Yours

E A Poe.

Poe's three poems ("For Annie," "Annabel Lee," and "Lenore") were printed by Griswold in his 10th edition of *Poets and Poetry of America*, which was noticed in the *New York Tribune*, December 15, 1849 (see J. L. Neu, *Studies in English*, No. 5, University of Texas, 1925, p. 122). Regarding Poe's statement about his birth, see the notes to Letter 112. Willis' praise of "The Raven" was probably that prefacing the poem in the *Evening Mirror*, January 29, 1845: ". . . it is the most effective single example of 'fugitive poetry' ever published in this country, and unsurpassed in English poetry for subtle conception, masterly ingenuity of versification, and consistent sustaining of imaginative lift and 'pokerishness' " (Quinn, *Poe*, p. 438). Poe's chief literary interests at this time were in establishing a magazine with the aid of E. H. N. Patterson (see Poe's letters to him). [CL 796]

318 ⊁ TO JOHN R. THOMPSON

New-York — June 9 — 49.

My Dear Sir,

It was my design to be in Richmond about the first of this month — but now it will be the 18th or 20th before I can leave New-York — and I will wait until I hear from you. Please send me $10 if you can possibly spare it. The June Messenger has not yet come to hand — but I presume it is in the city by this time.

Most probably you will have received, ere this, a letter for me, addressed to your care at Richmond. In such case, may I ask you to forward it here under cover with your reply? — but if it has not reached you when this letter does, please retain it (when it arrives) until you see me in Richmond.

Very truly your Friend,

John R Thompson Esqʳ   Edgar A Poe.

> For Poe's actual departure for Richmond, see the note to Letter 326. If Thompson answered Poe, no MS. or printing of his letter is known. Another installment of Poe's "Marginalia" was printed in the June issue of the SLM (reprinted in H, XVI, 160–168), scarcely enough at $2 a page to make the sum asked for in the present letter; perhaps Thompson owed him for previous installments of the "Marginalia," which had been running since April 1849, and Poe was trying to collect the debt. Poe had suggested to E. H. N. Patterson (see Letter 316) to write him in care of Thompson. This is the last known letter from Poe to John R. Thompson. [CL 799]

319 ⊁ TO ANNIE L. RICHMOND

Fordham — June 16. [1849]

My own *darling* Annie —

You must have been thinking all kinds of hard thoughts of your Eddie for the last week — for you asked me to write before I started for Richmond and I was to have started last Monday (the 11th) —

so perhaps you thought me gone, and without having written to say "good bye" — but indeed, my Annie, I *could not* have done so. The truth is, I have been *on the point* of starting every day since I wrote — and so put off writing until the last moment — but I have been disappointed — and can no longer refrain from sending you at least a few lines to let you see *why* I have been so long silent. *When* I can go now, is uncertain — but perhaps I may be off to-morrow, or next day: — all depends upon circumstances beyond my control. Most probably, I will not go until I hear from Thompson (of the S. L. Messenger) to whom I wrote 5 days ago — telling him to *forward* the letter from Oquawka, instead of retaining it until he sees me. The reason of the return of my draft on Graham's Magazine (which put me to such annoyance and mortification while I was with you) was, that the articles I sent (by mail) did not come to hand. No *insult* (as I had half anticipated) was meant — and I am sincerely glad of this; for I did not wish to give up writing for Graham's Mag. just yet. — I enclose the publishers' reply to my letter of enquiry. The Postmaster here is investigating the matter & in all probability the articles will be found & the draft paid by the time you get this: — so all this will be right, *dear, dearest* Annie.

You see I enclose you again quite a budget of papers — the letter of Mrs L to Muddy — Mrs L's long MS. poem — the verses by the "Lynn Bard" which you said you wished to see, and also some lines to me (or rather about me) by Mrs. O — in which she *imagines me writing to her.* I send, too, another notice of "Eureka", from Greeley's Tribune. The letter of Mrs. L. you can retain if you wish it.

Have you seen The "Moral for Authors", a new satire by J. E. Tuel? — who, in the name of Heaven *is* J. E. Tuel? The book is miserably [*page 2*] stupid. He has a long parody of the Raven — in fact nearly the whole thing seems to be aimed at me. If you have not seen it & wish to see it, I will send it.

Since I saw you, Annie, I have discovered your friend [Dr. Locke] to be a consummate scoundrel and no friend either to you or me. For my sake & your own, have as little to say to him as possible. If I were you I would not speak to him at all.

I will surely write to "Abby" before I go — or at all events immediately on getting to R. Give her my kindest love — for I have a right (have I not?) to send her my love — since she loves & is loved by *my* Annie. — I cannot tell you, darling, how sad I felt about parting with dear Sarah so coldly as I was forced to do. I did so long to kiss her and hold her to my heart — and I thought *she*, too, looked sad. Tell her I hope to see a great deal more of her when I return to Lowell.

No news of Mrs Locke yet. If she comes here I shall refuse to see her.

Remember me to your parents, Bardwell, *dear Caddy*, Mr & Miss C., and Mr R. How *dared* you send my love to Miss B.? Look over my letter and see if I even so much as mentioned her name. *Dear* Annie, my heart reproached me (after I parted with you) for having, even in jest, requested Bardwell to "remember me to Miss B." I thought it might have *pained* you in some measure — but indeed, darling Annie, no one in this whole world except your sweet self, is *more than a friend* to me.

And now Heaven forever bless you, my darling —

Your own Eddie.

I enclose, also, an autograph of the Mr. Willis you are so much in love with. Tell Bardwell I will send him what I promised, very soon.

Write soon — *soon* — dear, *dear* Annie. Muddy sends you her dearest — most devoted love.

> Poe wrote John R. Thompson, June 9, 1849. Concerning the "letter from Oquawka," see Letter 316. The reference to *Graham's* indicates an exchange of letters between Poe and the Samuel D. Patterson & Company, publishers of the magazine between George R. Graham's losing control of it in July 1848, and regaining control in April 1850 (see Mott, *History of American Magazines*, I, 544); both letters are presumably lost. For the references to Mrs. L[ocke], see Letters 309 and 311. The "Lynn Bard" was Alonzo Lewis (P, II, 1411); he wrote "To Edgar A. Poe," which appeared in *Godey's*, April 1847, p. 192. For Mrs. O[sgood]'s lines, see P, II, 1410, or Mrs. Clemm's letter to Mrs. Richmond, January 11, 1849 (Ingram, II, 202). John E. Tuel wrote in verse *The Moral for Authors* (as contained in the autobiography of Eureka, a manuscript novel, discovered by J. E. Tuel), published by Stringer and Townsend, New York, 1849. "Abby" and "Caddy" refer to Mrs. Richmond's daughter; "Mr. and Miss C" may refer to the Rev. Warren H. Cudworth family of Lowell (see the note to Letter 301); "Mr. R." to Mr. Richmond; Sarah was Mrs. Richmond's sister; Bardwell was Mrs. Richmond's brother. Nathaniel P. Willis was author, poet, and editor of the *Home Journal*. "Muddy," of course, was Mrs. Clemm. [CL 802]

320 ➤ TO GEORGE W. EVELETH

New-York — June 26. 49.

Dear Sir,

On the principle of "better late than never", I avail myself of a few moments' leisure to say a word or two in reply to your last letter — the one from Brunswick.

The essay you enclose, on the igneous liquidity of the Earth, embodies some truth, and evinces much sagacity — but no doubt ere this you have perceived that you have been groping in the dark as regards the general subject. Before theorizing ourselves on such topics, it is always wisest to make ourselves acquainted with the actually ascertained facts & established doctrines. You see I treat you unceremoniously — deal with me in the same manner. Let me know frankly how "Eureka" impresses you. It is accomplishing all that I prophecied — even more.

In respect to Draper: — By a singular coincidence, he is the chief of that very sect of Hog-ites to whom I refer as "the most intolerant & intolerable set of bigots & tyrants that ever existed on the face of the Earth". I had him especially in view when I wrote the passage. A merely perceptive man with no intrinsic force — no power of generalization — in short a pompous nobody. He is aware (for there have been plenty to tell him) that I intend *him* in "Eureka".

I do not exactly comprehend you about my being the "autobiographer of Holden's Mag." I occasionally hear of that work, but have never seen a number of it. (over[ ])

[*page 2*] "The Rationale of Verse" appeared in the last November & December numbers of "The S. Lit. Messenger". In the Feb. number (I think) I published (editorially) a review of "The Fable for Critics": — it is not much. Lowell might have done better.

I have never written any poem called "Ullahannà". What makes you suppose I did?

I enclose the last poem (of any length) which I have published. How do you like it? — you know I put much faith in your poetical judgments. It is from Willis's "H. Journal".

Do you ever see "The Literary World"?

Touching "The Stylus": — Monk Lewis once was asked how he came, in one of his acted plays, to introduce *black* banditti, when, in the country where the scene was laid, black people were quite un-known. His answer was: — "I introduced them because I truly anticipated that blacks would have more *effect* on my audience than whites — and if I had taken it into my head that, by making them sky-blue, the *effect* would have been greater, why sky-blue they should have been". To apply this idea to "The Stylus" — I am await-ing the *best opportunity* for its issue — and if by waiting until the day of judgment I perceive still increasing chances of ultimate suc-cess, why until the day of judgment I will patiently wait. I am now going to Richmond to "see about it" — & *possibly* I may get out the first number on next January.

Write soon & more frequently. I always receive your letters with interest.

Cordially your friend,

Please reënclose the verses   Edgar A Poe.

Most of Eveleth's letters were sent from his home in Phillips, Maine; Brunswick was the location of the Maine Medical School, where Eveleth was a student (see PE (reprint), p. 23). Since Poe's last letter, Putnam had published *Eureka* (see Letter 269), to which Poe is obviously re-ferring. According to Phillips (II, 1260), 750 copies were printed, a third of which were still on hand a year later. Wilson (PE (reprint), p. 23) cites Mabbott's identification of John W. Draper as a professor in New York University. For Poe's reference to *Holden's Magazine*, see Note 146. Poe enclosed his poem "For Annie," which had appeared in the *Home Journal*, April 28, 1849 (but see Letter 310). In 1849, the *Literary World* was owned and edited by Evert A. and George L. Duyckinck; it was the "first important American weekly to be devoted chiefly to the discussion of current books" (see Mott, *History of American Magazines*, I, 766). Poe left New York for Richmond, June 29 (see the note to Letter 326). [CL 803]

321 ➤ TO RUFUS W. GRISWOLD

New-York — June 28 — 49.

Dear Griswold,

Since I have more critically examined your "Female Poets" it oc-curs to me that you have not *quite* done justice to our common friend, Mrs. Lewis; and if you could oblige me so far as to substitute, for your no doubt hurried notice, a somewhat longer one prepared by myself (subject, of course, to your emendations) I would reciprocate the favor when, where, and *as* you please. If you *could* agree to this, give me a hint to that effect, and the MS. is ready. I will leave it sealed with Mrs. L. who is unaware of my design — for I would rather she should consider herself as indebted to *you* for the favor, at all points. By calling on Mrs. L., and asking for a package to your address, you can at any moment get it. I would not, of course, put you to any *expense* in this matter: — all cost shall be promptly defrayed.

Truly yours,

Edgar A Poe.

Griswold's *Female Poets of America* was "off the press" by December 30, 1848, according to a notice in the *Literary World* of that date (see J. L. Neu, *Studies in English,* No. 5, 1925, p. 144), and the second edition appeared in 1854 (*ibid.,* p. 145). Poe wrote the longer notice of Mrs. Lewis and Griswold called for it, as indicated by Mrs. Clemm's letter to Griswold, September 4, 1849: "I understand from Mrs. Lewis you received the package Mr. Poe left at her house for you" (see H, XVII, 395); Griswold published the article in the *Works* (1850), I, 242–249, as "Estelle Anna Lewis." Costs for furthering Mrs. Lewis' literary reputation were customarily defrayed by the Lewises, directly or indirectly; Mrs. Louise Shew-Houghton wrote J. H. Ingram, April 3, [1875]: "Mr. Poe was indebted to her [Mrs. Lewis], that is, she paid Mrs. Clemm in advance when they were needy and poor Poe had to notice her writings" (original MS. in Ingram collection, University of Virginia). It has been suggested that Poe wrote the sketch of Mrs. Lewis in Griswold's 1849 edition of *Female Poets of America,* but the above letter and the facts of publication of that edition disprove such a contention. [CL 805]

322 ➤ TO H. S. ROOT

[New York] June 28, 1849

Dear Sir,

I regret to say that I am unable to answer your query. I have not seen a volume of Dr. Earle's very beautiful poetry for many years, and I fancy the edition — (one only was published) — is out of print. The Doctor himself, when I last heard of him, was Superintendent of the Asylum for the Insane, at Bloomingdale, near this city.

[Edgar A. Poe]

Poe included Dr. Pliny Earle in "Autography," in *Graham's,* December 1841 (reprinted in H, XV, 230, in which he said that Dr. Earle "has become well known to the literary world, of late, by a volume of very

fine poems . . ."; see Letter 102). The identity of H. S. Root is unknown. [CL 806]

323 ⊱ TO MARIA CLEMM

New York [Philadelphia],
July 7. [1849]

My *dear, dear* Mother, —

I have been *so* ill — have had the cholera, or spasms quite as bad,
and can now hardly hold the pen[. . .]

The very instant you get this, *come* to me. The joy of seeing you
will almost compensate for our sorrows. We can but die together.
It is no use to reason with me *now*; I must die. I have no desire to
live since I have done "Eureka." I could accomplish nothing more.
For your sake it would be sweet to live, but we must die together.
You have been all in all to me, darling, ever beloved mother, and
dearest, truest friend.

I was never *really* insane, except on occasions where my heart was
touched[. . .]

I have been taken to prison once since I came here for getting drunk;
but *then* I was not. It was about Virginia.

[*No signature*]

Eureka had been published in the summer of 1848, probably in June
(see Letter 269). For Poe's reference to prison, see Woodberry (II, 313),
and John Sartain (*Reminiscences of a Very Old Man*, p. 206 ff.), the
former suggesting that the "imprisonment" was a "lingering hallucination," and the latter reconstructing the prison scene; see also Quinn,
Poe, p. 617, where a note indicates that a search of the records of
"Moyamensing Prison" yielded no evidence that Poe had been detained
there.

Poe enclosed the above letter to Mrs. Clemm in a brief note to Estelle
Anna Lewis, dated July 7, 1849 (Letter 324). [CL 808]

324 ⊱ TO SARAH ANNA LEWIS

[Philadelphia, July 7, 1849]

Dearest Anna,

Give the enclosed *speedily* to my darling <Anna.> mother. It
might get into wrong hands.

[*Unsigned*]

Poe left New York, June 29, 1849 (see the note to Letter 326). Phillips (II, 1414) quotes from a letter Mrs. Clemm wrote on August 4, 1849, to a friend (probably Annie Richmond); in it Mrs. Clemm states that for a fortnight after leaving Mrs. Lewis (the day following Poe's departure for Richmond — see Clemm to Annie Richmond, July 9, 1849, in H, XVII, 393), Mrs. Clemm heard nothing from "Stella," and when at last she went to see Mrs. Lewis, a letter from Poe awaited her; it had been enclosed in a "two" line note to Mrs. Lewis. "If I had received it," said Mrs. Clemm, "I should have gone on to Philadelphia . . ."; Poe's July 7 letter had begged her to come to him at once. Thus the present three-line note to Mrs. Lewis is undoubtedly the "two"-line note referred to by Mrs. Clemm; Poe was under the impression that his "mother" was still a guest of Mrs. Lewis in New York. [CL 809]

325 ➤ TO MARIA CLEMM

> Near Richmond
> [Saturday, July 14, 1849]

The weather is awfully hot, and, besides all this, I am so homesick I don't know what to do. I never wanted to see any one half so bad as I want to see my own darling mother. It seems to me that I would make any sacrifice to hold you by the hand once more, and get you to cheer me up, for I am terribly depressed. I do not think that any circumstances will ever tempt me to leave you again. When I am with you I can bear anything, but when I am away from you I am too miserable to live.

> *[Signature missing]*

The above letter may be complete in itself, it may be a fragment of a letter dated "Near Richmond," or it may be a portion of the Saturday night letter but printed separately by Burr; without the MSS. there is no way of identifying the above letter positively. Accepting Burr's printing, which is the only available source, we must date the letter "Saturday, July 14," since Poe left Philadelphia by train on Friday and probably caught the night boat from Baltimore to Richmond (see Letters 326 and 327). [CL 810]

326 ➤ TO MARIA CLEMM

> [July 14, 1849]
> Richmond, Saturday Night.

Oh, my darling Mother, it is now more than three weeks since I saw you, and in all that time your poor Eddy has scarcely drawn a breath except of intense agony. Perhaps you are sick or gone from

Fordham in despair, or dead. If you are but alive, and if I but *see you again,* all the rest is nothing. I love you better than ten thousand lives — so much so that it is cruel in you to let me leave you; nothing but sorrow *ever* comes of it.

Oh, Mother, I am *so* ill while I write — but I resolved that come what would, I would not sleep again without easing your dear heart as far as I could.

My valise was lost for ten days. At last I found it at the depot in Philadelphia, but (you will scarcely credit it) they had opened it and stolen *both lectures.* Oh, Mother, think of the blow to me this evening, when on examining the valise, these lectures were gone. All my object here is over unless I can recover them or re-write one of them.

I am indebted for more than life itself to B——. Never forget him, Mother, while you live. When all failed me, he stood my friend, got me money, and saw me off in the cars for Richmond.

I got here with two dollars over — of which I inclose you one. Oh God, my Mother, shall we ever again meet? If possible, oh COME! My clothes are *so horrible,* and I am *so ill.* Oh, if you *could* come to me, *my mother.* Write instantly — oh *do* not fail. God forever bless you.

Eddy.

Poe's "three weeks" is wrong; it should be "two." Poe left New York Friday afternoon at 5 o'clock, June 29, 1849 (see Mrs. Lewis' letter to G. W. Eveleth, February 11, 1854, Ingram collection, University of Virginia: "Edgar Poe dined with me at 3 o'clock, P.M. on the 29th of June, 1849, and left at 5, the same afternoon, for Richmond, Virginia. He never returned to New York again."; this testimony conflicts with that given by Ingram, II, 220–222, and subsequent biographers. Her information given Eveleth antedates that given Ingram by some twenty years; on the other hand, Ingram may have misconstrued the dating). Poe was therefore in Philadelphia from late that night or early Saturday morning, June 30, until Friday, July 13 (his letter of July 7, Saturday, was written in Philadelphia, and his letter of July 19 speaks of having been put on the cars for Baltimore "Friday last," July 13). His next letter ("Near Richmond"), together with that of "Richmond, Saturday Night" (July 14) places him in Richmond on Saturday, July 14, after an overnight passage from Baltimore. Though he is *"so ill"* as he writes the letter of Saturday night, July 14, he is "much better in health and spirits" by the time of his Thursday, July 19, letter. Moreover, the admonition to Mrs. Clemm to "write instantly" (in Poe's

July 14, Saturday Night, letter) was complied with by the time Poe wrote his letter of July 19. "B——" refers to C. Chauncey Burr, who saw Poe off on the cars, not to Richmond, but to Baltimore (see Letter 327). Burr bought Poe's ticket from Philadelphia to Baltimore and the boat passage cost Poe seven dollars of the ten with which he set out from Philadelphia, leaving him the above-mentioned "two dollars," after certain necessary expenses en route to Richmond. [CL 811]

327 ➤ TO MARIA CLEMM

Richmond, Thursday, July 19. [1849]

My Own Beloved Mother —

You will see at once, by the handwriting of this letter, that I am better — much better in health and spirits. Oh, if you only knew how your dear letter comforted me! It acted like magic. Most of my suffering arose from that terrible idea which I could not get rid of — the idea that you were dead. For more than ten days I was totally deranged, although I was not drinking one drop; and during this interval I imagined the most horrible calamities. . . .

All was hallucination, arising from an attack which I had never before experienced — an attack of *mania-à-potu.* May Heaven grant that it prove a warning to me for the rest of my days. If so, I shall not regret even the horrible unspeakable torments I have endured.

To L—— and to C—— B—— (and in some measure, also, to Mr. S——) I am indebted for more than life. They remained with me (L—— and B——) all day on Friday last, comforted me and aided me in coming to my senses. L—— saw G——, who said everything kind of me, and sent me five dollars; and P—— sent another five. B—— procured me a ticket as far as Baltimore, and the passage from there to Richmond was seven dollars. I have not drank anything since Friday morning, and then only a little Port wine. *If possible,* dearest Mother, I *will* extricate myself from this difficulty for your *dear, dear sake.* So keep up heart.

All is not lost yet, and "the darkest hour is just before daylight." Keep up heart, my own beloved mother — all may yet go well. I will put forth all my energies. When I get my mind a little more composed, I will try to write something. Oh, give my *dearest, fondest* love to Mrs. L. Tell her that *never, while I live,* will I forget her kindness to my darling mother.

[Signature missing]

Poe's "more than ten days" is hardly exact, for he was able to write to Mrs. Clemm on July 7, that is, on the eighth day after leaving her in New York (see Letter 323 and the note to Letter 326). "Mania à potu" is a medical term for delirium tremens and induces the torments Poe speaks of. "L——" was George Lippard (see Lippard to R. W. Griswold, November 22, 1849, original in Boston Public Library, for this and the following name identifications; see also notes in Quinn, *Poe,* p. 621); "C—— B——" was C. Chauncey Burr; "Mr. S——" was John Sartain; "G" was Louis A. Godey, and "P" was Samuel D. Patterson, who had taken over *Graham's* magazine in August 1848 (see the note to Letter 319). This letter is probably Poe's most overt testimonial to his difficulty in abstaining from alcoholic drink, and its extreme effects upon his system. Much has been written about Poe as a drunkard. Evidence from his own letters and from those of his friends indicates that on occasion he did drink, but the evidence points consistently to wine and that in small quantities. Letter 109 should be read in this connection, but the present letter seems the more sincere explanation of his problem. Poe's visit to Richmond was in the interest of establishing his own magazine with the aid of E. H. N. Patterson, of Oquawka, Illinois. Poe planned to solicit subscribers in certain cities and towns and to lecture as he went in order to pay his traveling expenses (see Letter 312). That Poe did "write something" is proved by his delivery of the lecture on "The Poetic Principle" on August 17 (see Quinn, *Poe,* p. 624), which may have been a rewritten version of the lecture of the same title given in Providence, December 20, 1848 (see Quinn, *Poe,* p. 583), and lost in the station in Philadelphia (see Letter 326). "Mrs. L." was Estelle Anna Lewis, who, according to a letter from Mrs. Clemm to a friend, had agreed to look after "Muddy" during Poe's absence (see P, II, 1414). [CL 813]

328 ✥ TO EDWARD H. N. PATTERSON

Richmond July 19 — [1849]

My Dear Sir,

I left New-York six weeks ago on my way to this place, but was arrested in Philadelphia by the Cholera, from which I barely escaped with life. I have just arrived in Richmond and your letter is only this moment received — or rather your two letters with the enclosures ($50. etc.) I have not yet read them and write now merely to let you know that they are safe. In a few days — as soon as I gather a little strength — you shall hear from me in full.

Truly Yours ever,

E. H. N. Patterson Esq.   Edgar A Poe.

For Poe's departure from New York, visit in Philadelphia, and arrival in Richmond, see the note to Letter 326. For "the enclosures," see Poe's requests in Letter 316. [CL 815]

329 ⤳ TO EDWARD H. N. PATTERSON

Richmond, Aug. 7. 49.

My Dear Sir,

The date of your last letter was June 7 — so that two months have elapsed since you wrote it, and I am only just now sitting down to reply. The fault, Heaven knows, has not been mine. I have suffered worse than death — not so much from the Cholera as from its long-continued consequences in debility and congestion of the brain — the latter, possibly, attributable to the calomel taken.

I have at length, however, been able to give your propositions full consideration — and I confess that I hesitate. "To fail" would be ruinous — at least to me; and a $3 Magazine (however well it might succeed (temporarily) under the guidance of another) would inevitably fail under mine. I could not undertake it *con amore*. My heart would not be in the work. So far as regards all *my* friends and supporters — so far as concerns all that class to whom *I* should look for sympathy and nearly all of whom I proposed to see personally — [*page 2*] the mere idea of a "$3 Magazine" would suggest namby-pamby-ism & frivolity. Moreover, even with a far more diminished circulation than you suggest, the *profits* of a $5 work would exceed those of a $3 one.

I most bitterly lament the event which has detained me from St Louis — for I cannot help thinking that, in a personal interview, I could have brought you over to my plans. I fear that *now* it is too late. But a Mag. might be issued *in July* very well — and if you think it *possible* that your views might be changed, I will still visit you at St L. As yet, I am too feeble to travel; but by the time your reply to this reaches me, I shall have gained sufficient strength to set out. It is not impossible, indeed, that, with energy, the first number might yet be issued in January. I will, therefore, await, in Richmond, your answer to this.

Very cordially yours,

Edgar A Poe.

For Patterson's reply to this letter, see H, XVII, 365–366, in which he agrees to publish "a $5 magazine, of 96 pp., monthly." Patterson published a note on Poe's death in his Oquawka *Spectator*, October 24, 1849, and a defense, on November 7 (see SLP, pp. 28–29). [CL 817]

330 ➤ TO MARIA CLEMM

[Richmond, August 28–29(?), 1849]

[*page* 3 (?) . . .] possible. Every body says that if I lecture again & put the tickets at 50 cts, I will clear $100. I *never* was received with so much enthusiasm. The papers have done nothing but praise me before the lecture & since. I enclose one of the notices — the only one in which the slightest word of disparagement appears. It is written by Daniel — the man whom I challenged when I was here last year. I have been invited out a great deal — but could seldom go, on account of not having a dress coat. To-night Rose & I are to spend the evening at Elmira's. Last night I was at Poitiaux's — the night before at Strobia's, where I saw my dear friend Eliza Lambert (Gen. Lambert's sister). She was ill in her bed-room, but insisted upon our coming up, & we stayed until nearly 1 o'clock. In a word, I have received nothing but kindness since I have been here, & could have been quite happy but for my dreadful anxiety about you. Since the report of my intended marriage, the McKenzies have overwhelmed me with attentions. Their house is so crowded that they *could* not ask me to stay. — And now, my own precious Muddy, the very moment I get a definite answer about everything, I will write again & tell you what to do. Elmira talks about visiting Fordham — but I do not know whether that would do. I think, perhaps, it would be best for you to give up everything there & come on here in the Packet. Write immediately & give me your advice about it — for you [*page* 4 (?)] know best. Could we be happier in Richmond or Lowell? — for I suppose we could never be happy at Fordham — and, Muddy, I *must* be somewhere where I can see Annie. — Did Mrs. L. get the Western Quarterly Review? Thompson is constantly urging me to write for the Messenger, but I am so anxious that I cannot. — Mr Loud, the husband of Mrs. St Leon Loud, the poetess of Philadelphia, called on me the other day and offered me $100 to edit his wife's poems. Of course, I accepted the offer. The whole labor will not occupy me 3

days. I am to have them ready by Christmas. — I have seen Bernard
often. Eliza is expected but has not come. — When I repeat my lecture here, I will then go to Petersburg & Norfolk. — A Mr. Taverner
lectured here on Shakspeare, a few nights after me, and had 8 persons, including myself & the doorkeeper. — I think, upon the whole,
dear Muddy, it will be better for you to say that I am ill, or something of that kind, and break up at Fordham, so that you may come
on here. Let me know immediately what you think best. You know
we could easily pay off what we owe at Fordham & the place is a
beautiful one — but I want to live *near Annie.* — And now, dear
Muddy, there is one thing I wish you to pay particular attention to.
I told Elmira, [*page* 5 (?)] when I first came here, that I had one of
the pencil-sketches of her, that I took a long while ago in Richmond;
and I told her that I would write to you about it. So, when you
write, just copy the following words in your letter:

I have looked again for the pencil-sketch of Mrs. S. but cannot
find it anywhere. I took down all the books and shook them one by
one, and unless Eliza White has it, I do not know what has become
of it. She was looking at it the last time I saw it. The one you spoilt
with Indian Ink ought to be somewhere about the house. I will do
my best to [fin]d it.

I got a sneaking letter to-day from Chivers. — Do not tell me anything about Annie — I cannot bear to hear it now — unless you can
tell me that Mr. R. is dead. — I have got the wedding ring. — and
shall have no difficulty, I think, in getting a dress-coat.

Wednesday Night.

[T****ll] n(m?)ight [**d *****o(w?)n *****] dear Muddy,
[. . . *page* 6 (?)] also the letter. *Return the letter when you write.*

[*Signature missing*]

On August 17, 1849, Poe lectured in Richmond on "The Poetic Principle"; the price of admission was twenty-five cents (Quinn, *Poe*, p.
624). John M. Daniel, editor of the Richmond *Examiner*, in his report
of the lecture, August 21, disparaged especially Poe's "recitations" (see
P, II, 1444–1445). Quinn (*Poe*, p. 571), after weighing certain evidence regarding Poe's possible visit to Richmond in 1848, quotes Poe's
sentence in the present letter ("the man whom I challenged when I was
here last year") as "the only evidence . . . that seems authentic"; but

Poe wrote Chivers, July 13, 1848, that he proposed going to Richmond on "Monday" (July 17); and wrote Mrs. Whitman (October 18, 1848) that her verses had reached him in Richmond. Rose was Poe's sister. As a youth, Poe had been interested in Elmira Royster; now in 1849, Elmira Royster Shelton was a widow. The Poitiaux, Strobia, Lambert, and Mackenzie families had been acquaintances of Poe's earlier Richmond days (see P, II, 1478–1479, and Quinn, *Poe*, p. 627). According to Killis Campbell (*Modern Language Notes*, XXXII, 270), Poe's review of Estelle Anna Lewis' poems (*The Child of the Sea and Other Poems*) appeared anonymously in the *Western Quarterly Review*, I (April 1849), 404–408, and was a recasting of his review in the SLM, September 1848, pp. 569–571. Peter D. Bernard was Thomas W. White's son-in-law; Eliza was White's daughter. Poe repeated his lecture on "The Poetic Principle" in Richmond, September 24 (Quinn, *Poe*, p. 635), but it was after his lecture in Norfolk, September 14, not before (Quinn, *Poe*, p. 629). The letter from Thomas H. Chivers to Poe is lost; concerning it, see Chivers' letter to Griswold, March 28, 1851 (H, XVII, 408). The references to Annie and R., of course, are to Annie Richmond and her husband. [CL 821]

331 ➤ TO SUSAN V. C. INGRAM

[Norfolk] Monday Evening
[September 10, 1849]

I have transcribed "Ulalume" with much pleasure, dear Miss Ingram, — as I am sure I would do any thing else, at your bidding — but I fear that you will find the verses scarcely more intelligible to day in my [*page 2*] manuscript than last night in my recitation. I would endeavor to explain to you what I really meant — or what I really fancied I meant by the poem, if it were not that I remember Dr Johnson's bitter and rather just remarks about [*page 3*] the folly of explaining what, if worth explanation, should explain itself. He has a happy witticism, too, about some book which he calls "as obscure as an explanatory note." Leaving "Ulalume" to its fate, therefore, & in good hands, I am

Yours truly

Edgar A Poe.

Poe delivered his lecture, "The Poetic Principle," at the Academy in Norfolk, Virginia, on September 14, 1849 (see Quinn, *Poe*, p. 629). [CL 822]

332 ⋗ TO MARIA CLEMM

Richmond V^a
Tuesday — Sep 18 — 49.

My own darling Muddy,

On arriving here last night from Norfolk I received both your letters, including Mrs Lewis's. I cannot tell you the joy they gave me — to learn at least that you are well & hopeful. May God forever bless you, my *dear dear* Muddy — Elmira has just got home from the country. I spent last evening with her. I think she loves me more devotedly than any one I ever knew & I cannot help loving her in return. Nothing is yet definitely settled [*The foregoing resembles the handwriting of Maria Clemm; the following is Poe's*] and it will not do to hurry matters. I [lec]tured at Norfolk on Monday & cleared enough to settle my bill here at the Madison House with $2 over. I had a highly fashionable audience, but Norfolk is a small place & there were 2 exhibitions the same night. Next Monday I lecture again here & expect to have a large audience. On Tuesday I start for Phil^a to attend to Mrs Loud's Poems — & *possibly* on Thursday I may start for N. York. If I do I will go straight over to Mrs Lewis's & send for you. It will be better for me not to go to Fordham — don't you think so? Write immediately in reply & direct to Phil^a. For fear I should not get the letter, sign no name & address it to *E. S. T. Grey Esqre*

If possible I will get married before I start — but there is no telling. Give my dearest love to Mrs L. My poor poor Muddy I am still unable to send you even one dollar — but keep [*The following resembles the handwriting of Maria Clemm*] up heart — I hope that our troubles are nearly over. I saw John Beatty in Norfolk.

God bless <you> & protect you my own darling Muddy. I showed your letter to Elmira and she says "it is such a darling precious letter that she loves you for it already"

Your own Eddy.

Don't forget to write immediately to Phil^a so that your letter will be there when I arrive.

The papers here are praising me to death — and I have been received everywhere with enthusiasm. Be sure & preserve all the printed scraps I have sent you & keep up my file of the Lit. World.

For Mrs. Lewis' letter, see Letter 333. According to Elmira Shelton, when Poe left Richmond late in September 1849, there was a partial understanding between them, but no definite engagement (see Quinn, *Poe*, p. 629); yet Mrs. Whitman wrote J. H. Ingram, January 4, 1874 (Ingram collection): "Poe, in the last of the two letters . . . to Mrs. Clemm in the month before his death, said his engagement to Mrs. Shelton was fixed"; but unless Mrs. Whitman is referring to the lost note of September 12–13, there is no evidence to corroborate her statement. Concerning Mrs. St. Leon Loud's poems, see Letter 330. "E. S. T. Grey" was used by Poe as a pseudonym on various occasions. That Poe showed Muddy's letter to Elmira is confirmed in Mrs. Shelton's letter to Mrs. Clemm, September 22, 1849 (Quinn, *Poe*, p. 634). Mrs. Clemm undoubtedly wrote to Poe at Philadelphia, but no MS. is known. The present letter is the last he is known to have written to Mrs. Clemm. [CL 826]

333 ➤ TO SARAH ANNA LEWIS

> [Richmond]
> [Tuesday 18th Sept.   1849]

My dear, dear Mrs. Lewis —

My dear sister Anna (for so you have permitted me to call you) — never while I live shall I forget you or your kindness to my mother. If I have not written you in reply to your first cherished letter, think anything of my silence except that I am ungrateful or unmindful of you — or that I do not feel for you the purest and profoundest affection — ah, *let* me say *love*. I hope very soon to see you and clasp your dear hand. In the meantime, may God bless you, my sweet sister.

> Your *always*,
>
> Edgar.

For data concerning Mrs. Lewis, see the note to Letter 257. Poe, in Richmond, is planning soon to leave for New York (see Letter 332 and Note 332). This is Poe's last known letter to Mrs. Lewis; in fact, this or Poe's letter to Mrs. Clemm of the same date seems to be the last letter he ever wrote. [CL 827]

NOTES

1. Source: photostat of original MS. (1 p.) in the Virginia State Library, Richmond. The letter was first printed in the *Calendar of Virginia State Papers*, x (1892), 518. The envelope is addressed to "His Excellency the Governor/ and/ Executive Council/ of/ *Virginia*." Endorsement on the envelope reads: "Application of Junior/ Volunteers for Arms/ Rec^d 17 Nov 1824." There is no postmark. No reply is known.

2. Source: photostat of original MS. (2 pp.) in the Virginia State Library, Richmond. The letter was written by Poe and addressed to "Mr. Peter V. Daniel/ Council Chamber/ of/ Virginia." There is no postmark. No reply from Daniel is known.

3. Source: facsimile in *Edgar Allan Poe Letters till Now Unpublished*, edited by Mary Newton Stanard (hereafter referred to as VL), pp. 41–42, from the original MS. (2 pp.) in the Valentine Museum, Richmond, Virginia, where it is first printed. The letter is not fully dated, but postmarked May 25, and directed to "John Allan Esqr/ Richmond,/ *Va*/ care Wm & Wm Galt Jr." Poe may be answering an unknown letter, which accompanied the clothes sent by John Allan.

The Poe–Allan correspondence between February 21 (?), 1826–April 12, 1833, includes 42 known letters, probably 43, and undoubtedly others for which there is no specific evidence. Of the known items, Poe wrote 30, Allan, 12–13. The collection in the Valentine Museum contains 27 holographs from Poe to Allan, and 2 from Allan to Poe. Mrs. Stanard (VL, p. 5) states erroneously, "There is, after Poe left the University, evidence of one missing letter, and one only [June 10, 1829]"; but there is at least one more, that cited by Allan, May 18, 1829 (VL, p. 121): "I duly rec^d your letter from Baltimore on Saturday . . . [May 14 (?), 1829]"; she adds that there is but one missing letter in the whole correspondence. On the contrary, Quinn (*Poe*, p. 71) quotes from Allan's letter to George Dubourg, August 14, 1817: "Enclosed is a letter for Edgar . . ."; thus Poe received at least one letter from John Allan, unless it was from Mrs. Allan, while the family was in England and Edgar was attending the Misses Dubourg's boarding school; also there are undoubtedly two letters to be added to those written at the University: one, about February 21, 1826, shortly after Poe's matriculation (see Letter 28); and another in December 1826, requesting money, which Allan sent (Letter 28). Although the Valentine Museum has but two MS. letters from Allan to Poe, at least ten or eleven others must have been written (see allusions in Poe's letters). Fourteen of Poe's known letters, and seven of Allan's were written during 1829 while Poe was in Baltimore, struggling to establish himself independently in life. A glance at Poe's salutations shows that the intimacy of "Dear Pa" prevailed from March 10, 1829, through November 6, 1830, with the exception of "Dear Sir," August 4, 1829, when Poe felt strongly that John Allan was offended. From January 3 until November 18, 1831, Poe begins with "Sir" or "Dear Sir." The successive letters of November 18 and December 15, 1831, have "Dear Pa," that of December 29, 1831, "Dear Sir," and his last letter, April 12, 1833, no salutation. John Allan's first extant letter to Poe, March 20, 1827, begins "Sir," and that of May 18, 1829, "Dear Edgar." On the evidence of known letters, the Poe–Allan correspondence during the second quarter of 1829 possessed an intimacy that was never again enjoyed; moreover, it is interesting to note that this intimacy first appears in Poe's letter of March 10, 1829, following the death of Frances Keeling Allan, from whose funeral Poe had just returned to Fortress Monroe (Poe arrived in Richmond too late to attend the services). The extant correspondence does not reveal in full the business and personal relations existing between Poe and Allan for the period covered by their letters; but the written words do not tell the whole story: inferences to be drawn from ideas expressed or half-expressed, chirography and pointing, salutations and closes — all these form the strange compound that represents the young Poe, a compound that must be read intelligently and sympathetically before one can pass fair judgment. Poe's letters to Allan are often careless in spelling and pointing; especially difficult to read correctly are his commas, periods, and dashes. Questionable readings in the facsimiles were collated with the MS. letters; all the original letters were examined for postmarks, addresses, and endorsements by John Allan. Notes to the Poe–Allan letters have been kept to a minimum; for fuller treatments, see the VL and the various biographies, especially Quinn's *Poe*.

The following letters comprise the known correspondence between Poe and John Allan; the starred items are those for which MSS. exist (possible additional items are treated in the preceding notes):

Poe to Allan		Allan to Poe	
1826	February *ca* 21		
		1826	February *post* 22
* 1826	May 25		
1826	September 21		
		1826	*ca.* December
* 1827	March 19		
* 1827	March 20		
		* 1827	March 20
* 1828	December 1		
* 1828	December 22		
* 1829	February 4		
* 1829	March 10		
1829	May 14		
		* 1829	May 18
* 1829	May 20		
* 1829	May 29		
		1829	June 8
1829	June 10		

Poe to Allan	Allan to Poe
* 1829 June 25	
* 1829 July 15	
	1829 July 19
* 1829 July 26	
* 1829 August 4	
	1829 August 7
* 1829 August 10	
	1829 August 19
	1829 October 27–28
* 1829 October 30	
* 1829 November 12	
	1829 November 15
* 1829 November 18	
	1830 May 21
* 1830 June 28	
* 1830 November 6	
	1830 December 27–28
* 1831 January 3	
* 1831 February 21	
* 1831 October 16	
	1831 *ante* November 18
* 1831 November 18	
* 1831 December 15	
* 1831 December 29	
* 1833 April 12	

4. Source: facsimile in VL, pp. 47–48, from original MS. (2 pp.) in the Valentine Museum, Richmond. The letter was first printed in VL. The envelope is lacking, but the letter is unquestionably to John Allan.

5. Source: facsimile in VL, pp. 59–61, of original MS. (3 pp.) in the Valentine Museum, Richmond; first printed in VL. The bracketed readings on page 3 indicate tears in the MS. The letter was dated by Mrs. Stanard (see VL, pp. 51–52). John Allan's reply, undated but probably written on March 20 before receipt of Poe's letter of the same date (Letter 6), is printed in VL, pp. 67–68.

6. Source: facsimile in VL, p. 65, of original MS. (1 p.) in the Valentine Museum, Richmond; first printed in VL. The letter was dated by Mrs. Stanard (see VL, pp. 51–52, and the notes to Letter 5). The present letter was written before Poe received Allan's of March 20.

7. Source: facsimile in VL, pp. 79–81, of original MS. (3 pp.) in the Valentine Museum, Richmond; first printed in VL. The envelope is postmarked "Dec. 3" (the envelope-address forms the verso of page 3 of the letter). Leaf two of the MS., comprising page 3 of the correspondence and

the cover, is worn at the folds, and a fragment missing from the left margin had been restored incorrectly at the right margin. This is Poe's first known letter to Allan since that of March 20, 1827. However, even if Poe did not write to Allan concerning his publication of *Tamerlane* in Boston, 1827, the tone of the present letter suggests some kind of communication, perhaps a lost letter, to his foster-father since the letter of March 20, 1827.

8. Source: facsimile in VL, pp. 91–94, of original MS. (4 pp.) in the Valentine Museum, Richmond; first printed in VL. The address is on page 4; postmarked December 24 from Old Point Comfort. The bracketed reading on page 3 indicates a section torn from the MS.

9. Source: facsimile in VL, pp. 103–106, of original MS. (4 pp.) in the Valentine Museum, Richmond; first printed in VL. Bracketed readings on page 3 represent tears in the MS., and the editorial asterisks indicate the possible number of letters in an indistinct word. The address appears on page 4, with the postmark February 9 at Old Point Comfort. John Allan had not answered Poe's last two letters, nor is there any evidence that he replied to the present one.

In connection with the correspondence between Poe and John McKenzie, cited in the present letter, Poe states that McKenzie wrote to him prior to Poe's reply. Poe probably refers to the son of Mr. and Mrs. William Mackenzie of Richmond, who at the time of Mrs. Poe's death took Rosalie Poe, Edgar's sister. No letter from John Mackenzie to Poe is known to be extant, but a letter from Poe to "MacKenzie" is listed for sale in Henkel's sale catalogue, November 20, 1935. This catalogue letter and Poe's "John McKenzie" letter are not the same, the Henkel item being an undated quarto asking about the possibility of buying T. W. White's subscription list of the *Southern Literary Messenger* (see Letter 159). Thus the letters exchanged between John Mackenzie and Poe early in 1829 have apparently been lost.

10. Source: facsimile in VL, pp. 115–116, of original MS. (2 pp.) in the Valentine Museum, Richmond; first printed in VL. The holograph is badly burned at both sides, bottom, and center fold; however, the wording of the first paragraph is complete, and probably only one line is missing at the foot of the leaf. The present printing of the letter is the most complete to date, the emended readings being based upon a close examination of the original manuscript. In all probability, Poe is not answering a letter from Allan, but reporting the progress of plans made while Poe was at home.

11. Source: facsimile in VL, pp. 127–128, of original MS. (2 pp.) in the Valentine Museum, Richmond. The letter was first printed in the VL. The envelope is postmarked May 20. John Allan recorded on the verso of the cover: "Answered in anticipation/ to Washington/ gave Edgar $50/ remitted him 100/ pd his draft 50/ [total] $200." On page 1, bracketed reading indicates tear in MS. Poe is answering Allan's letter of May 18, 1829, which was a reply to a lost letter from Poe, probably dated May 14, from Baltimore (see Allan's letter in the VL, p. 121).

12. Source: photostat of original (3 pp.) formerly in the Drexel Institute (MS. sold by Parke-Bernet Galleries, October 17–18, 1944, Drexel Institute

sale, item 199); also reproduced in Quinn, *Poe*, pp. 139–141. The autograph MS. has ink blots and smears. The envelope is directed to I. Lea, Esq., and was delivered by hand. Lea's address is on the back of the last page. The letter is folded and sealed with wax; it probably accompanied the MS. of the poem. There is no positive clue to the date except Lea's note at the top of page 1: "Ans' May 27." At the bottom of page 3 appears in pencil: "at City Hotel" (not in Poe's hand).

13. Source: facsimile in VL, pp. 137–140, of original MS. (4 pp.) in the Valentine Museum, Richmond; first printed in VL. The letter is addressed on page 4, and postmarked from Baltimore, May 31. The MS. is torn at the right edge of page 3, but no words are lacking.

The third and fifth paragraphs of the letter suggest an exchange of letters between Poe and Robert Walsh. Their location is unknown. They would have been written between Poe's letter to Wirt, May 11, and Poe's letter to Isaac Lea, *ante* May 27, 1829.

14. Source: facsimile in VL, pp. 149–152, of original MS. (4 pp.) in the Valentine Museum, Richmond; first printed in VL, with the omission of part of paragraph three on page two, alluding to Edward Mosher (the line is here first printed). The envelope is postmarked from Baltimore, June 25. The postmark and address appear on page 4, center, with the correspondence above and below; at the right margin appears Allan's notation: "Edgar A Poe/ June 25th 1829."

15. Source: facsimile in VL, pp. 155–156, of original MS. (2 pp.) in the Valentine Museum, Richmond; first printed in VL. The extra leaf, used as an envelope, was postmarked from Baltimore, July 17.

16. Source: facsimile in VL, pp. 163–166, of original MS. (4 pp.) in the Valentine Museum, Richmond; first printed in VL. Page 4 carries a Baltimore postmark of July 26, and in the center of the page, the address. The MS. is slightly torn at several places. Poe is replying to Allan's letter of July 19, which is unlocated.

17. Source: photostat of original MS. (2 pp.) in the Berg collection, New York Public Library. The letter was first printed by Charles Brombach of Philadelphia in a limited edition of 25 copies, 1917; also in A, 1, 250–251, and P, 1, 335, both in 1926. Beneath Poe's dating is a notation, presumably by Isaac Lea: "Rec^d July 30/ Ans Aug. 3" (the location of the MS. reply is unknown, nor has it ever been printed).

18. Source: facsimile in VL, pp. 175–176, of original MS. (2 pp.) in the Valentine Museum, Richmond; first printed in VL. The outside cover carries the address and a Baltimore postmark of August 4.

19. Source: facsimile in VL, pp. 185–187, of original MS. (3 pp.) in the Valentine Museum, Richmond; first printed in VL. The letter is postmarked at Baltimore, August 10. John Allan notes on the cover: "Answd Aug 19, 1829/ inclosed him $50." Poe is replying to a lost letter from Allan, dated probably August 7–8, 1829.

20. Source: facsimile in VL, pp. 197–198, of original MS. (2 pp.) in the Valentine Museum, Richmond; first printed in VL. The envelope carries the

postmark of Baltimore, October 30. Poe is answering Allan's letter of October 28 (?), 1829, the location of which is unknown.

21. Source: transcript made by Neal in a letter to Ingram, May 10, 1875, now in the Ingram collection, University of Virginia; lining and mechanics are Neal's. The letter was first printed in full by Neal (with poetic selections submitted by Poe) in *The Yankee and Boston Literary Gazette*, VI (December 1829), 295–298 n.s. The existence of Poe's original is unknown. The dating of this letter was established by the inclusive issues of *The Yankee* cited above. In a letter to Ingram, *supra*, Neal admitted Poe's letter was directed to him. It is possible that a concluding portion of the original letter was omitted by Neal in his printings of it in *The Yankee* and in the Portland *Advertiser*, Friday, April 26, 1850, and in his letter to Ingram. It seems probable, also, that the above letter to Neal is Poe's second, at least, an earlier one accompanying the verses "Heaven" noted in *The Yankee* in September (see Neal's introductory comment, Quinn, *Poe*, 152).

22. Source: facsimile in VL, p. 205, of original MS. (1 p.) in the Valentine Museum, Richmond; first printed in VL. The letter is postmarked Baltimore, November 12. For Allan's prompt reply, see Letter 23.

23. Source: facsimile in VL, p. 215, of original MS. (1 p.) in the Valentine Museum, Richmond; first printed in VL. The letter is postmarked at Baltimore, November 19. Poe is replying to John Allan's letter of November 15–16 (?), 1829, the location of which is unknown.

24. Source: photostat of original MS. (fragment of one (?) leaf) in the William H. Koester collection, Baltimore; also, for the material enclosed in daggers, W, I, 369. The present printing is the fullest known, former versions using either the Portland *Daily Advertiser*, April 26, 1850, or reprints from it; the *Advertiser* omitted everything before "I thank you, Sir" and for "anxiously," in the last line of page 1 of the MS., printed "consciously." The passage used from Woodberry is an exact reprinting of the passage in the *Advertiser*. The MS. being undated, the only available dating is that of the *Advertiser*, which places "Dec. 29, 1829," though without authority, at the end of the letter.

The Poe–Neal correspondence of 1829 seems to include at least three letters from Poe and at least one from Neal: Poe to Neal, *ante* September 1829, and October–November 1829 (see the latter letter and notes), and the present letter, December 29, 1829; Neal to Poe, *ante* December 29, 1829, in which he not only suggested corrections for some of the poems sent him but also refused to have the volume dedicated to him (see Neal's article in the Portland *Advertiser*, April 26, 1850, ". . . E. A. P. had written me a letter, offering to dedicate a volume of these poems [*Al Aaraaf, Tamerlane and Other Poems*, Baltimore: Hatch and Dunning, December 1829] to me — and that I said, no for his sake . . ."; see also a restatement of the foregoing in Neal's letter to Mary Gove, November 30, 1846, in Quinn, *Poe*, p. 153). If there is a missing portion to Poe's letter to Neal, October–November, 1829 (Letter 21), it may have contained an offer to dedicate the forthcoming volume of poems to Neal; if not, there must have been another letter from Poe that made the offer. Also, it seems probable that Neal would have replied to the present letter, or at least to a presentation copy of a volume of poems dedicated to him.

25. Source: facsimile in VL, pp. 225–227, of original MS. (3 pp.) in the Valentine Museum, Richmond; first printed in VL. The letter is postmarked Richmond, May 3, and addressed, on page 4, to Samuel Graves, Old Point Comfort, Virginia. The MS. is written in an unusually large hand for Poe; and there is a portion of page 3 torn away, though no words are missing. Poe is apparently replying to two letters from Graves, one of which was not received: the letter Bully said was sent to Washington never reached Poe, and may be dated conjecturally as April 1830; the letter Poe received was directed to him, probably, in Richmond, and may be dated May 1, 1830, though it may have been written at Fortress Monroe and not postmarked at Old Point Comfort station until later, May 1, therefore, being the latest date for Poe to answer it on May 3. Both letters from Graves are unlocated.

26. Source: facsimile in VL, pp. 237–238, of original MS. (2 pp.) in the Valentine Museum, Richmond; first printed in VL. Though the year date is not given, the references to West Point indicate 1830; moreover, Allan's note on the cover reads: "Edgar A Poe/ June 28th 1830/ West Point." The letter was postmarked from West Point, June 28. Allan's letter of May 21, 1830, which Poe is answering, was the first since November 15–16 (?), 1829 (see Letter 23 and notes).

27. Source: facsimile in VL, pp. 247–248, of original MS. (2 pp.) in the Valentine Museum, Richmond; first printed in VL. The letter is postmarked at West Point, November 10. John Allan, apparently, has not written since May 21, 1830.

28. Source: facsimile in VL, pp. 259–262, of original MS. (4 pp.) in the Valentine Museum, Richmond; first printed in VL. Poe dated the letter incorrectly 1830; its content proves 1831, as well as its postmark: West Point, January 5. The address appears in the center portion of page 4, the last paragraph of the letter coming at the bottom of the page. According to the editor of the VL, a portion of leaf 2 of the MS. broke off and was improperly restored (see VL, p. 261). Below the address, John Allan wrote: "I recd. this on the 10th, & did not from its conclusion deem it necessary to reply. I make this note on the 13th. & can see no good Reason to alter my opinion, I do not think the Boy has one [*tear*] good quality. He may do or act as [he] [*tear*] pleases, tho' I w^d have saved him [*tear*] but on his own terms & conditions since [*tear*] I cannot beleive a word he writes, His [*tear*] letter is the most barefaced one sided statem[ent]." The torn part of the MS. seems due to the breaking off of the sealing wax; therefore no words are lacking in Allan's note, for he was forced to write on both sides of the wax. The letter that Poe is answering cannot be dated exactly, but a conjectural date would be December 27–28, 1830; its location is unknown.

29. Source: facsimile in VL, pp. 271–273, of original MS. (3 pp.) in the Valentine Museum, Richmond; first printed in VL. The letter is postmarked at New York, February 21. The MS. has an ink blot in the center of each

page and a piece torn from the right margin of leaf 2. On page 3, just below the postscript, John Allan wrote: "Apl 12, 1833 it is now upwards of 2 years since I received the/ above precious relict of the Blackest Heart & deepest ingratitude/ alike destitute of honour & principle every day of his life/ has only served to confirm his debased nature — / Suffice it to say my only regret is in Pity for/ his failings — his Talents are of an order that can/ never prove a comfort to their possessor."

30. Source: photostat of original MS. (1 p.) at the U. S. Military Academy Library at West Point. The letter was first printed in the New York *Sun*, October 30, 1902 (see L and L, II, 449). The envelope, postmarked March 10 at New York, is addressed to "Lt. Col. S. Thayer, Superintendent, U.S.M.A., West Point." Also on the envelope is a memorandum which reads: "Edgar A. Poe / New York March 10. 1831 / Wishes a letter respecting him, / addressed to Genl Lafayette / &c. as he wishes to join the / Polish Army." No reply by Colonel Thayer is known.

31. Source: photostat of original (1 p.) in Pennsylvania Historical Society. First printed in full in Woodberry (1885), pp. 63–64.

32. Source: facsimile in VL, pp. 283–284, of original MS. (2 pp.) in the Valentine Museum, Richmond; first printed in VL. The letter is postmarked at Baltimore, October 16. The letter is rather carelessly written: words are over-written, certain letters ill-constructed, and "altho" appears to have had its *t* put in last. John Allan has not written to Poe since December 27–28, 1830.

33. Source: facsimile in VL, p. 293, of original MS. (1 p.) in the Valentine Museum, Richmond; first printed in VL. The letter is postmarked at Baltimore, November 18. Though Poe does not seem to be answering a letter from John Allan, his allusion to a "late kindness" suggests a recent letter with some sort of assistance, perhaps financial, from his foster-father, though the letter is unlocated.

34. Source: facsimile in VL, pp. 303–304, of original MS. (2 pp.) in the Valentine Museum, Richmond; first printed in VL. The letter is postmarked at Baltimore, December 15. Though Allan did not mail any reply to Poe's letter of November 18, nor to Mrs. Clemm's letter of December 5 (see VL, p. 295), he wrote on the present letter, just below Poe's signature: "Wrote on the 7th Decr 1831 to John Walsh/ to procure his liberation & to give him $20 besides to keep him out of farther/ difficulties & value on me for such/ amt as might be required — neglected/ sending it on till the 12th Jany 1832/ Then put in the office myself." Allan's last statement is confusing; but if he sent a letter to Poe with the money, it is unlocated.

35. Source: facsimile in VL, p. 307, of original MS. (1 p.) in the Valentine Museum, Richmond; first printed in VL. The letter is postmarked Baltimore, December 29. Allan had not answered Poe's last two letters.

36. Source: facsimile in VL, p. 315, of original MS. (1 p.) in the Valentine Museum, Richmond; first printed in VL. The letter is postmarked at Baltimore, April 12.

37. Source: photostat of original (4 pp.) in the Bradley Martin collection, New York. Page 1 of the MS., comprising all the letter except the "P.S.," is

reproduced by Quinn (*Poe,* p. 200), from a facsimile of the original. The letter was first printed in full in a French translation by Andre Fontainas in his *Edgar Poe Lettres à John Allan,* pp. 10–11, though he dates it "1823" (probably a typographical error). The letter covers the top third of page one of a four-page MS. that includes Poe's print-like copy of "Epimanes"; at the foot of p. 4, Poe added his "P.S." In the center of p. 4 appears: "Messrs. Buckingham/ Editors of the N. England Magaz^{ine}/ Boston, Mass^{tts}."

38. Source: photostat of original MS. (1 p.) in the Peabody Institute Library, Baltimore. The letter was first printed in the *Century Magazine,* XLVIII (August 1894), 573–574. In his letter to Kennedy, December 19, 1834, Poe says: "About four weeks ago I sent you a note respecting my Tales of the F. Club . . ."; thus the date of the present letter may be placed at *ca.* 19 November. The present letter is a MS. of a single sheet, written on one side only; therefore Quinn's statement (*Poe,* p. 204, n. 36) that Kennedy wrote a note on "the third leaf" is incorrect.

The Poe–Kennedy correspondence consists of 12 known letters from Poe and 5 known and two probable letters from Kennedy; the starred items below indicate letters known to be or to have been extant. Nine of Poe's original MSS. are in the Peabody Institute, Baltimore, to which they came in a sealed chest some forty years ago.

Poe to Kennedy		Kennedy to Poe	
* 1834	November *ca.* 19		
* 1834	December 19		
		* 1834	December 22
* 1835	March 15		
		1835	March 15
* 1835	March 15		
		1835	May 21–25 (?)
* 1835	September 11		
		* 1835	September 19
* 1836	January 22		
		* 1836	February 9
* 1836	February 11		
		* 1836	April 26
* 1836	June 7		
* 1840	December 31		
* 1841	June 21		
* 1844	February 1		
* 1845	October 26		
		* 1845	December 1

39. Source: an auctioneer's transcript in the collection of Thomas O. Mabbott; the original MS., a half-page octavo, was offered for sale in Sotheby's Catalogue, December 18–19, 1934, and at present is unlocated. The letter is here first printed.

40. Source: photostat of original MS. (1 p.) in the Peabody Institute Library. The letter was first printed in the *Century Magazine*, XLVIII (August 1894), 574. That 1835, the year date usually assigned to this letter, is correct, is established by the following advertisement in the *Baltimore Patriot*, Thursday, March 12, 1835, p. 3: "A Teacher Wanted — At male Public School No. 3 Aisquith St. The commissioners of Public Schools will appoint on Wednesday next, the 18th inst. a Teacher to supply a vacancy which has occurred at Male School No. 3. Satisfactory recommendations as to character, with testimonials of capacity for conducting a School on the Monitorial System, will be required. Salary one thousand dollars per annum, payable quarterly. Applications addressed to the commissioners, may be left with either of them or the Secretary, No. 8 Courtland Street [a list of the commissioners then follows]." The present letter is one of those MSS. that came to the Peabody Institute in the sealed chest containing the Kennedy papers (see Note 38).

41. Source: photostat of original MS. (1 p.) in the Peabody Institute Library. The letter was first printed in the *Century Magazine*, XLVIII (August 1894), 574. For the year date, Harrison (H, XVII, 2) suggested 1833; subsequent editors give 1835. In a letter to Ingram, March 2, 1909, Amelia Poe assigns the letter to March 15 (see Ingram collection, University of Virginia); in the unpublished MS. revision of his *Life* of Poe (Ingram collection), Ingram places Poe's letter concerning the teaching vacancy (Sunday, March 15, 1835) first, with the present letter next, dating both 1835. Poe's last sentence, above, especially "I must submit to my fate," suggests very strongly that the present letter is a follow-up of the one dated "Sunday, 15th March" [1835]. Kennedy's invitation was probably a written note, same date, unlocated.

42. Source: photostat of original (1 p.) in Huntington Library (HM 21868). The letter is here first printed in full. It is an undated fragment, written on one side of a quarto leaf measuring at present $9\frac{1}{4} \times 8\frac{1}{2}$ inches; both top and bottom are torn off, about equally, with text missing definitely at the top. The leaf is folded twice, into envelope shape, and addressed to T. W. White; the postal cancellation is Baltimore, April 30, and White wrote on back of letter: "April 30, 1835." The MS. a little split in folds and the right center edge is damaged. Poe is replying to certain criticisms and queries by White, as the content indicates.

I am of the opinion that the bracketed fragment missing at the head of the present MS. letter is to be identified with the paragraph concerning a swimming feat printed in the SLM, 1 (May 1835), 468. The paragraph, which is unsigned, alludes to a swimming adventure by the writer, the allusion being an answer to a passage in an article entitled "The Doom," which appeared in the SLM, January 1835, and in which "E—— P——" is cited as making the swim. Biographers have accepted testimonials of early Richmonders to Poe's dexterity and strength in the water. The paragraph printed in the May issue is headed: "A valued correspondent, who was the bold swimmer alluded to [in "The Doom"] writes to us as follows . . ." The paragraph could have been the first six lines of the present letter, which is a quarto leaf measuring at present $9\frac{1}{4} \times 8\frac{1}{2}$ inches. The original size of the leaf must have been at least $10 \times 8\frac{1}{2}$ inches, if not more than 10 inches in length. Poe's letter to White, May 30, 1835, measures $9\frac{3}{4} \times 7\frac{3}{4}$ inches; his letter to White of June 12, 1835, $7\frac{5}{8} \times 6$ inches; and that of June 22, 1835, $9\frac{5}{8} \times 7\frac{1}{2}$ inches; thus the length of leaves increased in proportion to the width. A leaf $8\frac{1}{2}$ inches wide would be at least 10, if not $10\frac{1}{2}$ or 11 inches in length. Poe's April 30, 1835, letter is closely written, and averages about $\frac{2}{3}$ of a line for each $\frac{1}{8}$ inch. Thus if the original leaf were $10\frac{1}{2}$ or 11 inches, the missing fragment could be six lines long, still allowing space for the date and salutation. There seems to be no way of proving that the paragraph in the SLM is printed from the missing portion of the present letter. However, since a few lines have been torn from the MS. and since the paragraph appeared in the issue of the SLM following the date of the present letter, and since the present editor believes the missing fragment could have contained the number of lines represented by the wording of the printed paragraph, the paragraph is printed at the head of the present letter. Following "Calais" there were probably a few words suggesting that White add the present comment to what was said in the January article. If the present hypothesis is correct, White probably tore off the lines from the head of the letter and used them for printing the paragraph.

43. Source: photostat of original MS. (3 pp.) in the Boston Public Library. The letter was first printed in H, XVII, 4–6. The envelope is postmarked at Baltimore, May 31. Poe is replying to White's letter of May 20, 1835 (unlocated).

44. Source: photostat of original (1 p.) in the Boston Public Library. The letter was first printed by Woodberry in the *Century Magazine*, XLVIII (August 1894), 575. Poe is replying to White's letter of June 8, the location of which is unknown.

45. Source: photostat of original (2 pp.) in the Boston Public Library. The letter was first printed in H, XVII, 8–10. The postal cancellation is Baltimore, June 23. Poe is replying to White's letter of June 18, the location of which is unknown.

46. Source: the original MS. (2 pp.) in the private collection of Merrill Griswold, Boston. The letter was first printed by Woodberry in the *Century Magazine*, XLVIII (August 1894), 575–576. The envelope is directed to "Thos. W. White, Esqr., Southern Messenger, Richmond, Va.," and cancelled July 20. Paragraph two of page two shows one faded portion of MS. and several smears. Poe is replying to White's letters of July 14 and 16, locations of originals unknown.

47. Source: photostat of original MS. (2 pp.) in the Berg collection, New York Public Library. The letter was first printed in *Gulf States Historical Magazine*, I (January 1903), 281–283 (Harrison's printing, XVII, 13–16, is less full). The envelope is postmarked Richmond, August 20, and is directed to William Poe, Augusta, Georgia. A portion of the MS. has been torn out, and the bracketed emendations, above, are suggested restorations. Poe is replying to William Poe's letter of *ca.* August 17 (?), 1835, which is unlocated.

48. Source: original MS. (3 pp.) in the Enoch Pratt Library, Baltimore.
The letter was first printed (with facsimile) in Pratt, facing p. 6. The year
date was established by internal and external evidence: Poe was in Richmond
in August 1835, and Mrs. Clemm was in Baltimore; the postal cancellation
shows Richmond, Virginia, August 29; and the envelope is directed to Mrs.
William Clemm, Baltimore, Maryland. Mrs. Clemm and Virginia joined Poe in
Richmond on October 3, 1835, according to a letter from Mrs. Clemm to William Poe, October 7, 1835 (see Quinn, *Poe,* p. 230, n.16). The MS. is badly
torn and worn, page three especially. Poe is replying to Mrs. Clemm's letter
written sometime between August 20–26 (?) after receipt of one from Poe
saying William Poe had written him offering to assist her; and to a letter just
received from her (probably dated Aug. 27–28?).

49. Source: photostat of original (1 p.) in the William H. Koester collection, Baltimore. The letter is here first printed.

50. Source: photostat of original MS. (2 pp.) in the Peabody Institute
Library. The letter was first printed in H, XVII, 16–18. It is written on both
sides of a single leaf; there is no cover extant. Poe is not replying to a letter
from Kennedy; but Kennedy seems to have written Poe a note to accompany
some money that he forwarded from Thomas W. White to Poe (see Letter
43); the note or letter, unlocated, may be dated May, *ca.* 21–25, 1835.

51. Source: Anderson Galleries Catalogue, November 13–14, 1916, item
71, where the letter is first printed; the location of the original is unknown.
The American Art Association Catalogue, April 20–21, 1921, part 3,
item 493, cites a Poe to Bird letter that solicits contributions to the SLM
under the date of October 6, 1835; this date is undoubtedly an error: at
times Poe's 8's are like his 6's, but his 6's are less likely to resemble his 8's;
furthermore, the Thomas Madigan Catalogue, November, 1923, No. 145,
p. 19, gives the letter under the later date. The letter, a 1 page quarto was
addressed to Dr. R. M. Bird, Philadelphia.

51a. Source: printed fragment in the Anderson Galleries sale catalogue,
April 25–27, 1916, item 465. The Merwin-Clayton sales catalogue, January
18, 1911, item 255, described the MS. as a 1 page octavo. Both catalogues
agree that the letter was written by Poe but signed by Thomas W. White,
and that Poe addressed the envelope to Lucian Minor, the Anderson Galleries
catalogue giving his address as Charlottesville, Virginia. The original MS. is
unlocated.

52. Source: photostat of original MS. (2 pp.) in the George P. Coleman
collection in Colonial Williamsburg Architectural Department, Williamsburg,
Virginia. The letter was first printed in the *Century Magazine,* CVII (March
1924), 653–655. The envelope is addressed to "Judge Beverly Tucker/
Williamsburg/ Va:" and is postmarked at Richmond, December 3. Poe is
replying to Tucker's letter to T. W. White, November 29, 1835 (MS. in
the Boston Public Library; printed in part in Quinn, *Poe,* pp. 234–235).
Tucker replied to the present letter, December 5, 1835 (MS. in the Boston
Public Library; printed in H, XVII, 21–24).

53. Source: photostat of original MS. (1 p.) in the Enoch Pratt Library,

Baltimore. The letter was first printed in Woodberry (1885), pp. 78–79. The envelope is postmarked Richmond, January 12, and directed to George Poe, Mobile, Alabama. The signature, including the complimentary close, and perhaps part of the postscript have been cut away, but Poe is obviously the writer. This is the first known letter between Poe and George Poe.

54. Source: photostat of original MS. (2 pp.) in the Peabody Institute Library. The letter is here first printed in full. Poe is replying to Kennedy's letter of September 19, 1835 (the MS. is in the Boston Public Library; printed in H, XVII, 19–20).

55. Source: photostat of original (1 p.) in Boston Public Library. The letter was first printed in W, II, 370–371. The envelope is directed to Charlottesville, Virginia, shows a postal cancellation of February 13, and has a note, in Minor's (?) hand: "rec^d 16th Feb. 1836."

56. Source: data in American Art Association catalogue, May 4–5, 1925, item 466, where the letter is listed and where the above unbracketed phrase is quoted. The letter is described as a 1 page quarto, signed, with the address on last page of sheet. The catalogue states that the letter is addressed to "an author of Savannah, Ga." and states in the next item for sale, No. 467, that the correspondent in each letter is the same. Evidence from the Poe letter in No. 467 tends to show the correspondent in the present item is Stephen G. Bulfinch, not of Savannah, but of Augusta, Georgia (see Letter 69, and notes). Location of the present manuscript is unknown.

57. Source: photostat of original MS. (2 pp.) in the Peabody Institute Library. The letter was first printed in H, XVII, 29–31, though he omits Hubard's name and places the postscript just before the complimentary close. Poe is replying to Kennedy's letter of February 9, 1836 (MS. in the Boston Public Library, not at Peabody as Quinn states — *Poe*, p. 241 n.; printed in H, XVII, 28–29).

58. Source: printed letter in Armistead C. Gordon's *Memories and Memorials of William Gordon McCabe*, I, 16–17. The original MS. is now owned by William Gordon McCabe, Charleston, South Carolina, but is inaccessible. Poe is answering McCabe's letter of February 24, 1836, which is unlocated.

59. Source: photostat of original MS. (1 p.) in the William H. Koester collection, Baltimore. The letter was first printed in facsimile in Anderson Galleries Catalogue (No. 1906), January 14–15, 1925, item 380, p. 61. The original is a one-page letter, with inside and postal cancellation dated the same. Minor's name does not appear in the letter itself, but does appear on the envelope; further identification is made by reference to "Liberian Literature," which was by Minor (see Letter 55; see also the letter of T. W. White to Minor, November 9, 1835, in Jackson's *Contributors to the Southern Literary Messenger, 1834–1864*, p. 14). Poe, acting as White's amanuensis, is answering Minor's letter to White, March 6, 1836; location of the original of which is unknown.

60. Source: letter printed in W, I, 377–378 (though he gives the *New York Times*, February 15, 1908, as his source, which would also be its first printing, the letter does not appear in that number). The original MS. is

unlocated. Poe is replying to William Poe's letter of March 29, 1836, also unlocated. Washington Poe's letter to Poe, *ante* March 29, 1836, and Poe's reply, March 30 (?), 1836, are both unlocated.

61. Source: photostat of original MS. (2 pp.) in the William H. Koester collection, Baltimore. The letter was first printed in full in Quinn, *Poe*, pp. 238–239. The envelope is addressed to "Mrs. L. H. Sigourney/ Hartford/ *Connec*¹" and is postmarked Richmond, April 12. The envelope is endorsed, presumably by Mrs. Sigourney, "Edgar A. Poe. Richmond. April 12, 1836./ ans^d April 25th"; but the original MS. letter from Mrs. Sigourney in reply to Poe's, above, is clearly dated "April 23^d" (a.l.s. in Boston Public Library). Poe is replying to a letter from Mrs. Sigourney to Thomas W. White, owner of the *Southern Literary Messenger*. For Mrs. Sigourney's answer to Poe's present letter, see H, XVII, 33–35.

62. Source: photostat of original MS. (1 p.) in the George P. Coleman collection in Colonial Williamsburg Architectural Department, Williamsburg, Virginia. The letter was first printed in the *Century Magazine*, CVII (March 1924), 655–656. No reply to the present letter is known.

63. Source: photostat of original (1 p.) in Harvard College Library. The letter is here first printed. Poe is acting for White in replying to Sparks's letter of May 17, 1836, location of original of which is unknown.

64. Source: photostat of original MS. (1 p.) in the William H. Koester collection, Baltimore. Reproduced in facsimile in the Anderson Galleries Catalogue (No. 4073), January 4–5, 1934, item 350. The letter was first printed in the *Daughters of the American Revolution Magazine*, LXVII (September 1933), 539–546. The location of Causten's reply is unknown, but on Poe's MS. is this note: "Ans Dec 9 J H C."

65. Source: photostat of original MS. (1 p.) in the William H. Koester collection, Baltimore. The letter was first printed in New York *Independent*, March, 1901, p. 940. The envelope is addressed to "Dr Robert M. Bird / Philadelphia / *Pa*," and is postmarked from Richmond, June 7. Bird's reply is unlocated.

66. Source: letter as first printed in *Correspondence of James Fenimore-Cooper*, edited by James Fenimore Cooper, I, 356–357. A copy in pencil, probably by Cooper's grandson, James Fenimore Cooper, is in the Yale University Library; the original MS. is apparently not in the Cooper collection, Cooperstown, New York.

67. Source: photostat of original MS. (1 p.) in the William H. Koester collection, Baltimore. A facsimile appears in the American Art Association catalogue, December 16–17, 1929, item 105. The letter was first printed in James Grant Wilson's *Life and Letters of Fitz-Greene Halleck*, pp. 396–397. Poe's letter is one of several seeking contributions to the *Southern Literary Messenger* (see Letters 65, 66, 68).

68. Source: photostat of original MS. (2 pp.) in the Bradley Martin collection, New York. The letter was first printed in Ingram, I, 140–141.

69. Source: letter in American Art Association catalogue, May 4–5, 1925, item 467, where it is first printed. It is described as an a.l.s., 1 page quarto,

with the address on the last page of the sheet; and addressed to the Georgia author whose contributions were solicited in a letter from Poe, February 9 (see letter 56). The present location of the original MS. is unknown. The letter to which Poe is replying is also unlocated.

70. Source: original MS. (1 p.) in the J. K. Lilly, Jr., collection, Indianapolis. The letter was first printed in the Richmond *Times-Dispatch*, Sunday, November 11, 1923, pt. 7, p. 3. The letter carries no postmark but is addressed to "Littleton W. Tazewell Esqr/ Norfolk/ V^a." It is also endorsed in an unknown hand: "Edgar A Poe/ July 16, 1836." No reply from Tazewell is known.

71. Source: photostat of original MS. (2 pp.) in the Historical Society of Pennsylvania. The letter was first printed in W, II, 371–372. Poe's apology implies a letter from Carey, probably dated in latter half of July; location of the original unknown.

72. Source: original (1 p.) in the Poe Foundation, Richmond. The letter was first printed by John W. Ostrom in *Americana*, XXXVI, No. 1 (January 1942), pp. 67–71. The letter is undated, but postal cancellation shows "Aug. 19"; the year is established as 1836 by Poe's review of Willis' *Inklings of Adventure* in SLM, II (August 1836), 597–600. The envelope is addressed to "H. Haines Esqr/"Constellation"/Petersburg."

73. Source: photostat of the letter as printed in the Richmond *Courier and Daily Compiler*, p. 2, cols. 4–5, September 2, 1836, from files in the Virginia State Library, Richmond. The original MS. was probably destroyed by the *Compiler* editor. The printed letter was reproduced in L and L, II, 458–460, but with numerous changes. Poe was replying to a paragraph in the *Courier* of August 31, 1836, p. 2, col. 4 (also in file of Virginia State Library); thus the letter is reasonably dated August 31 or September 1. Though the letter is signed "Editor of the Messenger," Poe certainly wrote it.

74. Source: photostat of original MS. (3 pp.) in the Haverford College Library. The letter was first printed in the *Sewanee Review*, XXXVI (April 1928), 172–174. The text appears on pages 1–3 of a folded leaf, the address on page 4; the envelope shows "To / Harrison Hall Esqr / Philadelphia / Pa."; and was postmarked Richmond, September 2.

75. Source: photostat of original MS. (1 p.) in the Bradley Martin collection, New York. Reproduced in facsimile in the Anderson Galleries Catalogue, No. 1956, April 27, 1925, item 224, p. 27. The letter was first printed in the *Nation*, LXXXIX (July 1, 1909), 9–10. Poe's year date is incorrect; it should be 1836, which is established by the copyright date of the *Ladies' Wreath*. Though Poe is not answering a letter addressed to him, he cites a recent letter to Mrs. Hale: probable date about June 7, since he wrote to Bird, Halleck, Cooper, Mrs. Sigourney, and, as he tells Kennedy (June 7, 1836), "many others," soliciting contributions for the SLM; for her probable response to this June letter, see the note to Letter 75.

76. Source: letter printed from MS. in W, II, 372–373, its only other printing. The present location of the MS. (probably 1 p.) is unknown. Poe is replying to Magruder's letter of December 24, 1836, which is unlocated.

Very little is known of Poe's correspondence in 1837; only two letters in MS. or printed form have been preserved: this one to Magruder and that to Carpenter, Norris, and Brown, February 28. However, others seem to have been written, both by and to Poe. White's letter of January 17, cited in the note to the letter, implies a note from Poe; and White's letter to Tucker suggests other notes from Poe to the publisher of the SLM. Lambert A. Wilmer (*Our Press Gang*, pp. 35, 39; see also, *Merlin*, edited by T. O. Mabbott, pp. 26–27, where Wilmer's statements are reprinted) refers to letters between him and Poe, though none is extant or known to be in print; however, the most datable is that in which Wilmer says, "Poe gave me to understand that he was preparing to leave Richmond [as editor of the SLM] and advised me to come hither without delay — as he was quite sure I could obtain the situation he was about to vacate." Charles Anthon, in his letter to Poe, June 1, 1837 (see H, XVII, 42–43), speaks of ". . . yours [Poe's] of the 27th [May]," which is unlocated; Poe used the material supplied by Anthon's letter in his review of John L. Stephens' *Incidents of Travel in Egypt*, published in the New York *Review*, October 1837. On the authority of Henry B. Hirst, Woodberry (I, 378) accepts a letter from Dr. Francis L. Hawks to Poe; but the letter, supposedly an invitation to write for the New York *Review*, could hardly have been written by Hawks in 1837, for Hawks did not join the editorial staff of the magazine until January 1838 (see Mott, *History of American Magazines*, I, 669). Moreover, in his unpublished MS.-revision of his *Life* of Poe (p. 234), Ingram quotes from a letter from Caleb S. Henry, founder and editor of the *Review* in 1837, to the Reverend Mr. Hopkins: "Poe was never engaged as a writer on the New York Review. He contributed of his own accord. It was a review of Stephen's Incidents of Travel in Egypt, Arabia, Petrea, and the Holy Land, etc. . . . in the 2d number . . . Oct. 1837." Thus, with the single exception of his letter to Brooks, September 4, 1838, Poe is not known to have written a letter between May 27, 1837, and May 1839. Still, Poe must have dashed off notes to editors to accompany his MSS., submitted for publication; for example, in the *Aristidean* (October 1845, p. 318) appears the following, as if Poe had written the article or had supplied the information: " 'The Haunted Palace,' . . . was originally sent to O'Sullivan, of the 'Democratic Review,' and by him rejected, because 'he found it impossible to comprehend it.' " [This passage supplied by T. O. Mabbott] The passage suggests not only an unlocated letter to Poe from O'Sullivan, but probably a note from Poe, as was his custom frequently, to offer the MS.; many such notes surely have been lost.

77. Source: letter printed in the *Poe Census* by Charles F. Heartman, II, 78–79, from an undated newspaper clipping supplied by Thomas O. Mabbott; the original MS. is advertised in the American Art Association Galleries catalogue, April 21, 1910, item 2595, but is at present unlocated. The letter was first printed in the unidentified newspaper clipping, cited above. Poe seems to be replying to a letter (unlocated) from Carpenter, Norris, and Brown, datable *ante* February 28, 1837.

78. Source: letter reprinted in an unidentified newspaper clipping from an

issue of the Baltimore *Gazette,* undated; the clipping is in the Ingram collection, University of Virginia. Ingram (I, 154–155) apparently printed from the same clipping, but omitted the allusion to Neilson Poe. The source of the present letter is probably its first full printing; the location of the MS. is unknown, but is probably lost. Poe is replying to a letter from Brooks, unlocated, but datable *ante* September 4, 1838. Poe seems to have written at least two other letters to Brooks, June 26, 1839 (the letter is lost, but the envelope is in the New York Public Library) and *ca.* January 1, 1841, which were not answered (see Letter 107).

79. Source: fragments of a letter as printed by Sir Edmund T. Bewley in an article entitled "The True Ancestry of Edgar Allan Poe," in the *New York Genealogical and Biographical Record,* XXXVIII (1907), 55–69, the excerpts from Poe's letter appearing on pages 57–58. Bewley says: "I am indebted for a copy of this letter to Mrs. E. D. Latta of Dilworth, Charlotte, North Carolina, whose maternal grandmother was a member of the American branch of the Poe family." He also says he quotes from "an unpublished letter, dated 14th July, 1839, written to his [Poe's] cousin, George W. Poe, of Mobile, Alabama." The present location of the MS. is unknown. Poe seems to be answering a letter from George Poe, *ante* July 14, 1839, which is unlocated.

80. Source: facsimile of the original MS. in the Parke-Bernet Galleries catalogue, February 25, 1947, item 239, where it was first printed, with the exception of page 2. The present location of the MS. is unknown. The catalogue describes the letter as a 1 page quarto (apparently ignoring the postscript on verso of page 1) of about 280 words addressed to J. Beauchamp Jones, Esqr., Baltimore, Maryland. Jones, presumably, wrote across the top of the letter: "Edgar Allen Poe Privately Squelches His Critics In Baltimore"; and at the foot of the page added: "over." Partial reconstruction of the content of the postscript on the verso of page 1 is made possible by portions of the letter as printed in *The Collector,* LVIII, No. 7 (November 1945), 185–187, and is bracketed in the present letter under page 2. Completeness and order of the text of the postscript are, of course, conjectural. Poe is replying to Jones's letter of August 6, 1839, which is unlocated. No reply to Poe's letter is known.

81. Source: facsimile of original (2 pp.) in Bixby, pp. 6–7. The text is missing from the lower right portion of page 1 and the lower left of page 2, the verso; numerous other portions of the MS. are damaged; all restorations in the body of the letter have been made from a collation with William Hand Browne's original transcript made for Ingram. The letter was first printed in W, I, 218–221, from the Spencer press-copy. Poe's reference to his forthcoming *Tales of the Grotesque and Arabesque* (December 1839) and to his review of Willis' *Tortesa* in the *Literary Examiner and Western Monthly Review,* July 1839, identifies the year as 1839. (The *Literary Examiner* began in May 1839, the third number being that for July: see Mott, *History of American Magazines,* I, 390.) The MS. letter is now owned by Thomas Ollive Mabbott, New York. This letter, Poe's first known correspondence with Joseph Evans Snodgrass, probably was not a reply to a letter from the Balti-

more friend; it is possible, however, that Snodgrass sent Poe a note in connection with his sending the St. Louis *Bulletin*, but, if so, it is unlocated.

Following Snodgrass' death in 1880, his wife released Poe's letters to her husband. She lent to William H. Carpenter, editor of the Baltimore *Sun*, the following nine holographs: the letters for September 11, October 7, December 12, and December 19, 1839; January 20, and June 17, 1840; January 17, July 12, and September 19, 1841. Carpenter permitted William Hand Browne, a professor of English at Johns Hopkins University, to make transcripts for John H. Ingram, who received them too late for inclusion in his edition of the *Life* of Poe (1880), but kept them with his MS. revision of the *Life*, now in the Ingram collection, University of Virginia. At Carpenter's request, Browne made from his transcripts press-copies, which he lent to Edward Spencer, who six months later edited and published them in the *New York Herald* for March 27, 1881. Woodberry's source for his printings of the letters was the press-copies themselves, and Harrison used Spencer's printed article. Harvey Allen and Mary E. Phillips depended upon both Woodberry and Harrison. In *Americana* for July 1940, the present editor in an article entitled "A Poe Correspondence Re-edited" presented in full for the first time the twelve known letters from Poe to Snodgrass, including the nine items in the Browne transcripts, an April 1, 1841, letter later found by Mrs. Snodgrass and published in the Baltimore *American*, April 4, 1881, a letter dated November 11, 1839, found in the W. K. Bixby collection, and a twelfth letter, dated June 4, 1842, sold with the Frank Maier library, New York, November 22, 1909. A collation of Spencer, Harrison, and Woodberry with Browne's transcripts shows that the transcripts were not followed in detail, and though a collation of Browne's transcripts with available original MSS. or facsimiles reveals that even Browne made a few minor errors, chiefly in punctuation, the transcripts, in the absence of Poe's original letters, must serve as the basic text. For a more detailed discussion of the Poe–Snodgrass series, see *Americana*, XXXIV (July 1940), 409–446.

82. Source: letter as first printed in the *Century Magazine*, XLVIII (September 1894), 726–729, from a MS., which at present is unlocated. Poe is replying to Cooke's letter (MS. in the Boston Public Library) of September 16, 1839, postmarked September 19. Cooke's letter was an answer to one from Poe (unlocated) which asked Cooke's opinion of "Ligeia" and encouraged Cooke to contribute to *Burton's*, of which Poe was editor from June 1839–June 1840. "Ligeia" had appeared in the *American Museum*, September 1838. Thus Poe's first known letter to Cooke may be dated August (?), 1839, since Cooke (September 16) speaks of its having been received "a long time ago."

83. Source: William Hand Browne's original transcript (Ingram collection) for J. H. Ingram (see Note 81); Poe's MS. letter is probably lost. The letter was first printed in full by the present editor in *Americana*, XXXIV (July 1940), 420, all biographers having omitted the second paragraph. In the margin of Browne's transcript Ingram made the notation to omit sentences 3–8; at the end of his transcript, Browne penciled this note: "In the original this P.S. is written lengthwise on right hand margin." The location

of the Snodgrass letter that Poe is answering is unknown, but undoubtedly is to be dated October 1–6 (?), 1839.

84. Source: facsimile of the original (2 pp.) in Bixby, pp. 24–25, where the letter is first printed. The present location of the MS. letter is unknown. (See also notes to Letter 81.) Poe's reference to two letters from Irving, the second of which was dated November 6, 1839 (see W, I, 216–217), and to Burton and the *Gentleman's Magazine* place the letter in 1839; though Snodgrass is nowhere mentioned by name, the content of the letter, especially in connection with that of Letter 81, identifies the Baltimore friend as the one addressed. Poe is answering two unlocated letters from Snodgrass: one, ". . . *perdu* in the P. Office for some 10 days," with the possible dating of November 1–2, 1839, and the second with the possible dating of *ante* November 11, 1839.

85. Source: facsimile of original MS. (1 p.) in the Anderson Galleries Catalogue (No. 2029), February 1–3, 1926, Part 2, item 514, p. 61, where the letter was first printed. The original MS. is unlocated. The letter is addressed to Mr. J. C. Cox, Philadelphia.

86. Source: photostat of original MS. (1 p.) in the Berg collection, the New York Public Library. The letter is here first printed. Poe's connection with Burton and the *Gentleman's* establishes this December letter as written in 1839. No reply from Carey or Hart is known.

87. Source: William Hand Browne's original transcript (Ingram collection) for J. H. Ingram (see Note 81); Poe's MS. letter is probably lost. The letter was first printed in W, I, 222, from the Spencer press-copy. According to Spencer, the letter was postmarked December 13, a date that fits the content of the letter and the text of the subsequent one, December 19.

88. Source: William Hand Browne's original transcript (Ingram collection) for J. H. Ingram (see Note 81); Poe's MS. letter is probably lost. According to Ingram's penciled note on the transcript, the holograph was worn and mutilated in several places. The letter was first printed in W, I, 237–239. Bracketed portions are Browne's emendations. Poe is replying to Snodgrass' letter postmarked December 16, 1839, which is unlocated. Poe errs in saying his own was "dated 2 days before" [the 16], for it was actually dated December 12 (Letter 87).

89. Source: facsimile of original MS. (1 p.) in the American Art Association catalogue, April 20–21, 1921, Part 3, item 494, where it is first printed. The original MS. is in the Berg collection of the New York Public Library. Poe is replying to Boyd's letter of November 15, 1839, which is unlocated.

90. Source: William Hand Browne's original transcript (Ingram collection) for J. H. Ingram (see Note 81); Poe's MS. letter is probably lost. The letter was first printed in W, I, 239–240. Harrison (XVII, 73) does not date the letter, and Woodberry dates it January 21, an error that Ingram corrected to January 20 in his personal copy of Woodberry's *Life of Edgar Allan Poe*, now in the University of Virginia library. Snodgrass' letter, date unknown, which Poe is answering, is unlocated.

91. Source: facsimile of original MS. (1 p.) in the William D. Morley

Catalogue, May 19, 1941, item 289; present location of the MS. is unknown. The letter carries no inside address or year date, but only 1840 and 1844 are possible, since the letter was written in a leap year and only in those two years were both Poe and Mitchell in Philadelphia, where Dr. Mitchell practiced medicine from 1822 until his death in 1858 (see the *Dictionary of American Biography*, XIII, 54–55). It seems impossible to determine which year date is correct, and the earlier has been chosen tentatively. Poe seems to be replying to a note from Dr. Mitchell, *ante* February 29, 1840.

92. Source: original MS. (1 p.) in the Poe Foundation, Richmond. The letter was first printed in Quinn, *Poe*, pp. 273–274 (see also Ostrom, *Americana*, XXXVI (January 1942), 70–71). The envelope is cancelled at Philadelphia, April 27, and addressed to "H. Haines Esqʳ/ Editor of "Virginia Star" / Petersburg /Va." The MS. is worn in folds and browned with age; is a one-leaf letter, folded once: page 1 serves for the communication, with pages 2 and 3 blank, and the address occurs on part of page 4; the chirography is unusually large, clear, and neat. Poe is replying to Haines's letter of March 24, 1840, location of original unknown.

93. Source: copy of original made by William Rouse for J. H. Ingram. The location of the original is not known, but Rouse's copy is in the Ingram collection, University of Virginia; Annie Richmond wrote Ingram, May 27, 1877, that the copy was exact in every detail, ". . . a perfect copy, for he is most reliable and he assured me that every erasure was precisely like the original." According to Mrs. Richmond, in letter to Ingram, October 8, 1877, she had given the original to her friend, Mr. Rouse, as a souvenir. The Poe MS. in Rouse's possession was undoubtedly a draft; the clean copy, if written and sent to Burton, is unknown. Mrs. Richmond probably got the MS. from Mrs. Clemm after Poe's death. The letter is here first printed in full (Quinn, *Poe*, pp. 297–300, as earlier biographers, prints with omissions). The Rouse copy gives no year date, but 1840 cannot be doubted. Bracketed readings, illegible in the Rouse copy, are from Ingram's printing (Ingram, I, 175–179). Poe is replying to Burton's letter of Saturday, May 30, 1840, location of the original unknown.

94. Source: facsimile of original MS. (1 p.) in the Parke-Bernet Galleries catalogue, November 6 and 8, 1944, item 549. The letter was first printed in John Neal's *Wandering Recollections of a Somewhat Busy Life*, p. 256. No year date is given, but 1840 is established by Neal's reply, June 8, 1840, the original of which is in possession of Mr. Edwin B. Hill, Ysleta, Texas, who printed it in the *New York Times Book Review*, June 17, 1917, p. 233. Neal's letter, fully dated, begins, "Yours of June 4, directed to New York, reached me but yesterday [in Portland]." On the MS. below Poe's signature appears: "Portland February 3/67 — This autograph the last / I have of Hon Poe / [signed] John Neal." Neither the facsimile nor the catalogue indicates that the letter was written on a blank page of the *Penn Magazine* prospectus; however, Neal's corrections of Poe's phraseology in this prospectus seem to suggest that Poe used the June prospectus for his letter to Neal, as he did with other correspondents, and that the distribution of the June pros-

pectus was almost simultaneous with Poe's leaving *Burton's* and prior to announcement of the *Penn* in the Philadelphia *Saturday Courier,* x (June 13, 1840), No. 481, p. 2 (see Quinn, *Poe,* p. 306, n.).

95. Source: William Hand Browne's original transcript (Ingram collection) for J. H. Ingram (see Note 81); Poe's MS. letter is probably lost. The letter was first printed in W, I, 248–251. The general content of the letter, particularly the reference to Snodgrass' poem in the February 1840, issue of *Burton's Gentleman's Magazine,* establishes the year date as 1840. The bracketed emendation is Woodberry's, not Browne's; on his transcript at this point, Browne noted that the MS. original was mutilated and he supplied "You," which Woodberry changed to "I" with greater justification, it would seem, considering the sense. Snodgrass' letter of June 12, 1840, is unlocated.

96. Source: photostat of original MS. (1 p.) in the William H. Koester collection, Baltimore. The letter was first printed in Heartman and Canny, p. 40. The letter is written on the second blank page of the June 1840 prospectus of the *Penn.* The MS. is somewhat worn in the folds. The letter is addressed to "C. W. Thompson Esqr / Bank of the U. S. / Phila" and is postmarked June 29. Poe is answering Thomson's note of June 26, 1840, which is unlocated. No reply to the present letter is known.

97. Source: photostat of original (2 pp.) in Huntington Library (HM 24220). The letter was first printed in H, xvii, 55–57. The envelope is addressed to Mr. William Poe, Augusta, Georgia. Though the letter is dated August 15, postal cancellation is August 14; the address occupies the center portion of page 2 of the letter. (The letter is probably written on page 3 of a June prospectus of the *Penn,* or, more likely, the revision, and the address on page 4.) The MS. is worn at the folds and torn at the right edge so that last word or two for eleven lines are wanting; in several places ink has faded. The location of William Poe's original letter is unknown.

98. Source: facsimile of original (1 p.) in Gill, facing p. 114; location of the original MS. is unknown. The letter was first printed in Gill. The year date is not given; W, I, 335, gives "1842"; however 1840 must be correct, for Poe to William Poe, August 14, 1840, says he will write to Washington Poe and send a prospectus (compare also the contents of both letters).

99. Source: facsimile in the American Art Association sale, January 30–31, 1923, item 491. Original MS. in the Charles C. Hart collection, Washington. The letter is here first printed in full except for whatever may be written on the verso of page 1. The text of the MS., which is at present inaccessible, was probably written on a revised form of the June prospectus of the *Penn* and represents one of the numerous solicitations sent out by Poe during the summer (see other letters of this period). The letter was addressed to Lucian Minor, Charlottesville, Virginia. No reply from Minor is known.

100. Source: photostat of original (1 p.) in Historical Society of Pennsylvania. The letter is here first printed. The postal cancellation is dated September 3 at Philadelphia; the letter directed to Joseph B. Boyd, Esqr., Cincinnati, Ohio.

101. Source: photostat of original MS. (1 p.) in the Huntington Library

(HM 24209). The letter was first published in facsimile in the *Bookman*, V
(May 1897), 218. It is written on a prospectus of the *Penn*, probably the
revision of the June printing: the letter is on page 3 of the prospectus, the address on page 4. The address reads: "John Tomlin Esqr / Jackson / Tennessee"
and is marked "Single — Paid." The letter carries a Philadelphia postmark,
dated September 17. Poe is replying to Tomlin's letter, dated *ante* September
16, which was possibly an answer to one from Poe, dated *ca.* August–September, soliciting subscriptions for the *Penn*.

102. Source: photostat of original MS. (1 p.) in the William H. Koester
collection, Baltimore. The envelope is addressed to "Dr Pliny Earle, / Frank-
ford, / Pa." and in lower left corner appears "Friends' Asylum"; it is postmarked Philadelphia, October 12. Poe is replying to Earle's letter of October 2, 1840, which is unlocated.

103. Source: fragment as first printed in Whitty, p. 218. The original
MS., though unlocated, was offered for sale in the Merwin-Clayton catalogue,
May 14, 1906, item 455; and in the Anderson Galleries catalogues, January 10,
1908, item 219, and November 11, 1924, item 663. According to Whitty, the
letter and the MS. of the sonnet "To Zante," referred to in the letter, were
sold by E. C. Stedman, executor of Mr. Stoddard's estate. The Anderson Galleries catalogue of November 11, 1924, says: "A note at foot of the mount
states that 'This letter was addressed to Richard H. Stoddard, and by him
given to his nurse Pedro N. Piedro a short time before his death.' " Stoddard's
own statement (*Recollections Personal and Literary*, p. 213) that Griswold
gave him the MS. of the sonnet as a souvenir of Poe's autograph, is discredited
by the evidence: namely, that various catalogues identify the author of the
letter and the correspondent, and cite the letter, including the poem, as a one-
page MS. Stoddard's letter, *ante* November 6, 1840, is unlocated; it obviously
asked Poe for a sample of his handwriting.

104. Source: photostat of original MS. (1 p.) in the William H. Koester
collection, Baltimore. The letter was first printed in the *Century Magazine*,
XLVIII (September 1894), 731. The envelope is addressed to "F. W. Thomas
Esqr/ St Louis / Mo" and is postmarked from Philadelphia, November 23.
This is Poe's first known letter to Thomas, and is an answer to Thomas' letter
of November 6, 1840, which is unlocated. The Poe–Thomas correspondence
contains more items than does any other correspondence that Poe engaged in;
Thomas wrote at least 39 letters to Poe's 31.

The following letters comprise the known correspondence between Poe and
Thomas; the starred items are those for which MSS. or printings from MS.
exist:

	Thomas to Poe		Poe to Thomas
1840	November 6		
		* 1840	November 23
* 1840	December 7		
* 1841	March 7		
		1841	April 1

Thomas to Poe	Poe to Thomas
* 1841 May 11	
* 1841 May 20	
	1841 May 26
* 1841 May 29 [28]	
	1841 May 29–June 7
	1841 June 11–12
* 1841 June 14	
	* 1841 June 26
* 1841 July 1	
	* 1841 July 4
1841 July 6	
* 1841 July 7	
	1841 July 17–18
* 1841 July 19 (2)	
1841 July–August	
* 1841 August 30	
	* 1841 September 1
* 1841 August 3 [September 3]	
	1841 September 20
* 1841 September 22	
* 1841 October 14	
	* 1841 October 27
* 1841 November 6	
	1841 November 8–9
* 1841 November 10	
* 1841 November 23	
	* 1841 November 26
* 1842 January 13	
	* 1842 February 3
* 1842 February 26	
	1842 March 13
* 1842 May 21	
	* 1842 May 25
	1842 June 27–28
	* 1842 August 27
1842 September 2	
	* 1842 September 12
	* 1842 September 21
1842 November 14	
	* 1842 November 19
	1843 *ante* January 29
	1843 January 30–31
* 1843 February 1	
* 1843 February 8 (?)	

Thomas to Poe	Poe to Thomas
	1843 February 15–18
	* 1843 February 25
	* 1843 March 16
* 1843 March 27	
* 1844 September 2	
	* 1844 September 8
* 1844 October 10	
* 1844 December 10	
	* 1845 January 4
1845 January 5–May 3 (2)	
	* 1845 May 4
* 1845 May 12	
	* 1845 May 14
* 1845 July 10	
* 1845 September 29	
* 1846 August 14	
* 1846 August 24	
1848 November 27	
	* 1849 February 14

105. Source: photostat of original MS. (1 p.) in the Bradley Martin collection, New York. The letter is here first printed. Cist's letter of December 7, 1840, is unlocated.

106. Source: photostat of original MS. (1 p.) in the Peabody Institute Library. The letter was first printed in W, I, 266–267. This is Poe's first known letter to Kennedy since that of June 7, 1836; no letters from Kennedy for the same period are known.

107. Source: facsimile of original (2 pp.) in Bixby, pp. 14–15, where the letter is first accurately presented; though Woodberry prints the letter in full, with variations (I, 267–271), he was using a copy as source (see his 1885 edition, p. 142, n.) which had undoubtedly been prepared by Spencer from William Hand Browne's transcripts of the originals (see Note 81). The original MS. is now in the Berg collection, New York Public Library. A penciled note at the end of Browne's transcript, made for J. H. Ingram, reads: "The Prospectus which follows [*the one mentioned in the letter*] was printed on the 3d page of this sheet. In other words, Poe took one of his prospectuses, folded it the other way, & wrote his letter." Ingram then added the note that the prospectus was dated January 1, 1841 (Ingram collection, University of Virginia). Actually, the letter is written on what appears to be the first leaf of the January 1, 1841, prospectus, but the two leaves of the prospectus have become entirely separated and are now connected with mending tape. Snodgrass' address is on page [4] of the prospectus, according to John D. Gordan, Curator of the Berg collection in the New York Public Library. Poe is an-

swering a letter from Snodgrass, date and location of the original unknown, which must have been written sometime between June 17, 1840, and January 16, 1841. Bracketed emendations in the above letter are from the original transcript made by Dr. Browne for Ingram, and emended from collation made by Mr. Gordan.

108. Source: photostat of original MS. (1 p.) in the Morgan Library. The letter was first printed in Heartman and Canny, pp. 47–48. The letter appears on the second leaf of the prospectus of the *Penn* for January 1, 1841.

109. Source: photostat of the letter printed in the *Baltimore American*, April 4, 1881, where it was first printed. The original MS. is probably lost (see notes to Letter 81). Poe is replying to Snodgrass' letter of March 8, 1841, which is unlocated.

110. Source: Used original MS. (2 pp.) now preserved in the Longfellow House, Cambridge, Massachusetts. The letter was first printed in Samuel Longfellow's *Henry Wadsworth Longfellow: Final Memorials* (Boston: Ticknor and Company, 1887), pp. 13–14; the third paragraph, however, was there omitted and is, to the best of my knowledge, here first printed. The letter occupies pages 1 and 2 of a folded leaf; the address, which is on page 4, reads: "Professor H. W. Longfellow,/ Cambridge,/ Mass:." The letter bears a Philadelphia postmark of May [11], the date being indistinct. Longfellow's reply of May 19, printed in Samuel Longfellow's *Life of Longfellow*, 3 vols. (Boston: Houghton Mifflin, 1891), I, 389–390, is the only known letter from Longfellow to Poe; it is unlocated but was advertised for sale in the Anderson Galleries catalogue, November 22, 1918, from the Robert H. Dodd collection.

111. Source: photostat of original MS. (1 p.) in the Wrenn Library of the University of Texas. The letter is here first printed. The MS. is a small piece of paper torn from a larger leaf and folded twice; on the outside appears "Rev. Rufus W. Griswold," and inside there is neither place identification nor date. This is the earliest known written communication between Poe and Griswold (for the so-called "first" letter of Poe to Griswold given heretofore erroneously under the date of March 29, 1841, see Letter 112 and notes). Conjectural dating of the letter is based upon the following evidence: in the spring of 1841 Poe was with *Graham's* and Griswold with the *Daily Standard*, both in Philadelphia; the present letter indicates that Poe "spoke" with Griswold, and the MS. shows that the letter was not mailed but delivered by hand; moreover, Griswold says he first met Poe in the spring of 1841 (see "Preface" to *Works of Poe*, I (1856 ed.), xxi). Probably before May 8 Griswold left Philadelphia for Boston to serve on the editorial staff of George Roberts' *Times and Notion* (see letter of George Roberts to Griswold, April 23, 1841, in the Boston Public Library, sent from the office of the *Times and Notion*, Boston, to Griswold's office at the *Standard*, Philadelphia: ". . . I am glad that you have at length made up your mind to come with me, for I truly believe it will prove to be your own interest as well as mine . . . I prefer you would commence on Saturday May 8th . . ."; see

also Jacob L. Neu, *Rufus Wilmot Griswold*, Studies in English, No. 5, University of Texas, 1925, p. 113).

Griswold edited the *Works of the Late Edgar Allan Poe* in three volumes in 1850. Volume 3, the *Literati*, appeared last and included Griswold's "Memoir" and the accompanying "Preface." When the 1853 edition of the *Works* appeared, the "Preface" and the "Memoir" were moved to the first volume as pages xxi–xxiii and pages xxiii–lv, respectively. The "Preface" contained what purported to be 11 letters from Poe to Griswold; for which, however, there are only 7 extant MSS., the 4 unauthenticated items being, in all probability, forgeries by Griswold. In printing the 11 letters, Griswold remained faithful to the texts of only 3 (in the present edition Letters 112, 190, 211, though he changed the date of the first and omitted the postscript of the last). Three others (Letters 193, 196, 321) he revised at will. To one other (Letter 317) he added a postscript. The remaining 4 are probably spurious. The 4 doubtful letters are not authenticated by extant MSS. They are printed in Harrison (xvii), from the "Preface" under the following datings: "Without date, 1843?"; June 11, 1843; January 10, 1845; and November 1, 1845. The January 10 letter is certainly a forgery (see Letter 190 and notes); and the November 1 letter is also undoubtedly forged (see Note 211). The first 2 of the 4 doubtful letters cited above are less easily disposed of. The first ("Without date, 1843?") echoes phrases found in Poe's review of Griswold's *Poets and Poetry of America,* in the *Boston Miscellany,* November 1842, a fact that lends weight to Poe's having written the letter but that does not rule out Griswold's imitating Poe's style and appropriation of phrases in a letter printed after Poe's death. Also, Woodberry prints the letter, as he says, from the "Griswold MSS." (I, 354–355). However, there is no other evidence that the MS. letter ever existed. In addition, no prospective review of Griswold's book is mentioned in the Poe–Lowell correspondence, though all Poe's known contributions to the *Pioneer* are referred to. Furthermore, the letter could hardly have been written prior to Poe's first letter to Lowell, November 16, 1842; yet, during the summer of 1842, Poe had written a review of the book (see Letter 143), which Griswold had published in the *Miscellany.* The nature of the present letter seems belied by the facts, and the letter, therefore, is regarded as spurious. For the doubtful "June 11, 1843" letter, there is little evidence to prove it either false or genuine. However, its only source is the "Preface"; even Woodberry cites no MS. for it. Yet Woodberry accepts the letter as genuine and quotes from the "Memoir" to support Griswold's visit to Poe at this time, as requested in the letter (see W, II, 34–35). If written by Poe, the letter would be the only authentic one between those of May 29, 1841, and January 16, 1845, for which MSS. are extant. Also, it would be the only letter or note Poe wrote to Griswold and signed with only his initials. Finally, of all the Poe letters printed in Griswold's "Preface," it would be the only one, unauthenticated in any way by a MS. original, that would be fully accepted as genuine. Thus, in the light of available evidence, the present editor considers that the genuineness of the letter is highly doubtful.

SARAH HELEN WHITMAN

Courtesy of the New York Historical Society

EDGAR ALLAN POE, ABOUT 1845

Because the June 11, 1843, letter has not been admitted into the canon of Poe's letters, it is here printed for purposes of reference:

Philadelphia, June 11, 1843.

Dear Griswold: — Can you not send me $5? I am sick, and Virginia is almost gone. Come and see me. Peterson says you suspect me of a curious anonymous letter. I did not write it, but bring it along with you when you make the visit you promised to Mrs. Clemm. I will try to fix that matter soon. Could you do anything with my *note?*

Yours truly,

E.A.P.

Only the following letters are admitted to the canon. Starred items are authenticated by extant MSS.; unstarred, by references in Poe's MS.-letters.

Poe to Griswold	Griswold to Poe
* 1841 *ante* May 8	
	1841 *ante* May 29
* 1841 May 29	
	1841 late August
	* 1845 January 14
* 1845 January 16	
* 1845 February 24	
* 1845 April 19	
* 1845 September 28	
* 1845 October 26	
* 1849 May (?)	
* 1849 **June 28**	

112. Source: photostat of original MS. (1 p.) in the Boston Public Library; also collated with the MS. The letter was first printed in Griswold's "Preface," to the *Literati* (1850), the third volume of his edition of the *Works* of Poe (see notes to Letter 111). The letter is undated; but Griswold, presumably, docketed it "March 29 / 1841," and inked out the month in the postmark. Biographers of Poe have accepted the March dating; the correct dating, however, is May 29, 1841. Poe's MS. has been divided into two pieces, one of which is in the Boston Public Library, the other now on indefinite loan from the Griswold collection to the Poe Foundation, Richmond. The portion in the Boston Public Library bears the Philadelphia postmark with the inked out month date, and shows part of the address as: "R.W.Grisw / Bo." The portion in the Poe Foundation, Poe's famous "Memo" of biographical data, shows: "ld, Esqre / oston, / *Mass.*" Ultra-violet lamp, microscope, and opinion by a hand-writing expert established the month date as May 29; the joining of the two pieces of MS., which fit each other, gave the address of Griswold as Boston, and a letter from George Roberts to Griswold, April 23, 1841 (MS. in the Boston Public Library), urging Griswold to join the staff of the

Times and Notion by May 8, if possible, confirmed the year date. Thus the two pieces of MS. are fragments of the original letter Poe sent from Philadelphia, May 29, 1841, to Rufus W. Griswold in Boston. Poe is undoubtedly replying to a Griswold letter, datable *ante* May 29, 1841 (which is unlocated); though the requests for contributions and biographical data could have been made by Griswold prior to his leaving Philadelphia, support for the existence of a letter is given in a letter from F. W. Thomas to Griswold, June 8, 1841 (see *Some Passages in the Correspondence of Rufus W. Griswold*, ed. W. M. Griswold, p. 66). For a fuller discussion of the present letter, see *Modern Language Notes* (May 1943), pp. 394–396, for an article by the present editor, entitled "Another Griswold Forgery in a Poe Letter."

113. Source: photostat of original MS. (2 leaves) in the Mrs. Sherburne Prescott collection, Greenwich, Connecticut. The letter was first printed in the *New York Times*, January 12, 1930, pt. 2, p. 4. The letter is addressed to "Washington Irving Esqr/ Tarrytown/ N.Y." and bears the postmark: "Philadelphia/ Jun 21." On the outside cover presumably in Irving's hand is: "Edgar A Poe/ June 21 [. . . *illegible*]/ answd June 24th."

A letter, similar to this one, to James Fenimore Cooper, which is unlocated, was advertised for sale by the Libbie Sales catalogue, April 24–25, 1898, item 648, which quoted the opening lines. Letters to William Cullen Bryant, James K. Paulding, and Nathaniel P. Willis, also presumably written, are unlocated. Irving's memo on the present cover is the only known indication of a reply to Poe's letters to these correspondents. Though the present letter represents the only extant letter from Poe to Irving, one other seems to have existed, and Irving seems to have written to Poe at least three times. Irving's letter to Poe, November 6, 1839 (MS. unlocated; printed in H, xvii, 54), says: "I have read your little tale of 'William Wilson' with much pleasure . . . I repeat what I have said in regard to a previous production, which you did me the favor to send me . . . ." The "previous production" seems to refer to "The Fall of the House of Usher" (*Burton's*, September 1839), for Poe wrote Cooke, September 21, 1839, that Irving had praised that story. Poe may have sent Irving only a copy of *Burton's*, or he may have sent a letter too. Thus Irving's praise must have reached Poe in a letter, datable *ante* September 21, 1839 (but after issuance of *Burton's* September number). The tone of Irving's November 6 letter also suggests that Poe sent Irving a copy of the October number of *Burton's* and a note requesting criticism of "William Wilson"; this Poe letter may be dated *ante* November 6, 1839 (but after issuance of *Burton's* for October). Thus, in late 1839 Poe seems to have written Irving at least one letter, and Irving seems to have written Poe two (for further confirmation, see Letter 84, in which Poe says that "Washington Irving has addressed me 2 letters"). Irving's third letter to Poe is cited on the cover of the present letter.

114. Source: photostat of original MS. (3 pp.) in the Peabody Institute Library, Baltimore. The letter was first printed in full (but with inaccuracies and omissions) in Quinn, *Poe*, pp. 318–320. The letter is not fully dated, but the cover carries a Philadelphia postmark of June 21, and a Baltimore mark

(it was forwarded to Washington) of June 22; moreover, Poe told F. W. Thomas, July 4, 1841, that he had written to Kennedy "about ten days ago." No reply from Kennedy is known.

115. Source: original MS. (2 pp.) now preserved in the Longfellow House, Cambridge, Massachusetts. The letter was first printed in the *Century Magazine*, XLVIII (September 1894), 729. The letter is addressed to "Professor H. W. Longfellow / Cambridge / Mass.:." It is postmarked from Philadelphia, June 22. Poe is replying to Longfellow's letter of May 19, 1841 (see Note 110).

116. Source: photostat of original MS. (2 pp.) in the Huntington Library (HM 24210). The letter was first printed in H, XVII, 89–91. Page 1 of the MS. is very faded.

117. Source: photostat of original MS. (2 pp.) in the Manuscript Division of the New York Public Library. The letter was first printed in Stoddard, "Memoir" to *Select Works of Edgar Allan Poe,* pp. xcii–xciv. The postscript is very faded. This is Poe's first extant letter since that of November 23, 1840, though he wrote at least four in the interim (see the table in Note 104): the first, April 1, 1841, unlocated, concerning Thomas' request that Poe arrange for the periodical publication of a proposed novel, and the failure of such arrangements (see Thomas to Poe, May 11, 1841, in the Boston Public Library). The second, May 26, 1841, unlocated, enclosing a draft due Thomas from Graham, requested in Thomas' letter of May 20 (original MS. in the Boston Public Library), and acknowledged as received in Thomas to Poe, May 29 (MS. in the Boston Public Library), though Thomas' letter should be dated May 28, since it was postmarked May 28 and speaks of "Yours of the 26" as received "yesterday." A third, May 29–June 7, unlocated, stating that Griswold was desirous of biographical sketches of Pinckney of Baltimore and Amelia of Kentucky (see Thomas to Griswold, June 8, 1841, in *Some Passages in the Correspondence of Rufus W. Griswold,* ed. W. M. Griswold, p. 66: "My friend Edgar A. Poe . . . wrote me the other day . . ."), the letter following one from Griswold to Poe, *ante* May 29, 1841 (see Note 112), for Thomas' letter of May 29 [28] makes no allusion to the Griswold request. And a fourth, June 11–12, unlocated, received by Thomas, June 13 (see Thomas to Poe, June 14, 1841, MS. in the Boston Public Library).

118. Source: photostat of two pages of original 3-page MS. owned by the Authors' Club, New York. The letter was first printed in Stoddard, "Memoir" to *Select Works of Edgar Allan Poe,* pp. xciv–xcvi. Page 3 of the letter does not appear in the photostat used for the present text and seems to be lost, but the sentence is printed in Stoddard and is given in Thomas' letter to Poe, July 7, 1841 (the original MS. of which is in the Boston Public Library) and is reprinted in H, XVII, 94. Poe's reproduction of the symbols used in the cryptogram is here first printed. The envelope is postmarked July 5, and carries Thomas' note: "Received July 6th / Answered 7th." Poe is replying to Thomas' letter of July 1 (the MS. of which is in the Boston Public Library; reprinted in H, XVII, 92–93, with Poe's interlinear solution of the cryptogram, from the Thomas a.l.s.).

119. Source: photostat of original MS. (1 p.) in the William H. Koester collection, Baltimore; formerly in Drexel Institute, Philadelphia, but sold by Parke-Bernet Galleries, October 17–18, 1944 (Drexel sale), item 200. The letter is here first printed. It is directed to William Landor, Philadelphia. Poe is replying to two notes from Landor, location of originals not known, the first written probably late in June, the second early in July.

120. Source: photostat of original (2 pp.) in the Morgan Library. The letter was first printed in full in W, I, 283–285 (but "of Soran" is omitted in the first sentence of paragraph five). The letter is postmarked "July 12." Poe is replying to Snodgrass' letter of July 10, 1841, which is unlocated, the first since March 8.

121. Source: photostat of original (1 p.) in the Boston Public Library; first printed in H, XVII, 100. Poe's letter to McJilton must have had an outside leaf which carried McJilton's Baltimore address and the postal cancellation, for they are missing; McJilton, in replying on August 13, wrote Poe's address on the back of Poe's original letter to him; the Baltimore cancellation is also there. Thus Whackemwell wrote to Poe on August 10, Poe replied to McJilton on August 11, and McJilton answered on August 13, penning his remarks at the foot of Poe's letter to him. The MS. is torn at the right; the bracketed emendation of "infinitely" is warranted by "i . . . f . . . tely" with three dots as if for letter *i* being quite clear; "exc . . ." is clear.

122. Source: photostat of original (1 p.) formerly in the Drexel Institute, Philadelphia, but sold by the Parke-Bernet Galleries, October 17–18, 1944, Drexel sale, item 201. The letter was first printed in *The Library of George W. Childs,* described by F. W. Robinson, pp. 13–14. In the upper left corner of the MS., probably in Lea's hand, is the notation: "Rc' Aug 14 / An^d 16."

123. Source: letter as first printed in *The Dial,* XLIV (January 16, 1908), 32–33, from the MS. owned by Weld's daughter, Mrs. A. H. Heulings. The present location of the MS. is unknown. According to *The Dial* the MS. was a single sheet. Weld's reply is unlocated.

124. Source: facsimile of original MS. (1 p.) in the American Art Association catalogue, March 11–12, 1930, facing p. 88, where it was first printed. The letter is here first collected. The original MS. is now owned by Mrs. Sherburne Prescott, Greenwich, Connecticut. Since Poe's last extant letter to Thomas, seven letters passed between them: six from Thomas, one from Poe (see table in Note 104): Thomas' letter of July 6 (MS. unlocated, but printed in H, XIV, 136–137), of July 7 (MS. in the Boston Public Library; printed in H, XVII, 94–95), Poe's letter of July 17–18 (unlocated), implied in Thomas' second of two letters, July 19 (MSS. mailed in one cover, in Boston Public Library; unpublished), Thomas' letter of late July–early August (unlocated, but implied in Thomas' next as containing information not in extant letters), and Thomas' letter of August 30 (MS. in Boston Public Library; printed in H, XVII, 102–103). On the verso of Thomas' second letter of July 19, Poe made some notations on cryptography, which, it would seem, he took from Rees's *Cyclopedia* (see W. K. Wimsatt, Jr., *Publications of the Modern Language Association,* LVIII (September 1943), 771–772, for further

discussion and for the first printing of the notations as given by Poe): "I never terminate a word — a & u seldom. Order of frequency e a o i. / d h n r s t v y c f g l m w b k p q x z / observe a word of 4 letters the first & last the same. — *that* — then / look for *this*. — then *the*. H beging a word is foll by vowel, so also / l m n v — K by a e in. / Shiottus has computed that 1000,-000,000 of men in / as many years cd not write down the different [*illegible*] of [*illegible*] / letters, each completing 40 pp a day, every p conting 40 / [*illegible*]. Mr. Falconer has shown this supposition to be visibly / too low./ Vowels are more frequently doubled at the beginning of words than consonants. / The vowels exceed conso. in short words — where double cons: are preceded by / a single letter that letter is a vowel. The single cons: which precedes or / follows double cons: is l m n or r. When 2 dif: characters occur, the / latter of wh: is often joined with other letters, but the former never found / alone, nor joined with any than the latter, those characters stand / for qu — always foll. by vowel. Y seldom in middle of word. so, / ty ly. ing & tion common terminations. Em in con com fre- / quent prepos. o often followed with u. [*illegible*] more frequent in beg & end / than middle. In polysyllabic words double letters in the middle [*illegible*] is cons:"

125. Source: photostat of original MS. (2 pp.) in the William H. Koester collection, Baltimore; reproduced in facsimile in the Barnet J. Beyer catalogue, item 364, no date, in the Alderman Library at the University of Virginia. The letter was first printed in the Beyer catalogue. Quinn (*Poe*, p. 342, n.) incorrectly gives the date as "September 21, 1841." Poe is replying to Cist's letter of August 30, 1841, which is unlocated.

126. Source: facsimile of original (1 p.) in Bixby, pp. 20–21, where the letter is first accurately presented; Woodberry, however, first printed the letter, with variations (I, 285–287), from the Spencer press-copies made from William Hand Browne's transcripts of the original MS. (see Note 81). Poe's original letter is now in the Huntington library (HM 21865). The location of Snodgrass' letter to Poe, September 6, 1841, is unknown.

127. Source: letter published in *American Literature*, VI (March 1934), 66–68, where it was first printed, from a copy of the original MS. owned by Dr. Thomas R. Boggs. The present location of the MS. is unknown, for after Dr. Boggs's death it was not found among his papers. Poe is replying to Thomas' letter of October 14, not, as Lewis Chase, who published the letter, stated incorrectly, that of August 3 [September 3]. The Thomas letter of October 14 (MS. in the Boston Public Library; unpublished) asks if Poe received the manuscript of Thomas' song, "sent you the other day"; it also says that Dow is publishing the *Index* at Alexandria, and asks if Judge Upshur is author of the *Partisan Leader*. Poe also posted a letter to Thomas, September 20 (MS. unlocated), which Thomas answered, September 22 (MS. in the Boston Public Library; unpublished).

128. Source: facsimile of original (1 p.) in G. S. Haight's *Mrs. Sigourney, the Sweet Singer of Hartford*, facing p. 118, where it was first printed; the original MS. is in the Connecticut Historical Society. For similar solicitation,

see Sigourney to Poe, June 11, 1836, in Haight, pp. 84–85 (original MS. in the Boston Public Library).

129. Source: photostat of original MS. (2 pp.) in the Connecticut Historical Society. The letter was first printed in Haight, *Mrs. Sigourney, the Sweet Singer of Hartford*, pp. 119–120. The year date should be 1841; for in November 1842, Poe was no longer editor of *Graham's*. Poe is replying to Mrs. Sigourney's letter of November 13, 1841, which is unlocated.

130. Source: photoprint of original (2 pp.) in the *Commercial Appeal* (Memphis, Tennessee), November 15, 1925, section 4, p. 7, where the letter is first printed. The location of the original MS. is unknown. Poe is replying to Bolton's letter of November 4, 1841, location of the original of which is unknown.

131. Source: photostat of original MS. (3 pp.) in the Dumbarton Oaks Research Library, Georgetown, D.C. The letter was first printed in Ernest Dressel North's *Catalogue of a Choice Collection of Autograph Letters and MSS.*, October 1905 (New York), No. 357, pp. 58–59 (title supplied by Thomas O. Mabbott). On the verso of page 3 appears the address: "F. W. Thomas Esqr / Washington / D.C."; the letter was postmarked Philadelphia, November 26. Thomas noted on the envelope: "Received November 27." The MS. has a hole in the right side of page 3, and in two places in the cover where the seal was applied. Poe is answering Thomas' letter of November 23, 1841 (MS. in the Boston Public Library; unpublished). However, Thomas wrote on November 6 (MS. in the Boston Public Library; unpublished); Poe replied on November 8–9 (unlocated), according to Thomas' letter of November 10 (MS. in the Boston Public Library; unpublished).

132. Source: letter printed in *The Autograph*, I (January–February 1912), 42–43), where it was first printed. The original MS. is unlocated, but extant; it was last known to be in the possession of the late P. F. Madigan, New York. Poe is replying to Thomas' letter of January 13, 1842 (MS. in the Boston Public Library; unpublished).

133. Source: photostat of original MS. (1 p.) in the William H. Koester collection, Baltimore. The letter was first printed in the Parke-Bernet Galleries catalogue, November 19–20, 1945, item 422. The envelope is addressed to the "Revd J. N. McJilton,/ Baltimore/ Md," and initialed "E A P." in the lower left corner of the envelope. It is postmarked at Philadelphia, March 15. Poe is replying to McJilton's letter of February 14, 1842, which is unlocated.

134. Source: photostat of original MS. (2 pp.) in the William H. Koester collection, Baltimore. The letter was first printed by Woodberry in the *Century Magazine*, XLVIII (September 1894), 732–733. Thomas made an "x" after "here," page 1, paragraph 2, following the words "Custom House," and in the left margin wrote: " x I had been promised a place in the Philadelphia Custom House by the powers that were for Poe, but some small beer politician or other got the place and genius was left to its fate. T." The letter is addressed to "F. W. Thomas Esqre / Washington / D. C," and is postmarked from Philadelphia, May 25, and docketed by Thomas "Received May 26.

1842." Prior to Poe's present letter, Thomas had written February 26, 1842 (MS. in the Boston Public Library; printed in H, xvii, 105–106, and in W, i, 318–321, both under the wrong date of February 6); Poe replied March 13 (unlocated), according to Thomas' next letter, May 21, 1842 (MS. in the Boston Public Library; printed in H, xvii, 108–110).

135. Source: photostat of original MS. (a fragment) in the William H. Koester collection, Baltimore. The fragment is here first printed in full and with proper identification. The fragment is undated, but seems to belong to the first part of June 1842; it certainly follows F. W. Thomas' letter to Poe, May 21, 1842 (H, xvii, 108–110), in which Thomas speaks of a possible opening in the custom house for Poe, and it seems to precede Poe's letter to Herron, June 30, 1842 (Letter 138). The MS. is a fragment, apparently of one leaf, written on both sides; the top portion has been cut off, carrying with it probably only a half dozen lines from each side of the leaf. Most of the present fragment was combined with the last paragraph of the letter to Herron of June 30, 1842, and printed as one item under that date in the *World* [N.Y.?], May 1, 1921 (see clipping in the Ingram collection, University of Virginia); but the present fragment is certainly a separate item. When David K. Jackson (*American Literature*, xiii (November 1941), 283) suggests the existence of a draft of Poe's letter to Herron, June 30, 1842, he is undoubtedly thinking of the present fragment. Poe seems to be answering a lost letter from Herron, datable May (?), 1842.

136. Source: original MS. (2 pp.) in the J. K. Lilly, Jr., collection, Indianapolis. The letter was first printed in H, xvii, 112–113. The letter is postmarked Philadelphia, Pennsylvania, June 4, and is addressed to "George Roberts Esqre/ Boston "Times"/ *Boston*," with "EAP" in the lower left corner. The letter is also endorsed: "Edgar A Poe/ Phil. June 4. 1842." No reply by Roberts is known.

137. Source: photostat of original (4 pp.) in the Morgan Library. The letter was first printed in the Anderson Galleries catalogue, November 22, 1909, item 1700 (see Note 81). The address is written on page 4; directed to "Dr. J. Evans Snodgrass/ Ed. of "Visiter"/ Baltimore/ M^d." The MS. has several ink blots, and was postmarked at Philadelphia, June 5.

138. Source: photostat of original MS. (1 p.) in the William H. Koester collection, Baltimore. The letter was first printed in Quinn, *Poe*, pp. 360–361. The envelope is postmarked Philadelphia, June 30, and directed to "James Herron Esqre/ Civil Engineer/ Washington/ D.C." Herron's letter, which Poe is answering, can be conjecturally dated *ante* June 30; for Poe wrote Thomas, August 27, 1842, "I wrote a few words to you, about two months since, from New York . . ."; and Poe wrote Mrs. Elizabeth Tutt, July 7, "About ten days ago, however, I was obliged to go on to New York on business . . ."; thus Herron's letter seems to have reached Philadelphia after Poe's departure for New York, which may have been about June 25–26. Herron's letter is unlocated.

139. Source: photostat of original MS. (3 pp.) in the Iowa State Department of History and Archives, Des Moines, Iowa. The letter was first

printed in the *Critic*, April 16, 1892 (reprinted in L and L, II, 462–464). The communication is written on a single leaf, folded, and fills three pages. The address, on page 4, reads: "Dan¹ Bryan Esqʳᵉ / Alexandria / D.C." Though the center portion of the MS. is torn, the only text missing is that represented by the bracketed emendations on page 3. Prior to Poe's present letter, Bryan had written at least three to Poe: May 13 (MS. in the Boston Public Library), submitting a poem for *Graham's; ca.* June 15, implied in the present letter as sent "about three weeks since," and different from the May 13 item; June 27 (MS. in the Boston Public Library), in which Bryan, hearing of Poe's leaving *Graham's*, asks that poems, lately sent, be withheld from publication in that magazine and kept by Poe for his own use later on; Bryan also speaks of "an attack upon you by a writer in one of the Philadᵃ journals."

140. Source: letter printed in the New York *Independent*, March 1901, pp. 940–941, in an article, "Memorials of Edgar Allan Poe," by James Grant Wilson, who seems to have used the original MS. The autograph letter was offered for sale in Henkels' catalogue, May 5, 1903, item 953, but its present location is unknown. The letter, first printed in the *Independent*, was copied by Harrison (XVII, 113–115) under the wrong date of June; Woodberry merely cites the letter, but gives the June dating. The July dating is supported by Chivers' letter to Poe, July 12, 1842 (H, XVII, 115–117). Poe is replying to three unanswered letters from Chivers: August 27, 1840 (H, I, 190–191), one, late in November 1841, remonstrating against Poe's sketch of him in "Autography" (*Graham's*, December 1841), and another, dated by Poe, June 11, 1842; the last two are unlocated.

Because the Poe–Chivers correspondence covered a period of nine years and because numerous letters, now lost, are alluded to by both Poe and Chivers in the extant items, the following list is offered; the starred items are those for which MSS. exist; or printings from MS.:

Poe to Chivers	Chivers to Poe
1840 *ca.* August 20	
	* 1840 August 27
	1841 November–June 10 (?), 1842 (2 letters)
	1842 June 11
* 1842 July 6	
	* 1842 July 12
	1842 September 15
	* 1842 September 26
* 1842 September 27	
	* 1842 December 7
	1843 early summer
	* 1844 June 15
* 1844 July 10	

Poe to Chivers	Chivers to Poe
	* 1844 August 6
	* 1844 September 24
	1845 *ante* August 11
* 1845 August 11	
	1845 August 11
	1845 August 25
* 1845 August 29	
	* 1845 September 9
	* 1845 October 30 (suggests others)
* 1845 November	
	1845 November–July 1846 (6 letters or more)
* 1846 July 22	
1847 *ante* January 30(?)	
	* 1847 February 21
	* 1847 April 4 (suggests others)
* 1848 July 13 [14?]	
	1849 *ante* August 27 (?)

141. Source: fragment as first printed in the Anderson Galleries catalogue, January 18, 1922, item 229. The present location of the MS. (2½ pp.) is unknown. Though the printed letter is unsigned, the sales catalogue and the content of the letter identify it as Poe's. No letter from Mrs. Tutt to Poe is known.

142. Source: letter printed in W, I, 335–337, where it was first published. The present location of the MS. is unknown. Following Thomas' last letter, May 21, 1842, Poe wrote to Thomas, from New York, June 27–28 (unlocated), cited above; the following data establish the approximate time of the letter: Poe wrote James Herron, June 30, 1842, "Upon return from a brief visit to New-York, last night . . ."; and to Elizabeth R. Tutt, July 7, 1842, "About ten days ago, however, I was obliged to go on to New York on business . . ." No letter from Thomas is known between that of May 21 and September 2, 1842.

143. Source: photostat of original MS. (3 pp.) in the Manuscript Division of the New York Public Library. The letter was first printed in Stoddard, "Memoir" to the *Select Works of Edgar Allan Poe*, pp. xcvii–xcviii. The edges of the MS. are ink-smeared, but the wording is readable. Thomas endorsed the letter: "Did not get this until my return — Saw Poe in Philadelphia — " Poe is replying to Thomas' letter of September 2, 1842 (unlocated).

144. Source: photostat of original MS. (2 pp.) in the Huntington Library (HM 21871). The letter was first printed in the *Century Magazine*, XLVIII (September 1894), 733. The postmark: Philadelphia, September 21, and Poe's last line, page 1, establish the date of the letter. The envelope is

directed to "F. W. Thomas Esqre / Washington / *D.C.*" Thomas endorsed
the envelope, "Received Sep. 22nd and answered — ." No "answer" is known,
unless it is the letter of November 14 (see Letter 148).

145. Source: photostat of original MS. (3 pp.) in the Huntington Library (HM 24211). The letter was first printed in the *Century Magazine,*
LXV (January 1903), 439. The envelope is postmarked Philadelphia, September 28, and is addressed to "Dr. Thos. H. Chivers/ New-York." Chivers'
letter of September 15, 1842, is unlocated.

146. Source: letter as first printed in *Holden's Dollar Magazine,* II (December 1848), 718, where it appeared with letters by other people in an
article entitled "Autobiography of a Monomaniac," edited by Joe Bottom,
Esqr. The original MS. is probably lost. Poe is replying to Tomlin's letter
of September 21, which is unlocated. T. O. Mabbott in *Notes and Queries,*
CLXII, 437, identifies John Tomlin, of Jackson, Tennessee, as the recipient of
the letters in the article (and probably the author); though the article was
magazine material, Dr. Mabbott feels the letters were genuine.

147. Source: photostat of original MS. (1 p.) in the Harvard College
Library. The letter was first printed in Woodberry (1885), pp. 176–177. The
Poe–Lowell correspondence consists of 14 letters from Poe (12 in MS., 1 in
copy of original MS., and 1 unlocated) and 12 letters, possibly 13, from
Lowell (1 in MS., 9 in printings from MS. at present unlocated, 1 from sales
catalogue, and 2 unlocated). The two writers did not meet during the period
of their known correspondence, but one meeting apparently took place sometime late in the spring of 1845. The following list gives the letters in the
series: with the Poe items, the asterisk indicates known MS., and with the
Lowell items, the single asterisk indicates printings from MS. and the double
asterisk identifies known MS.:

Poe to Lowell	Lowell to Poe
* 1842 November 16	
	* 1842 November 19
	* 1842 December 17
* 1842 December 25	
* 1842 December 27	
* 1843 February 4	
	* 1843 March 24
* 1843 March 27	
	* 1843 April 17
	* 1843 May 8
	* 1843 May 16
* 1843 June 20	
* 1843 September 13	
	1843 October 13
* 1843 October 19	
1843 December–1844 January	* 1844 January

Poe to Lowell	Lowell to Poe
	* 1844 March 6
* 1844 March 30	
	1844 May *ca.* 23
* 1844 May 28	
	* 1844 June 27
* 1844 July 2	
* 1844 August 18	
	** 1844 September 27
* 1844 October 28	
	* 1844 December 12

148. Source: photostat of a transcript of the original MS. Though the original letter is unlocated, it was offered for sale by the Anderson Galleries catalogue, April 24, 1911, item 2641. The transcript, now in the Boston Public Library, carries the following notation: "The above copied from the original in the possession of 'Fred' for Geo H Morse Esq. Lenox Library. May 30/78 C. W. F[rederickson]." The copy seems to be a very careful reproduction, line for line, of the holograph. The letter was first printed in the *Century Magazine*, XLVIII (September 1894), 733–734. Poe is replying to Thomas' letter of November 14, 1842 (unlocated).

149. Source: photostat of original MS. (1 p.) in the Harvard College Library. The letter was first printed in Woodberry (1885), pp. 177–178, the only date given being that of the postmark. The envelope is addressed to "James Russell Lowell Esqre / Boston / Mass:"; in the lower left corner appears: "Single — / E A P." Though the signature is cut off the handwriting is Poe's. Lowell endorsed the letter: "E. A. Poe, 1843"; a different hand entered "Dec. 23 / 1842." The content of the letter places it in 1842, and the envelope is postmarked Philadelphia, December 25. Poe's second sentence refers to Lowell's letter of November 19, 1842 (MS. unlocated; printed in W, I, 345–346), and of December 17 (MS. unlocated; printed *ibid.*, pp. 346–347).

150. Source: photostat of original MS. (1 p.) in the William H. Koester collection, Baltimore. The letter was first printed in Quinn, *Poe*, p. 365, with variations in pointing and with the signature incorrectly given as "Edgar Poe." The letter was postmarked at Philadelphia, December 27.

151. Source: photostat of original MS. (2 pp.) in the Harvard College Library. The letter was first printed in Woodberry (1885), pp. 178–180. In the margin opposite the third paragraph from the end appears: "E.A.Poe / 4th Feby — 1843." Since Poe's last letter of December 27, 1842, no letter from Lowell is known.

152. Source: original MS. (1 p.) in the J. K. Lilly, Jr., collection, Indianapolis. The letter is here first printed (?). The year date is established by the reference to the *Pioneer* (January–March 1843). The verso of the folded leaf is postmarked Philadelphia, Pennsylvania, February 16; and is addressed

to "R. Carter Esqre / Editor of "The Pioneer"/ Boston/ Mass:," with the initials *"EAP."* in the lower left corner. The letter is also endorsed "E. A. Poe/ Feb. 16. 1843." The letter is the lower third of page 1 of a folded leaf, the upper portion carrying a transcription of "Eulalie," sent as a contribution to the *Pioneer*. Poe is replying to Carter's letter of *ante* February 16, 1843 (unlocated).

153. Source: photostat of original MS. (2 pp.) in the Boston Public Library. The letter was first printed in the *Century Magazine*, XLVIII (September 1894), 733–734. The envelope is directed to F. W. Thomas, Treasury Department, Washington, D.C., and postmarked February 26. Since his last known letter to Thomas, November 19, 1842, Poe wrote *ante* January 29, 1843 (unlocated, but implied in Thomas' letter of February 1, 1843, as probably written in connection with the biography of Poe that Thomas was to write); January 30–31, 1843 (unlocated, but cited as received in Thomas' letter of February 1, 1843, MS. in the Boston Public Library; printed in H, XVII, 128–129; Thomas also quotes from it; this letter is not the same as that of *ante* January 29, given above); on February 8, 1843, Thomas wrote a letter to Robert Tyler (MS. in the Boston Public Library), introducing Poe, and noted on it that it would "be handed to you by my friend, Poe": thus the letter was sent to Poe, probably with an accompanying note of the same date (unlocated); Poe wrote to Thomas, February 15–18, 1843, a letter introducing his friend Professor Wyatt (unlocated; but see the above letter).

153a. Source: photostat of original MS. (1 p.) in the William H. Koester collection, Baltimore. The letter is here first printed. No reply from Carter is known.

154. Source: letter as first printed in P, 1, 803. The present location of the MS. (1 p.) is unknown. Miss Phillips seems to have printed from a copy provided by Lewis M. Thompson of Boston. The MS. was advertised for sale in the Anderson Galleries catalogue, November 15–16, 1926. Superficially, the letter seems genuine, though proof is not possible without an examination of the holograph. Thus the present letter is not admitted unreservedly to the canon.

155. Source: facsimile in L and L, II, facing p. 134; original MS. (1 p.) is in the Berg Collection, New York Public Library. The letter was first printed in Gill, p. 120. The MS. is carelessly written, with a portion so heavily scratched out as to be illegible; "Thomas" in the second paragraph has a line through it.

156. Source: photostat of original MS. (3 pp.) in the Boston Public Library. A facsimile of the draft of this letter, showing certain variations, is printed in Pratt, pp. 17–18. The letter was first printed in the *Century Magazine*, XLVIII (September 1894), 735–736. The envelope is postmarked at Philadelphia, March 17.

157. Source: original MS. (1 p.) in the Virginia State Library, Richmond. The letter was first printed in H, 1, 178. The postal cancellation is dated March 26.

158. Source: photostat of original MS. (3 pp.) in the Harvard College

Library. The letter was first printed in Woodberry (1885), pp. 183–185. The envelope is addressed to "James Russell Lowell Esqre / Editor of "The Pioneer"/ Boston / Mass."; and postmarked at Philadelphia, March 28. Poe is replying to Lowell's letter of March 24, 1843 (MS. unlocated; printed in W, II, 19–20).

159. Source: photostat of original MS. (1 p.) in the William H. Koester collection, Baltimore. The letter was first printed in Henkels' catalogue, November 20, 1935, item 185a. The upper portion of the MS. is missing, as well as the date; however, a conjectural dating would be April, 1843: Rosalie Poe seems to have written to Edgar sometime after March 26 (see Letter 160), and Poe's promise to write to her seems further evidence of a letter received from his sister; Poe's letter to Bernard (March 24, 1843) probably preceded the present letter to Mackenzie, for Bernard was the person more likely to have the desired information (see Letter 157 and note); Poe's letter to Thomas, March 16, speaks of Virginia's health as "about the same" and adds that her distress of mind is great, evidence that points to the present letter's being of a later date. Poe's letter to Lowell, June 20, 1843, says the plans for the *Stylus* "exploded" with his partner's withdrawal, and since the partner was Thomas C. Clarke, the "capitalist" of the present letter, Poe's letter to Mackenzie was written prior to June 20. April has, therefore, been given as the conjectural dating, though May is not impossible. The MS. is a fragment, though only the inside address, date, and salutation seem to be missing; a portion of the lower left corner of the MS. is gone and part of "W^m" is missing.

160. Source: original MS. (1 p.) in the Poe Foundation, Richmond. The letter is here first printed. The envelope portion of the letter is cut off. No letter from Rosalie Poe to Poe conveying Miss Henry's request is known, beyond this reference.

161. Source: photostat of original MS. (1 p.) in the William H. Koester collection, Baltimore. The letter was first printed in H, XVII, 149 (but wrongly headed "to James T. Fields"). The envelope is addressed to "James Russell Lowell Esqre / Boston / Mass." and initialed "E A P." in the lower left corner. It is postmarked from Philadelphia, June 20. Since Poe's last letter of March 27, 1843, Lowell wrote on April 17, May 8, and May 16, 1843 (MSS. unlocated; but printed from the Griswold MSS. in W, II, 23–28). No intervening Poe letter is indicated.

162. Source: letter as printed in W, II, 39–42; original MS. unlocated. The letter was first printed in Woodberry (1885), pp. 190–192. Poe is answering Tomlin's letter postmarked August 9 (MS. in the Boston Public Library).

163. Source: photostat of original MS. (1 p.) in the Harvard College Library. The letter was first printed in W, II, 44. The MS. is endorsed by Lowell, "E. A. Poe, 13th Septr. 1843."

164. Source: photostat of original MS. (3 pp.) in the Harvard College Library. The letter was first printed in Woodberry (1885), pp. 192–194. The envelope is addressed to "James Russell Lowell Esqre / Cambridge /

Mass:"; and postmarked at Philadelphia, October 19. Poe is replying to Lowell's letter of October 13, 1843 (unlocated).

165. Source: fragment as first printed in Whitty, p. 196. The location of the original MS. is unknown; it was offered for sale in the Henkels' catalogue, February 22, 1907, item 161. Poe is replying to Hedges' note of November 14, 1843, which is unlocated.

166. Source: photostat of original MS. (1 p.) in the Haverford College Library, Haverford, Pennsylvania. The letter is here first printed. The envelope is addressed: "Joel B. Sutherland Esqre. / *Present* / Per Mr Robert Travers."

167. Source: original fragment (1 p.) in the William H. Koester collection, Baltimore. The letter is here first printed in the fullest available form. The Robert H. Dodd sales catalogue No. 27, March, 1918, prints part of the letter and adds: "The page has been cut in half and the signature pasted over it. The part of the letter destroyed revealed Poe's financial troubles and was removed by one of his admirers who did not wish his favorite's urgent need of money to become public property." In the text of the present letter the omitted portion is represented by the ellipsis, and the MS. portion containing the signature shows along its top edge, though indistinctly, what appears to have been the last line of the original letter. The dating of the letter is based upon the fact that Poe lectured in Baltimore, January 31, 1844 (see Letter 168), and also upon the presumption that he lectured there early in 1846, for Mary E. Hewitt, writing to Poe, April 14, 1846, regrets hearing of his illness in Baltimore (see original MS. in the Boston Public Library; also printed in *A Christmas Book,* p. 120). However, the proposed lectures may never have been delivered, or the letter date may have been earlier or later than the dates suggsted here. The MS. carries neither addressee, date, or postal information. No reply is known.

168. Source: copy made by Dr. John C. French, Librarian, Johns Hopkins University, of his own transcript of the original MS. The holograph, which was in private hands in Baltimore over twenty years ago, is unlocated. The letter is here first printed. The undated MS. was certainly written on January 31, 1844, Wednesday, for several Baltimore papers of that date carry puffs for Poe's lecture.

168a. Source: letter as first printed in Sotheby Sales catalogue (London), June 2–3, 1924, item 321, where the MS. is described as an a. l. s., 1 page quarto to John P. Kennedy, Esq. The letter is here first collected. The identification of place and full date of the letter is conjectural, but is based upon Poe's visit to Baltimore for a lecture on Wednesday evening, January 31, 1844 (see Letter 168 and note, and Note 168) and Kennedy's continued friendliness toward Poe which would encourage Poe to visit his benefactor whenever he was in Baltimore. The present text may or may not be complete.

169. Source: letter as first printed in Lippard's novel, *Herbert Tracy* (Philadelphia: R. G. Berford, 1844), pp. 167–168. The original MS. is probably lost. Poe seems to be replying to a letter from Lippard, which is un-

located. One other letter from Poe to Lippard is known but is also unlocated; it was dated July 19, 1849, and asked Lippard to find the lectures
Poe lost in Philadelphia (see Quinn, *Poe*, p. 622, where Poe's letter is cited
by Lippard in a letter to Griswold, Lippard's letter being in the Boston Public
Library).

170. Source: photostat of original MS. (1 p.) in the William H. Koester
collection, Baltimore. The letter was first printed in facsimile in the American
Art Association catalogue, March 18–19, 1925, item 569. The envelope is
postmarked at Philadelphia, March 3, and is addressed to "Mess: Jno: C.
Myers/ Sam: Williams/ or Will: Greaff Jr./ Reading/ P^{a}" and is initialed
"E A P" in the lower left corner. Poe is replying to a letter from Myers,
Williams, and Greaff [Graeff], dated December 29, 1843, which is unlocated.

171. Source: a transcript furnished by Thomas O. Mabbott, with the following authentication: "Copy made from my original copy of transcript of
the letter made by a former owner . . . Thomas F. Madigan"; the present
location of the original MS. (1 p.) is unknown. The letter was first printed
in P, 1, 858. Poe is replying to a letter from Williams and Graeff dated
March 5, 1844, which is unlocated. The text of Poe's present letter and the
later delivery of the lecture imply another letter from Williams and Graeff
about March 9–10, 1844, which is unlocated.

172. Source: facsimile of original MS. (1 p.) in Bixby, pp. 22–23, where
it was first printed in full. The original MS. is now in Huntington Library
(HM 21864). The Poe–Horne correspondence includes 5 known letters,
3 by Horne (original MSS. now in the Boston Public Library), and 2 by
Poe (original MSS. not known save through internal evidence in Horne's letters to Poe); the first letter in the correspondence was from Poe, March 20–
26 (?), 1844, and the last, from Horne, May 17, 1845.

173. Source: photostat of original MS. (4 pp.) in the Harvard College
Library. The letter was first printed in Woodberry (1885), pp. 197–199.
The envelope is addressed to "James Russell Lowell Esqre / Elmwood / Cam-
bridge / Mass."; and postmarked at Philadelphia, March 30. Following his
letter of October 19, 1843, Poe wrote to Lowell, probably in December–
January (unlocated), regarding a lecture before the Boston Society (see
Lowell to Poe, March 6, 1844, W, II, 56–59); Poe's present letter is a reply
to Lowell's, just cited.

174. Source: original MS. (2 pp.) in the Enoch Pratt Free Library, Baltimore. Reproduced in facsimile in Quinn and Hart, facing p. 20. The letter
was first printed in Woodberry (1885), pp. 201–204. The year was lacking,
but it has been established by Letter 175. The envelope is directed to Mrs.
Maria Clemm (street address cut out), Philadelphia; cancelled at New York,
April 7. Poe's autograph is lacking; the excision also carried away completely three half-lines and part of the letters of a fourth; portions of the MS.
are damaged by holes and tears. The extent of emendations by various biographers is at times misleading, owing to the lining of the printed letter.

175. Source: photostat of original MS. (2 pp.) in the Harvard College
Library. The letter was first printed in Woodberry (1885), pp. 208–209.

The letter was endorsed by Lowell, "E.A.Poe / 28th May — 1844." Poe is replying to Lowell's letter, *ca.* May 23, 1844 (unlocated).

176. Source: the fragment printed in the *New York Times*, Magazine Section, p. 14, January 28, 1917; a less full printing appeared in the Anderson Galleries catalogue, January 25, 1917, item 48, with the following variants: in line 3, next "Opal" ; line 7, Mr. Willis' ; line 8, to state, ; line 9, I am as usual, . The present location of the original MS. is unknown. Though the above fragment is unsigned, it was printed by the *Times* and the Anderson Galleries as a genuine Poe item. There seems to be no reason to doubt its authenticity. Mrs. Hale replied May 30 (?) (unlocated).

177. Source: photostat of original (1 p.) in the Huntington Library (HM 21875). The letter was first printed in facsimile in the Anderson Galleries catalogue, January 25–6, 1917, frontispiece; see also the *New York Times*, Magazine Section, January 28, 1917, p. 14. Poe is replying to Mrs. Hale's letter of May 30 ?, which replied to Poe's of May 29 (Letter 176).

178. Source: clipping from the Philadelphia *Ledger*, January 12, 1912 (no p.), in Ingram's unpublished MS. revision of his *Life* of Poe, in the Ingram collection, University of Virginia. The letter was first printed in the *Ledger*. The above note was added by Poe to his June 4, 1844, news-letter from Gotham, which was printed in the Columbia (Pennsylvania) *Spy*, June 8. The original MS. is unlocated. No reply from Bowen is known.

179. Source: photostat of original MS. (4 pp.) in the Harvard College Library. The letter was first printed in Woodberry (1885), pp. 211–214. The envelope is addressed to James Russell Lowell, Elmwood, Cambridge, Massachusetts, and was postmarked at New York, July 3. The MS. shows numerous changes and careted additions due to afterthought. Poe is replying to Lowell's letter of June 27, 1844 (unlocated; but printed in W, II, 87–89).

180. Source: photostat of original MS. (3 pp.) in the Huntington Library (HM 24212). The letter was first printed in the *Century Magazine*, LXV (January 1903), 441–442. The MS. is badly ink-stained, and the bracketed emendations indicate the illegible letters or words. The letter is definitely to Chivers, who wrote Poe, August 6, 1844: "Your beautiful, friendly, abstruse, and transcendental letter of July the 10th in answer to mine of June the 15th . . ." Chivers' letter of June 15 is in the Boston Public Library.

Chivers has written four letters since Poe's last reply (see the notes to Letter 140): September 26, 1842 (H, XVII, 119–120); December 7, 1842 (*Century Magazine*, LXV (January 1903), 440–441, the full date given on page 56 of the Miller-Townsend Scrapbook of Dr. Thomas H. Chivers — a collection of letters, news clippings, and so on in the Alderman Library, University of Virginia; the Scrapbook also states that the letter was written soon after the death of Chivers' daughter); May–June 1843 (cited in Chivers to Poe, June 15, 1844, where he says, "When I wrote to you last, I believe it was strawberry-time . . . I have just been eating strawberries and honey" — see H, XVII, 171, where the letter is incorrectly dated; the MS. letter shows a postmark of Washington, Georgia, June 15, and Poe to Chivers, July 10, and Chivers to Poe, August 6, 1844, both speak of it as June 15); and June 15,

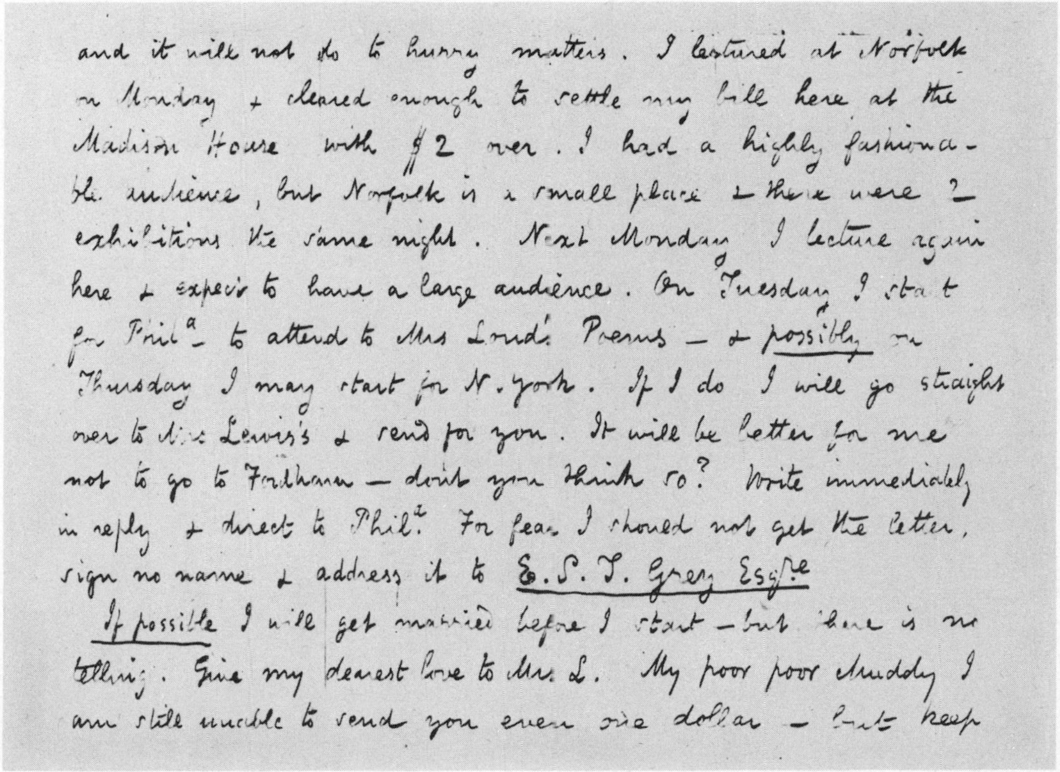

POE TO MRS. CLEMM, 28 SEPTEMBER 1849

(Letter 332)

Tuesday 18ᵗʰ Sept. 1849

My dear, dear Mrs. Lewis — My dear
sister Anna (for so you have permitted me to call you) — never while I live
shall I forget you or your kindness to
my mother. If I have not written
you in reply to your first cherished letter, think anything of my silence except that I am ungrateful or unmindful of you — or that I do not feel for you
the purest and profoundest affection — ah,
let me say love. I hope very soon to see
you and clasp your dear hand. In the
meantime, may God bless you, my sweet
sister. Your always,

Edgar.

POE TO MRS. LEWIS, 18 SEPTEMBER 1849
(Letter 333)

1844 (H, XVII, pp. 170–173, under wrong date, see above), which asks for details concerning a Poe-Chivers partnership in publishing the *Penn* (*Stylus*).

181. Source: photostat of original MS. (2 pp.) in the Harvard College Library. The letter was first printed in Woodberry (1885), pp. 215–216. Lowell's endorsement: "E.A.Poe / 18th Aug. 1844" and the content of Lowell to Poe, September 27, 1844 (W, II, 100), identify Poe's correspondent.

182. Source: letter printed in W, II, 98–100. The original MS. is unlocated, but is listed for sale as a 2-page quarto in Bangs and Company catalogue, April 11, 1896, item 102. The letter was first printed by Woodberry in the *Century Magazine*, XLVIII (October 1894), 863. This is Poe's first known letter to Thomas since March 16, 1843, but Thomas, meanwhile, wrote two: March 27, 1843 (MS. in the Boston Public Library; printed in H, XVII, 140–141) and September 2, 1844, posted at Washington, September 2, directed to Philadelphia, forwarded to New York, September 4 (MS. in the Boston Public Library; unpublished).

183. Source: photostat of a copy of the original MS. (unlocated) in the hand of Maria Clemm, now in the Boston Public Library. The letter was first printed in H, XVII, 190. At the top of the MS.-copy appears: "Copy of a letter sent to Mr. Craig. Oct. 25. mailed by me." At first Mrs. Clemm wrote "Nov."; then smudged the entry and wrote over it, "Oct." The notation is signed, "Maria Clemm." Poe is replying to a letter from Craig, datable *ante* October 24, 1844, which is unlocated.

184. Source: photostat of original MS. (1 p.) in the Pennsylvania Historical Society, Philadelphia. The letter was first printed in Woodberry (1885), pp. 204–205. Poe is answering Duane's letter of October 15, 1844, which is unlocated.

185. Source: photostat of original MS. (2 pp.) in the Harvard College Library. The letter was first printed in Woodberry (1885), pp. 216–218. Lowell's endorsement: "E.A.Poe / 28th Oct. 1844" and the content of the letter identify Poe's correspondent. Poe is replying to Lowell's letter of September 27, 1844 (MS. in the New York Public Library; printed in W, II, 100). This is Poe's last known letter to Lowell. However, Lowell wrote one more, December 12, 1844 (W, II, 106–108), providing Poe a means of introduction to Lowell's friend, Charles F. Briggs, then about to start the *Broadway Journal*.

186. Source: photostat of original draft (7 pp.) in the Huntington Library (HM 21870. The letter was first printed by Woodberry in the *Century Magazine*, XLVIII (October 1894), 855–857, as a clean copy, not as a draft with Poe's corrections. The letter is here first printed as it was originally written. The original MS. is undated; biographers, with one exception, have followed Woodberry's dating of June 1844; Quinn (*Poe*, p. 426) questions the dating. Woodberry (II, 79) credits his source to the Griswold MSS., and he was obviously following the original draft, as a collation will show; it was then probably part of the Griswold MSS., which were subsequently dispersed, a large portion going to the Boston Public Library, the rest to various collections. The MS. is unsigned, though clearly Poe's, and has no writing on the

verso of the leaves. Anthon's letter to Poe, November 2, 1844 (original in the Boston Public Library), is an answer to the above draft, which indicates that Poe later sent a clean copy; moreover, the contents of Anthon's reply prove the fact: "I have called upon the Harpers, as you requested . . . they have retained . . . the letter which you sent me." Thus Poe's letter to Anthon was written probably late in October 1844, and destroyed by "the Harpers." (For Anthon's letter to Poe, see Quinn, *Poe*, p. 427.) In the above draft, matter between daggers indicates Poe's deletions in the MS.

187. Source: fragment as first printed by Graham in an open letter to Willis, entitled "The Late Edgar Allan Poe," in *Graham's*, March 1850. The original MS. is unlocated. According to Graham, Poe wrote the letter, from which the above fragment is taken, long after Poe left Philadelphia and after Graham, at Poe's request, returned the unpublished MS. of "The Gold Bug." Since Poe won the *Dollar Newspaper* prize in June 1843, nearly 10 months prior to his leaving Philadelphia in April 1844, the letter must have been written later than April 1844. Moreover, since Poe included a lengthy criticism, equal to about four and one-half to five pages of *Graham's*, of Longfellow's *Spanish Student* in his "American Drama" in the *American Whig Review*, August 1845, it is probable that the present letter was written before this date, for the *Whig Review* article undoubtedly contained the original criticism of the *Spanish Student*, either in its entirety or in revision for the article at hand, and Poe probably did not make use of the material until either Graham returned the MS. to him or Poe despaired of its ever being published in *Graham's*. Thus the letter may conjecturally be dated between April 1844, and August 1845, with allowance for the time during which the article on the drama lay in the *Whig* office. In an effort for a more specific dating, "early 1845" is given.

188. Source: letter as first printed in full in Quinn, *Poe*, p. 420, from a copy of original MS. then in possession of Mrs. Thomas F. Madigan; the present location of the MS. is unknown. Libbie catalogue, April 24–25, 1895, item 648, lists the MS. for sale and says it has an outer envelope, is postmarked, and is a quarto MS. No reply from Bush is known.

189. Source: photostat of original MS. (2 pp.) in the Huntington Library (HM 21866). The letter was first printed in Quinn, *Poe*, p. 435. Poe is replying to Thomas' letters of October 10 and December 10, 1844 (MSS. in the Boston Public Library; unpublished).

190. Source: photostat of original MS. (1 p.) in the Boston Public Library. The letter was first printed in Griswold's "Preface" to the *Literati* (1850; see Note 111), with the introductory "Confidential" deleted; Griswold also crossed out the word on the holograph. Poe is answering Griswold's letter of January 14, 1845 (original in the Boston Public Library). The letter is directed to "Rufus W. Griswold / Present," but bears postal mark of January 17. Harrison (XVII, 196) prints from the "Preface" a letter from Poe to Griswold, dated January 10, 1845, and also, p. 197, a reply from Griswold, dated January 11; the first is a completely forged letter by Griswold to prepare for the January 11 letter, also partly forged, the first sentence being

largely the first sentence of the genuine letter of January 14, and the second sentence being wholly spurious. Poe's letter of January 16 — in tone, contents, and manner — supports the fact that the January 10 letter was never written by him. (For supplementary treatment of these letters, with parallel printings, see Quinn, *Poe,* 443–446.)

191. Source: photostat of original MS. (1 p.) in the Pennsylvania Historical Society, Philadelphia. The letter was first printed in Woodberry (1885), pp. 205–206. Poe is answering Duane's letter of *ante* January 28, 1845, which is unlocated.

192. Source: photostat of original MS. (1 p.) in the Morgan Library. The letter was first printed in an unidentified newspaper clipping, reprinted in H, I, 218. The year is certainly 1845; the month date probably February 3, since the corrected lines in the letter were incorporated in the printing of the poem in the *New York Tribune,* February 4 (see *The Raven and Other Poems,* ed. Mabbott, pp. xxv–xxvi). The letter was not mailed but delivered by hand; on the cover appears: "J. Augustus Shea Esqr/ To be delivered as soon as he / comes in."

193. Source: photostat of original (1 p.) in the Boston Public Library. The letter was first printed in H, XVII, 200–201 (with Griswold's manipulation of the letter, pp. 201–202); Quinn, *Poe,* pp. 446–448, gives parallel printings of the two forms, and a facsimile of the original. The letter is addressed to Rev. Rufus W. Griswold, Philadelphia, Pennsylvania, and posted February 25. Griswold printed his manipulated form of the letter in his "Preface," p. xxii, with the statement that this letter was Poe's next after that of January 10, 1845; but the January letter was forged and the statement covered his not printing Poe's letter of January 16 (Letter 190).

194. Source: letter printed under "Correspondence" in the *Broadway Journal,* I (March 8, 1845), 159. The original MS. is probably lost. The date of the letter is taken from the issue of the *Broadway Journal* in which it appeared. Though the letter is not strictly a personal one, it is here reprinted to make it more accessible.

195. Source: photostat of original (3 pp.) in the Huntington Library (HM 24213). The letter was first printed by Woodberry in the *Century Magazine,* LXV (February 1903), 550. The MS. has a torn portion in the postscript.

196. Source: photostat of original (1 p.) in the Boston Public Library. The letter was first printed in H, XVII, 202–203; it was previously printed in manipulated form by Griswold in his "Preface," pp. xxii, and this forgery was reprinted in H, XVII, 169–170; the genuine and forged letters are printed in parallel columns by Quinn, *Poe,* pp. 449–450. The envelope was cancelled at New York, April 19. The lecture establishes the year as 1845 (see the note to Letter 193 for the date of publication of Griswold's *Poets and Poetry of America;* see also the note to Letter 195 for the date of the lecture in New York). If a letter from Griswold accompanied the proof, its location is unknown; moreover, there is no evidence that Griswold replied to Poe's question about alteration.

197. Source: photostat of original MS. (3 pp.) in the Boston Public Library. The letter was first printed in the *Century Magazine*, XLVIII (October 1894), 863. The envelope is directed to F. W. Thomas, Washington City, and postmarked at New York, May 4; Thomas endorsed the envelope: "Recd May 5. 1845." Poe is replying to at least two letters from Thomas, written between January 5 and May 3 (unlocated).

198. Source: photostat of the original MS. (1 p.) in the William H. Koester collection, Baltimore. The letter was first printed, in facsimile, in the American Art Association catalogue, December 16–17, 1929, item 285, facing page 68. The envelope is addressed: "F. W. Thomas Esqr / Washington *D. C.*" and postmarked at New York, May 15. On the envelope Thomas noted: "And as Moses lifted up the serpent in the Wilderness, even so must the son of man be lifted up, That whosoever believeth in him should not perish, but have eternal life — John III. 14 15." He also noted on envelope: "Recd May 18, 1845." Poe is answering Thomas' letter of May 12, 1845 (MS. in the Boston Public Library; unpublished; in which Thomas says the secret writing is sent at the request of C. S. Frailey).

199. Source: photostat of the original MS. (1 p.) in the William H. Koester collection, Baltimore. The letter was first printed in the American Art Association catalogue, November 13–14, 1935, item 299, without salutation or close. Poe's letter to Keese, June 9 [1845], the year being established by the reference to the *Broadway Journal*, serves to establish the year date of the present letter, which is addressed to "Mr John Keese/ 254 *Pearl Street*." and is postmarked "City Despatch Post, May 27, 9 oclock." Poe is replying to Keese's letter of May 24, 1845, which is unlocated.

200. Source: photostat of the original MS. (1 p.) in the William H. Koester collection, Baltimore. The letter is here first printed. The year date is established by the reference to the *Broadway Journal* (see also Letter 199 and notes).

201. Source: photostat of original MS. (1 p.) in the Manuscript Division of the New York Public Library. The letter was first printed in the *New York Public Library Bulletin*, VI (January 1902), 8, with a wrong date. Harrison (XVII, 222) dates it "[Nov. 13? 1845]"; Woodberry (II, 157) suggests late summer, 1845; Quinn (*Poe*, p. 493), though using the original MS., gives "[Nov. 13? 1845?]." With the year date established by the reference to the *Broadway Journal*, what seems to be the month date is supported by "June 26" which is entered in pencil on the original MS., and which was first noticed by Thomas O. Mabbott, who recorded the fact in his edition of *The Raven and Other Poems*, p. xii. Misdatings of the letter have probably been due to the "Nov. 13, 1845?" entered on the mounting of the MS. The envelope is addressed: "E. A. Duyckinck Esqr/ 20 Clinton Place / 8th St." Contributory evidence to the acceptance of the above dating for the letter is to be found in the similar tone of despondency cited in Mrs. Lynch's letter to Poe, June 27, 1845 (see Letter 237; Mrs. Lynch's letter, without date, is printed in H, XVII, 258–259); also, in June 1845 Poe had a third interest or

share in the *Broadway Journal,* but in November he was full owner (see Letter 211 and note).

The Poe–Duyckinck correspondence, which must have contained many more items than are extant, is unique. Thirteen (possibly 14) Poe MSS. are at present extant or are known to have been extant, but not one Duyckinck MS. is known to exist, and only one letter from Duyckinck is definitely cited by Poe. Heretofore, only 11 letters by Poe were known; the present edition includes 3 others, 2 from dealers' sales catalogues and 1 from a private collection. In the list below, the new items are indicated by asterisks.

Poe to Duyckinck		Duyckinck to Poe
1845	June 26	
1845	September 10	
		1845 September 10
1845	September 11	
1845	November 13	
* 1845	December 10	
* 1845	———	
1846	January 8	
* 1846	January 30	
1846	April 28	
1846	June 29	
1846	December 24	
1846	December 30	
1849	February 16	
1849	March 8	

202. Source: letter as printed in H, XVII, 250–251, from the Philadelphia *Spirit of the Times,* XVI, No. 164 (July 10, 1846), p. 1, cols. 4–6, where it was first published. No original MS. of the letter is known. It is undated, but elicited Thomas' reply of July 5, 1845 (see H, XVII, 251). Poe's note is difficult to date; if actually written and sent, it probably reached Thomas after June 27, the date on which, according to his letter to Poe, he saw the person "from whom the report [of forgery] originated," though it may have been written earlier. Thomas' letter contains no reference to the receipt of Poe's note.

203. Source: photostat of original MS. (1 p.) in the Enoch Pratt Library, Baltimore. The letter was first printed in W, II, 373–374. The MS. is a one leaf quarto, with the letter on page 1 and the address: "Neilson Poe Esq./ Baltimore/ *Md.*" on page 4; the letter was postmarked at New York, August 8. Poe is replying to Neilson Poe's letter of July (?), 1845, which is unlocated.

204. Source: photostat of original MS. (1 p.) in the Bradley Martin collection, New York. The letter was first printed, in facsimile, on the cover of the rare William E. Benjamin catalogue, No. 30, April, 1890; one of these catalogues is now in the American Antiquarian Society library, Worcester, Massachusetts. Poe is replying to a note from Field, *ca.* July 15, 1845, which is unlocated.

205. Source: photostat of original MS. (1 p.) in the Huntington Library (HM 21863). The letter was first printed in the *New York Observer*, April 26, 1900, p. 528. The MS. is badly ink-stained from some composition written by Chivers on both recto and verso of the leaf; the postscript is especially illegible, but a collation with James Grant Wilson's printing of the letter in the *Observer* provides the above restoration. Both Wilson and the contents of the letter establish Chivers as the "Friend." Chivers has written Poe three letters since Poe's last reply, thirteen months before: August 6, 1844 (see H, xvii, pp. 184–186), September 24, 1844 (see H, xvii, 188–190), and *ante* August 11, 1845 (see Chivers to Poe, September 9, 1845, in H, xvii, 210–215).

206. Source: Anderson Galleries catalogue, December 7–8, 1909 (part 2), item 1316, pp. 190–191, where it was first printed. The MS. letter is cited as a 2 page quarto, bearing "the scarce 2 cents green Boyd's City Express" stamp, but its present location is unknown. The Osborn letter, which Poe is answering and which accompanied the Poe MS. letter at the sale, was written from 219 Eighth Avenue [New York], and was dated August 14, 1845.

207. Source: photostat of original MS. (2 pp.) in the Huntington Library (HM 24214). The letter was first printed in the *Century Magazine*, lxv (February 1903), 545–546. The year date is established by Chivers' letter to Poe, September 9, 1845: "I have just received your letter, dated the 29th of August (see H, xvii, 210–215); the "Friend" is identified by Chivers' letter, just cited, and by the contents of the present one. Poe is replying to Chivers' letter of August 25, 1845, which is unlocated.

208. Source: photostat of original MS. (1 p.) in the Manuscript Division of the New York Public Library. The letter was first printed in the *New York Public Library Bulletin*, vi (January 1902), 7. On the mounting of the MS., in an unknown hand, is written: "Sept. 10, 1845?"; the date is established by the appearance of the cited poetic passages in *The Raven and Other Poems*, printed by November 12, actually published November 19, and first reviewed in the *Evening Mirror*, November 26, 1845 (see *The Raven and Other Poems*, ed. Mabbott, pp. xi and xiv, and *passim*). In this connection, see also Letter 210.

209. Source: letter as first printed in *The Raven and Other Poems*, ed. Mabbott, p. vii, from a copy in the New York Public Library. The original MS. (unlocated) was offered for sale in the Anderson Galleries catalogue, May 15, 1922, item 512, as an a.l.s., 1 p. octavo, n.d. The date of the present letter was suggested by Mabbott, in his edition of *The Raven*, and in its plausible relation to Poe's letter of September 10 and in the absence of any contradictory evidence in the Poe–Duyckinck correspondence seems justifiable.

210. Source: photostat of original (1 p.) in the Boston Public Library. The letter was first printed by T. O. Mabbott in his "Introduction" to his edition of *The Raven and Other Poems*, p. viii. Someone docketed the MS. with "[1845?]." The envelope was cancelled in New York, September 29, and was addressed to Griswold in Philadelphia. Poe's letter to Duyckinck (Letter 208), dated only "Wednesday 10th," belongs certainly to 1845, for *The Raven* volume was published November 19, 1845; therefore this letter to Griswold belongs to 1845. Since "Wednesday 10th" in 1845 fell only in September and December, the Duyckinck letter can be dated Wednesday 10th [September, 1845], and the Griswold letter, September 28 [1845]. Since Griswold was living in Philadelphia in 1845, the contents of Poe's letter suggest either a conference with Griswold during one of his visits to New York, or an earlier letter from Poe, for which there is no other evidence.

211. Source: photostat of original (1 p.) in the Boston Public Library. The letter was first printed in Griswold's "Preface," p. xxii, but without the postscript; H, XVII, 216, reprinted from the "Preface." The envelope is directed to Dr. Rufus W. Griswold, Philadelphia, Pennsylvania, and cancelled at New York, October 27. Harrison (XVII, 220–221) also prints a letter from Poe to Griswold, dated November 1, 1845, which thanks Griswold for sending $25 with a promise of $25 more, and which implies a letter from Griswold. The "Preface," p. xxii, prints the November 1 letter, but it is undoubtedly spurious, since the "Preface" is the sole authority. Moreover, had it been sent with the money, Poe would probably have published the "article about you [Griswold]" in the *Broadway Journal*, as the letter implies, but the magazine has no such article after the date of the letter.

212. Source: photostat of original MS. (1 p.) in the William H. Koester collection, Baltimore. The letter was first printed in full in the American Art Association catalogue (4201), November 13–14, 1935, item 300, with facsimile facing p. 188. The envelope is postmarked at New York, October 27, and is addressed to "Mrs. S. J. Hale / Philadelphia / Pa." Poe is replying to Mrs. Hale's letter of October 15–16 (?), which is unlocated.

213. Source: photostat of original MS. (1 p.) in the Peabody Institute Library. The letter was first printed in H, XVII, 217. This is the last known letter from Poe to Kennedy; the last known one from Kennedy is dated December 1, 1845 (MS. in the Boston Public Library; printed in H, XVII, 224–225).

214. Source: photostat of original fragment (1 p.) in the Wrenn Library of the University of Texas. The letter was first printed in the *Literary Review*, March 5, 1921, p. 14; but neither place, date, nor signature is given. Reference to the *Broadway Journal* fixes the place and year, and "late October" is suggested by his lecture engagement before the Boston Lyceum, October 16 (Quinn, *Poe*, p. 485), and by the press of business incident to his taking over the control of the *Broadway Journal*, October 24, 1845 (Quinn, *Poe*, pp. 752–753; see also Letter 212). Though the letter is unsigned, the handwriting is definitely Poe's. The original letter seems to have been a small single leaf, folded once, the message being written on page 1, the lower portion

of which has been removed. The message may have been continued on the verso of page 1, though there are no ink marks to support this contention, or on page 3 with the address on the verso of page 3, but the original pages 3 and 4 have been torn off.

215. Source: photostat of original MS. (2 pp.) in the Manuscript Division of the New York Public Library. The letter was first printed in the *New York Public Library Bulletin*, VI (January 1902), 7–8. On the mounting of the letter, in an unknown hand, appears: "Nov. 13, 1845"; since the thirteenth fell on Thursday only in February, March, and November in 1845, the November dating is corroborated by the reference to the *Tales*, which had been published in June of that year. The envelope is addressed: "Evert A. Duyckinck Esqr./ 20 Clinton Place." No reply to the present letter is known.

216. Source: photostat of original MS. (3 pp.) in the Huntington Library (HM 24215). The letter was first printed in the *Century Magazine*, LXV (February 1903), 546–547. The identity of Chivers as the "Friend" is established by Chivers' letters to Poe, September 9 (H, XVII, 210–215, concerning the "Florida bank" and the "broken money"), and October 30, 1845 (H, XVII, 217–220, concerning the pronunciation of *Archytus*). Chivers has written two letters (others are suggested) since Poe's last letter of August 29, 1845: one, September 9; the other, October 30, 1845, both cited in this letter of Poe's.

217. Source: photostat of original MS. (1 p.) in the Enoch Pratt Library, Baltimore. The letter was first printed in H, XVII, 223–224. The envelope (page 4 of a folded leaf) is addressed to "George Poe Jr Esqr / (late of Mobile)/ Georgetown / D. C." and is postmarked at New York, December 1. George Poe endorsed the letter: "Edgar A. Poe / 30th Nov 1845 / recd 3 Decr / [blot, *probably* "not"] ans." The holograph has been cut off at the bottom of page 1, though probably not more than one line and the signature are missing. This is the last known letter from Poe to George Poe, and no reply is known.

218. Source: photostat of original anastatic letter in the Library of Congress. Reproduced in facsimile in *The South in the Building of the Nation*, vol. XII, facing p. 294, where it was first printed, from the anastatic letter to Watterston, now in the Library of Congress, for, according to St. George L. Sioussat, chief of the Division of Manuscripts, the facsimile carries the pressmark once used by the Division. The letter was addressed to "Geo. Watterston Esqr./ Washington/ D.C.," and was postmarked at New York, December 2. Mr. Sioussat states that the address appears on page 4 of the folded leaf, and that the inner two pages are blank. No letter from Watterston to Poe is known.

The Watterston letter (in volume II of the Watterston Papers, in the Library of Congress) is but one of several which were made from some facsimile copying process, or from anastatic printing (see Poe's article, "Anastatic Printing," reprinted in H, XIV, 153–159); the original letter from which the printing was done is undoubtedly lost. There are at least four of these circular letters extant, each carrying a different address. Besides the Watterston letter, there is one in the Huntington Library, addressed to "Wm. Green Esq./ Culpepper C. H./ Va." and postmarked New York, December 8; it differs from the Watterston letter only in having a silverfish hole in the lower right portion of the text. Another is in the Pierpont Morgan Library, addressed to Charles Campbell, Petersburg, Virginia, and postmarked New York, December 5. Still another is reproduced in John W. Robertson's *Edgar A. Poe: A Psychopathic Study,* facing page 324; this letter differs from the others in having only one dot after the "A" in the signature, and no period after the "Poe"; thus it is a fourth letter, though Robertson gives no address or postmark, unless his reproduction of it is from a retouched plate. All the above letters are alike in wording, lining, and dating, and, except for the Robertson item, alike in punctuation; each is written on page 1 of a quarto leaf, and addressed on page 4 (except, again, the Robertson item, which was not available for inspection, but probably conforms to the others). It is interesting that each of the first three given differs in the postal date. No reply from any of these correspondents is known.

219. Source: letter printed in James Grant Wilson's *Life and Letters of Fitz-Greene Halleck,* p. 431, its first printing. The original MS. is probably lost. This is Poe's third and last known letter to Halleck.

220. Source: fragment as first printed in the Anderson Galleries catalogue, May 27, 1914, item 208, where the letter is called an a.l.s. "Poe" to Duyckinck, and described as a quarto, dated December 10, with edges worn and stained. The MS. is unlocated. The letter undoubtedly belongs to 1845, for by December 1846, Poe and Elizabeth F. Ellett were not on friendly terms.

220a. Source: facsimile in the Anderson Galleries catalogue, January 17–18, 1928, item 369, where it is first printed. The note is described as tipped on a fly-leaf of the first volume of Poe's *Tales of the Grotesque and Arabesque.* Neither place, date, nor correspondent is given, but the reference to the "B. J." (*Broadway Journal*) almost certainly identifies the year as 1845. The correspondent may very well have been Evert A. Duyckinck, who was associated with Wiley and Putnam, New York publishers. He selected the stories for Poe's 1845 edition of *Tales,* published in June. The original MS. (probably 1 page) is unlocated. No reply to the present letter is known.

220b. Source: photostat of original MS. (1 p.) in the collection of Miss Helen Ingersoll Tetlow, but now on deposit in the Longfellow House, Cambridge. The letter is here first printed. The MS. is a small folded sheet, with the letter on page 1 and is addressed on page 4 to "Mr. W. M. Gillespie / 30 *Dey St.*" Reference to the *Broadway Journal* dates the letter 1845; the month-date must remain uncertain, though late spring is possible. No other letters to Gillespie are known, but Gillespie wrote to Poe, March 1, 1845 (original in Boston Public Library). If Poe was answering a letter from Gillespie, it is unlocated.

221. Source: original fragment in the Alderman Library, University of Virginia. The fragment appears to be middle section of original letter. Neither the correspondent's name nor the date is given. The tone of the letter suggests 1845–1846.

222. Source: original MS. (1 p.) in the Valentine Museum, Richmond. The letter was first printed in W, II, 374. Poe is replying to Percival's letter of December 19, 1845, in which Percival sent a cipher for solution; the present location of the Percival original is unknown, but it was announced for sale in the Bangs and Company catalogue, April 11, 1896, item 113½.

223. Source: photostat of original MS. (1 p.) in the Manuscript Division of the New York Public Library. The letter was first printed in the *New York Public Library Bulletin*, VI (January 1902), 8. The envelope, not mailed, is addressed: "Evert A. Duyckinck Esqr."

224. Source: photostat of original MS. (1 p.) in the Koester collection, Baltimore. The letter is here first printed. The letter must be dated 1846, for Saturday, January 10, fell only in that year during Poe's New York period and his visits to Anne Lynch's soirees. The letter came to light recently, attached to the flyleaf of a copy of the *Museum*, volume XL, Philadelphia, 1840. The present letter was written on Poe's own letter paper, embossed with his initials "E A P."

224a. Source: photostat of original MS. (1 p.) in the William H. Koester collection, Baltimore. The letter is here first printed. The year date is established by an almost identical letter written by Poe to Fitz-Greene Halleck of the same date (see Letter 224 and Note 224). Like the letter paper to Halleck, the present item carries the blind embossing "E A P" in the upper left corner of the MS. The correspondence appears on page 1 of a folded sheet of note paper; on page 4 appears: "C. Edwards Lester Esqr / *Present*."

225. Source: photostat of original MS. (3 pp.) in the Huntington Library (HM 24216). The letter is here first printed in full. Poe is replying to Mrs. Hale's letter of November 14, 1845, which is unlocated.

226. Source: original MS. fragment (1 p.) in the J. K. Lilly, Jr., collection, Indianapolis. The letter is here first printed. The top third of the holograph has been cut off, and some ten lines are missing. The fragment lacks address and postmark, but seems genuine. Though the correspondent's name is missing, the content of the letter suggests Evert A. Duyckinck as the recipient: for he was editor of Poe's *Tales* of 1845, published by Wiley and Putnam; and though Martin F. Tupper's review of the *Tales* did not appear in the *Literary Gazette* (London) until January 31, 1846, a letter from Tupper to Mr. Wiley late in 1845 asking, "Shall we make Edgar Poe famous by a notice in the *Literary Gazette*" (see P, II, 1021), would have given Poe's publisher and editor the information Poe solicits in the present letter. Moreover, Poe often sent letters to Duyckinck by Mrs. Clemm. Finally, Duyckinck would probably have been able to furnish Poe with the data about the writers cited in the present letter. Thus, with some reservation, this letter is assigned to the Poe–Duyckinck correspondence. The letter is undated in full; but 1846 is given to it on the basis of the above external evidence relative to the publication of the *Tales* and the Tupper review and letter to Wiley concerning it. Furthermore, Poe lived at 85 Amity Street from October 1, 1845 (see the note to Letter 215) to sometime early in 1846 (see Letter 227). Why Poe did not know the addresses of many of the men listed in this letter and why

he did not refer to the New York City Directory may reasonably be questioned; still, in the absence of other controverting evidence the letter is admitted to the canon as genuine.

227. Source: photostat of original MS. (2 pp.) in the Bradley Martin collection, New York. The letter is here first printed. The poem "Power of the Bards," which appeared in Colton's *American Review,* III (June 1846), 587–588, and was signed "P. P. Cooke, Virginia," identifies the correspondent; moreover, Cooke's reply, August 4, 1846 (original in Boston Public Library), is clearly an answer to the present letter. Poe's reference to his having left 85 Amity Street [early in 1846] coupled with the date of Cooke's reply, cited above, proves Poe's own misdating of the present letter by four years. The correct year date is 1846. Cooke's "three last letters" (unlocated) may be dated *ca.* January late–April early, 1846. Correspondence between Poe and William T. Porter is untraceable.

228. Source: photostat of original MS. (1 p.) in the William H. Koester collection, Baltimore. Reproduced in facsimile in the American Art Association catalogue, May 2–3, 1934 (Pt. 1), item 214. The letter was first printed in Ingram, II, 72. Poe is answering Eveleth's letters of December 21, 1845, January 5, and April 3, 1846 (original MSS. in the New York Public Library).

Eveleth never met Poe, but while a medical student he corresponded with Poe from his home in Phillips, Maine, and from the Maine Medical School in Brunswick. In a letter dated October 1, 1878 (Ingram collection, University of Virginia), Eveleth copied his letters from Poe, as well as letters, in whole or in part, from Mrs. Clemm, Mrs. Whitman, John P. Kennedy, and others, which he had received during a correspondence with them following Poe's death. He defended Poe against charges of intoxication in an article in the *Portland* (Maine) *Transcript,* June 8 and July 6, 1850. Numerous errors in Eveleth's copies of the letters were carried into Ingram's printing of them. James Southall Wilson edited Eveleth's copies for the University of Virginia *Alumni Bulletin,* XVII (January 1924), 34–59, the article being reprinted as *The Letters of Edgar A. Poe to George W. Eveleth* (hereinafter referred to as PE (reprint)). Thomas Ollive Mabbott edited Eveleth's letters to Poe for the *New York Public Library Bulletin,* XXVI (March 1922), 171–195, the article being reprinted as *The Letters of George W. Eveleth to Edgar Allan Poe* (hereinafter referred to as EP (reprint)). For a fuller treatment of the Poe–Eveleth correspondence, see the two articles cited. Since the errors in the Eveleth transcripts were unavoidably reproduced in the Ingram and Wilson printings, and continued by other writers using them as sources, the present printing, taken from photostat or facsimile copies of original MSS., is the most accurate presentation to date of the letters as Poe wrote them. Eveleth wrote Poe 13 letters, 1 of which is lost and unprinted; Poe wrote Eveleth 7 letters, all accounted for, the one cited by Wilson as "lost" (PE (reprint), p. 3) being part of the letter of January 4, 1848. The items in the Poe–Eveleth correspondence follow; the starred item is that for which no known MS. or printing has come down to the present time:

Eveleth to Poe		Poe to Eveleth	
1845	December 21		
1846	January 5		
1846	April 3		
		1846	April 16
1846	June 9		
1846	October 13		
		1846	December 15
1847	January 19		
		1847	February 16
1847	February 21		
		1847	March 11
1847	July 27		
		1848	January 4
1848	January 11		
		1848	February 29
1848	March 9		
1848	July 9		
1849	February 17		
		1849	June 26
* 1849	*ante* October 7		

229. Source: photostat of original MS. (2 pp.) in the Manuscript Division of the New York Public Library. The letter was first printed in the *New York Public Library Bulletin*, VI (January 1902), 8–9. The year date seems established by "1846" noted on both the envelope and the mounting of the letter, and by Poe's request for autographs of a number of persons who later in the year appeared in his "Literati." The envelope was not mailed, but delivered probably by messenger, and was addressed: "Evert A. Duyckinck Esqr / *Present.*"

230. Source: photostat of original MS. (1 p.) in the William H. Koester collection, Baltimore. The letter was first printed in the Anderson Galleries catalogue, March 14–15, 1921, item 332. Accompanying this letter at the sale was a copy of a poem, "The Toilette," by Jerome A. Maubey, to which Poe refers, and certain other "correspondence relating to it." Items of this correspondence are unlocated. Poe is replying to Maubey's letter, datable only *ante* April 28, 1846, which is unlocated.

231. Source: letter, as first printed, in Adrian H. Joline, *Meditations of an Autograph Collector*, p. 159. The original MS. is unlocated, but was offered for sale in the Anderson Galleries catalogue, December 15, 1914, item 832, which states the item was ". . . an a.n.s. [autograph note signed] of Edgar Allan Poe to T. Honland," which had been inserted in a copy of Woodberry's *Life* of Poe (1909); the catalogue then quotes the letter, identical with the note printed in Joline. Joline merely gives Poe's middle initial, the above signature in full being taken from the note supplied by the Anderson cata-

logue. Honland's request for the autograph, probably a letter, is unlocated, but may be dated *ante* May 25, 1846.

232. Source: copy of original MS. (probably 1 p.) sent by Mrs. Marie Louise Houghton (formerly Shew) to Ingram, now in the Ingram collection, University of Virginia; the original letter is probably lost. The letter was first printed by Ingram in *Appleton's Journal*, IV (May 1878), 421. Ingram, II, 88–89, reprints the letter, and says that it was "written on a page of Poe's rough pocket notebook paper." Mrs. Houghton's letter to Ingram, May 2 [1875] (in the Ingram collection, University of Virginia), says: "I sent the original [her daughter Dora kept a copy] thinking you would like to have it as he wrote it"; yet Ingram noted on the letter: "It never came. Only the copy — " In the unpublished MS. revision of his *Life* of Poe (Ingram collection), he copies the letter to Virginia and says that it is taken from the "M.S." (p. 571). Thus it would appear that Ingram at one time had the original letter in his possession. Harrison (XVII, 232) prints the letter from the Griswold collection, though it is not now there; if it was ever in the Griswold MSS. it probably was among those items that did not go to the Boston Public Library. (Intriguing is a statement by Ingram in a letter to Mrs. H. M. Thomas, July 14, 1913: "I offered three very interesting letters from Poe to the British Museum they would only buy one and only gave me £2. 2/ — about $10½," quoted in Pratt, p. 80. Could Poe's letter to Virginia have been this one?) Mrs. Houghton is undoubtedly responsible for the errors in spelling and pointing in the letter. Ingram's various printings of the letter give varying changes: in *Appleton's* he has three dots after "tomorrow," no comma after "remembrance," a comma after "words," and italics for "fervent prayer"; in his published *Life*, as in *Appleton's*, he corrects the misspellings, puts a comma after "remembrance" and after "words," italicizes "fervent prayer," and places a caret after "tomorrow"; in his unpublished MS. he carets the space before "P.M." Harrison follows the printing of the letter in Ingram's *Life* (which may have been his source, not a letter in the Griswold MSS.). Ingram's *Life* seems to have been the source of subsequent printings; however, Mrs. Houghton's copy, which was from the original, seems to be the safer, despite its minor errors.

233. Source: photostat of original (3 pp.) in Huntington Library (HM 21872). The letter was first printed in Lillian Whiting's *Life of Kate Field*, pp. 21–22. The envelope is addressed to J. M. Field, Esqr., Editor of the St. Louis *Reveilé*, St. Louis; postmarked at New York, June 18. There are a few torn places in the MS. This is the only known letter between Poe and Field, though Field seems to have printed one of the editorials and sent Poe a copy of the *Reveilé*, perhaps with a letter (see Letter 237). On the MS. brackets have been drawn around Poe's entire editorial, beginning with paragraph three on page 2, probably by Field.

234. Source: letter as first printed in the Anderson Galleries catalogue, May 1–3, 1916, item 642, where the MS. is cited as a 1 page octavo, inlaid in a quarto sheet. According to an earlier, shorter version of the present text in Anderson Galleries catalogue, December 15, 1914, item 832, the MS. is cited

as having no postmark. The correspondent's name is not given. The present location of the MS. is unknown. No reply to the present letter is known.

235. Source: facsimile of original MS. (1 p.) in *Current Opinion*, LXX (June 1921), 823, where it was first presented in full. The original MS. is in the Huntington Library (HM 21867).

236. Source: photostat of original MS. (1 p.) in the Manuscript Division of the New York Public Library. The letter was first printed in the *New York Public Library Bulletin*, VI (January 1902), 9. The year date is established by the publication of Poe's "Reply to English" in the Philadelphia *Spirit of the Times*, July 10, 1846 (see H, XVII, 239–253; also Letter 237); and in 1846, Monday 29 fell only in June. Moreover, the mounting of the letter is docketed "June 29, 1846."

237. Source: photostat of original MS. (2 pp.) in the Boston Public Library. The letter was first printed in the *Century Magazine*, XLVIII (October 1894), 860. The envelope is addressed to Godey, as editor of the *Lady's Book*, Philadelphia, and is postmarked July 16. Poe is replying to a letter from Godey, *ca.* July 14, 1846, which is unlocated. The present letter suggests an exchange of correspondence numbering four items: two from Poe and two from Godey, only the present letter being extant. The only evidence that Godey replied to Poe's letter of July 16 is found in the following fact: the cover of Poe's present letter shows on the verso the West Farms address; thus Godey reversed the cover and directed his reply to Poe at the address given in the postscript of the present letter.

The one known letter from Anne C. Lynch to Poe (see H, XVII, 258–259) has hitherto been undated or wrongly assigned to 1846. Because it refers to a "note" from Poe, it should be properly dated. In the letter Miss Lynch thanks Poe for "your very kind notice of my poems, no less than for your kind and friendly note." In the *Broadway Journal*, June 21, 1845 (I, 390), accompanying her poems, appears: "The two noble poems subjoined . . . are the composition of one of our most justly distinguished poetesses — Miss Anne Charlotte Lynch . . . In modulation and force of rhythm — in dignity and loftiness of sentiment — and in terse energy and expression — they equal if they do not excel any thing of the same character written by an American. — Eds. B. J." After telling Poe that she is about to leave New York, she adds: "I shall take the Tales with me . . . Many thanks for them." The *Tales* (that is, the title page) was entered for copyright, June 13, 1845. A bookseller advertised it on June 26, Thursday. Thus the actual publication date (the day on which it was offered for sale) was probably June 25–26, and Poe would have had copies a few days in advance. Miss Lynch's letter, dated only "Friday morning — 27," was written June 27, 1845. Thus Poe's note to her must have been dated *ca.* June 25–26.

238. Source: facsimile of original (1 p.) in the Parke-Bernet Galleries catalogue (No. 248), January 15–16, 1941, item 321, where it was first printed. The location of the original MS. is not known. This is the only known letter between Poe and Bisco. Reproduced in the Parke-Bernet catalogue with the letter were four receipts, each signed "Edgar A Poe":

(1) "New-York: Jany: 20th 45. Rec[d] of Mr John Bisco eighteen dollars, in full for two articles in Broadway Journal." (2) "New-York: April 7th — 45. Received of John Bisco ten dollars, on account of the Southern Literary Messenger. 10$." (3) "New-York: April 16./ 45. Received of John Bisco three dollars on a/c of Southern L. Messenger." (4) "New-York: April 30th 1845. Received of John Bisco five dollars account of the Southern Literary Messenger." Item (1) above refers to Poe's critique of Elizabeth Barrett's *Drama of Exile and Other Poems* which appeared in the *Broadway Journal*, 1 (January 4 and 11), 4–8, 17–20, for which apparently he received $2 per page. Concerning the other items, see Allen, *Israfel*, p. 521.

239. Source: photostat of original MS. (3 pp.) in the Huntington Library (HM 24217). The letter was first printed in the *Century Magazine*, LXV (February 1903), 547. The identity of Chivers as the "Friend" was established by the reference to his "Luciferian Revelation" (see Chivers to Poe, September 9, 1845, in H, XVII, 213). As Poe states, Chivers has written six letters (perhaps more), all lost, since Poe's last, November 15, 1845. Chivers placed a cross after "Reveilé," on page 3 of the MS., and then noted at the end of the letter: "The following, is the article from the *Home Journal* to which he refers."

240. Source: photostat of original MS. (4 pp.) in the Berg Collection of the New York Public Library. The letter was first printed in H, XVII, 265–268. Pages 1 and 2 appear to have been scorched by an iron. It is clear from Poe's allusion to "the hair-splitting of my French friend" that he is replying to Cooke's letter of August 4, 1846 (see H, XVII, 262–264).

241. Source: photostat of original MS. (3 pp.) in the Berg collection of the New York Public Library. The letter was first printed in PE (reprint), pp. 7–12. Neither Ingram, who printed the letter incorrectly and incompletely from the copy sent him by Eveleth, October 1, 1878 (MS. in the Ingram collection, University of Virginia), nor Harrison, using Ingram, presents a true reading; and Wilson, using the Eveleth copy, likewise unavoidably prints the letter with the errors contained in Eveleth's transcript. Quinn (*Poe*, pp. 521–524), though printing from the original Poe MS., made certain minor variations. The envelope was addressed to "G. W. Evelett Esqr./ Phillips / *Maine*," and was postmarked New York, December 16. Pages 1 and 3 of the MS. are torn in several places along the right margin; the bracketed *not*, page 3, was written in by a strange hand at a torn place in the MS. Poe is replying to Eveleth's letter of June 9, 1846; this letter has never been printed in full, but when the holograph was up for sale, portions of the text were printed in the Bangs and Company catalogue, April 11, 1896; P, II, 1100, reprints parts from the Bangs catalogue. Thus this June 9 letter, which thanks Poe for returning money sent him as a subscription to the *Broadway Journal*, is a reply to Poe's letter of April 16, 1846, and is the "lost" item suggested by Wilson (PE (reprint), p. 3). Poe's present letter is also replying to Eveleth's of October 13, 1846, original MS. in the New York Public Library, and printed in EP (reprint), pp. 7–8.

242. Source: photostat of original MS. (1 p.) in the Manuscript Division

of the New York Public Library. The letter was first printed in the *New York Public Library Bulletin*, VI (January 1902), 9–10.

243. Source: photostat of original MS. (1 p.) in the Library of Congress (Oliver Wendell Holmes collection). The letter was first printed in Allen, *Israfel*, II, 725. No reply to Poe's letter or request is known.

244. Source: photostat of original MS. (1 p.) in the Manuscript Division of the New York Public Library. The letter was first printed in the *New York Public Library Bulletin*, VI (January 1902), 10.

245. Source: facsimile of original (1 p.) in John W. Robertson's *Commentary on Edgar A. Poe*, II, facing p. 234. The original MS. was then in the Robertson collection, but its present location is unknown. The letter was first printed by J. H. Whitty in the *Bookman*, XLIV (September 1916), 20–21. The envelope is directed to A. Ramsay, Esqr., Stonehaven, Scotland; postmarked at New York, December 30, and at Stonehaven, January 16, 1847. Poe is replying to a letter from Ramsay, dated November 30, 1846, the original MS. of which is in the Boston Public Library; printed in H, XVII, 268–269. The only other known letter in this correspondence is that of Ramsay, April 14, 1847, original MS. in Boston Public Library; printed in H, XVII, 284–285.

246. Source: letter printed in the *Home Journal*, January 9, 1847, where it was first published. The page containing the letter from this particular issue of the *Home Journal*, which is very rare, is in the Ingram collection at the University of Virginia. No other issue of the *Home Journal* of this date was located. Though the page used shows no dating, it does indicate the title of the journal. Corroboration of the date is to be found: in Ingram's statement (II, 100) that the letter appeared in the *Home Journal* (though his dating is wrong); in the appearance of Willis' editorial, that called forth Poe's reply, in the issue for December 26; in the fact that Poe's letter was written too late for inclusion in the issue for January 2 and would therefore appear in that of January 9; and in a note to the effect that the letter appeared in the January 9, 1847, issue, taken by Dr. Mabbott years ago when he saw a now inaccessible issue of the *Home Journal* of that date. Poe is replying to a letter from Willis (MS. in the Boston Public Library), which is undated, save for "Wednesday," but certainly belonging to December 23, 1846; on the holograph appears "Edgar A. Poe, Esq., New York City (to be called for)." Willis' letter (printed in H, XVII, 272) enclosed the *Home Journal* editorial, which is reprinted in Quinn, *Poe*, pp. 525–526.

247. Source: photostat of original MS. (1 p.) in the William H. Koester collection, Baltimore. The letter is here first printed in full.

248. Source: photostat of original MS. (1 p.) in the Huntington Library (HM 24221). The letter was first printed by Ingram in *Appleton's Journal*, May 1878, p. 421; and is reproduced in facsimile in Ingram, II, 107. Poe is probably replying to an unlocated letter from Mrs. Shew, dated January 28–29, 1847.

249. Source: photostat of original MS. (2 pp.) in the Berg collection of the New York Public Library. The letter was first printed in Ingram, I,

167 (see also PE (reprint), pp. 12–13). The envelope is addressed to "G. W. Evelett Esqre / Phillips / *Me*" and postmarked "New York 17 Feb.," page 4 of the folded leaf being used as the cover. Poe is replying to Eveleth's letter of January 19, 1847; the original MS. of which is in the New York Public Library, and which is printed in EP (reprint), pp. 9–12.

250. Source: photostat of original MS. (2 pp.) in the Morgan Library. The letter is here first printed in full. The envelope is directed to Horace Greeley, Esqr., Washington, D.C., but bears no postal cancellation. The "tr" in the close is scarcely decipherable and may be just a pen mark, though probably intended to represent "truly."

251. Source: photostat of original MS. draft (3 pp.) in the Boston Public Library. The letter is reproduced in facsimile in P, ii, 1215–1219, where it was first printed. No clean copy MS. is known; the original draft is unsigned and was not sent through the mail, though there is a strong presumption that Poe sent a corrected version. The printings of the letter in Ingram, ii, 116–117, and in H, xvii, 280–282, are undoubtedly corrected versions by the respective editors, as collation with the above printing will show; moreover, Harrison's citing the Griswold MS., which, as far as the Boston Public Library knows, could refer only to the draft, and the uncertainty of the nature of his printing, expressed in his footnote, tend to confirm his use of the draft. The identity of Poe's correspondent is to be found in the last paragraph, and her letter of February 21, 1847 (wrongly dated in P, ii, 1214), is unlocated.

252. Source: photostat of original MS. (2 pp.) in the William H. Koester collection, Baltimore. The letter was first printed in PE (reprint), pp. 13–14; Ingram (ii, 87) had printed but a small portion of the letter, even changing the proper order of the text. The envelope is addressed to "Geo. W. Evelette Esqr / Phillips / *Me*," and initialed in lower left corner "E A P."; it is postmarked New York, March 12. Poe is answering Eveleth's letter of February 21, 1847, the original MS. of which is in the New York Public Library, and which is printed in EP (reprint), pp. 13–14.

253. Source: transcript made by William Hand Browne for J. H. Ingram (now in the Ingram collection, University of Virginia). The present location of the original MS. is unknown, and it is probably lost. The letter was first printed in Ingram, ii, 118. Poe is replying to a letter from Reinman and Walker, February 24, 1847, concerning which Browne wrote on verso of the transcript: "Copy of Edgar A. Poe's letter of acceptance of honorary membership of the 'Philosophian Society' of Wittenberg College, Springfield, Ohio. He was elected (as the Cor. Secy. informs me) Feby. 19, 1847." The location of the Reinman and Walker letter to Poe is also unknown.

254. Source: Dora Houghton's copy of the original MS. The copy is in the Ingram collection, University of Virginia; the original MS. is probably lost. The letter was first printed by Ingram in *Appleton's Journal*, May 1878, p. 422, under the date of "May, 1848"; and on Dora Houghton's copy, he wrote "May 1848," but later changed it to "1847." However, in his unpublished MS. revision of his *Life* of Poe (in the Ingram collection), he inclines

toward 1848. "May" is probably Ingram's dating, but the Houghton–Ingram correspondence does not confirm it. The rather formal salutation, the reference to "months," probably a few, the reference to Virginia's death — all suggest 1847 instead of 1848, and the month may tentatively be given as May, since Ingram may have had justification for it. Moreover, by May 1848 Mrs. Shew (later Mrs. Roland Houghton) was breaking off her friendship with Poe, at the insistence of John H. Hopkins, Jr., then a theological student and friend of Mrs. Shew (see Letter 273 and note). Ingram's printings of the letter omit: "I should return the money, if I did not know it would grieve you, as" and "deserving a place in a palace or church & "; Harrison (XVII, 297), who says his source is in the Griswold collection, omits the same passages. They are, therefore, here first printed. The language of the letter suggests that Poe is replying to Mrs. Shew's note of Saturday night, May (?), 1847, which is unlocated.

254a. Source: fragment printed in the Dodd, Mead and Company sales catalogue No. 59, March 1901, item 269, where the MS. is described as an a.l.s. of 1 page, duodecimo, addressed to Professor C. P. Bronson. No reply to the present letter is known, and the present MS. is unlocated.

255. Source: original MS. (2 pp.) in the Alderman Library, University of Virginia. The letter was first printed in H, I, 270–271. That the letter is written to Robert T. Conrad is proved by Letter 256.

256. Source: facsimile of original MS. (1 p.) in the N. A. Kovach catalogue (Los Angeles, California), September 22, 1933, p. 1, where it was first presented in full. The original MS. is unlocated.

257. Source: photostat of original MS. (1 p.) in the Yale University Library. The letter was first printed in Ingram, "Memoir" to *The Works of Edgar Allan Poe*, I, lxxxii, though he dates it "1848"; however, in Ingram, II, 127–128, it is dated 1847. The 1847 dating is established by the sonnet, "An Enigma," referred to in the letter, and published in *Sartain's Magazine*, March 1848 (see Campbell, *Poems*, p. 276). In his unpublished MS. revision of his *Life* of Poe, p. 627 c (Ingram collection, University of Virginia), Ingram says: "M.S. presented to me by Mrs. Lewis together with other letters and autograph writings by Poe." Former printings of the present letter do not show the above deletion; who made it can scarcely be determined. There is no evidence of a postmark on the letter, though it may have been on a lost cover. Poe is replying to Mrs. Lewis' letter of *ante* November 27, 1847, which is unlocated.

258. Source: letter printed in W, II, 233; the original MS. being unlocated. The letter was first printed in Woodberry (1885), p. 281, from MS. The year date is lacking, but 1847 is established by the appearance of the poem in the *American Whig Review*, December 1847. Willis' "note" of "three or four weeks ago" is unlocated.

259. Source: facsimile in Quinn, *Poe*, pp. 536–537, of the original MS. (2 pp.) in the A. S. W. Rosenbach collection, Philadelphia. The letter was first printed in full as one letter in PE (reprint), pp. 15–19; however, the bracketed five lines following the first signature, not then known to belong

to the present letter, were first printed by the present editor in an article, "Two 'Lost' Poe Letters," *American Notes and Queries*, 1 (August 1941), 68–69. Bracketed emendations in some places are due to the state of the facsimile print used; the original MS., which was not available, is probably clear. The bracketed five lines at the end of the present letter are printed from the Anderson Galleries catalogue, January 21–24, part 2, 1929, item 934. Wilson (PE (reprint), pp. 2–3) suggested, from an Eveleth letter to J. H. Ingram, that these lines made up a separate letter, but he corrected Eveleth's improper dating. The lines, however, turned out to be an enclosure sent with the present letter. They were written in pencil on the verso of a prospectus of the *Stylus*. Eveleth had given it to a friend who requested a specimen of Poe's handwriting (see Eveleth's letter to Ingram, October 30, 1878, in the Ingram collection, University of Virginia). Evidence that identifies these lines as the supposed "lost" letter is combined in Eveleth's replies to Poe, January 11, March 9, and July 9, 1848 (see EP). Poe is answering Eveleth's eighth letter, dated July 27, 1847, the original MS. of which is in the New York Public Library. (Although Poe gives the date as July 26, Eveleth's MS. is dated "27 Tues. eve." and is postmarked July 28.)

260. Source: letter as first printed in Ingram, II, 135. The original MS. is probably lost.

261. Source: fragment as first printed in the American Art Association catalogue, November 23–24, 1937, item 353. The MS. is unlocated, but is cited by the catalogue as a 1 page quarto from Poe to Godey. Godey's probable reply, unlocated, may be dated *post* January 17, 1848. The present letter is the last known item in the Poe–Godey correspondence, the paragraph published over Poe's signature in *Godey's*, December 1849, being a hoax.

262. Source: letter printed in Willis' "Death of Poe," *Home Journal*, October 20, 1849, p. 2, where it was first printed. The location of the original MS. is unknown, and is probably lost.

263. Source: photostat of the original MS. (2 pp.) in the Morgan Library, New York. The letter was first printed in PE (reprint), pp. 19–22; however, Wilson printed from a copy of the letter made by Eveleth for Ingram (in the Ingram collection, University of Virginia), and his printing varies in certain details with the original reading, especially in his omission of sentence twelve, page 1. The original MS. in the Morgan Library does not contain the bracketed passage following the signature — the last line of the letter, the close, and the signature all being written on the same line at the foot of the page; the ellipsis represents the long discussion of *Eureka* (see H, XVI, 337–346, reprinted from the *Methodist Review*, January 1896); thus the bracketed passage, including the addenda, began on page 3 of the letter, the original MS. of which is unlocated, though Eveleth's copy is in the Ingram collection. Except for the addenda, the bracketed portion was first printed by Ingram, II, 141–142. Poe is replying to Eveleth's letter of January 11, 1848, the original of which is in the New York Public Library, and printed in EP (reprint), pp. 16–18.

264. Source: photostat of original MS. (2 pp.) in the J. K. Lilly collection,

Indianapolis. The letter was first printed in H, I, 277–278, without the post-script. For the letter Poe used a printed prospectus of the *Stylus*, dated "New-York City, April, 1848"; the advertisement appears on page 1, the letter on pages 3 and 4, and the address: "George E. Irbey [Isbell] Esq / Binghamp-ton, / Broome Co./ *New-York*" occupies page 2; the letter is postmarked: "New York/, Mar 3 / 5 cts." In the salutation of the letter, an unidentified hand has struck out "Irbey" and written above, "Isbell." The same change was not made on the envelope. Poe is replying to Isbell's letter of February 10, 1848, which is unlocated.

265. Source: printed letter in Ingram, II, 143; the original MS. being un-located. Ingram assigned it to 1848; Harrison (XVII, 344), to 1849; subse-quent biographers vary in the year date. March 30 fell on Thursday in 1848, not in 1847 or 1849; moreover, Poe wrote Eveleth, February 29, 1848: "I mean to start for Richmond on the 10th March."

266. Source: photostat of original MS. (1 p.) in the Huntington Library (HM 21869). The letter is here first printed in full. The location of Hirst's letter to Poe is unknown.

267. Source: photostat of original MS. (4 pp.) in the William H. Koester collection, Baltimore. The letter is here first printed in full. The envelope is directed to "Mrs Jane E. Locke/ Wamesit Cottag[e]/ Lowell/ Mass:/." The letter was written on two leaves, the verso of leaf 2 carried correspond-ence at both top and bottom, with the address in the center; the address-portion of the leaf is badly ink-stained, some of the ink soaking through on the recto, but not obscuring the words. Poe's first sentence suggests at least two letters from Mrs. Locke (both undatable and unlocated); however, "your last" may refer to a letter of some time past, and Poe's present letter may be in answer to a follow-up note just received.

268. Source: photostat of original MS. (1 p.) in the William H. Koester collection, Baltimore. The cover is not postmarked but bears the direction: "To / Charles H. Marshall Esqre." The folds of the manuscript are con-siderably frayed.

269. Source: photostat of original MS. (1 p.) in the William H. Koester collection, Baltimore. The letter was first printed, in facsimile, in the American Art Association catalogue, November 11–12, 1937, item 332, facing p. 130. The letter, which is unpostmarked, was probably sent by messenger.

270. Source: photostat of a handwritten copy (3 pp.) in the J. K. Lilly collection, Indianapolis. The present location of the original MS. is unknown; Quinn, *Poe*, p. 574, incorrectly assigns it to the Lilly collection. The letter is here first printed in full. On the verso of sheet 2 of the Lilly copy appears "To Anna Blackwell," and below, in an unidentified hand, "J R Bartlett's copy"; Bartlett may have been the Hon. John R. Bartlett, of New York, a friend of Sarah Helen Whitman (see P, II, 951). Ingram, Harrison, Wood-berry, and Phillips misdate the letter; Quinn dates it correctly. In a transcript of the present letter, made by Mrs. Whitman for Ingram (Ingram collection, University of Virginia), is copied the address given by Poe: "Miss Anna

Blackwell / care of Prof. de Bonneville / Providence / *R. I."* Poe is replying to Miss Blackwell's letter of *ca.* May 24, 1848, which is unlocated.

271. Source: photostat of original MS. (1 p.) in the William H. Koester
collection, Baltimore. The letter was first printed in W, II, 374–375. Poe's
"P.S." suggests a possible letter from Taylor, though it is unlocated.

272. Source: letter published in Ingram, II, 219–220, where it was first
printed. The correct year date is 1848, not 1849 as given in the various biographies; for Poe reviewed *The Child of the Sea and Other Poems,* published
by Putnam, in the SLM, September 1848, and again in *Graham's,* April 1849.
Apparently no second edition appeared, though Poe suggested that Putnam
bring it out (see Letter 315). In the *Democratic Review,* XXIII (August
1848), 160, Poe says that the volume "is now in press." Thus, the present
letter, which speaks of the MS. of the work, belongs to 1848. Ingram identifies the letter as to Mrs. Lewis, and, of course, the content corroborates the
identity. The ellipsis probably indicates the omission of but a few words,
perhaps a phrase of endearment.

273. Source: transcript of original MS. made by Mrs. Roland S. Houghton
(Mrs. Marie Louise Shew) for John H. Ingram (see her letter to him,
April 3 [1875?] in the Ingram collection, University of Virginia). The
original MS. is probably lost. The letter was first printed in full (from the
Shew transcript) in Quinn, *Poe,* 609–611, but with minor variations; it is
here printed just as Mrs. Shew copied it for Ingram. On her transcript, just
preceding her quotation from "The Raven," Mrs. Shew interpolated the
direction that here Poe copied a "whole stanza" from the poem; apparently
she quoted only enough to identify the stanza for Ingram. The accuracy
of her quotation is highly questionable (see Campbell, *Poems,* p. 112, lines
63–66). For the bracketed "say" following the quotation, Ingram and Quinn
give "repeat"; but the Shew transcript shows "say" written over "repeat."
Ingram's printings of the letter with omissions in *Appleton's Journal,* May
1878, and in his *Life* (1880), which are followed by most subsequent biographers, assign the letter to 1848; Quinn, *Poe,* pp. 609–611, without authority dates the letter June 19, but gives "1849," the date on Mrs. Shew's
transcript. In her letter to Ingram cited above, Mrs. Houghton said, "The
following [letter] was his last and was written in June / 49"; but clearly she
was wrong: the contents of the letter point to June (assuming her month
date is correct) 1848. Poe is replying to Mrs. Shew's letter of June (?) 1848,
which is unlocated.

274. Source: photostat of the original MS. (1 p.) in the Huntington
Library (HM 24218). The letter was first printed in the *Century Magazine,*
LXV (February 1903), 549. Though the letter is dated July 13, the reference
to "tomorrow and Sunday" points clearly to its having been written on Friday, July 14. The envelope is directed to "Dr Thomas Holley Chivers/ New-
York City." At the top of the MS. Chivers noted: "The following is the last
letter that I ever received from him." Though no letter from Chivers to Poe
is known for 1848, the present letter suggests a note of recent date. Between
Poe's letter of July 22, 1846, and his present one, there is a lost letter, *ante*

January 30, 1847, for Chivers to Poe, February 21, 1847, said: "I received the paper, containing your letter and the notice of your writings, some time ago. I was delighted with your letter — that is, with the idea that you had got well again . . . from what you say, she [Virginia] is nigh to the angels . . ." (see H, xvii, 278). The lost letter was undoubtedly a note that accompanied the enclosures. Virginia Poe died January 30, 1847. Two letters from Chivers followed Poe's lost letter: February 21 (just cited), and April 4, 1847 (H, xvii, 282–284), which also seems to suggest a lost letter from Chivers. Though the present letter is Poe's last to Chivers, Poe wrote Mrs. Clemm, August 28–29 (?), 1849, "I got a sneaking letter today from Chivers"; however, Chivers' letter is otherwise unknown.

275. Source: original MS. (1 p.) in the J. K. Lilly, Jr., collection, Indianapolis. The letter was first printed, in facsimile, in the Washington (D. C.) *Post*, Sunday, January 17, 1909 (Ingram collection, University of Virginia). The letter carries no postmark and is merely addressed: "Mrs. Osborne." It is also inscribed, in an unknown hand: "My aunt who was at the country seat of my brother in law Max [?] Lindsay near that of Poe's cottage at Fordham."

276. Source: photostat of original (1 p.) in the J. K. Lilly, Jr., collection, Indianapolis. The letter was first printed in P, ii, 1313. Postmarked New York, September 5, and directed to "Mrs Sarah Helen Whitman,/ Providence,/ R. I." Though Poe made an effort to disguise his handwriting in the letter, that of the outside address is quite natural. With the exception of Quinn (*Poe*, p. 575), who dates it correctly, Poe biographers have dated the above letter "September 8," incorrectly. This is Poe's first known letter to Mrs. Whitman. For further discussion of the Poe–Whitman correspondence, see Note 278.

277. Source: Griswold's "Memoir" of Poe in the edition of the *Literati* (New York: J. S. Redfield, 1850), pp. xxvii–xxix, where it was first printed. The original MS. is probably lost.

278. Source: original MS. (12 pp.) in the J. K. Lilly, Jr., collection, Indianapolis. The letter is here first printed in its fullest possible text, some portions of the letter being past restoration. Until Dr. John G. Varner's research (culminating in his unpublished dissertation, "Sarah Helen Whitman, Seeress of Providence," University of Virginia, 1941), printed forms of the present letter were incomplete; but he succeeded in piecing together three manuscript fragments in the Lilly collection that proved to be the final, or sixth, leaf of the original letter (pages 11 and 12). Then, Mr. Lilly and Dr. Varner subjected to powerful electric lights and infrared photography those passages in the letter that had been heavily scratched out by Mrs. Whitman. Their resulting restorations of the original text, with a few additional ones by the present editor, have been indicated by brackets. The present MS. carries neither postmark nor address, but there can be no question to whom it was sent. In the left margin of page 1 of the MS. is written, presumably by Mrs. Whitman: "Edgar Allan Poe/ to Sarah Helen Whitman/ Fordham Oct. 1. 1848." In the left margin of page 2 Mrs. Whitman wrote opposite

the poem: "I simply showed him the/ lines that I might ask his/ opinion of a verse which/ the publisher wished me to alter." In the second sentence of page 3 she scratched out the restored reading, "half sneers at," and above wrote, "allusions to." In the right margin of page 3, opposite the words "I passed through Providence with Mrs Osgood," she wrote: "1845." In the left margin of page 4, opposite the reference to the valentine, she wrote "Feb 1848." In the lower left margin of page 6, appears, "Last lines or stanzas," the exact allusion being unknown. On page 10, the editorial asterisks indicate the approximate number of letters in illegible words. Mrs. Whitman deleted extensively in transcribing this letter for J. H. Ingram. Poe is answering Mrs. Whitman's letter of September 27–29 (?), 1848 (unlocated), her first to him, according to his letter of October 18 (see also Mrs. Whitman's letter to Ingram, March 23, 1874, Ingram collection, University of Virginia, in which she admits that the present letter is an answer to one from her in September).

The Poe–Whitman romance has been treated in the various biographies. Their correspondence has never before been fully discussed, and because of misinformation, misdatings, and omissions (see notes to the letters here printed), the following list of items is presented: the starred items are extant in MS. originals by Poe, except the last, for which there is a copy from the original; no original letters by Mrs. Whitman are known to exist —

Poe to Mrs. Whitman	Mrs. Whitman to Poe
* September 5, 1848	
	September 27–29, 1848
* October 1, 1848	
	ca. October 10, 1848
* October 18, 1848	
	November 1–2, 1848
* (?) November 3, 1848	
* November 7, 1848	
	November 7, 1848 (?)
November 8, 1848	
November 14, 1848	
	November 17, 1848
	November 18–20, 1848
* November 22, 1848	
* November 24, 1848	
* November 26, 1848	
	December 14–15, 1848
* December 16, 1848	
* January 21, 1849	

279. Source: letter printed in Anderson Galleries catalogue, April 29, 1924, item 956, where it was first printed. No other publication is known. The MS. is a 1 page quarto, addressed on the verso to T. L. Dunnell, Esq.,

Providence, R. I.; location of the MS. is unknown. Poe is answering Dunnell's letter of October 17 (?), location of the original of which is unknown.

280. Source: original MS. (9 pp.) in the J. K. Lilly, Jr., collection, Indianapolis. The letter was first printed in LL, pp. 19–29, without restoration of the obliterated portion on page 3; that portion is here first printed. The letter is undated; but "Oct 18, 48" has been penciled in at top of page one, "October 18, 1848" has been noted on the envelope that presumably belongs to this letter, and the envelope bears a very faded postmark of "New York [Oct.] 18." The envelope is addressed to "Mrs Sarah Helen Whitman/ Providence/ R. I." Besides the lock of hair Poe is said to have sent in this envelope, Poe probably sent the present letter, for on the envelope under the postmark is a "10" indicating the postal rate, too high for a small piece of paper and a lock of hair (Poe's September 5, 1848, letter (1 p.) to Mrs. Whitman carried a five-cent rate). The bracketed reading on page 3 is based on the restoration made by Dr. Varner and Mr. Lilly (see Note 278). Poe is answering Mrs. Whitman's letter of _ca._ October 10, which is unlocated.

281. Source: photostat of original MS. (1 p.) in the William H. Koester collection, Baltimore. The letter was first printed, in facsimile, in the Parke-Bernet catalogue, May 24, 1939. No exact dating seems possible.

282. Source: facsimile of the MS. (1 p.) in the American Art Association catalogue, April 24–25, 1935, p. 127, item 252, where the letter was first printed, from the collection of Frederick Locker-Lampson, the original carrying the endorsement "F. Locker" on the verso. In a letter to Ingram, February 6 [1877 (?)], Locker-Lampson said he had a note from Poe to "Mrs. Richmond, dated Fordham, Oct 1848" (Ingram collection, University of Virginia). No exact dating seems possible. The original MS. may be in the Gimble collection, but is inaccessible.

283. Source: photostat of an original fragment in the William H. Koester collection, Baltimore. The letter is here first printed. When it was sold by the Swann Auction Galleries, January 20, 1944, from the Titus C. Geesey collection, the fragment was described as written to Mrs. Annie L. Richmond of Providence to whom Poe was to have been married. The fragmentary nature of the manuscript almost defies identification; however, the present editor believes that the correspondent is not Mrs. Richmond, to whom Poe was never engaged to be married, and who did not live in Providence, R. I., but rather is Mrs. Sarah Helen Whitman, to whom he was engaged in December 1848, and who did live in Providence. Moreover, the tone of the fragment suggests that of Poe's other letters to Mrs. Whitman, rather than those to Mrs. Richmond. And finally, Poe did not sign himself "Edgar" in his letters to Mrs. Richmond, but did in those to Mrs. Whitman. Accurate dating of the letter is most difficult; but assuming that the lines are to Mrs. Whitman, the present editor assigns them to a lost letter from Poe to Mrs. Whitman, November 3, 1848. In a letter to Ingram, October 25, 1875 (Ingram collection, University of Virginia), Mrs. Whitman mentions sending Poe a note [about November 1–2] that "perplexed and agitated him"; and added that

Poe's reply [November 3] stated that he "should be at Providence on the following evening" [November 4]. The rest of the present manuscript is un-located, and is probably lost. Mrs. Whitman probably tore off the portion containing the signature, as was her habit at times, for some friend. Poe is presumably answering a letter from Mrs. Whitman, November 1–2, 1848, which is unlocated.

284. Source: original MS. (1 p.) in the J. K. Lilly, Jr., collection, In-dianapolis. The letter was first printed in LL, pp. 30–31. Ingram (II, 174–175), followed by Harrison (XVII, 311), printed all but one sentence. All printings show no signature. Though undated by Poe, the MS. carries the following endorsements, presumably by Mrs. Whitman: in lower left corner, "Tuesday Nov 7"; and in lower right corner, "Edgar Poe to S H W. Nov 7 48/ 76 Benefit St — Providence R. I." On the verso appears Mrs. Whitman's note: "Written the day on which Mr Poe returned from Lowell. I sent him word I would meet him in half an hour at the Atheneum. S H W." Whether she wrote Poe a note or sent word by messenger is not known. The bottom portion of the original letter seems to have been torn off, probably by Mrs. Whitman as a souvenir of Poe's autograph. Other correspondence between Poe and Mrs. Whitman at this time must have existed (all items are unlocated, with the possible exception of one frag-ment), for in a letter to Ingram, October 25, 1875, she mentions sending Poe a note [about November 1–2] that "perplexed and agitated him" (see also W, II, 277; Quinn, *Poe*, p. 579). In the same letter she cited Poe's answer [November 3]. See the MS. fragment conjecturally assigned to this date, Letter 283.

285. The original MS. is lost, so I have used the copy Mrs. Whitman made for John H. Ingram (Ingram collection, University of Virginia). The letter is here first printed as Mrs. Whitman transcribed it; the first printed, with minor variations, was by Ingram (II, 178). Several printings of this letter have appeared, no two agreeing in all details; one, a copy by Mrs. Whitman (?), appeared in *Cosmopolitan Magazine* in facsimile (Ingram collection, University of Virginia, n.d.) as reprinted from " 'The Complete Works of Edgar Allan Poe.' Thomas Y. Crowell & Co., New York City"; but no edi-tion containing such a facsimile has been found. The original letter had a postscript in which Poe thanked William J. Pabodie for kindness extended him during a recent illness in Providence; Pabodie borrowed the letter, after Mrs. Whitman made a copy, and later told her that he had either mislaid or lost it (see LL, p. 33).

286. Source: Annie Richmond's transcript made from the original MS. for Ingram (now in the Ingram collection, University of Virginia). Ingram printed incomplete texts in *Appleton's Journal,* May 1878, pp. 424–425, and in Ingram, II, 193–194 (H, XVII, 312–314, prints from the *Appleton's* text, but cites the source as from the "Griswold Collection?"); the location of the original MS. is unknown, and is probably lost. Quinn (*Poe,* pp. 589–592), though using the Annie Richmond transcript, changes the pointing and for Poe's "(if it can be called saving) saved me" prints the less satisfactory "(if

it can be called easing) eased me." At the head of her transcript, Mrs. Richmond wrote: "Copy of a letter written at Fordham Nov. 16th 1848 — " Ingram noted on the transcript: "This *must* be burnt. *J. H. I.*" Though the letter was first printed in Quinn, *Poe*, pp. 589–592, it is here first given as Mrs. Richmond wrote it, which is undoubtedly the only extant source.

287. Source: transcript of the original MS. made by Edward V. Valentine of Richmond, Virginia, for John H. Ingram (now in the Ingram collection, University of Virginia); the original MS. is unlocated. The letter was first printed in Ingram, II, 197–198. At the head of the MS. copy, Mr. Valentine wrote: "A letter from Edgar Allan Poe to my cousin Mr Edward Valentine, of Buchanan, Botetourt County, Virginia. Mr Valentine is now 84 years of age. This is the letter I mentioned to you." There is no evidence that Mr. Valentine replied.

288. Source: original MS. (1 p.) in the J. K. Lilly, Jr., collection, Indianapolis. The letter was first printed in LL, pp. 34–35; Ingram (II, 180–181), followed by Harrison (XVII, 317–318) and Woodberry (II, 290–291), prints under this date the letter for November 26, 1848, and omits the above letter. A penciled notation, presumably by Mrs. Whitman, appears on the verso of page 1: "November 22, 1848/ 3 Letters written on the 22. 24 & 26 of November"; moreover, the verso of page 1 carries the postmark: "New York/ 22 Nov/ 5 cts"; and the address: "Mrs. Sarah H. Whitman/ Providence/ R.I." Poe is answering Mrs. Whitman's "note" of November 17, location of the original of which is unknown.

289. Source: transcript of Poe's original, made by Annie Richmond for J. H. Ingram (Ingram collection, University of Virginia). The original MS. is probably lost. The letter is here first printed in full. Ingram printed incomplete versions in *Appleton's Journal*, May 1878, p. 425, and in Ingram, II, 195–196; Harrison (XVII, 319–320) followed the *Appleton's* text, but cited as his source, "Griswold collection?"

290. Source: original (4 pp.) in the J. K. Lilly, Jr., collection, Indianapolis. The letter was first printed in full in LL, pp. 36–40; Ingram (II, 70–71, 182–184) prints it only in part and under proper date, but Harrison (XVII, 320–322), reprinting Ingram, prints it wrongly under "November 25." The entry "November 1848," in handwriting resembling Mrs. Whitman's, appears just above Poe's dating, and at the end of page 4, Mrs. Whitman, presumably, wrote: "Fordham/ November 24th 1848"; in the lower right corner of page 4, parallel to the edge of the leaf, she wrote: "From Edgar Poe/ to Sarah Helen Whitman." On page 3, toward the bottom, following "the," is an obliterated passage preceded by an asterisk, and at the foot of the page Mrs. Whitman supplied (which I include in brackets): " * the insults of your mother & sister still rankle at." Her restoration seems accurate as far as it goes, but the obliterated space calls for additional filler; a clue is suggested for the missing word in Mrs. Whitman's letter to Mrs. Mary Hewitt, September 25 or 27, 1850 (see Quinn, *Poe*, p. 585), where she quotes Poe's epithet of resentment against her family: "intolerable insults"; the same phrase would fit the spacing and might well have been used both in the letter and on the occasion alluded

to by Mrs. Whitman. Poe is replying to Mrs. Whitman's letter of November 18–20 (?), promised in her note of November 17 (see Note 288), and clearly sent, as the content of the above letter proves.

291. Source: original MS. (3 pp.) in the J. K. Lilly, Jr., collection, Indianapolis. The letter was first printed in LL, pp. 41–43. The full dating is established by the following evidence: November 26, 1848, fell on Sunday; a strange hand noted in upper right corner of the MS.: "Nov 26 / 1848"; on the verso of Poe's original to Mrs. Whitman, November 22, 1848, presumably in her hand, appears: "3 Letters written on the 22. 24 & 26 of November"; and finally, the content of the present letter supports the dating. On page 3 the portion of original MS. beginning with "Edgar" and ending with "enclosures" was cut out by Mrs. Whitman and given to James T. Fields in 1865. She then replaced the original with a copy, which accompanied the original MS., until Mr. Lilly purchased a volume of *Poetical Works of E. A. Poe* (London: Sampson Low & Co., 1857) that had once been in the Fields collection. Tipped in was the original fragment, with Fields' endorsement: "given to me by Mrs. S. H. Whitman in 1865." The fragment is here first printed as Poe wrote it. No reply to the present letter is known.

292. Source: facsimile of original MS. (1 p.) in Ingram's *Works of Edgar Allan Poe* (1874), I, between lxxvii–lxxviii, where the letter is first printed. The original MS. is probably lost.

293. Source: original MS. (1 p.) in the J. K. Lilly, Jr., collection, Indianapolis. The letter was first printed in LL, p. 44, under the date of "Dec. 17, 1848," but December 16, 1848, fell on Saturday. The holograph carries neither postmark nor address. The MS. was cut in two after the third line, and on the basis of the paper of the present MS. and that of the November 26 letter, both having the same width and the same embossed design, some eight or nine lines of the original MS. seem to be missing; evidence of wording belonging to the lost portion appears along the line of cutting and the word "mail" has been careted by a strange hand following "afternoons," the inference being that "mail" was the first word of the original fourth line and was preserved in this manner. Poe is answering Mrs. Whitman's letter of December 14–15 (?), 1848, the location of which is unknown.

294. Source: original MS. (1 p.) in the J. K. Lilly, Jr., collection, Indianapolis. The letter was first printed in LL, p. 50. The MS. has neither postmark nor address. Evidence for the authenticity of the letter is found in William J. Pabodie's letter to Griswold, June 11, 1852 (H, XVII, 413) and in Mrs. Whitman's letter to Mrs. Hewitt, September, 1850 (see Quinn, *Poe*, p. 584; Stanley T. Williams, "New Letters About Poe," *Yale Review*, XIV (July 1925), 761–763); Mrs. Whitman, however, speaks of the "second train of cars." The dating is supported by the two letters just cited, Mrs. Whitman giving the exact date. The present letter could be an unfinished fragment; moreover, it may never have been sent.

295. Source: original MS. (1 p.) in the J. K. Lilly, Jr., collection, Indianapolis. The letter was first printed in LL, p. 46. Poe delivered his lecture on "The Poetic Principle" before the Franklin Lyceum of Providence on the evening

of December 20 (W, II, 283–284; Quinn, *Poe*, p. 583); according to William J. Pabodie, in a letter to R. W. Griswold, June 11, 1852 (H, XVII, 413–414), Poe's letter to Dr. Crocker was written within a few days after the lecture; Mrs. Whitman, writing to Mrs. Hewitt, in September 1850, gives the date of the letter as December 23 (see Stanley T. Williams, *Yale Review*, XIV (July 1925), 755–773). Since Poe was back in New York on December 28 (see his letter to Mrs. Richmond), the letter above must have been written prior to the Sunday on which the banns were to be published; December 23, Saturday, is the most likely date and agrees with Mrs. Whitman's dating. In the J. K. Lilly collection is the original draft of the letter Poe wrote to Dr. Crocker. It reads: "Dear Sir,/ Will you have the/ kindness to publish the banns/ of matrimony between Mrs./ Sarah Helen Whitman and/ myself on Sunday and/ Monday. When we have."

296. Source: Ingram, II, 196–197, where the letter was first printed, though not in full. No original or transcript by Mrs. Richmond is known. Though not fully dated, the letter belongs to December 1848.

297. Source: original letter, written on page 4 of a MS. of the poem, "The Prisoner of Peroté," in the Ingram collection, University of Virginia. On the front page of the MS. appears: "These corrections and the note in pencil on the last page are Poe's in his hand writing — Estella." On the last page is Ingram's note: "Poe MS. JHI." The letter was first printed by Ingram in the *Albany Review* (London), 1 (July 1907), 420–421. The MS. is undated, and the present dating is suggested on the following basis: in the known letters from Poe to Mrs. Lewis, a familiar tone does not appear until May 17, 1849, though this evidence is, of course, scarcely conclusive; on the other hand, "The Prisoner of Peroté" was included by Mrs. Lewis in *Myths of the Minstrel* (New York: D. Appleton and Company, 1852, pp. 29–32). The "prose paragraph," a translation from a "Spanish paper," appeared as a note in the appendix (p. 94); and in the "Advertisement" Mrs. Lewis said: "These Poems, with one or two exceptions, have been written since the publication of 'Child of the Sea, and other Poems.' " Though the subject matter and tone of the present poem are typical of the other poems in *Myths of the Minstrel*, "The Prisoner of Peroté" may have been one of the "exceptions." Available evidence from the tone of Poe's note on the MS. of the poem and from the statement by Mrs. Lewis suggests a dating for the note between the summer of 1848, when the *Child of the Sea* was published (see Letter 272), and May 1849. A date as early as 1845 is also possible: Poe was living in New York at that time, and Phillips (II, 1374) quotes Mrs. Lewis' husband as saying that he first knew Poe in 1845. Ingram's statement in the *Albany Review*, cited above, that "The Prisoner of Peroté" was published in Mrs. Lewis' *The Records of the Heart* (deposited in Clerk's Office for the Southern District of New York, April 20th, 1844, and published by George S. Appleton, 1844) is erroneous. In view of the available evidence, the present editor inclines to the later dating. Poe may be answering a lost letter from Mrs. Lewis or an oral request.

298. The present text is a composite of that portion of the letter printed

by Ingram in *Appleton's Journal,* May 1878, p. 425, and that printed in Ingram, II, 202–203 (H, XVII, 318–319, though ascribing the source as the "Griswold collection?", is clearly following the *Appleton* printing; he also misdates the letter by placing it among those for 1848). The *Appleton's* fragment was here used as the basic text; daggers enclose readings not found in the *Life* text; brackets, except for the date and place, supplied by the editor, enclose readings not found in *Appleton's.* No printing is complete, though the present one is the fullest known. Ingram (II, 201) says Poe's letter to Mrs. Richmond, undated, was enclosed in one from Mrs. Clemm to Mrs. Richmond, which he dates January 11, 1849. A search of the items in the Ingram collection (University of Virginia) failed to reveal Ingram's source for his printings, though it was probably a transcript of the original made by Mrs. Richmond. Poe's preceding letter to Mrs. Richmond (December 28, 1848) was but two weeks before the present one. The texts of most of Poe's letters to Annie Richmond are necessarily of a composite nature, derived from Ingram's versions in *Appleton's Journal* (1878) and in his *Life* of Poe (1880), location of original MSS. or Annie's transcripts being unknown. Subsequent to the appearance of the *Appleton's* article, Mrs. Richmond's letters to Ingram (University of Virginia) revealed her surprise and displeasure at Ingram's publishing for the eyes of the world what she had transcribed only for the eyes of the biographer; perhaps Annie's feelings controlled Ingram's further editings of the *Life* texts.

In printing Poe's letters to Mrs. Richmond, Ingram omits quotation marks with Annie's name, in the *Appleton's* text, but uses them in the *Life* text; I have followed Annie's own procedure, based upon her known transcripts made for Ingram. Both "Eddy" and "Eddie" appear in the Ingram versions; Annie and Poe used "Eddy."

299. Source: photostat of original (2 pp.) in the Huntington Library (HM 21874). The letter is here first printed in full; P, II, 1367–1368, prints the letter in part, but misdates it "January 18." Poe's first sentence implies a previous letter to Thompson, but no MS. or printing is known, except Woodberry's statement (II, vii) that the Poe signature on the frontispiece was taken from a letter to Thompson, December 7, 1848 (unlocated). Poe's first sentence might allude to a request for the "two Messengers" made in that letter, except that the signature of the present letter differs from that of the frontispiece.

300. Source: letter printed for first time in Whitty, p. lxxi, from MS.; the bracketed readings, given above, are not found in the Whitty printing, but in P, II, 1368, probably from MS. The present location of the MS. is unknown. Whitty says the letter is to Priestly, proprietor of the *American Whig Review;* this is confirmed and the year date established by Poe's letter to Mrs. Richmond, January 21, 1849, in which he says: "I sent yesterday an article to the *Am. Review,* about 'Critics and Criticism.' " This is the only known letter between Poe and Priestly.

301. The present text is a composite of that portion of the letter printed by Ingram in *Appleton's Journal,* May 1878, pp. 425–426, and that printed

in Ingram, II, 203–205 (H, XVII, 327–329, follows the *Life* text). The *Appleton's* fragment was used as the basic text; daggers enclose readings not found in the *Life* text; brackets, except for the date, enclose readings not found in *Appleton's*. No printing is complete, though the present one is the fullest known. According to Ingram, the letter was undated and was sent to Annie with one Poe wrote to Mrs. Whitman (see Letter 302 and notes). Consultation of the notes to the Poe–Whitman letter just cited is requisite to an understanding of various allusions in the present letter. Poe is answering a Mrs. Richmond letter (January 20 (?) or earlier), of which no MS. or printing is known, save the part quoted by Poe. A search of the items in the Ingram collection (University of Virginia) failed to reveal Ingram's source for his printings, though it was probably a transcript of the original made by Mrs. Richmond.

302. Source: the MS. copy (Ingram collection, University of Virginia) of the original (probably 2 pp.) made by Annie Richmond for J. H. Ingram (see her letter to Ingram, January 14, 1877); the location of Poe's original is unknown. The letter is here first printed in full. The dating of this letter presents a curious problem. Without the MS. letter, there is no evidence to prove Poe dated it "January 25, 1849," the date given by Quinn (*Poe*, p. 586); the source for this dating is Annie Richmond's copy enclosed in her letter to Ingram, January 14, 1877 (Ingram collection, University of Virginia). But Poe wrote the letter and enclosed it in one to Mrs. Richmond in January 1849 (see Letter 301). Poe may have dated the letter ahead, under the circumstances, Mrs. Richmond copying that date correctly in her transcript for Ingram; or Poe may have entered no date, Mrs. Richmond supplying a dating for Ingram that corresponded with her posting of the letter; in neither instance was the date of composition given. On the other hand, Poe's letter to John Priestly, Saturday, January 20, 1849, accompanied a contribution to the *American Whig Review*, and Poe's letter to Annie Richmond in January [January 21 (?), 1849] says: "I sent yesterday an article to the *American Review* . . ." Though Poe was not always accurate as to dates, it is reasonable to suppose him correct in this one. Therefore, since his letter to Mrs. Whitman was enclosed in that to Mrs. Richmond, its compositional date seems to have been January 21 (?), 1849. Dr. Quinn (*Poe*, pp. 586–587, and n.) calls attention to a curious reading found in the MS. copy made by Mrs. Richmond; however, the MS. reads clearly, not "I have assigned on reason . . . ," as Dr. Quinn gives it, but "I have assigned no reason . . . ," as printed above.

303. Source: photostat of extant portion of original (fragments of 2 pp.) in the Morgan Library, supplemented by J. H. Ingram's two texts as printed in *Appleton's Journal*, May 1878, p. 426, and in Ingram, II, 205–207 (the *Life* text is fuller, but the *Appleton* text includes words not in the *Life*; H, XVII, 330–331, follows the *Life* text). The letter is here first printed in its fullest known form, though a portion is still lacking and probably lost; the original MS. was certainly no longer than two pages, a recto and verso of one leaf. The unbracketed portions come from the *Appleton's Journal* text; material

in daggers comes from the Morgan Library fragment; material in brackets, except for address, date, and pagination, comes from the *Life* text. Though the MS. has the top portion of pages 1 and 2 torn off, identification of the addressee is established by the last three lines of the letter; the publication of "Hop-Frog" in *The Flag of Our Union,* March 17, 1849 (Wyllie, *Poe's Tales,* p. 327), and Poe's statement that he ". . . returned from Providence — six weeks ago" (by December 28, 1848 — see Letter 296) suggest the correct dating of the above letter as February 8, 1849, which, incidentally, was on Thursday. The missing portion of page 2 of the MS. was equivalent to that represented by all the material on page 1 preceding the passage in daggers, beginning "How I wish my Annie . . ."; emendations of lines destroyed by the tearing or cutting of the MS. were made from Ingram's *Life* text, as indicated.

Poe's statement that the proprietor of *The Flag* "wrote to me . . . and I accepted . . ." suggests at least one exchange of letters between Poe and Gleason. In his letter to Mrs. Richmond, January 21 (?), 1849, Poe says he "had two proposals within the last week *from Boston*"; perhaps Gleason made one of them in a letter that can be dated only between January 18 (?) and February 5, 1849, and Poe's acceptance may have been in the letter dated Feb. 5, 1849, unlocated, but sold by Dodd Mead Company, catalogue 46, March, 1897, item 76.

304. Source: photostat of original MS. (2 pp.) in the Boston Public Library. The letter was first printed in the *Century Magazine,* XLVIII (October 1894), 863–864. The envelope is covered with addresses and postmarks, which seem to indicate: first, Poe directed the letter to F. W. Thomas, Louisville, Kentucky, from which it was returned to New York, February 27; then Poe directed it to Editor of "The Chronicle," 47 Wall St.; next it was sent to Frankfort, Kentucky, from which it was redirected, April 5, to Washington, D.C., the last address having no line drawn through it. Thomas noted on the envelope: "Recd April 10, 1849." Page 3 of the holograph contains a review of Mrs. S. Anna Lewis' *Child of the Sea and Other Poems.* Under the review appears, probably in Thomas' hand, "This notice was never published." The bracketed restorations on pages 1 and 2 of the present letter appear in the MS. over Poe's lines crossed out; the restorations are certainly not Thomas'. Since Poe's last letter, May 14, 1845, Thomas wrote at least five, but Poe does not seem to have replied until the present letter, though such a long silence toward Thomas seems incredible. Thomas' letters, all unpublished, were as follows: July 10, 1845 (MS. in the Boston Public Library), September 29, 1845 (MS. in the Boston Public Library), August 14, 1846 (MS. in the New York Public Library), August 24, 1846 (MS. in the Boston Public Library), and November 27, 1848 (unlocated). This is Poe's last known letter to Thomas, and no further letters from Thomas have been located.

305. Source: photostat of original MS. (1 p.) in the Manuscript Division of the New York Public Library. The letter was first printed, from a transcript, in H, XVII, 335. The MS. letter is an extra illustration in Duyckinck's own copy of his *Cyclopedia,* at present in the New York Public Library.

306. Source: Mrs. Richmond's transcript made from the original MS. for Ingram (now in the Ingram collection, University of Virginia). Ingram printed incomplete texts in *Appleton's Journal*, May 1878, pp. 426–427, and in Ingram, II, 207–210 (H, XVII, 335–338, prints from the *Appleton's* text, but cites his source as from the "Griswold Collection"); location of the original MS. is unknown. Quinn (*Poe*, pp. 597–599) prints from the Annie Richmond transcript, but changes her pointing, fills in abbreviations, and, in one or two instances, varies in wording. "February 19, 1849" has been the accepted dating, despite the fact that the 19th fell on Monday, and the letter is headed "Sunday"; Poe was more likely to have erred in the date than the day, and the correct dating of the letter, therefore, is probably "Feb. 18. Sunday 1849." Though Poe is known to have written four letters to Mrs. Richmond between his of November 16, 1848, and the present one, the number of her letters to him is less certain: she wrote the one to which his of January 21 (?), 1849, is a reply, and of the "letters to me & my mother," cited above, one or two must have been to Poe himself; no letter from Mrs. Richmond to Poe, either in MS. or in print, is known.

307. Source: original MS. (1 p.) in the J. K. Lilly, Jr., collection, Indianapolis. The letter is here printed for the first time. On the verso of the MS. appears: "The handwriting of / Edgar Allan Poe." The letter carries neither postmark nor address, and its content, especially its salutation, suggests it may have been enclosed in a letter to Mrs. Annie Richmond (unlocated). Originally Poe seems to have written "kiss dear Annie for me"; but "Ca" appears written over "An" by someone in such a way that the second "n" of *Annie* would be read as the "rr" of *Carrie*. The change may or may not have been Poe's.

308. Source: photostat of original MS. (3 pp.) in the Manuscript Division of the New York Public Library. The letter was first printed in the *New York Public Library Bulletin*, VI (January 1902), 10. The year date is established by Duyckinck's printing of "Ulalume" in the *Literary World*, March 3, 1849 (see Letter 305). On the envelope, which was not mailed, appears: "Evert A. Duyckinck Esqr." In upper left corner, page 1, of MS., is the entry: "1849." This is Poe's last known letter to Duyckinck, and no subsequent letter from Duyckinck is known.

309. The present text is a composite of that portion of the letter printed by Ingram in *Appleton's Journal*, May 1878, pp. 427–428, and that printed in Ingram, II, 210–212 (H, XVII, 342–344, follows the *Life* text). The *Appleton's* fragment was used as the basic text. Daggers enclose readings not found in the *Life* text; brackets, except for the remark on the signature, enclose readings not found in *Appleton's*. No printing is complete, though the present one is the fullest known. Both of Ingram's versions omit a salutation, and in the *Appleton's* text (p. 427) he states that the letter is "too lengthy to quote in full." A search of the items in the Ingram collection (University of Virginia) failed to reveal Ingram's source for his printings, though it was probably a transcript of the original made by Mrs. Richmond. Poe seems to be answering a letter from Mrs. Richmond (no MS. or printing known), for

he apparently quotes portions of it and implies queries put by her; a conjectural date for it would be between February 18, 1849 (his last to her) and March 22, 1849.

310. Source: Willis' article, "Death of Edgar A. Poe," first printed in the *Home Journal,* October 20, 1849, p. 2 (reprinted in H, I, 362–363). The original MS. is probably lost.

311. The present text is a composite of that portion of the letter printed by Ingram in *Appleton's Journal,* May 1878, p. 428, and that printed in Ingram, II, 213–215 (H, XVII, 345–346, follows the *Life* text). The *Life* fragment, in this instance, was used as the basic text; daggers enclose readings not found in the *Life* text; brackets, except for the date line and place and the note on the signature, enclose readings not found in *Appleton's.* No printing is complete; Quinn (*Poe,* pp. 603–605) prints a composite text that is essentially the same as the one above, but his pointing varies in minor details and he shows but half the ellipses necessary to an understanding of Ingram's editing. Both of Ingram's versions omit signature. A search of the items in the Ingram collection (University of Virginia) failed to reveal Ingram's source for his printings, though it was probably a transcript of the original made by Mrs. Richmond. Definite dating of the letter seems impossible: Ingram, Harrison, and Phillips leave it undated; Woodberry (II, 417) dates it "May, 1849," Allen (II, 804–805) quotes part and dates it "March, 1849," and Quinn, *supra,* suggests "the spring of 1849" and after April 21, 1849. "For Annie" appeared in the *Home Journal,* April 28, 1849, which was probably in advance of date (see Letter 310 and note); thus Mrs. Richmond could have received the *Home Journal* and written to Poe by April 28. Since Poe visited Mrs. Richmond during the last week in May (see Letter 316), leaving Fordham on May 23, the present dating of the letter has been adopted; however, a date late in April is more probable. Poe is answering a letter from Mrs. Richmond (no MS. or printing known); a conjectural dating of which would be April 26–May 21, 1849. (See Note 312.)

312. Source: facsimile of original MS. (3 pp.) in SLP, between pp. 14–15. The original MS. is unlocated. The letter was first printed by Eugene Field in *America,* II (April 11, 1889), 45–46, in an article entitled "Poe, Patterson and Oquawka." Allen, without authority, dates the letter April 8 (A, II, 809–810); there is no address or postmark on the fourth page of the letter, a separate cover apparently having been used and since lost. Patterson's May 7, 1849, letter to Poe was answered May 23, after a week's delay; thus up to a week or ten days can be allowed for the transit of a letter between New York and Oquawka. Since Patterson introduced his May 7 letter with "I hasten to reply . . ." Poe's letter must have been written at least a week before, but in April. Furthermore, Poe's letter to Mrs. Richmond, April 28 (?)–May 23 (?), 1849, does not mention Patterson's offer nor carry the note of optimism that the December 18, 1848, letter from Oquawka certainly must have inspired. Thus, the letter to Mrs. Richmond was written probably prior to Poe's reply to Patterson, and his letter to Mrs. Richmond is dated April 28 (?)–May 23 (?), 1849, though very likely before the last day of April,

and his reply to Patterson is dated April 30 (?) in order to place it after the letter to Mrs. Richmond and still place it in the April dating which the holograph carries (see Letter 311).

The Poe–Patterson correspondence consists of 9 letters. Of these, the 4 from Poe (April 30 (?), May 23, July 19, and August 7, 1849) and 2 of Patterson's (the memoranda of May 7 and the letter of August 21, 1849) are printed in SLP, the last cited having been printed in Gill, pp. 232–233. These letters do not include three unlocated ones from Patterson (December 18, 1848, and 2 between May 23 and June 7, mentioned by Poe in his letter of July 19, 1849).

313. Source: photostat of original (1 p.) in the Huntington Library (HM 21873). The letter was first printed (without date) in the Anderson Galleries Catalogue, November 29, 1920, item 346 (P, II, 1403–1404, prints the letter from MS. with date). Poe is answering a letter from Thompson of unknown date (location of original unknown).

314. Source: photostat of original MS. (1 p.) in the William H. Koester collection, Baltimore; reproduced in facsimile in the American Art Association Catalogue, February 28–March 1, 1935, item 344, facing p. 84, where it was first printed. The year date is established by the reference to "For Annie" (see Letter 309 and note). "Edgar Poe" is written in the upper left corner of the MS., perhaps by Mrs. Lewis. Poe is replying, it seems, to a letter from Mrs. Lewis, *ante* May 17, 1849, unlocated; and the present letter implies a further note from Mrs. Lewis, also unlocated.

315. Source: photostat of original MS. (2 pp.) in the William H. Koester collection, Baltimore. The letter was first printed in Henkels' Catalogue, April 10, 1935, item 78. The MS. is torn along upper left margin but no words are missing. In the upper left corner of the MS. is a notation: "ans^d May 20," which indicates that Putnam replied promptly to Poe's letter, though the item is unlocated.

316. Source: facsimile of original MS. (2 pp.) in SLP, between pp. 20–21 and 22–23. The original MS. is unlocated. The letter was first printed by Eugene Field in "Poe, Patterson and Oquawka," in *America*, II (April 11, 1889), 47. Allen (A, II, 811, 815) misdates it "May 7." The cover of the letter was postmarked May 25 at New York. Poe is answering Patterson's letter of May 7, only the memoranda of which are known (see SLP, p. 16).

317. Source: photostat of original (1 p.) in the Wrenn Library of the University of Texas. The letter was first printed in Griswold's "Preface" to the *Literati* (1850; reprinted in *Works*, I (1853), xxii–xxiii), not only with additions and omissions in the first part of the letter, but also an added "P.S." not found in the MS. (see also Quinn, *Poe*, p. 670). The MS. is undated, but has been assigned by various editors to March or June; also the MS. has been docketed "about '45," in a strange hand, but this date is clearly wrong. In his letter to Annie Richmond, March 23, 1849, Poe speaks of "For Annie" as of recent composition, and to her, April 28 (?)–May 23 (?), 1849, he mentions "Annabel Lee" for the first time; since Poe, in order to have "a true copy," sent "For Annie" to the *Home Journal,* where it was printed, April 28,

1849, and since Griswold says he knew of "Annabel Lee" in June 1849 (see Campbell, *Poems,* p. 293), the most probable date for the above letter to Griswold seems to be between April 28 and June, 1849; therefore, May (?), 1849, is here given as a satisfactory guess. Quinn (*Poe,* p. 670) suggests the possibility of a "P.S." that mentioned "Annabel Lee," to which Griswold added the forged references to Graham, Godey, and Eveleth; but besides Quinn's statement that such a postscript would scarcely be cut off for the sake of framing the letter, certainly both Poe and Griswold knew at this time that Graham no longer owned *Graham's* (see Letter 319), and "Annabel Lee" could not be sold to him, though it might have been sent to Godey. In all probability, there was no postscript to Poe's original letter.

318. Source: photostat of original (1 p.) in the Pierpont Morgan Library. The letter is here first printed.

319. Source: photostat of original MS. (2 pp.) in the William H. Koester collection, Baltimore. The letter is here first printed in full. Ingram presumably had a transcript from Mrs. Richmond, but deleted portions; subsequent printings have followed Ingram (*Appleton's Journal,* May 1878, p. 428; Ingram, II, 216–217), with or without further deletions. References to Oquawka, Illinois, the home of E. H. N. Patterson (see Poe's letters to him), and to Tuel place the present letter in 1849. The first few lines of the above letter suggest an exchange of correspondence between Poe and Mrs. Richmond, following his visit with her during the last week in May (see Note 311). In the second paragraph of page 2, the bracketed emendation is due to a heavily scratched out name in the MS. Concerning Poe's actual departure for Richmond, see the note to Letter 324. This is the last known letter from Poe to Annie Richmond.

320. Source: photostat of original MS. (2 pp.) in the Berg collection of the New York Public Library. The letter is here first printed in its correct form; Ingram (II, 217–219) and Wilson (PE (reprint), pp. 22–24), used Eveleth's copy made for Ingram (now in the Ingram collection, University of Virginia), but Eveleth omitted all of the second paragraph, except the last two sentences, replacing the omission with: "You have had time to form an opinion of 'Eureka'." He also omitted from the third paragraph, "I had him especially in view when I wrote the passage." He made certain other minor changes. Harrison (XVII, 360–362) followed Ingram. Poe is replying to Eveleth's letter of February 17, 1849, the original MS. of which is in the New York Public Library, and which is printed in EP (reprint), pp. 22–23; however, Eveleth had written Poe on March 9 and July 9, 1848, but Poe had not answered. The present letter is Poe's last to Eveleth, but Eveleth appears to have written one more to Poe, which is unlocated; it is cited by Eveleth from an undated letter to him from Mrs. Clemm, while she was visiting Annie Richmond in Lowell: she wrote, "Your last letter to him was sent to me from Richmond after he had gone to dwell with the angels" (see PE (reprint), p. 3).

321. Source: photostat of original (1 p.) in the Boston Public Library. The letter was first printed by Woodberry, *Century Magazine,* XLVIII (Octo-

ber 1894), 864. Griswold did not print the letter, but did insert in his "Preface," p. xxii, under the date of "early 1849," for which there is no known original, a longer letter that is undoubtedly a forgery of the present one. The Griswold version of the letter (reprinted in H, XVII, 326–327) cites at least two articles Poe did not write and strikes a fawning note not characteristic of Poe's dealings with Griswold.

This is probably the last letter between Poe and Griswold; certainly it is the last known to have been written. Mrs. Susan Archer Talley Weiss (see H, I, 323) says Poe wrote to Griswold inviting him to become Poe's literary executor, and that Poe showed her the reply. Neither letter has ever appeared in MS. or in printed form, and almost certainly never existed, though many biographers of Poe have leaned kindly to the possibility of existence of one or both. Mrs. Clemm, in signing over to Griswold the right to publish Poe's works, mentioned that it was Poe's "express wish and injunction" that Griswold edit the MSS., but there is no indication of written correspondence to that effect. Griswold himself states in his "Memoir" that he did not know of such a wish on Poe's part until after Poe's death. If Mrs. Weiss's statement were to be accepted as true, the date of the letters would probably be late August or September 1849 (see Quinn, *Poe*, pp. 635–636); Miss Mary Phillips (II, 1557) dates Poe's, "June 29, 1849," from Fordham; Woodberry (II, 450) inclines to a June dating. Until evidence appears that is more reliable than that now at hand, it must be supposed that Poe did not invite Griswold by letter to become his literary executor, Griswold did not accept by letter, and the present letter, above, is the last known one between the two men.

322. Source: letter printed in the Merwin-Clayton catalogue, May 13, 1912, item 965-A, where it was first printed. The catalogue states that the letter is an a.l.s., 1 page octavo, with envelope; its present location is unknown. Poe is replying to Root's letter of *ante* June 28, 1849, which is unlocated.

323. Source: printed letter in C. Chauncey Burr's "Character of Edgar A. Poe," *The Nineteenth Century*, v (February 1852), 29, where it was first printed, with Mrs. Clemm's permission, but as extracts only, from the original MS., which is now lost. Burr begins each paragraph with quotation marks; where he uses end quotation the present text uses ellipses to indicate an obvious omission from the MS. The letter was written in Philadelphia, not New York (see John Sartain, *Reminiscences of a Very Old Man*, p. 206 ff.; see also Letters 326, 327 and 328).

324. Source: photostat of original MS. (1 p.) in the William H. Koester collection, Baltimore. The letter was first printed in Quinn, *Poe*, p. 633, but without date and with the implication that it belongs at the time of the September letters to Mrs. Clemm and Mrs. Lewis.

325. Source: printed letter in C. Chauncey Burr's "Character of Edgar A. Poe," *The Nineteenth Century*, v (February 1852), 29, where it was first printed with Mrs. Clemm's permission, but as extracts only, from the original MS., which is now lost.

326. Source: printed letter in C. Chauncey Burr's "Character of Edgar A. Poe," *The Nineteenth Century*, v (February 1852), 30, where it was first printed with Mrs. Clemm's permission from the original MS., which is now lost; the absence of end quotation marks and the presence of the signature may suggest that the present letter is printed in full. Though not fully dated, the letter certainly belongs to July 14, 1849, since its content generally and tone in particular belong prior to the letter of July 19. Enclosed in this letter may have been that of "Near Richmond," same date.

327. Source: printed letter in C. Chauncey Burr's "Character of Edgar A. Poe," *The Nineteenth Century*, v (February 1852), 30–31, where it was first printed with Mrs. Clemm's permission, but as extracts only, from the original MS., which is now lost. The letter belongs unquestionably to 1849 (see Letter 326 and note), and according to Burr's pointing and omission of signature is certainly incomplete. Poe is answering Mrs. Clemm's letter of July 15–18 (?), 1849, which was in reply to his request of July 14, Saturday Night; no printing or MS. of her letter is known.

328. Source: facsimile of original MS. (1 p.) in SLP, between pp. 24–25. The original MS. is unlocated. The letter was first printed by Eugene Field in "Poe, Patterson and Oquawka," in *America*, II (April 11, 1889), 24. The letter belongs unquestionably to 1849 (see Letter 316); it is postmarked July 21 from Richmond. The letter is written on page 1 of a folded leaf, pages 2–3 are blank, and page 4 carries the address. Poe is replying to Patterson's two letters, written between May 23–June 7, the location of which is unknown (see Letter 329).

329. Source: facsimile of original MS. (2 pp.) in SLP, between pp. 26–27. The original MS. is unlocated. The letter was first printed in Gill, pp. 232–233; also in SLP, pp. 24–26, from the article in *America*, II (April 11, 1889), 47. The letter, written on a folded leaf, occupies pages 1–2, with page 3 blank and on page 4 the address. It is postmarked from Richmond, August 1[?]; thus it was mailed not before August 10 and perhaps as late as August 16, since Patterson's reply is dated August 21 and states: ". . . I hasten to reply" (see H, XVII, 365–366). Poe is replying to two unlocated letters from Patterson, written between May 23–June 7, 1849.

330. Source: photostat of the MS. fragment (4 pp.) in the Boston Public Library. The letter was first printed by Woodberry in the *Century Magazine*, XLVIII (October 1894), 865–866, from the fragment; the complete letter has never been printed, and the missing portions of the MS. are unlocated, and are undoubtedly lost. The MS. fragment of four pages probably begins with the text of page 3, for the suggested pagination of the fragment is based on pages 3 (?) and 4 (?) being recto and verso of one leaf, and pages 5 (?) and 6 (?) being recto and verso of another leaf. Some eight lines are missing from the bottom portion of page 3 (?), above; the tearing off of these lines destroyed most of the wording of the first line of the "Wednesday Night" message. Only "dear Muddy" is clear; suggested emendations are highly conjectural, and asterisks have been used, as accurately as possible, to represent missing letters. Dating the present letter presents diffi-

culties. Poe seems to have written Mrs. Clemm a letter that can be dated
only tentatively as August 2–14, and that arrived in New York after she
mailed her letter to Annie Richmond, August 4 (MS. in the Ingram collection, University of Virginia). Mrs. Clemm told Annie that she had received no word from Poe for two weeks, probably referring to Poe's letter
of July 19, 1849; also, she is undoubtedly alluding to this July 19 letter in
her communication to Griswold, August 27 (H, XVII, 394–395) wherein
she says that Poe "is getting better and hopes he will soon be able to attend
to business." Another letter from Poe to Mrs. Clemm, the one printed
above, can be dated August 28–29 (?), 1849; either through Poe's delay
in mailing it or through Mrs. Clemm's in calling for it at the post office,
this letter must have reached her after she wrote to Mrs. Richmond, September 3 (MS. in Ingram collection), and before she wrote to Griswold, September 4 (H, XVII, p. 395), for she told Annie that she had had no letter
for three weeks, but told Griswold, "I have just heard from him, he writes
in fine spirits and says his prospects are excellent." In Mrs. Clemm's letter
to Mrs. Richmond, September 15 (Ingram collection), she says she is enclosing "the only one I received for nearly four weeks"; that is, the only
one since the letter of August 2–14. In the same letter to Mrs. Richmond,
Mrs. Clemm mentions a "note" received "yesterday." Thus, the letter enclosed would be that of August 28–29 (?), and the "note" would be still
another communication from Poe, with the plausible dating of September 12–
13. The next letter in the series, and his final to Mrs. Clemm, is that of
Tuesday, September 18, 1849. Biographers and editors have given various
datings to the present letter, actuated partly by the docketing in a strange
hand at the head of the MS.: "Sept. 1849" (W, II, 326, gives "Sept. [5]";
H, XVII, 368, "Sept"; P, II, 1462, "September early"; and Quinn, *Poe*, p. 626,
n., points out that Wednesday, September 5, would be correct for the
"Wednesday Night" portion of the letter, but that the first portion would
have been earlier). Between July 19 and September 18, the only letters
known to have been written by Mrs. Clemm to Poe are the two mentioned
in his letter to her, September 18, 1849.

331. Source: photostat of original MS. (3 pp.) in the Morgan Library,
New York. The letter was first printed in the *New York Herald*, February 19,
1905, from which it was reprinted in W, II, 331. The dating of the letter
seems established by Miss Ingram's statement (see Quinn, *Poe*, pp. 629–631)
that Poe read "Ulalume" to a group of people at the Hygeia Hotel at Old
Point Comfort on Sunday evening, September 9, 1849, and that she received
a MS. copy of the poem the next day, which would have been Monday,
September 10. The envelope carries no postmark and is addressed merely
"Miss Susan Ingram."

332. Source: photostat of a MS. fragment in Poe's hand and of a transcript
of the whole letter in Maria Clemm's hand (probably), both items being in
the Enoch Pratt Library; the original Poe letter was undoubtedly two pages
in length. Although C. Chauncey Burr printed one paragraph, the letter was
first printed in full in Woodberry (1885), pp. 339–340, the sources being

apparently those used for the present text. The two letters from Mrs. Clemm that Poe is answering are probably her replies to his letter of August 28–29 (?) and his note of September 12–13. Poe lectured on "The Poetic Principle" in Norfolk, not on "Monday" as he says, but on Friday, September 14 (see Quinn, *Poe,* p. 629). If Susan V. C. Ingram's account of her being with Poe in Old Point Comfort, September 9, is true (see Quinn, *Poe,* pp. 629–631), and of Poe's later calling on her family near Norfolk, he may have left Richmond shortly after his letter to Mrs. Clemm, August 28–29 (?), probably wrote the "note" from Old Point Comfort or Norfolk, delivered his lecture, and returned to Richmond, as he says, "last night from Norfolk," on September 17. No MS. or printing of Mrs. Clemm's two letters is known.

333. Source: photostat of original MS. (1 p.) in the William H. Koester collection, Baltimore. The letter was first printed in Quinn, *Poe,* p. 633. Someone, probably Mrs. Lewis, entered the bracketed date at the head of the letter; though the date may indicate the day received, it may well be the date written, for Poe wrote a letter to Mrs. Clemm on Tuesday, September 18, 1849 (Letter 332), in which he says he has just returned to Richmond and found letters from her and a letter from Mrs. Lewis. Poe is replying to two letters from Mrs. Lewis, written sometime between June 30 and September 16, 1849, both of which are unlocated.

BIBLIOGRAPHY AND LIST OF MANUSCRIPT COLLECTIONS

BIBLIOGRAPHY

The following bibliography contains only those items actually used in printing and editing the letters of the canon. It is divided into three units: first, works containing matters pertinent to the editing of the letters; second, works that contained not only printings of letters necessarily used in the canon, but also in some instances editorial comment; and, third, reliable auction sales catalogues which contained letters in facsimile or printed form, originals of which were unavailable.

I

Biographies, bibliographies, edited texts, studies, articles, etc.

Allen, Hervey. *Israfel: the Life and Times of Edgar Allan Poe,* 2 vols. (New York: George H. Doran and Company, 1926), revised, 2 vols. in one (New York: Farrar and Rinehart, 1934). In the notes, when no volume is given, the reference is to the one-volume edition.

American Book-prices Current, vol. I– (New York: Dodd, Mead, 1895–1917; E. P. Dutton, 1918–1928; R. R. Bowker, 1930–).

"American Library, The," *Blackwood's Magazine,* LXII (November 1847), 574–592.

Baltimore *Gazette* (unsigned, undated clipping in the Ingram collection, University of Virginia Library).

Bayless, J. "Another Rufus W. Griswold as a Critic of Poe," *American Literature,* VI (March 1934), 69–72.

Brigham, Clarence S. "Edgar Allan Poe's Contributions to *Alexander's Weekly Messenger,*" *Proceedings of the American Antiquarian Society,* LII (April 1942), 45–125.

Broadway Journal, The [New York], vols. I–II (1845–1846).

Bronson, Walter C. *American Literature* (New York: D. C. Heath, 1900), p. 262.

Brooks, Nathan C. Editorial, *American Museum* [Baltimore], vol. II (May 1839).

Burton's Gentleman's Magazine [Philadelphia], vols. I–VII (1837–1840).

Campbell, Killis. "Gleanings in the Bibliography of Poe," *Modern Language Notes,* XXXII (1917), 267–272.

——. "The Kennedy Papers," *Sewanee Review,* XXV (April 1917), 197–198.

——, ed. *The Poems of Edgar Allan Poe* (Boston: Ginn, 1917).

Cappon, Lester J. *Virginia Newspapers: 1821–1935* (New York: D. Appleton-Century, 1936).

Charleston [S.C.] *Southern Patriot,* Review of Thomas Holley Chivers, *The Lost Pleiad,* August 7, 1845, p. 2, col. 2.

Dictionary of American Biography (New York: Charles Scribner's Sons), IV (1930), 388–389; V (1930), 469; VI (1931), 166; VII (1931), 628; IX (1932), 68–69; XI (1933), 285–286; XIII (1934), 54–55; XVII (1935), 546–547; XVIII (1936), 222–223, 528–529, 618; XIX (1936), 579–580; XX (1936), 120.

Evans, May G. "Poe in Amity Street," *Maryland Historical Magazine*, XXXVI (December 1941), 363–380.

Friedman, William F. "Edgar Allan Poe, Cryptographer," *American Literature*, VIII (November 1936), 266–280.

Gill, William F. *The Life of Edgar Allan Poe* (New York: C. T. Dillingham, 1877).

Godey's Lady's Book [Philadelphia], vols. X–XL (1835–1849).

Graham's Magazine [Philadelphia], vols. XV–XXXVI (1839–1850).

"Hale, Sarah Josepha," *Appleton's Cyclopedia of American Biography* (New York: D. Appleton and Company, 1888), III, 35.

Harrison, James A., ed. *The Complete Works of Edgar Allan Poe*, 17 vols. (New York: T. Y. Crowell, 1902).

Heartman, Charles F., and James R. Canny. *A Bibliography of Edgar Allan Poe* (Hattiesburg, Miss.: The Book Farm, 1940).

Heartman, Charles F., and Kenneth Rede. *A Census of First Editions and Source Materials by Edgar Allan Poe in American Collections*, 2 vols. (Metuchen, N. J.: Charles F. Heartman, 1932).

Hudson, Ruth L. "Poe and Disraeli," *American Literature*, VIII (January 1937), 402–416.

Hull, William D., Jr. "A Canon of the Critical Works of Edgar Allan Poe" (Unpublished University of Virginia Doctoral Dissertation, 1940).

Ingram, John H. *Edgar Allan Poe: His Life, Letters and Opinions*, 2 vols. (London: J. Hogg, 1880).

——. University of Virginia Library MS. revision of *Edgar Allan Poe: His Life, Letters and Opinions*.

Jackson, David K. "Brief Mention," *American Literature*, XIII (November 1941), 283.

——. *Contributors to the Southern Literary Messenger: 1834–1864* (Charlottesville, Virginia: The Historical Publishing Co., 1936).

——. *Poe and the Southern Literary Messenger* (Richmond: Dietz Press, 1934).

"Lecture of Edgar A. Poe, Esq.," Baltimore *Sun*, January 31, 1844, p. 2, col. 2.

Lewis, Estelle Anna. *Myths of the Minstrel* (New York: D. Appleton, 1852).

——. *Records of the Heart* (New York: George S. Appleton, 1844).

"Literati of New York, The," *Democratic Review*, XXIII (August 1848), 158–160.

Mabbott, Thomas O. "A Few Notes on Poe," *Modern Language Notes*, XXXV (1920), 374.

——, ed. *Al Aaraaf, Tamerlane and Minor Poems* (New York: Facsimile Text Society, 1933).

——. "English Publications of Poe's 'Valdemar Case,'" *Notes and Queries,* CLXXXIII (November 21, 1942), 311–312.

——, ed. *Merlin, Baltimore, 1827, Together with Recollections of Edgar A. Poe,* by Lambert A. Wilmer (New York: Scholars' Facsimiles and Reprints, 1941).

——, ed. *Politian, an Unfinished Tragedy by Edgar A. Poe* (Richmond: The Poe Shrine, 1923).

——, ed. *Tamerlane and Other Poems* (New York: Facsimile Text Society, 1941).

——, ed. *The Raven and Other Poems* (New York: Facsimile Text Society, 1942).

Minor, Benjamin B. *The Southern Literary Messenger: 1834–1864* (New York: Neale Publishing Co., 1905).

More, Paul Elmer. "Margaret Fuller," *Cambridge History of American Literature* (New York: Macmillan, 1933), I, 343.

Mott, Frank Luther. *A History of American Magazines,* 3 vols. (Cambridge, Mass.: Harvard University Press, 1938–1939).

New York *Morning Express,* Editorial, December 15, 1846, p. 2, col. 1.

Neu, Jacob L. "Rufus Wilmot Griswold," *Studies in English,* vol. v (Austin: University of Texas, 1925).

Opal, The, ed. by Mrs. S. J. Hale (New York: J. C. Riker, 1845).

Ostrom, John W. "Another Griswold Forgery in a Poe Letter," *Modern Language Notes,* LVIII (May 1943), 394–396.

——. "Two 'Lost' Poe Letters," *American Notes & Queries,* I (August 1941), 68–69.

Phillips, Mary E. *Edgar Allan Poe, the Man,* 2 vols. (Philadelphia: John C. Winston, 1926).

"Porter, Miss Jane," *Allibone's Dictionary of Authors* (Philadelphia: J. B. Lippincott, 1890), II, 1645–1646.

Quinn, Arthur H. *Edgar Allan Poe: a Critical Biography* (New York: D. Appleton-Century, 1941).

Robertson, John W. *Commentary on Edgar A. Poe,* 2 vols. (San Francisco: Edwin and Robert Grabhorn, 1934).

——. *Edgar A. Poe, a Psychopathic Study* (New York: Putnam, 1923).

Sartain, John. *Reminiscences of a Very Old Man* (New York: D. Appleton, 1899).

South in the Building of the Nation, The (Richmond: The Southern Historical Publication Society, 1909).

Southern Literary Messenger, The [Richmond], vols. I–XV (1834–1849).

"Tazewell, Littleton Waller," *The South in the Building of the Nation* (Richmond: The Southern Historical Publication Society, 1909), XII, 445–446.

"Teacher Wanted, A," Baltimore *Patriot,* March 12, 1835, p. 3, col. 3.

University of Virginia Library, Ingram Collection, n. d., "Miller-Townsend Scrap Book of Dr. Thomas H. Chivers."

Varner, John G. "Sarah Helen Whitman, Seeress of Providence," 2 vols. (Unpublished University of Virginia Doctoral Dissertation, 1941).

Weiss, Mrs. Susan Archer Talley. "The Last Days of Edgar A. Poe," *Scribner's*, XV (March 1878), 707–716.

Williams, Stanley T. "New Letters About Poe," *Yale Review*, XIV (July 1925), 755–773.

Wilmer, Lambert A. *Our Press Gang* (Philadelphia: J. T. Lloyd, 1860).

Wilson, James Southall. "The Devil Was In It," *American Mercury*, XXIV (October 1931), 214–220.

Wimsatt, W. K., Jr. "Poe and the Mystery of Mary Rogers," *Publications of the Modern Language Association*, LVI (March 1941), 230–248.

——. "What Poe Knew About Cryptography," *Publications of the Modern Language Association*, LVIII (September 1943), 754–779.

Woodberry, George E. *Edgar Allan Poe* (Boston: Houghton Mifflin, 1885).

——. *The Life of Edgar Allan Poe*, 2 vols. (Boston: Houghton Mifflin, 1909).

Wyllie, John C. "A List of the Texts of Poe's Tales," *Humanistic Studies in Honor of John Calvin Metcalf* (Charlottesville, Va.: University of Virginia Studies), I (1941), 322–338.

II

Works Chiefly Important as Sources of Letters

Beweley, Sir Edmund T. "The True Ancestry of Edgar Allan Poe," *New York Genealogical and Biographical Record*, XXXVIII (1907), 55–69.

Bixby, W. K. *Some Edgar Allan Poe Letters* (St. Louis: W. K. Bixby, 1915).

Burr, C. Chauncey. "Character of Edgar A. Poe," *The Nineteenth Century*, V (February 1852), 19–33.

Calendar of Virginia State Papers, X (arranged, edited, and printed under the authority and direction of H. W. Flournoy. Richmond, 1892), 518.

Campbell, Killis. "Poe and the Southern Literary Messenger in 1837," *The Nation*, LXXXIX (July 1, 1909), 9–10.

——. "Unique Poe Items," *Literary Review*, March 5, 1921, p. 14 (clipping in Ingram collection, University of Virginia Library).

Chase, Lewis. "A New Poe Letter," *American Literature*, VI (March 1934), 66–69.

Christmas Book, A (published by Hunter College of the City of New York, December 1937).

Cooper, James Fenimore, ed. *Correspondence of James Fenimore-Cooper*, 2 vols. (New Haven: Yale University Press, 1922).

Cosmopolitan Magazine (undated clipping in Ingram collection, University of Virginia Library).

Daughters of the American Revolution, LXVII (September 1933), 539–546.

Didier, Eugene L., ed. "Memoir" to *The Life and Poems of Edgar Allan Poe* (New York: W. J. Widdleton, 1877).

"Edgar Allan Poe: an Unpublished Letter," Baltimore *American*, April 4, 1881, and New York *Herald*, same date (clippings, n. p., in the Ingram collection, University of Virginia Library, filed under April 1, 1841).

Eveleth, George W. "Edgar A. Poe," Portland [Me.] *Transcript*, June 8 and July 6, 1850 (data through courtesy of Mr. Clarence S. Brigham of the American Antiquarian Society, Worcester, Mass.).

Field, Eugene, ed. *Some Letters of Edgar Allan Poe to E. H. N. Patterson of Oquawka, Illinois* (Chicago: Caxton Club, 1898). Printed earlier in *America*, vol. II (April 1889).

Fontainas, André, trans. *Edgar Poe Lettres à John Allan* (Paris: G. Crés et Cie, 1930).

Gordon, Armistead C. *Memories and Memorials of William Gordon McCabe*, 2 vols. (Richmond, 1925).

Graham, George R. "The Late Edgar Allan Poe," *Graham's Magazine*, XXXVI (March 1850), 224–226.

Griswold, Rufus W., ed. "Preface" and "Memoir" to *Works of Edgar A. Poe*, 3 vols. (New York: J. S. Redfield, 1853).

Griswold, W. M., ed. *Some Passages from the Correspondence of Rufus W. Griswold* (Cambridge, Mass., 1898).

Haight, G. S. *Mrs. Sigourney, the Sweet Singer of Hartford* (New Haven: Yale University Press, 1930).

Harrison, James A., ed. *Last Letters of Edgar Allan Poe to Sarah Helen Whitman* (New York: G. P. Putnam's Sons, 1909).

——, ed. *Life and Letters of Edgar Allan Poe*, 2 vols. (New York: T. Y. Crowell, 1903).

——, ed. *The Complete Works of Edgar Allan Poe*, 17 vols. (New York: T. Y. Crowell, 1902).

Howe, M. A. D. "Edgar Allan Poe," *The Bookman*, V (May 1897), 205–216.

Ingram, John H., ed. "Memoir" to *The Works of Edgar Allan Poe*, 4 vols. (Edinburgh: Adam and Charles Black, 1874).

——. "Poe and Stella," *Albany Review* [London], I (July 1907), 417–423.

——. "Unpublished Correspondence of Poe," *Appleton's Journal*, IV (May 1878), 425–428.

Joline, Adrian H. *Meditations of an Autograph Collector* (New York: Harper and Bros., 1902).

"Letters of E. A. Poe, 1845–1849," *Bulletin of the New York Public Library*, VI (January 1902), 7–11.

Lippard, George. *Herbert Tracy* (Philadelphia: R. G. Berford, 1844).

Longfellow, Samuel, ed. *Henry Wadsworth Longfellow: Final Memorials* (Boston: Ticknor, 1887).

Mabbott, Thomas O. "Correspondence of John Tomlin," *Notes and Queries*, CLXII (June 18, 1932), 437.

——. "Letters from Mary E. Hewitt to Poe," *A Christmas Book* (published by Hunter College of the City of New York, December 1937), pp. 116–121.

——. "On Poe's 'Tales of the Folio Club,' " *Sewanee Review*, XXXVI (April 1928), 171–176.

——. "The Letters of George W. Eveleth to Edgar Allan Poe," *Bulletin of the New York Public Library,* XXVI (March 1922), 171–195. Also separately printed.

——, ed. *The Raven and Other Poems* (New York: Facsimile Text Society, No. 56, 1942).

Neal, John. *Wandering Recollections of a Somewhat Busy Life* (Boston: Roberts, 1869).

New York *Times,* January 28, 1917, Magazine Section, p. 14; *ibid.,* June 17, 1917 (clipping, n. p., Ingram collection, University of Virginia Library); *ibid.,* January 12, 1930, part 2, p. 4.

"Notes on the Genealogy of the Poe Family," *Gulf States Historical Magazine,* I (January 1903), 281–283.

Ostrom, John W. "A Poe Correspondence Re-edited," *Americana,* XXXIV (July 1940), 409–446.

——. "Two Unpublished Poe Letters," *Americana,* XXXVI (January 1942), 67–71.

Philadelphia *Ledger,* January 12, 1912 (clipping, n. p., in J. H. Ingram, unpublished MS.-revision of his *Life* of Poe, University of Virginia Library).

Poe, Edgar Allan. "Correspondence," *Broadway Journal,* I (March 8, 1845), 159.

"Poe Letters Found in a Pillow-case," *Current Opinion,* LXX (June 1921), 823.

Portland [Me.] *Daily Advertiser,* April 26, 1850 (copy of article sent through the courtesy of Dr. Arthur H. Quinn).

Quinn, Arthur H., and Richard H. Hart. *Edgar Allan Poe Letters and Documents in the Enoch Pratt Free Library* (New York: Scholars' Facsimiles and Reprints, 1941).

Richmond *Courier and Daily Compiler,* September 2, 1836, p. 2, cols. 4–5.

Richmond *Times-Despatch,* November 11, 1923, pt. 7, p. 3.

Robinson, F. W. *The Library of George W. Childs* (Philadelphia: Collins, 1882).

Sears, Edward S. Memphis *Commercial Appeal,* November 15, 1925, sec. 4, p. 7.

Spannuth, Jacob E., and Thomas O. Mabbott. *Doings of Gotham* (Pottsville, Pa.: 1929).

[Spencer, Edward]. "The Memory of Poe," New York *Herald,* March 27, 1881, n. p. (clipping in the Ingram collection, University of Virginia).

Stanard, Mary Newton, ed. *Edgar Allan Poe Letters Till Now Unpublished* (Philadelphia: J. B. Lippincott, 1925).

Stedman, E. C., and George E. Woodberry, eds. "Memoir" to *Works of Edgar Allan Poe,* 10 vols. (Chicago: Stone and Kimball, 1894).

Stoddard, R. H., ed. "Memoir" to *Select Works of Edgar Allan Poe, Poetical and Prose* (New York: Widdleton, 1880).

——, ed. "Memoir" to *The Works of Edgar Allan Poe,* 6 vols. (London: Kegan Paul, Trench, 1884).

Tomlin, John, ed. "Autobiography of a Monomaniac," *Holden's Dollar Magazine*, II (December 1848), 718.

"Unpublished Letter of Edgar Allan Poe, An," *The Autograph*, I, No. 3 (January–February 1912), 41–43.

"Unpublished Letter of Poe, An," *The Dial*, XLIV (January 16, 1908), 32–33.

Washington [D. C.] *Post*, January 17, 1909 (clipping in Ingram collection, University of Virginia Library, filed under 1909).

Whiting, Lillian. *Life of Kate Field* (Boston: Little, Brown, 1899).

Whitty, James H., ed. "Introduction" to *The Complete Poems of Edgar Allan Poe* (Boston: Houghton Mifflin, 1911).

——. "Poe in England and Scotland," *The Bookman*, XLIV (September 1916), 14–21.

Willis, Nathaniel P. "Death of Edgar A. Poe," *Home Journal*, October 20, 1849, p. 2.

——. "Editorial," *Home Journal*, January 9, 1847.

Wilson, James Grant. *Life and Letters of Fitz-Greene Halleck* (New York: D. Appleton, 1869).

——. "Memorials of Edgar Allan Poe," *Independent* [New York], March 1901, pp. 940–941.

——. *Observer* [New York], April 26, 1900, p. 528.

Wilson, James Southall. "The Letters of Edgar A. Poe to George W. Eveleth." *Alumni Bulletin*, University of Virginia, XVII (January 1924), 34–59. Also separately printed.

——. "Unpublished Letters of Edgar Allan Poe," *Century Magazine*, CVII (March 1924), 652–656.

Woodberry, George E. "Selections from the Correspondence of Edgar Allan Poe," *Century Magazine*, XLVIII (August), 572–583; (September), 725–737; (October 1894), 854–866.

——. "The Poe–Chivers Papers," *Century Magazine*, LXV (1903), 435–447, 545–558.

III

Auction Sales Catalogues

American Art Association, New York. Catalogues: April 21, 1910; April 20–21, pt. 3, 1921; March 18–19, 1925; December 16–17, 1929; May 2–3, pt. 1, 1934; February 28–March 1, 1935; April 24–25, 1935; November 13–14, 1935; November 11–12, 1937; November 23–24, 1937.

Anderson Galleries, New York. Catalogues: October 14, 1904; January 10, 1908; November 22, 1909; December 7–8, pt. 2, 1909; April 24, 1911; May 27, 1914; December 15, 1914; November 13–14, 1916; January 25–26, 1917; March 17, 1920; November 29, 1920; March 14–15, 1921; January 18, 1922; May 15, 1922; April 29, 1924; November 11, 1924; January 14–15, 1925; April 27, 1925; February 1–3, pt. 2, 1926; November 15–16, 1926; January 21–24, pt. 2, 1929; January 4–5, 1934.

Bangs and Company, New York. Catalogues: April 11, 1896; February 16, 1898.

Barnet J. Beyer, New York. (Undated facsimile, item 364, in Ingram collection, University of Virginia Library, filed under Poe to Lewis J. Cist, September 18, 1841.)

Stan V. Henkels, Philadelphia. Catalogues: May 5, 1903; February 22, 1907; April 10, 1935; November 20, 1935.

N. A. Kovach, Los Angeles. Catalogue: September 22, 1933.

C. F. Libbie, Boston. Catalogue: April 24–25, 1895.

Thomas Madigan, New York. Catalogue: November, 1923.

Merwin-Clayton, New York. Catalogues: May 14, 1906; January 18, 1911; May 13, 1912.

William D. Morley, Philadelphia. Catalogue: May 19, 1941.

Ernest D. North, New York. Catalogue: October, 1905 (*Collection of Autograph Letters and MSS.*).

Parke-Bernet Galleries, Inc., New York. Catalogues: May 24, 1939; January 15–16, 1941; April 5–6, 1943; October 17–18, 1944; November 6–8, 1944.

Sotheby, London. Catalogue: December 18–19, 1934.

Swann Galleries, New York. Catalogue: January 20, 1944.

LIST OF MANUSCRIPT COLLECTIONS

Authors' Club, New York City
Boston Public Library, Boston, Massachusetts
Connecticut Historical Society, Hartford, Connecticut
Dumbarton Oaks Research Library, Georgetown, Washington, D. C.
Enoch Pratt Free Library, Baltimore, Maryland
Harvard College Library, Cambridge, Massachusetts
Henry E. Huntington Library and Art Gallery, San Marino, California
Hickory Hill Library, Greenwich, Conn.
Ingram Collection, Alderman Library, University of Virginia, Charlottesville, Virginia
Iowa State Department of History and Archives, Des Moines, Iowa
Library of Congress, Washington, D. C.
Longfellow House, Cambridge, Massachusetts
New York Public Library, New York City
Pennsylvania Historical Society, Philadelphia, Pennsylvania
Pierpont Morgan Library, New York City
Poe Shrine, Richmond, Virginia
United States Military Academy, West Point, New York
University of Texas Library, Austin, Texas
University of Virginia, Charlottesville, Virginia
Valentine Museum, Richmond, Virginia
Yale University Library, New Haven, Connecticut

Manuscript Collections (Individual):

  Coleman, George P., Colonial Williamsburg Architectural Division, Williamsburg, Virginia

  Cooper, James Fenimore, Cooperstown, New York

  Gimbel, Richard G., Philadelphia, Pennsylvania

  Hart, Charles C., Washington, D. C.

  Koester, William H., Baltimore, Maryland

  Lilly, Josiah K., Jr., Indianapolis, Indiana

  Mabbott, Thomas O., New York City

  Martin, H. Bradley, New York City

  McCabe, William G., Charleston, South Carolina

  Prescott, Mrs. Sherburne (See The Hickory Hill Library, *above*), Greenwich, Connecticut

  Rosenbach, Dr. A. S. W., Philadelphia, Pennsylvania

Auction Sales and Book Catalogues:

  American Art Association, New York

  Anderson Galleries, New York

  Bangs and Company, New York

  Benjamin, Walter R., New York

  Beyer, Barnet J., New York

  Dodd, Robert H., New York

  Dodd Mead Company, New York

  Goodspeed's, Boston

  Henkels, Stan V., Philadelphia

  Kovach, N. A., Los Angeles

  Libbie, C. F., Boston

  Madigan, Thomas, New York

  Merwin-Clayton, New York

  Morley, William D., Philadelphia

  Parke-Bernet Galleries, New York

  Sotheby, London, England

  Swann Galleries, New York

REVISED CHECK LIST OF
POE'S CORRESPONDENCE

ABBREVIATIONS

(for fuller information see Bibliography)

*	letter collected in *The Letters of Edgar Allan Poe*.
F	*facsimile available in item cited*.
(?)	following date of entry indicates item accepted as written, though unlocated in MS. or print; and included on basis of data acceptable to the editor.
[?]	following date of entry indicates uncertainty as to whether letter was ever written; after a book source, original MS., or correspondent's name, indicates questionable authenticity, though admission of entry with such restriction made on basis of extant data.
[ ]	editorial interpolations.
A	Allen, Hervey, *Israfel* (2 vols.).
ABC	*American Book-Prices Current*.
Allen, *Israfel*	Allen, Hervey, *Israfel* (1 vol.).
a.l.s.	autograph letter signed.
Bixby	*Some Edgar Allan Poe Letters in the Collection of W. K. Bixby*.
Cappon	Cappon, Lester J., *Virginia Newspapers: 1821–1935*.
EP and	Mabbott, Thomas O., "The Letters of George W.
EP (reprint)	Eveleth to Edgar Allan Poe."
Gill	Gill, William F., *The Life of Edgar Allan Poe*.
H	Harrison, James A., *The Complete Works of Edgar Allan Poe*.
Heartman and Canny	Heartman, Charles F., and Canny, James R., *A Bibliography of Edgar Allan Poe*.
Hull	Hull, William D., "A Canon of the Critical Works of Edgar Allan Poe."
Ingram	Ingram, John H., *Edgar Allan Poe*.
LL	Harrison, James A., *Last Letters of Edgar Allan Poe to Sarah Helen Whitman*.
L and L	Harrison, James A., *Life and Letters of Edgar Allan Poe*.
Life	see Ingram.
OCL	Ostrom, John W., ed., *Check List of Letters to and from Poe*.
P	Phillips, Mary E., *Edgar Allan Poe, the Man*.

PC	Heartman, Charles F., *A Census of First Editions and Source Materials of Edgar Allan Poe in American Collections.*
PE and PE (reprint)	Wilson, James S., "The Letters of Edgar A. Poe to George W. Eveleth."
Pratt	Quinn, Arthur H., and Hart, Richard H., *Edgar Allan Poe Letters and Documents in the Enoch Pratt Free Library.*
Preface	Griswold, Rufus W., *Works of Edgar Allan Poe,* "Preface" from vol. I.
Quinn, *Poe*	Quinn, Arthur H., *Edgar Allan Poe.*
Quinn and Hart	see Pratt.
SLM	*Southern Literary Messenger.*
SLP	Field, Eugene, *Some Letters of Edgar Allan Poe to E. H. N. Patterson of Oquawka, Illinois.*
Varner	Varner, John G., "Sarah Helen Whitman: Seeress of Providence."
VL	Stanard, Mary Newton, *Edgar Allan Poe Letters Till Now Unpublished.*
Whitty	Whitty, James H., *The Complete Poems of Edgar Allan Poe.*
W	Woodberry, George E., *The Life of Edgar Allan Poe.*
Woodberry (1885)	Woodberry, George E., *Edgar Allan Poe.*
Wyllie, *Poe's Tales*	Wyllie, John C., "A List of the Texts of Poe's Tales."

1817

Aug. 14   John Allan or Frances Allan (Cheltenham, England) to Poe (London). Cited in John Allan to George Dubourg, Aug. 14, 1817 (Quinn, *Poe*, 71).   1

1824

Oct. 25   William Henry Leonard Poe (Baltimore) to Poe (Richmond). Cited in John Allan to W. H. L. Poe, Nov. 21, 1824 (Quinn, *Poe*, 89).   2

* Nov. 17   Poe and John Lyle (Richmond) to Governor of Virginia (Richmond). Original in Virginia State Library   3

* Nov. 23   Poe and John Lisle [Lyle] (Richmond) to Peter V. Daniel (Richmond). Original in Virginia State Library   4

1826

ca. Feb. 21 (?)   Poe (Charlottesville) to John Allan (Richmond). Implied in Poe to Allan, Jan. 3, 1831.   5

ca. Feb. 24–27 (?)   John Allan (Richmond) to Poe (University of Virginia). Implied in Poe to Allan, Jan. 3, 1831.   6

* May [25]   Poe (University of Virginia) to John Allan (Richmond). VL 37–39 (F). Original in Valentine Museum.   7

* Sept. 21   Poe (University of Virginia) to John Allan (Richmond). VL 43–45 (F). Original in Valentine Museum.   8

ca. Dec.   John Allan (Richmond) to Poe (University of Virginia). Cited in Poe to Allan, Jan. 3, 1831.   9

late (?)   Poe (University of Virginia) to James Galt (Richmond). Implied in Poe to Allan, Jan. 3, 1831   10 *post* late (?) James Galt (Richmond) to Poe (University of Virginia). Implied in Poe to Allan, Jan. 3, 1831. 11

1827

* [March 19] Poe (Richmond) to John Allan (Richmond).
Monday VL 55–58 (F). Original in Valentine Museum. 12

* [March 20] Poe (Richmond) to John Allan (Richmond).
Tuesday VL 63–64 (F). Original in Valentine Museum. 13

March 20 John Allan (Richmond) to Poe (Richmond). VL 69–70 (F). Original in Valentine Museum. 14

March 25 E. G. Crump (Dinwiddie County, Virginia) to Poe (en route to Boston?). VL 52–53. A 1, 200. P 1, 270–271, 292. Original in Library of Congress. 15

n.d. Poe to Mills Nursery. Cited in Whitty (1917) xxix; P 1, 285; A 1, 189–190. Probably no letter.

1828

* Dec. 1 Poe (Fort Moultrie [Charleston, S. C.]) to John Allan (Richmond). VL 75–78 (F). Original in Valentine Museum. 16

* Dec. 22 Poe (Fortress Monroe [Old Point Comfort, Va.]) to John Allan (Richmond). VL 87–90 (F). Original in Valentine Museum. 17

ante Dec. 23, 1828– John Mackenzie (Richmond) to Poe (Fortress
Feb. 3, 1829 Monroe [Old Point Comfort, Va.]). Cited in Poe to Allan, Feb. 4, 1829. 18

Dec. 23, 1828– Poe (Fortress Monroe [Old Point Comfort,
Feb. 3, 1829 Va.]) to [John] Mackenzie (Richmond). Cited in Poe to Allan, Feb. 4, 1829. 19

1829

January Poe to Mackenzie. See No. 19. OCL 14 is a less satisfactory dating.

* Feb. 4 Poe (Fortress Monroe [Old Point Comfort, Va.]) to John Allan (Richmond). VL 99–102 (F). Original in Valentine Museum. 20

* March 10	Poe (Fortress Monroe [Old Point Comfort, Va.]) to John Allan (Richmond). VL 113–114 (F). Original in Valentine Museum.	21
May 11	William Wirt (Baltimore) to Poe (Baltimore). VL 131–132. Original in Boston Public Library.	22
May 12–27 (?)	Poe (Baltimore) to Robert Walsh (Philadelphia). Implied in Poe to Allan, May 29, 1829.	23
post May 12–27 (?)	Robert Walsh (Philadelphia) to Poe (Baltimore). Implied in Poe to Allan, May 29, 1829.	24
ca. May 14	Poe (Baltimore) to John Allan (Richmond). Cited in Allan to Poe, May 18, 1829, VL 121.	25
May 16	Poe to Allan. See No. 25. OCL 18 is a less satisfactory dating.	
May 18	John Allan (Richmond) to Poe (Baltimore). VL 121–122 (F). Original in Valentine Museum.	26
* May 20	Poe (Baltimore) to John Allan (Richmond). VL 125–126 (F). Original in Valentine Museum.	27
* [*ante* May 27]	Poe (Philadelphia) to Isaac Lea (Philadelphia). Quinn, *Poe*, 138–143 (F). Original formerly in Drexel Institute, but sold by Parke-Bernet Galleries, Oct. 17–18, 1944, item 199.	28
May 27	Poe to Isaac Lea. Misdated in Quinn, *Poe*, 156 n. See No. 28.	
May 27	Isaac Lea (Philadelphia) to Poe (Philadelphia ?). Cited on MS. of Poe to Lea, *ante* May 27, 1829.	29
* May 29	Poe (Baltimore) to John Allan (Richmond). VL 133–136 (F). Original in Valentine Museum.	30
June 8	John Allan (Richmond) to Poe (Baltimore). Cited in Poe to Allan, June 25, 1829.	31
June 10	Poe (Baltimore) to John Allan (Richmond). Cited in Poe to Allan, June 25, 1829.	32
ante June 25	Edward Mosher (Baltimore) to Poe (Baltimore). Cited in Poe to Allan, June 25, 1829.	33
* June 25	Poe (Baltimore) to John Allan (Richmond). VL 145–147 (F). Original in Valentine Museum.	34

* July 15	Poe (Baltimore) to John Allan (Richmond). VL 153–154 (F). Original in Valentine Museum.	35
July 19	John Allan (Richmond) to Poe (Baltimore). Cited in Poe to Allan, July 26, 1829.	36
* July 26	Poe (Baltimore) to John Allan (Richmond). VL 157–161 (F). Original in Valentine Museum.	37
* July 28	Poe (Baltimore) to Carey, Lea and Carey (Philadelphia). A I, 250–251. Original in New York Public Library.	38
Aug. 3	Carey, Lea and Carey (Philadelphia) to Poe (Baltimore). Cited on MS. of Poe to Carey, Lea and Carey, July 28, 1829	39
* Aug. 4	Poe (Baltimore) to John Allan (Richmond). VL 171–173 (F). Original in Valentine Museum.	40
ca. Aug. 7	John Allan (Richmond) to Poe (Baltimore). Cited in Poe to Allan, Aug. 10, 1829.	41
* Aug. 10	Poe (Baltimore) to John Allan (Richmond). VL 181–183 (F). Original in Valentine Museum.	42
Aug. 19	John Allan (Richmond) to Poe (Baltimore). Cited on MS. of Poe to Allan, Aug. 10.	43
ante Sept. (?)	Poe (Baltimore) to John Neal (Boston). Implied by Neal in *The Yankee . . . Gazette,* III (Sept. 1829) 168.	44
ca. Oct. 27–28	John Allan (Richmond) to Poe (Baltimore). Cited in Poe to Allan, Oct. 30, 1829.	45
* Oct. 30	Poe (Baltimore) to John Allan (Richmond). VL 193–195 (F). Original in Valentine Museum.	46
* [Oct.–Nov.]	Poe (Baltimore) to John Neal (Boston). W I, 58–60.	47
* Nov. 12	Poe (Baltimore) to John Allan (Richmond). VL 203–204 (F). Original in Valentine Museum.	48
ca. Nov. 15	John Allan (Richmond) to Poe (Baltimore). Cited in Poe to Allan, Nov. 18, 1829.	49
* Nov. 18	Poe (Baltimore) to John Allan (Richmond). VL 213–214 (F). Original in Valentine Museum.	50
Nov. (?)	Poe (Baltimore) to N. P. Willis. Possible letter similar to Poe to Neal, Sept. (?), 1829.	51
ante Dec. 29 (?)	John Neal (Boston) to Poe (Baltimore).	

Implied by Neal in Portland (Maine) *Advertiser*, April 26, 1850. See also Neal to Gove, Nov. 30, 1846 (Quinn, *Poe*, 153). 52

* [Dec. 29] Poe (Baltimore) to John Neal (Boston). W I, 369. Original in Koester collection. 53

n. d. Poe to Neal. See No. 47. Ingram I, 71–73; W I, 58–60; OCL 41 are less satisfactory datings.

1830

Jan. 3 Poe to Allan. Misdated by Poe. See No. 61.

ante May 1–3 Sergeant Samuel Graves (Old Point Comfort, Va.) to Poe (Washington). Cited in Poe to Graves, May 3, 1830. 54

May 1–3 Sergeant Samuel Graves (Old Point Comfort, Va.) to Poe (Richmond). Cited in Poe to Graves, May 3, 1830. 55

* May 3 Poe (Richmond) to Sergeant Samuel Graves (Old Point Comfort, Va.). VL 221–223 (F). Original in Valentine Museum. 56

May 21 John Allan (Richmond) to Poe (in Baltimore but forwarded to West Point). Cited in Poe to Allan, June 28, 1830. 57

* June 28 Poe (West Point) to John Allan (Richmond). VL 233–235 (F). Original in Valentine Museum. 58

* Nov. 6 Poe (West Point) to John Allan (Richmond). VL 243–245 (F). Original in Valentine Museum. 59

Dec. 27–28 John Allan (Richmond) to Poe (West Point). Cited in Poe to Allan, Jan. 3, 1831. 60

1831

* Jan. 3 Poe (West Point) to John Allan (Richmond). VL 253–258 (F). Original in Valentine Museum. 61

ca. Feb. 20 (?) Poe (New York) to William Henry Leonard Poe (Baltimore). Implied in Poe to Allan, Feb. 21, 1831. 62

* Feb. 21 Poe (New York) to John Allan (Richmond). VL 267–269 (F). Original in Valentine Museum. 63

* March 10 Poe (New York) to Colonel Sylvanus Thayer (West Point). VL 277. W I, 79–80. Original in West Point Library. 64

* May 6	Poe (Baltimore) to William Gwynn (Baltimore). W I, 88. Original in Pennsylvania Historical Society.	65
* Oct. 16	Poe (Baltimore) to John Allan (Richmond). VL 279–281 (F). Original in Valentine Museum.	66
ante Nov. 18 (?)	John Allan (Richmond) to Poe (Baltimore). Implied in Poe to Allan, Nov. 18, 1831.	67
* Nov. 18	Poe (Baltimore) to John Allan (Richmond). VL 291–292 (F). Original in Valentine Museum.	68
* Dec. 15	Poe (Baltimore) to John Allan (Richmond). VL 299–301 (F). Original in Valentine Museum.	69
* Dec. 29	Poe (Baltimore) to John Allan (Richmond). VL 305–306 (F). Original in Valentine Museum.	70

1833

March 15	Poe to Kennedy. Misdated in H XVII, 2. See No. 78.	
* April 12	Poe (Baltimore) to John Allan (Richmond). VL 313–314 (F). Original in Valentine Museum.	71
* May 4	Poe (Baltimore) to Messrs. Buckingham (Boston). Quinn, *Poe*, 200 (F). Original in Bradley Martin collection.	72

1834

Sept. 11	Poe to Kennedy. Misdated in ABC II (Nov. 1932) 290. See No. 101.	
* *ca.* Nov. [19]	Poe (Baltimore) to J. P. Kennedy (Baltimore). H I, 1–2. W I, 104–105. Original in Peabody Library.	73
November	Poe to Kennedy. See No. 73. H I, 1–2; W I, 104–105; A I, 363; OCL 61 are less satisfactory datings.	
November	Poe to Kennedy. Misdated in ABC II (Dec. 1932) 338; OCL 62. See No. 74.	
* Dec. 19	Poe (Baltimore) to J. P. Kennedy (Baltimore). [A follow-up note to the letter of *ca.* Nov. 19.] Sotheby Sales catalogue (London), Dec. 18, 1934.	74
Dec. 22	J. P. Kennedy (Baltimore) to Poe (Baltimore). W I, 105–106. H XVII, 3. Original in Boston Public Library.	75

1835

Jan. 21	Poe to Carey and Hart. Misdated in OCL 64. See No. 113.
* March 15	Poe (Baltimore) to J. P. Kennedy (Baltimore). H xvii, 4. W i, 107. Original in Peabody Library. 76
March 15	J. P. Kennedy (Baltimore) to Poe (Baltimore). Cited in Poe to Kennedy, Sunday 15th [March, 1835]. 77
* [March] Sunday 15	Poe (Baltimore) to J. P. Kennedy (Baltimore). H xvii, 2. W i, 107–108. Original in Peabody Library. 78
ante April 30 (?)	T. W. White (Richmond) to Poe (Baltimore). Implied in Poe to White, April 30, 1835. 79
* [April 30]	Poe (Baltimore) to T. W. White (Richmond). First portion of letter printed in SLM, 1 (1835) 468; Whitty, xxviii–xxix. Rest of letter (with few words missing) printed in *Modern Philology*, xxv (1927) 101–105; P i, 488–489. Original of second portion of letter in Huntington Library (HM 21868). 80
ante May 15	Poe (Baltimore) to E. L. Carey (Philadelphia). Cited in Carey to Kennedy, May 15, 1835. *Sewanee Review*, xxv (April 1917) 197–198. 81
May 15–18	Poe to Carey. Misdated in OCL 70. See No. 81.
May 20	T. W. White (Richmond) to Poe (Baltimore). Cited in Poe to White, May 30, 1835. 82
May 20–30	Kennedy to Poe. See No. 83. OCL 72 is a less satisfactory dating.
May 21–25 (?)	J. P. Kennedy (Baltimore) to Poe (Baltimore). Implied in Poe to White, May 30, 1835. 83
May 30	Poe to Kennedy. (Quinn, *Poe*, 209), actually Poe to White, No. 84.
* May 30	Poe (Baltimore) to T. W. White (Richmond). H xvii, 4–6. W i, 110–113. Original in Boston Public Library. 84
May	Poe to White. SLM 1 (1835) 468, and subsequent reprintings, such as Whitty, xxviii-xxix; P i, 200; OCL 69 are misdatings. See No. 80.

June 2	Poe to White. Misdated in A 1, 367. See No. 88.	
June 8	T. W. White (Richmond) to Poe (Baltimore). Cited in Poe to White, June 12, 1835.	85
* June 12	Poe (Baltimore) to T. W. White (Richmond). H XVII, 7. W I, 114–115. Original in Boston Public Library.	86
June 18	T. W. White (Richmond) to Poe (Baltimore). Cited in Poe to White, June 22, 1835.	87
* June 22	Poe (Baltimore) to T. W. White (Richmond). H XVII, 8–10. W I, 115–118. Original in Boston Public Library.	88
July 14	T. W. White (Richmond) to Poe (Baltimore). Cited in Poe to White, July 20, 1835.	89
July 16	T. W. White (Richmond) to Poe (Baltimore). Cited in Poe to White, July 20, 1835.	90
* July 20	Poe (Baltimore) to T. W. White (Richmond). H XVII, 10–12. W I, 118–121. Original in private collection of Merrill Griswold, but on loan at Poe Shrine, Richmond.	91
ca. Aug. 17	William Poe (Augusta, Ga.) to Poe (Richmond). Cited in Poe to William Poe, Aug. 20, 1835.	92
Aug. 19	William Poe to Poe. See No. 92. OCL 81 is a less satisfactory dating.	
* Aug. 20	Poe (Richmond) to William Poe (Augusta, Ga.). H XVII, 13–16. *Gulf States Historical Magazine,* 1 (1903) 281–283. Original in New York Public Library.	93
ca. Aug. 20	Poe (Richmond) to Mrs. Maria Clemm (Baltimore). Cited in Poe to Clemm, Aug. 29, 1835.	94
Aug. 20–26	Mrs. Maria Clemm (Baltimore) to Poe (Richmond). Cited in Poe to Clemm, Aug. 29, 1835.	95
Aug. 27–28	Mrs. Maria Clemm (Baltimore) to Poe (Richmond). Cited in Poe to Clemm, Aug. 29, 1835.	96
* Aug. 29	Poe (Richmond) to Mrs. Maria Clemm (Baltimore). Quinn, *Poe,* 219–224 (F). Original in Pratt Library.	97

* Sept. 4	Poe (Richmond) to John Neal (Boston). Original in Koester collection.	98
Sept. 7–9	Dr. Miller to Poe. See No. 100. OCL 88 is a less satisfactory dating.	
ante Sept. 8 (?)	Poe (Richmond) to Dr. J. H. Miller (Westminster, Md.). Implied in Poe to Kennedy, Sept. 11, 1835.	99
Sept. 8–9	Dr. J. H. Miller (Westminster, Md.) to Poe (Richmond). Cited in Poe to Kennedy, Sept. 11, 1835.	100
* Sept. 11	Poe (Richmond) to J. P. Kennedy (Baltimore). H xvii, 16–18. W i, 138–141. Original in Peabody Library.	101
Sept. 15–20 (?)	Poe (Richmond or Baltimore ?) to T. W. White (Richmond). Implied in White to Poe, Sept. 29, 1835.	102
Sept. 19	J. P. Kennedy (Baltimore) to Poe (Richmond or Baltimore ?). W i, 141–143. H xvii, 19–20. Original in Boston Public Library.	103
Sept. 29	T. W. White (Richmond) to Poe (Baltimore). W i, 144–146. H xvii, 20–21. Original in Boston Public Library.	104
ante Oct. 6	William Poe (Augusta, Ga.) to Poe (Richmond). Cited in Clemm to William Poe, Oct. 7, 1835 (H xvii, 379, where misdated 1836).	105
Oct. 6	Poe to Bird. No such letter. OCL 93 same as No. 106.	
* Oct. 8	Poe (Richmond) to R. M. Bird (Philadelphia). Anderson Galleries sale, Nov. 13–14, 1916, item 71.	106
* Oct. 31	Poe (Richmond) to Lucian Minor (Charlottesville, Va.). Merwin-Clayton sale, Jan. 18, 1911, item 255, cited. Anderson Galleries sale, April 25–27, 1916, item 465.	107
Nov. 29	Carey and Lea (Philadelphia) to Poe (Richmond). W ii, 375.	108
ante Dec. 1 [?]	P. P. Cooke (Winchester, Va.) to Poe (Richmond). Implied in Poe to Tucker, Dec. 1, 1835.	109
* Dec. 1	Poe (Richmond) to Beverley Tucker (Williamsburg, Va.). *Century Magazine*, cvii (1924) 653–655. Original in Coleman collection.	110

Dec. 5   Beverley Tucker (Williamsburg, Va.) to Poe (Richmond). H xvii, 21–24. Original in Boston Public Library.   111

1836

* Jan. 12   Poe (Richmond) to George Poe (Mobile, Ala.). Pratt 13–14. H xvii, 25–26. W i, 161–163. Original in Pratt Library.   112

Jan. 21   Poe (Richmond) to Carey and Hart (Philadelphia). Bangs sale, Feb. 16, 1898, item 690, cited.   113

* Jan. 22   Poe (Richmond) to J. P. Kennedy (Baltimore). H xvii, 26–27. Original in Peabody Library.   114

Jan. 23–24   Poe (Richmond) to Beverley Tucker (Williamsburg, Va.). Cited in Tucker to White, Jan. 26, 1836 (W i, 154).   115

Jan. 26 [?]   Beverley Tucker (Williamsburg, Va.) to Poe (Richmond). Inferred from P i, 521.   116

* Feb. 5   Poe (Richmond) to Lucian Minor (Charlottesville, Va.). W ii, 370–371. Original in Boston Public Library.   117

Feb. 9   J. P. Kennedy (Baltimore) to Poe (Richmond). H xvii, 28–29. W i, 148–149. Original in Boston Public Library.   118

* Feb. 9   Poe (Richmond) to S. G. Bulfinch [an Augusta, Ga., author]. American Art Association sale, May 4–5, 1925, item 466, cited.   119

* Feb. 11   Poe (Richmond) to J. P. Kennedy (Baltimore). H xvii, 29–31. Original in Peabody Library.   120

Feb. 12   George Poe (Mobile, Ala.) to Poe (Richmond). Cited on MS. of Poe to George Poe, Jan. 12, 1836.   121

Feb. 15   George Poe to Poe. Misdated in OCL 106. See No. 121.

ante Feb. 20   Poe (Richmond) to Carey and Lea (Philadelphia). Cited in Carey and Lea to Poe, Feb. 20, 1836.   122

Feb. 20   Carey and Lea (Philadelphia) to Poe (Richmond). W ii, 375.   123

Feb. 24   J. C. McCabe (Richmond) to Poe (Richmond). Cited in Poe to McCabe, March 3, 1836.   124

* March 3   Poe (Richmond) to J. C. McCabe (Richmond). Armistead C. Gordon, *Memories and Memorials of William Gordon McCabe* (Richmond, 1925. 2 vols.), I, 16–17. Original in McCabe collection.   125

March 10   Poe to Paulding or Thomas. OCL 109 wrongly includes Thomas. See No. 127.

* March 10   Poe (Richmond) to Lucian Minor (Charlottesville, Va.). Anderson Galleries sale, Jan. 14–15, 1925, item 380 (F). Original in Koester collection.   126

ante March 17 (?)   Poe (Richmond) to J. K. Paulding (New York). Implied in Paulding to Poe, March 17, 1836.   127

March 17   J. K. Paulding (New York) to Poe (Richmond). W I, 159–160. H XVII, 31–32. Original in Boston Public Library.   128

ante March 29   Washington Poe (Macon, Ga.) to Poe (Richmond). Cited in Poe to William Poe, April ·12, 1836.   129

March 29   William Poe (Augusta, Ga.) to Poe (Richmond). Cited in Poe to William Poe, April 12, 1836.   130

ca. March 30   Poe (Richmond) to Washington Poe (Macon, Ga.). Cited in Poe to William Poe, April 12, 1836.   131

* April 12   Poe (Richmond) to William Poe (Augusta, Ga.). W I, 377–378.   132

* April 12   Poe (Richmond) to Mrs. L. H. Sigourney (Hartford, Conn.). Quinn, *Poe*, 238–239. Original in Koester collection.   133

April 23   Mrs. L. H. Sigourney (Hartford, Conn.) to Poe (Richmond). H XVII, 33–35. Original in Boston Public Library.   134

April 26   J. P. Kennedy (Baltimore) to Poe (Richmond). H XVII, 32–33.   135

* May 2   Poe (Richmond) to Beverley Tucker (Williamsburg, Va.). *Century Magazine*, CVII (1924) 655–656. Original in Coleman collection.   136

* May 23   Poe (Richmond) to Jared Sparks (Cambridge, Mass.). Original in Harvard Library.   137

June 3 [possibly May 3]   S. G. Bulfinch (Augusta, Ga.) to Poe (Richmond). Cited in Poe to Bulfinch, June 8, 1836.   138

* June 3	Poe (Richmond) to J. H. Causten (Washington). Anderson Galleries sale, Jan. 4–5, 1934, item 350 (F). Original in Koester collection.	139
June 3	Poe (Richmond) to Harper & Brothers (New York). Cited in Harper & Brothers to Poe, June 19, 1836 (MS. in Boston Public Library).	140
June 4	Poe (Richmond) to Mrs. L. H. Sigourney (Hartford, Conn.). Cited in Sigourney to Poe, June 11, 1836 (H xvii, 37).	141
June 4 or later	Harper & Brothers to Poe. Incompletely dated in W i, 162, ii, 402; ABC ii (Dec. 1932) 339; Quinn, *Poe*, 250–251; OCL 124. See No. 152.	
ante June 7 (?)	R. M. Bird (Philadelphia) to Poe (Richmond). Implied in Poe to Bird, June 7, 1836.	142
* June 7	Poe (Richmond) to R. M. Bird (Philadelphia). H xvii, 35–36. Original in Koester collection.	143
* June 7	Poe (Richmond) to J. F. Cooper (Cooperstown, N. Y.). *Correspondence of James Fenimore Cooper*, ed. by James Fenimore Cooper (New Haven: Yale University Press, 1922), i, 356–357.	144
ca. June 7	Poe (Richmond) to Mrs. S. J. Hale (Boston ?). Cited in Poe to Hale, Oct. 20, 1836.	145
* June 7	Poe (Richmond) to Fitz-Greene Halleck (New York). American Art Association sale, Dec. 16–17, 1929, item 105 (F). J. G. Wilson, *Life and Letters of Fitz-Greene Halleck* (New York: D. Appleton, 1869), 396–397. Original in Koester collection.	146
* June 7	Poe (Richmond) to J. P. Kennedy (Baltimore). H xvii, 36–37. W i, 164–166. Original in Bradley Martin collection.	147
post June 7 (?)	R. M. Bird (Philadelphia) to Poe (Richmond). Possibly accompanied contribution to SLM solicited in Poe to Bird, June 7, 1836.	148
* June 8	Poe (Richmond) to S. G. Bulfinch (Augusta, Ga.). American Art Association sale, May 4–5, 1925, item 467.	149

June 11	Mrs. L. H. Sigourney (Hartford, Conn.) to Poe (Richmond). H xvii, 37–38. Original in Boston Public Library.	150
June 18	Poe (Richmond) to Francis Lieber (Columbia, S. C.). Cited in Lieber to Poe, June 28, 1836 (SLM ii [Aug. 1836] 535–538).	151
June 19	Harper & Brothers (New York) to Poe (Richmond). Original in Boston Public Library.	152
June 28	Francis Lieber (Columbia, S. C.) to Poe (Richmond). SLM ii (1836) 535–538	153
* July 16	Poe (Richmond) to L. W. Tazewell (Richmond). Richmond *Times-Dispatch*, Nov. 11, 1923. Original in Lilly collection.	154
July 29	Carey to Poe. See No. 155. OCL 133 is a less satisfactory dating.	
ante July 30 (?)	Mathew Carey (Philadelphia) to Poe (Richmond). Implied in Poe to Carey, July 30, 1836.	155
* July 30	Poe (Richmond) to Mathew Carey (Philadelphia). W ii, 371–372. Original in Pennsylvania Historical Society.	156
July	Poe to Kennedy. Misdated in A i, 399. See No. 147.	
Aug. 2	Poe to ——. Henkels sale, May 23–24, 1900, item 229, cited.	157
* [Aug. 19]	Poe (Richmond) to Hiram Haines (Petersburg, Va.). *Americana*, xxxvi (Jan. 1942) 67–71. Original in Poe Shrine, Richmond.	158
* [*ante* Sept. 2]	Poe (Richmond) to the Richmond *Courier and Daily Compiler*. H viii, xii–xv.	159
* Sept. 2	Poe (Richmond) to Harrison Hall (Philadelphia). *Sewanee Review*, xxxvi (1928) 172–174. Original in Haverford College.	160
Sept. 2	Poe to Richmond *Courier*. See No. 159. Richmond *Courier and Daily Advertiser*, Sept. 2, 1836, and subsequent reprintings, such as H viii, xii–xv; OCL 138; *et cetera*, are less satisfactory datings.	
Oct. 4 (?)	Poe (Richmond) to E. W. Johnston (New York). Possibly from Poe as amanuensis for T. W. White (see Quinn, *Poe*, 251, n. 45).	161
Oct. 12–15	Poe to Dew. See No. 162. OCL 140 is a less satisfactory dating.	
ante Oct. 17	Poe (Richmond) to T. R. Dew (Williamsburg, Va.). Cited in Dew to Poe, Oct. 17, 1836 (H xvii, 39).	162

Oct. 17	T. R. Dew (Williamsburg, Va.) to Poe (Richmond). H XVII, 39–40. Original in Boston Public Library. 163
* Oct. 20	Poe (Richmond) to Mrs. S. J. Hale (Boston). *Nation*, LXXXIX (1909) 9–10. Anderson Galleries sale, April 27, 1925, item 224 (F). Original in Bradley Martin collection. 164
Oct. 31	T. R. Dew (Williamsburg, Va.) to Poe (Richmond). Original in Boston Public Library. 165
Nov. 29	Carey and Lea to Poe. Misdated in W II, 375; OCL 144. See No. 108.
Dec. 9	J. H. Causten (Washington) to Poe (Richmond). Cited on MS. of Poe to Causten, June 3, 1836. 166
Dec. 24	A. B. Magruder (Charlottesville, Va. ?) to Poe (Richmond). Cited in Poe to Magruder, Jan. 9, 1837. 167

1837

* Jan. 9	Poe (Richmond) to A. B. Magruder (Charlottesville, Va. ?). W II, 372–373. 168
Jan. 14–16	Poe to White. OCL 148 same as No. 169.
ante Jan. 17 (?)	Poe (Richmond) to T. W. White (Richmond). Implied in White to Poe, Jan. 17, 1837 (H XVII, 41). 169
Jan. 17	T. W. White (Richmond) to Poe (Richmond). W I, 182–183. H XVII, 41–42. Original in Boston Public Library. 170
Jan. (?)	Poe (Richmond) to Lambert Wilmer (Baltimore). Implied by Wilmer in his *Our Press Gang* (1860), reprinted by T. O. Mabbott in *Merlin* (New York: Scholars' Facsimiles & Reprints 1941), 26. 171
Feb. 23	Poe to ——. Misdated in OCL 150. See No. 173.
ante Feb. 28 (?)	W. H. Carpenter, J. S. Norris, and James Brown (Baltimore) to Poe (New York). Implied in Poe to Carpenter *et al.*, Feb. 28, 1837. 172
* Feb. 28	Poe (New York) to W. H. Carpenter, J. S. Norris, and James Brown (Baltimore). PC II, 78–79. 173
May 27	Poe (New York) to Charles Anthon (New York). Cited in Anthon to Poe, June 1, 1837 (H XVII, 42). 174

June 1   Charles Anthon (New York) to Poe (New
                          York). W I, 189. H XVII, 42–43. Original
                          in Boston Public Library.   175

Sept. or Oct.   Poe to Hale. Misdated in OCL 154. See
                          No. 164.

Oct. 20   Poe to Hale. A misdating in *Nation*, LXXXIX
                          (1909) 9–10, due to Poe's own error.
                          See No. 164.

Oct. 23   Poe to Hale. Misdated in ABC III (April
                          1933) 246; OCL 155. See No. 164.

n.d.   Hawks to Poe. See No. 176. W I, 378; P I,
                          548; OCL 156 are less satisfactory datings.

late 1837 —   Dr. F. L. Hawks (New York) to Poe (New
  spring 1838 [?]   York). W I, 378 [?].   176

1838

ante Sept. 4   N. C. Brooks (Baltimore) to Poe (Phila-
                          delphia). Cited in Poe to Brooks, Sept. 4,
                          1838.   177

* Sept. 4   Poe (Philadelphia) to N. C. Brooks (Balti-
                          more). H XVII, 44–45.   178

1839

Feb. 19   Poe (Philadelphia) to Harper & Brothers
                          (New York). Cited in Harper & Brothers
                          to Poe, Feb. 20, 1838.   179

Feb. 20   Harper & Brothers (New York) to Poe
                          (Philadelphia). Original in Boston Public
                          Library.   180

ante April (?)   J. L. O'Sullivan (New York) to Poe (Phila-
                          delphia). Implied in *Aristidean*, I (Oct.
                          1845) 318.   181

May 1–10   Poe to Burton. OCL 158 same as No. 182.

May 10   Burton to Poe. Misdated in H XVII, 45–46;
                          W I, 202–203; A II, 450–451. See No. 183.

ante May 11 (?)   Poe (Philadelphia) to W. E. Burton (Phila-
                          delphia). Implied in Burton to Poe, May 11,
                          1839.   182

May 10 [11]   W. E. Burton (Philadelphia) to Poe (Phila-
                          delphia). W I, 202–203. H XVII, 45–46.
                          Original in Boston Public Library.   183

May 11–30   Poe (Philadelphia) to W. E. Burton (Phila-
                          delphia). Cited in Burton to Poe, May 30,
                          1839.   184

May 30	W. E. Burton (Philadelphia) to Poe (Philadelphia). Quinn, *Poe*, 279–281 (F). W I, 240–242. Original in Boston Public Library. 185
June 10	E. B. Fisher (Pittsburgh) to Poe (Philadelphia). American Art Association sale, Dec. 16–17, 1929, item 287. 186
June 26	Poe (Philadelphia) to N. C. Brooks (Baltimore). [Letter lost, but envelope is in New York Public Library.] 187
July 4	W. E. Burton (New York) to Poe [?] (Philadelphia). Original in Boston Public Library. 188
July 5	Poe (Philadelphia) to E. B. Fisher (Pittsburgh). Cited in Fisher to Poe, July 9, 1839. 189
July 9	E. B. Fisher (Pittsburgh) to Poe (Philadelphia). Original in Boston Public Library. 190
ante July 14 (?)	George Poe (Mobile, Ala.) to Poe (Philadelphia). Implied in Poe to George Poe, July 14, 1839. 191
* July 14	Poe (Philadelphia) to George Poe (Mobile, Ala.). *New York Genealogical and Biographical Record*, xxxviii (1907) 55–69. 192
July 19	Fisher to Poe. Misdated in ABC ii (Dec. 1932) 339. See No. 190.
July–Aug.	Poe (Philadelphia) to P. P. Cooke (Charlestown, Va.). Cited in Cooke to Poe, Sept. 16, 1839. 193
ante Aug. 6	J. Beauchamp Jones (Baltimore) to Poe (Philadelphia). Cited in Poe to Jones, Aug. 8, 1839. 194
* Aug. 8	Poe (Philadelphia) to J. Beauchamp Jones (Baltimore). *The Collector*, Nov. 1945, 185–187. Parke-Bernet Galleries sale, Feb. 25, 1947, item 239 (F). 195
post Sept. 1 (?)	Poe (Philadelphia) to Washington Irving (Newburg, N. Y.). Implied in Irving to Poe, Nov. 6, 1839, and in Poe to Cooke, Sept. 21, 1839. 196
Sept. 5	Poe (Philadelphia) to J. E. Heath (Richmond). Cited in Heath to Poe, Sept. 12, 1839. 197
* Sept. 11	Poe (Philadelphia) to J. E. Snodgrass (Baltimore). W I, 218–221. Bixby 6–7 (F). Original in Mabbott collection. 198

Sept. 12	J. E. Heath (Richmond) to Poe (Philadelphia). W I, 205–208. H xvii, 47–48. Original in Boston Public Library.	199
Sept. 13	Cooke to Poe. Misdated in ABC ii (Dec. 1932) 338. See No. 200.	
Sept. 16	Poe to Cooke. Quinn, *Poe*, 271 n. wrongly identified. See No. 200.	
Sept. 16	P. P. Cooke (Charlestown, Va.) to Poe (Philadelphia). W I, 208–212. H xvii, 49–51. Original in Boston Public Library.	200
ante Sept. 21	Washington Irving (Newburg, N. Y.) to Poe (Philadelphia). Cited in Poe to Cooke, Sept. 21, 1839.	201
ante Sept. 21 [?]	Isaac D'Israeli (England) to Poe (Philadelphia). Implied in Poe to Cooke, Sept. 21, 1839.	202
* Sept. 21	Poe (Philadelphia) to P. P. Cooke (Charlestown, Va.). H xvii, 51–54. W I, 212–216.	203
Sept. 22– Nov. 5 (?)	Poe (Philadelphia) to Washington Irving (Newburg, N. Y.). Implied in Irving to Poe, Nov. 6, 1839.	204
Sept. 22– Dec. 18 (?)	Poe (Philadelphia) to P. P. Cooke (Charlestown, Va.). Implied in Cooke to Poe, Dec. 19, 1839.	205
Sept. 27	Poe to Lea and Blanchard. OCL 171 same as No. 206.	
ante Sept. 28 (?)	Poe (Philadelphia) to Lea and Blanchard (Philadelphia). Implied in Lea and Blanchard to Poe, Sept. 28, 1839.	206
Sept. 28	Lea and Blanchard (Philadelphia) to Poe (Philadelphia). W ii, 375–376. Original in Boston Public Library.	207
ante Oct. 7	J. E. Snodgrass (Baltimore) to Poe (Philadelphia). Cited in Poe to Snodgrass, Oct. 7, 1839.	208
* Oct. 7	Poe (Philadelphia) to J. E. Snodgrass (Baltimore). Quinn, *Poe*, 291. Copy in Alderman Library.	209
Oct. 16	John Tomlin (Jackson, Tenn.) to Poe (Philadelphia). Original in Boston Public Library.	210
ante Oct. 30 (?)	Poe (Philadelphia) to Lea and Blanchard (Philadelphia). Implied in Lea and Blanchard to Poe, Oct. 30, 1839.	211

Oct. 30	Lea and Blanchard (Philadelphia) to Poe (Philadelphia). W II, 376.	212
Nov. 1–2	J. E. Snodgrass (Baltimore) to Poe (Philadelphia). Cited in Poe to Snodgrass, Nov. 11, 1839.	213
Nov. 6	Washington Irving (Newburg, N. Y.) to Poe (Philadelphia). W I, 216–217. H XVII, 54.	214
ante Nov. 11	J. E. Snodgrass (Baltimore) to Poe (Philadelphia). Cited in Poe to Snodgrass, Nov. 11, 1839.	215
* Nov. 11	Poe (Philadelphia) to J. E. Snodgrass (Baltimore). Bixby 24–25 (F).	216
Nov. 15	J. B. Boyd (Cincinnati) to Poe (Philadelphia). Cited in Poe to Boyd, Dec. 25, 1839.	217
Nov. 16–19	Poe to Lea and Blanchard. OCL 180 same as No. 219.	
Nov. 17	E. B. Fisher (Mt. Pleasant, Pa.) to Poe (Philadelphia). Bangs sale, April 11, 1896, item 110.	218
ante Nov. 20	Poe (Philadelphia) to Lea and Blanchard (Philadelphia). Cited in Lea and Blanchard to Poe, Nov. 20, 1839.	219
Nov. 20	Lea and Blanchard (Philadelphia) to Poe (Philadelphia). W I, 225.	220
* Dec. 6	Poe (Philadelphia) to J. C. Cox (Philadelphia). Anderson Galleries sale, Feb. 1–3, 1926, part 2, item 514 (F).	221
* Dec. 9	Poe (Philadelphia) to E. L. Carey and John Hart (Philadelphia). Original in New York Public Library.	222
* [Dec.] 12	Poe (Philadelphia) to J. E. Snodgrass (Baltimore). W I, 222. Copy in Alderman Library.	223
Dec. 16	J. E. Snodgrass (Baltimore) to Poe (Philadelphia). Cited in Poe to Snodgrass, Dec. 19, 1839.	224
* Dec. 19	Poe (Philadelphia) to J. E. Snodgrass (Baltimore). H XVII, 71–73. W I, 237–239.	225
Dec. 19	P. P. Cooke (Charlestown, Va.) to Poe (Philadelphia). P I, 617. Original in Boston Public Library.	226
* Dec. 25	Poe (Philadelphia) to J. B. Boyd (Cincinnati). American Art Association sale, April 20–21, 1921, part 3, item 494 (F). Original in New York Public Library.	227

1840

ante Jan. 20	J. E. Snodgrass (Baltimore) to Poe (Philadelphia). Cited in Poe to Snodgrass, Jan. 20, 1840.	228
* Jan. 20	Poe (Philadelphia) to J. E. Snodgrass (Baltimore). W I, 239–240.	229
Jan. 21	Poe to Snodgrass. Misdated in Woodberry, *Poe* (1885) 136 n.; W I, 239–240. See No. 229.	
ante Feb. 29	J. K. Mitchell (Philadelphia) to Poe (Philadelphia). Cited in Poe to Mitchell, Feb. 29 [1840].	230
* [Feb. 29]	Poe (Philadelphia) to J. K. Mitchell (Philadelphia). Morley sale, May 19, 1941, item 289 (F).	231
March 24	Hiram Haines (Petersburg, Va.) to Poe (Philadelphia). Cited in Poe to Haines, April 24, 1840.	232
* April 24	Poe (Philadelphia) to Hiram Haines (Petersburg, Va.). Quinn, *Poe*, 273–274. Original in Poe Shrine, Richmond.	233
May 10	Poe to Thompson. Misdated in ABC II (Dec. 1932) 339, 342; OCL 189. See No. 789.	
May 30 (?)	W. E. Burton (Philadelphia) to Poe (Philadelphia). Implied in Poe to Burton, June 1, 1840.	234
May	Burton to Poe. Misdated in Allen, *Israfel*, 378; P I, 620. See No. 234.	
* June 1	Poe (Philadelphia) to W. E. Burton (Philadelphia). H I, 163–167. Quinn, *Poe*, 297–300. Copy in Alderman Library.	235
post June 1	Poe (Philadelphia) to W. E. Burton (Philadelphia). Cited in Poe to Snodgrass, June 17, 1840.	236
* June 4	Poe (Philadelphia) to John Neal (New York: forwarded to Portland, Maine). H XVII, 86. A II, 897. Parke-Bernet Galleries sale, Nov. 6–8, 1944, item 549 (F).	237
June 8	Neal to Poe. OCL 192 same as No. 238.	
June 8	John Neal (Portland, Maine) to Poe (Philadelphia). A II, 898.	238
June 12	J. E. Snodgrass (Baltimore) to Poe (Philadelphia). Cited in Poe to Snodgrass, June 17, 1840.	239

* June 17	Poe (Philadelphia) to J. E. Snodgrass (Baltimore). W I, 248–251.	240
June 26	C. W. Thomson (Philadelphia) to Poe (Philadelphia). Cited in Poe to Thomson, June 28, 1840.	241
* June 28	Poe (Philadelphia) to C. W. Thomson (Philadelphia). Heartman and Canny 40. Original in Koester collection.	242
July 28	William Poe (Augusta, Ga.) to Poe (Philadelphia). Cited in Poe to William Poe, Aug. 15, 1840.	243
Aug. 14–15 (?)	Poe (Philadelphia) to Robert Poe (Augusta, Ga.). Implied in Poe to William Poe, Aug. 14, 1840.	244
Aug. 14–15	Poe to Washington Poe. OCL 199 same as No. 246.	
* Aug. 15 [14]	Poe (Philadelphia) to William Poe (Augusta, Ga.). H XVII, 55–57. Original in Huntington Library (HM 24220).	245
* Aug. 15	Poe (Philadelphia) to Washington Poe (Macon, Ga.). Gill 114 (F).	246
Aug. 15	Poe to William Poe. Misdated (due to Poe's error) in H XVII, 55–57; Quinn, *Poe*, 259. See No. 245.	
* Aug. 18	Poe (Philadelphia) to Lucian Minor (Charlottesville, Va.). P. 1, 635–636. American Art Association sale, January 30–31, 1923, item 491 (F). Original in Hart collection.	247
* Aug. 20	Poe (Philadelphia) to J. B. Boyd (Cincinnati). Original in Pennsylvania Historical Society.	248
ca. Aug. 20	Poe (Philadelphia) to T. H. Chivers (New York). Cited in Chivers to Poe, Aug. 27, 1840.	249
Aug. 24	Thomas to Poe. Misdated in ABC II (Dec. 1932) 339; OCL 203. See No. 656.	
Aug. 27	T. H. Chivers (New York) to Poe (Philadelphia). H I, 190–191. Original in Boston Public Library.	250
ca. Aug.– Sept. (?)	Poe (Philadelphia) to John Tomlin (Jackson, Tenn.). Implied in Joe to Tomlin, Sept. 16, 1840.	251
ante Sept. 16	John Tomlin (Jackson, Tenn.) to Poe (Philadelphia). Cited in Poe to Tomlin, Sept. 16, 1840.	252

* Sept. 16	Poe (Philadelphia) to John Tomlin (Jackson, Tenn.). H XVII, 57–58. *Bookman*, V (May 1897) 218 (F). Original in Huntington Library (HM 24209).	253
Sept. 30	Socrates Maupin (Richmond) to Poe (Philadelphia). Original in Boston Public Library.	254
Oct. 2	Pliny Earle (Frankford, Pa.) to Poe (Philadelphia). Cited in Poe to Earle, Oct. 10, 1840.	255
* Oct. 10	Poe (Philadelphia) to Pliny Earle (Frankford, Pa.). Original in Koester collection.	256
* [Nov. 6]	Poe (Philadelphia) to R. H. Stoddard (Philadelphia). Whitty, *Poems* (1911) 218.	257
Nov. 6	F. W. Thomas (St. Louis) to Poe (Philadelphia). Cited in Poe to Thomas, Nov. 23, 1840.	258
Nov. 22	John Tomlin (Jackson, Tenn.) to Poe (Philadelphia). H XVII, 61–62. Original in Boston Public Library.	259
* Nov. 23	Poe (Philadelphia) to F. W. Thomas (St. Louis). H XVII, 62–64. W I, 262–264. Original in Koester collection.	260
November	Poe to Stoddard. OCL 209 same as No. 257.	
Dec. 7	L. J. Cist (Cincinnati) to Poe (Philadelphia). Cited in Poe to Cist, Dec. 30, 1840.	261
Dec. 7	F. W. Thomas (St. Louis) to Poe (Philadelphia). H XVII, 65–67. Original in Boston Public Library.	262
* Dec. 30	Poe (Philadelphia) to L. J. Cist (Cincinnati). Original in Bradley Martin collection.	263
* Dec. 31	Poe (Philadelphia) to J. P. Kennedy (Baltimore). W I, 266–267. Original in Peabody Library.	264

1841

ca. Jan. 1	Poe (Philadelphia) to N. C. Brooks (Baltimore). Cited in Poe to Snodgrass, Jan. 17, 1841.	265
ante Jan. 17	J. E. Snodgrass (Baltimore) to Poe (Philadelphia). Cited in Poe to Snodgrass, Jan. 17, 1841.	266
* Jan. 17	Poe (Philadelphia) to J. E. Snodgrass (Baltimore). Bixby 14–15 (F). W I, 267–271. Original in New York Public Library.	267

* Jan. 22	Poe (Philadelphia) to R. T. Conrad (Philadelphia). Heartman and Canny 47–48. Original in Morgan Library.	268
ca. Jan. 22 (?)	Poe (Philadelphia) to Judge Joseph Hopkinson (Philadelphia). Implied in Hopkinson to Poe, Jan. 25, 1841.	269
Jan. 22–24	Poe to Hopkinson. See No. 269. OCL 215 is a less satisfactory dating.	
Jan. 25	Judge Joseph Hopkinson (Philadelphia) to Poe (Philadelphia). Original in Boston Public Library.	270
March 7	F. W. Thomas (Washington) to Poe (Philadelphia). H xvii, 81–82. Original in Boston Public Library.	271
March 8	J. E. Snodgrass (Baltimore) to Poe (Philadelphia). Cited in Poe to Snodgrass, April 1, 1841.	272
March 10	W. D. Gallagher (Cincinnati) to Poe (Philadelphia). Original in Boston Public Library.	273
March 12	John Tomlin (Jackson, Tenn.) to Poe (Philadelphia). H xvii, 82–83. Original in Boston Public Library.	274
March 13	Tomlin to Poe. Misdated (due to Tomlin's error) in ABC ii (Dec. 1932) 339. See No. 274.	
March 19	Poe to Griswold. Misdated in ABC ii (Dec. 1932) 338. See No. 289.	
March 29	Poe to Griswold. Misdated by Griswold's *Preface,* xxi, and all subsequent reprintings, such as H xvii, 83–84; W i, 351–352; Quinn, *Poe,* 351; OCL 222. See No. 289.	
March 29	Poe to Griswold. Memorandum sent with letter same date; thus wrongly dated March 29, 1841, wherever cited. See No. 289.	
* April 1	Poe (Philadelphia) to J. E. Snodgrass (Baltimore). H i, 158–161. W i, 252–256.	275
April 1	Poe (Philadelphia) to F. W. Thomas (Washington). Cited in Thomas to Poe, May 11, 1841.	276
April 11	Thomas to Poe. Misdated in ABC ii (Dec. 1932) 339. See No. 283.	
April 15	Poe (Philadelphia) to John Tomlin (Jackson, Tenn.). Cited in Tomlin to Poe, April 30, 1841.	277

April 21	S. D. L. (Stonington, Conn.) to Poe (Philadelphia). *Graham's*, XIX (1841) 36. [Represents many such letters.]	278
April 30	John Tomlin (Jackson, Tenn.) to Poe (Philadelphia). Original in Boston Public Library.	279
May 1	C. W. Thomson (Philadelphia) to Poe (Philadelphia). Original in Boston Public Library.	280
* May 3	Poe (Philadelphia) to H. W. Longfellow (Cambridge, Mass.). Quinn, *Poe*, 316–317. Original in Longfellow House, Cambridge, Mass.	281
* [*ante* May 8]	Poe (Philadelphia) to R. W. Griswold (Philadelphia). Original in University of Texas Library.	282
May 11	F. W. Thomas (Washington) to Poe (Philadelphia). Original in Boston Public Library.	283
May 19	H. W. Longfellow (Cambridge, Mass.) to Poe (Philadelphia). Samuel Longfellow, *Life of Longfellow* (1891), I, 390–391. Quinn, *Poe*, 317.	284
May 20	F. W. Thomas (Washington) to Poe (Philadelphia). H XVII, 84–85. W I, 289. Original in Boston Public Library.	285
May 26	Poe (Philadelphia) to F. W. Thomas (Washington). Cited in Thomas to Poe, May 28, 1841.	286
May 26–June 4	Poe to Thomas. See No. 290. OCL 235 is a less satisfactory dating.	
May 26–June 4	Griswold to Poe. See No. 288. OCL 234 is a less satisfactory dating.	
May 29 [28]	F. W. Thomas (Washington) to Poe (Philadelphia). Original in Boston Public Library.	287
ante May 29 (?)	R. W. Griswold (Boston) to Poe (Philadelphia). Implied in Thomas to Griswold, June 8, 1841 (*Some Passages in the Correspondence of Rufus W. Griswold*, Cambridge, 1898, 66).	288
* [May 29]	Poe (Philadelphia) to R. W. Griswold (Boston). [Includes "memorandum."] Original in Boston Public Library.	289
ca. May 29–June 7	Poe (Philadelphia) to F. W. Thomas (Washington). Cited in Thomas to Griswold,	

	June 8, 1841 (*Some Passages in the Correspondence of Rufus W. Griswold*, Cambridge, 1898, 66).	290
May	Thomas to Poe. Incomplete dating in Quinn, *Poe*, 321. See No. 285.	
June 4	Poe to Neal. Undated or misdated in Neal's *Wandering Recollections of a Somewhat Busy Life* (1869) 256; Ingram I, 225–226; H XVII, 86; P I, 668; OCL 237. See No. 237.	
June 7–11	Poe to Thomas. See No. 291. OCL 238 is a less satisfactory dating.	
June 11–12	Poe (Philadelphia) to F. W. Thomas (Washington). Cited in Thomas to Poe, June 14, 1841.	291
June 14	F. W. Thomas (Washington) to Poe (Philadelphia). Original in Boston Public Library.	292
June 17	Poe to Snodgrass. Misdated in W II, 409. See No. 240.	
* June 21	Poe (Philadelphia) to Washington Irving (Tarrytown, N. Y.). New York *Times*, Jan. 12, 1930, part 2, page 4. Original in Prescott collection.	293
* June [21]	Poe (Philadelphia) to J. P. Kennedy (Baltimore: forwarded to Washington). W I, 280–282. Quinn, *Poe*, 318–320. Original in Peabody Library.	294
* June 22	Poe (Philadelphia) to H. W. Longfellow (Cambridge, Mass.). H XVII, 86–88. W I, 277–280. Copy in Boston Public Library. Original in Longfellow House, Cambridge, Mass.	295
* June 24	Poe (Philadelphia) to Fitz-Greene Halleck (New York). H XVII, 89–91. Original in Huntington Library (HM 24210).	296
June 24	Washington Irving (Tarrytown, N. Y.) to Poe (Philadelphia). Cited on MS. of Poe to Irving, June 21, 1841.	297
* June 26	Poe (Philadelphia) to F. W. Thomas (Washington). Stoddard, *Select Works of Edgar Allan Poe* (1880) xcii–xciv. Original in New York Public Library.	298
June	Poe (Philadelphia) to W. C. Bryant (New York). Cited in Poe to Irving, June 21, 1841.	299

June	Poe (Philadelphia) to J. F. Cooper (Cooperstown, N. Y.). Libbie sale, April 24–25, 1898, item 648.	300
June	Poe to Kennedy. Incompletely dated in W I, 280–282; P I, 667–668; ABC II (Nov. 1932) 290; Quinn, *Poe*, 318–320. See No. 294.	
June	Poe (Philadelphia) to J. K. Paulding (New York). Cited in Poe to Irving, June 21, 1841.	301
June	Poe (Philadelphia) to N. P. Willis (New York). Cited in Poe to Irving, June 21, 1841.	302
July 1	F. W. Thomas (Washington) to Poe (Philadelphia). H XVII, 92–93. W I, 291–292. Original in Boston Public Library.	303
* July 4	Poe (Philadelphia) to F. W. Thomas (Washington). Stoddard, *Select Works of Edgar Allan Poe* (1880) xciv–xcvi. W I, 292–293. Original in New York Authors' Club.	304
July 6	F. W. Thomas (Washington) to Poe (Philadelphia). H XIV, 136–137. Ingram I, 198–199.	305
ante July 6	William Landor (Philadelphia) to Poe (Philadelphia). Cited in Poe to Landor, July 7, 1841.	306
ante July 7	William Landor (Philadelphia) to Poe (Philadelphia). [A second letter.] Cited in Poe to Landor, July 7, 1841.	307
July 7 or earlier	Landor to Poe. OCL 254 same as No. 307.	
* July 7	Poe (Philadelphia) to William Landor (Philadelphia). Parke-Bernet Galleries catalogue, Oct. 17–18, 1944, item 200. Original in Koester collection.	308
July 7	F. W. Thomas (Washington) to Poe (Philadelphia). H XVII, 94–95. Original in Boston Public Library.	309
July 10	J. E. Snodgrass (Baltimore) to Poe (Philadelphia). Cited in Poe to Snodgrass, July 12, 1841.	310
* July 12	Poe (Philadelphia) to J. E. Snodgrass (Baltimore). W I, 283–285. Original in Morgan Library.	311
ante July 15 (?)	E. St. J. to Poe (Philadelphia). Implied in *Graham's Magazine*, XIX (Aug. 1841) 96.	312
July 16–17	Poe to Thomas. OCL 258 same as No. 313.	

| July 17–18 (?) | Poe (Philadelphia) to F. W. Thomas (Washington). Implied in Thomas to Poe, July 19, 1841. | 313 |

| July 19 | F. W. Thomas (Washington) to Poe (Philadelphia). Original in Boston Public Library. | 314 |

| July 20–Aug. 29 | Thomas to Poe. See No. 315. OCL 260 is a less satisfactory dating. | |

| July–Aug. | F. W. Thomas (Washington) to Poe (Philadelphia). Cited in Thomas to Poe, Aug. 30, 1841. | 315 |

| Aug. 3 | Thomas to Poe. Misdated in H xvii, 95–100; ABC ii (Dec. 1932) 339; Quinn, *Poe*, 321 n. See No. 326. | |

| Aug. 10 | Timotheus Whackemwell to Poe (Philadelphia). H xiv, 138. | 316 |

| * Aug. 11 | Poe (Philadelphia) to Timotheus Whackemwell: addressed to J. N. McJilton (Baltimore). H xvii, 100. Original in Boston Public Library. | 317 |

| Aug. 11 | Lea and Blanchard to Poe. Misdated in ABC ii (Dec. 1932) 339. See No. 321. | |

| Aug. 11 | Whackemwell to Poe. Misdated in P i, 675–676. See No. 316. | |

| * Aug. 13 | Poe (Philadelphia) to Lea and Blanchard (Philadelphia). H xvii, 101. W i, 294–295. Original formerly in Drexel Institute, but sold by Parke-Bernet Galleries, Oct. 17–18, 1944, item 201. | 318 |

| Aug. 13 | J. N. McJilton (Baltimore) to Poe (Philadelphia). Original in Boston Public Library. | 319 |

| * Aug. 14 | Poe (Philadelphia) to Hastings Weld (New York). *Dial*, xliv (Jan. 16, 1908) 32–33. | 320 |

| Aug. 16 | Lea and Blanchard (Philadelphia) to Poe (Philadelphia). W i, 295–296. Original in Boston Public Library. | 321 |

| Aug. 26 | Poe to Thomas. Misdated in A ii, 476 n. See No. 298. | |

| Aug. 30 | L. J. Cist (Cincinnati) to Poe (Philadelphia). Cited in Poe to Cist, Sept. 18, 1841. | 322 |

| Aug. 30 | F. W. Thomas (Washington) to Poe (Philadelphia). H xvii, 102–103. W i, 293–294. Original in Boston Public Library. | 323 |

| Aug. 31 | Thomas to Poe. Misdated in ABC ii (Dec. 1932) 339. See No. 323. | |

Aug. late	R. W. Griswold (Philadelphia) to Poe (Philadelphia). Cited in Poe to Thomas, Sept. 1, 1841.	324
August	Griswold to Poe. See No. 324. OCL 267 is a less satisfactory dating.	
* Sept. 1	Poe (Philadelphia) to F. W. Thomas (Washington). American Art Association sale, March 11–12, 1930, item 284 (F). Original in Prescott collection.	325
Sept. 3	F. W. Thomas (Washington) to Poe (Philadelphia). H XVII, 95–100. Original in Boston Public Library.	326
Sept. 6	J. E. Snodgrass (Baltimore) to Poe (Philadelphia). Cited in Poe to Snodgrass, Sept. 19, 1841.	327
Sept. 9	Richard Bolton (Pantotoc, Miss.) to Poe (Philadelphia). Cited in Bolton to Poe, Nov. 4, 1841.	328
* Sept. 18	Poe (Philadelphia) to L. J. Cist (Cincinnati). Beyer sale, no date, item 364 (F). Anderson Galleries sale, Jan. 17, 1927, item 321. Original in Koester collection.	329
* Sept. 19	Poe (Philadelphia) to J. E. Snodgrass (Baltimore). W I, 285–287. Bixby 20–21 (F). Original in Huntington Library (HM 21865).	330
Sept. 20	Poe (Philadelphia) to F. W. Thomas (Washington). Cited in Thomas to Poe, Sept. 22, 1841.	331
Sept. 21	Poe to Cist. Misdated in Quinn, *Poe*, 342 n. See No. 329.	
Sept. 22	F. W. Thomas (Washington) to Poe (Philadelphia). P I, 681. Original in Boston Public Library.	332
Oct. 14	F. W. Thomas (Washington) to Poe (Philadelphia). Original in Boston Public Library.	333
* Oct. 27	Poe (Philadelphia) to F. W. Thomas (Washington). *American Literature*, VI (1934) 66–69.	334
Oct. 29	John Tomlin (Jackson, Tenn.) to Poe (Philadelphia). Original in Boston Public Library.	335
October	Poe (Philadelphia) to N. P. Willis (New York). Cited in Willis to Poe, Nov. 30, 1841.	336

Oct.–Nov.	N. P. Willis (New York) to Poe (Philadelphia). Cited in Willis to Poe, Nov. 30, 1841.	337
Nov. 4	Richard Bolton (Pontotoc, Miss.) to Poe (Philadelphia). Memphis *Commercial Appeal*, Nov. 15, 1925.	338
Nov. 6	F. W. Thomas (Washington) to Poe (Philadelphia). Original in Boston Public Library.	339
ante Nov. 8	W. B. Tyler to Poe (Philadelphia). *Graham's Magazine*, XIX (1841) 306–307.	340
Nov. 8–9	Poe (Philadelphia) to F. W. Thomas (Washington). Cited in Thomas to Poe, Nov. 10, 1841.	341
* Nov. 10	Poe (Philadelphia) to Mrs. L. H. Sigourney (Hartford, Conn.). G. S. Haight, *Life of Mrs. Sigourney* (New Haven: Yale University Press, 1930) 118 (F). Original in Connecticut Historical Society.	342
Nov. 10	F. W. Thomas (Washington) to Poe (Philadelphia). P I, 685. Original in Boston Public Library.	343
Nov. 13	Mrs. L. H. Sigourney (Hartford, Conn.) to Poe (Philadelphia). Cited in Poe to Sigourney, Nov. 16, 1841.	344
* Nov. 16	Poe (Philadelphia) to Mrs. L. H. Sigourney (Hartford, Conn.). G. S. Haight, *Life of Mrs. Sigourney* (New Haven: Yale University Press, 1930) 119–120. Original in Connecticut Historical Society.	345
* Nov. 18	Poe (Philadelphia) to Richard Bolton (Pontotoc, Miss.). Memphis *Commercial Appeal*, Nov. 15, 1925 (F).	346
Nov. 23	F. W. Thomas (Washington) to Poe (Philadelphia). Original in Boston Public Library.	347
* Nov. 26	Poe (Philadelphia) to F. W. Thomas (Washington). Original in Dumbarton Oaks Library.	348
Nov. 29	Poe to Willis. OCL 289 same as No. 349.	
ante Nov. 30 (?)	Poe (Philadelphia) to N. P. Willis (Glenmary, N. Y.). Implied in Willis to Poe, Nov. 30, 1841.	349
Nov. 30	N. P. Willis (Glenmary, N. Y.) to Poe (Philadelphia). W I, 287–288. H XVII, 104. Original in Boston Public Library.	350

Nov.–June 10, 1842   T. H. Chivers to Poe (Philadelphia). [2 letters.] Cited in Poe to Chivers, July 6, 1842.   351

Dec. 1   John Tomlin (Jackson, Tenn.) to Poe (Philadelphia). P I, 686. Original in Boston Public Library.   352

Dec. 12   John Tomlin (Jackson, Tenn.) to Poe (Philadelphia). Original in Boston Public Library.   353

Dec. 31   Poe to Kennedy. Misdated in ABC II (Nov. 1932) 290. See No. 264.

1842

Jan. 10   Richard Bolton (Pontotoc, Miss.) to Poe (Philadelphia). Memphis *Commercial Appeal*, Nov. 15, 1925.   354

Jan. 13   F. W. Thomas (Washington) to Poe (Philadelphia). Original in Boston Public Library.   355

Jan. 13–14   Thomas to Poe. OCL 293 same as No. 355.

* Feb. 3   Poe (Philadelphia) to F. W. Thomas (Washington). *The Autograph*, I (1912) 42–43.   356

Feb. 6   Thomas to Poe. Misdated in H XVII, 105–106; W I, 318–321; P I, 689–690. See No. 358.

Feb. 14   J. N. McJilton (Baltimore ?) to Poe (Philadelphia). Cited in Poe to McJilton, March 13, 1842.   357

Feb. 26   F. W. Thomas (Washington) to Poe (Philadelphia). W I, 318–321. H XVII, 105–106. Original in Boston Public Library.   358

March 1–6   Poe to Dickens. OCL 296 same as No. 359.

ante March 6 (?)   Poe (Philadelphia) to Charles Dickens (Philadelphia). Implied in Dickens to Poe, March 6, 1842.   359

March 6   Charles Dickens (Philadelphia) to Poe (Philadelphia). W I, 327. H XVII, 107.   360

* March 13   Poe (Philadelphia) to J. N. McJilton (Baltimore ?). Parke-Bernet Galleries sale, Nov. 19–20, 1945, item 422. Original in Koester collection.   361

March 13   Poe (Philadelphia) to F. W. Thomas (Washington). Cited in Thomas to Poe, May 21, 1842.   362

March 30   Poe to Tyler. Misdated in A II, 541, where original is wrongly cited as at University of Wisconsin; OCL 299. See No. 429.

March 31	Tyler to Poe. Misdated in W I, 321; ABC II (Dec. 1932) 339; OCL 300. See No. 430.	
April 16	Poe to Cooke. Misdated by Poe. See No. 621.	
May 13	Daniel Bryan (Alexandria, D. C.) to Poe (Philadelphia). Original in Boston Public Library.	363
May 21	F. W. Thomas (Washington) to Poe (Philadelphia). H XVII, 108–110. W I, 322–324. Original in Boston Public Library.	364
* May 25	Poe (Philadelphia) to F. W. Thomas (Washington). H XVII, 110–111. W I, 324–326. Original in Koester collection.	365
ca. May late (?)	James Herron (Washington) to Poe (Philadelphia). Implied in Poe to Herron, June (early) 1842.	366
* [*ca.* June early]	Poe (Philadelphia) to James Herron (Washington). Quinn, *Poe,* 360. Original in Koester collection.	367
* June 4	Poe (Philadelphia) to George Roberts (Boston). H XVII, 112–113. Original in Lilly collection.	368
* June 4	Poe (Philadelphia) to J. E. Snodgrass (Baltimore). Quinn, *Poe,* 355–357. Original in Morgan Library.	369
June 4 (?)	Poe (Philadelphia) to [T. W. White or M. F. Maury (Richmond) (as editor of SLM)]. Bangs sale, May 24, 1897.	370
June 6	Poe to Chivers. Misdated in H XVII, 113–115; W II, 382; P I, 752–753. See No. 378.	
June 10 or as early as Dec. 1841	Chivers to Poe. See No. 351. OCL 308 is a less satisfactory dating.	
June 10	Bolton to Poe. Misdated in Memphis *Commercial Appeal,* Nov. 15, 1925; OCL 307. See No. 354.	
June 11	T. H. Chivers (Middletown, Conn.) to Poe (Philadelphia). Cited in Poe to Chivers, July 6, 1842.	371
ca. June 15 (?)	Daniel Bryan (Alexandria, D. C.) to Poe (Philadelphia). Implied in Poe to Bryan, July 6, 1842.	372
June 27	Daniel Bryan (Alexandria, D. C.) to Poe (Philadelphia). Original in Boston Public Library.	373
ca. June 27	Poe (Philadelphia) to F. W. Thomas (Washington). Cited in Poe to Thomas, Aug. 27, 1842.	374

ante June 30	James Herron (Washington) to Poe (Philadelphia). Cited in Poe to Herron, June 30, 1842.	
* June 30	Poe (Philadelphia) to James Herron (Washington). Quinn, *Poe*, 360–361. Original in Koester collection.	375
* July 6	Poe (Philadelphia) to Daniel Bryan (Alexandria, D. C.). W I, 330–334. Original in Iowa State Department of History and Archives, Des Moines.	376
* July 6	Poe (Philadelphia) to T. H. Chivers (Middletown, Conn.). H XVII, 113–115.	377
* July 7	Poe (Philadelphia) to Mrs. E. R. Tutt (Woodville, Va.). Anderson Galleries sale, Jan. 18, 1922, item 229.	378
July 11	Daniel Bryan (Alexandria, D. C.) to Poe (Philadelphia). Original in Boston Public Library.	379
July 12	T. H. Chivers (New York) to Poe (Philadelphia). H XVII, 115–117. Original in Boston Public Library.	380
July 18	Poe (Philadelphia) to ——. Anderson Galleries sale, April 19, 1904, item 689, cited.	381
July 26	Poe to Bryan. Misdated in Quinn, *Poe*, 342. See No. 377.	382
July 26	Daniel Bryan (Alexandria, D. C.) to Poe (Philadelphia). Original in Boston Public Library.	383
July 27–Aug. 3 (?)	Poe (Philadelphia) to Daniel Bryan (Alexandria, D. C.). Implied in Bryan to Poe, Aug. 4, 1842.	384
July	Poe to Thomas. Erroneously stated as to Thomas, in A II, 542. See No. 377.	
Aug. 4	Daniel Bryan (Alexandria, D. C.) to Poe (Philadelphia). Original in Boston Public Library.	385
Aug. 15	Poe to Washington Poe. Misdated in W I, 335; OCL 322. See No. 246.	
* Aug. 27	Poe (Philadelphia) to F. W. Thomas (Washington). W I, 335–337.	386
Sept. 2	F. W. Thomas (Washington) to Poe (Philadelphia). Cited in Poe to Thomas, Sept. 12, 1842.	387
* Sept. 12	Poe (Philadelphia) to F. W. Thomas (Washington). W I, 352–354. Original in New York Public Library.	388

Sept. 15	T. H. Chivers (New York) to Poe (Philadelphia). Cited in Poe to Chivers, Sept. 27, 1842.	389
Sept. 15	Edgar Janvier and W. W. McNair to Poe (Philadelphia). Cited in Poe to Janvier and McNair, Sept. 27, 1842.	390
* Sept. [21]	Poe (Philadelphia) to F. W. Thomas (Washington). H xvii, 118–119. W i, 337–339. Original in Huntington Library (HM 21871).	391
Sept. 21	John Tomlin (Jackson, Tenn.) to Poe (Philadelphia). Cited in Poe to Tomlin, Oct. 5, 1842.	392
Sept. 26	T. H. Chivers (New York) to Poe (Philadelphia). H xvii, 119–120. Original in Boston Public Library.	393
* Sept. 27	Poe (Philadelphia) to T. H. Chivers (New York). *Century Magazine*, lxv (1903) 439. Quinn, *Poe*, 367–369. Original in Huntington Library (HM 24211).	394
Sept. 27	Poe (Philadelphia) to Edgar Janvier and W. W. McNair. Cited in *American Literature*, xiii, No. 3 (Nov. 1941) 283, but original not at Lafayette, as stated.	395
September	Poe to Thomas. OCL 329 same as No. 391.	
* Oct. 5	Poe (Philadelphia) to John Tomlin (Jackson, Tenn.). PC ii, 37.	396
Nov. 14	F. W. Thomas (Washington) to Poe (Philadelphia). Cited in Poe to Thomas, Nov. 19, 1842.	397
* Nov. 16	Poe (Philadelphia) to J. R. Lowell (Boston). W i, 344. Original in Harvard Library.	398
Nov. 16	Poe to Sigourney. Misdated by Poe. See No. 345.	
* Nov. 19	Poe (Philadelphia) to F. W. Thomas (Washington). W i, 339–342. Copy in Boston Public Library.	399
Nov. 19	J. R. Lowell (Boston) to Poe (Philadelphia). H xvii, 120–121. W i, 345–346.	400
Nov. 20–Dec. 16	Poe to Lowell. OCL 335 same as No. 405.	
Nov. 27	Charles Dickens (London) to Poe (Philadelphia). W i, 328–329. H xvii, 124–125. Original in Boston Public Library.	401
Dec. (early ?)	Poe (Philadelphia) to Editor *Boston Miscellany*. Implied as accompanying "The Tell-	

Tale Heart," offered for publication. See
Lowell to Poe, Dec. 17, 1842.   402

Dec. 7   T. H. Chivers (Augusta, Ga.) to Poe (Philadelphia). *Century Magazine,* LXV (1903)
440–441.   403

ante Dec. 16   Editor [H. T. Tuckerman] *Boston Miscellany*
to Poe (Philadelphia). Cited in Poe to
Lowell, Dec. 25, 1842.   404

ante Dec. 17 (?)   Poe (Philadelphia) to J. R. Lowell or Brad-
bury & Soden (Boston). Implied in Lowell
to Poe, Dec. 17, 1842.   405

Dec. 17   J. R. Lowell (Boston) to Poe (Philadelphia).
W I, 346–347. H XVII, 125.   406

Dec. 23   Poe to Lowell. Misdated in OCL 339. See
No. 407.

* [Dec. 25]   Poe (Philadelphia) to J. R. Lowell (Boston).
W I, 347–348. Original in Harvard Li-
brary.   407

* Dec. 27   Poe (Philadelphia) to J. R. Lowell (Boston).
Quinn, *Poe,* 365. Original in Koester collection.   408

n. d.   Poe to Graham. Undated in *Graham's Magazine,* XXXIV (March 1850) 224–226;
Quinn, *Poe,* 343. See No. 512.

1842–1843 n. d.   Poe to Griswold. Included in Griswold's
Preface, xxi; H XVII, 129; W I, 354–355;
P I, 781; OCL 340. Not an authentic
letter.

1843

ante Jan. 29 (?)   Poe (Philadelphia) to F. W. Thomas (Washington). Implied in Thomas to Poe, Feb. 1,
1843.   409

ca. Jan. 30–31   Poe (Philadelphia) to F. W. Thomas (Washington). Cited in Thomas to Poe, Feb. 1,
1843.   410

Feb. 1   F. W. Thomas (Washington) to Poe (Philadelphia). H XVII, 128–129. W II, 3–4.
Original in Boston Public Library.   411

* Feb. 4   Poe (Philadelphia) to J. R. Lowell (Boston).
W I, 348–350. Original in Harvard Li-
brary.   412

Feb. 8   Thomas to Poe. No such letter. Cited in
Quinn, *Poe,* 371, as to Poe. Actually from

	Thomas to Robert Tyler, the original MS. being in the Boston Public Library.	
Feb. 8 (?)	F. W. Thomas (Washington) to Poe (Philadelphia). Not in Boston Public Library as stated in Quinn, *Poe*, 371. However, this item implied in Thomas to Tyler, Feb. 8, 1843, original in Boston Public Library.	413
Feb. 15	Poe to Wyatt. OCL 346 same as No. 417.	
ante Feb. 16	Robert Carter (Boston) to Poe (Philadelphia). Cited in Poe to Carter, Feb. 16, 1843.	414
* [Feb. 16]	Poe (Philadelphia) to Robert Carter (Boston). Original in Lilly collection.	415
ca. Feb. 15–18	Poe (Philadelphia) to F. W. Thomas (Washington). Cited in Poe to Thomas, Feb. 25, 1843.	416
ca. Feb. 15–18	Poe (Philadelphia) to Prof. Wyatt (Washington). Cited in Poe to Thomas, Feb. 25, 1843.	417
* Feb. 25	Poe (Philadelphia) to F. W. Thomas (Washington). H xvii, 131–133. W ii, 5–8. Original in Boston Public Library.	418
March 1	John Tomlin (Jackson, Tenn.) to Poe (Philadelphia). H xvii, 133. Original in Boston Public Library.	419
* March 7	Poe (Philadelphia) to Robert Carter (Boston). Original in Koester collection.	419a
* March 9	Poe (Washington) to J. K. Townsend (Washington). P i, 803.	420
* March 11	Poe (Washington) to T. C. Clarke (Philadelphia). H xvii, 134. W ii, 8–9. Gill 120 (F). Original in New York Public Library.	421
ante March 16	Subscribers to *Stylus* [several] to Poe (Philadelphia). Cited in Poe to Thomas and Dow, March 16, 1843.	422
March 16	Poe (Philadelphia) to F. W. Thomas and J. E. Dow (Washington). [Original draft of letter of same date.] Pratt 17–18 (F). Original draft in Pratt Library.	423
* March 16	Poe (Philadelphia) to F. W. Thomas and J. E. Dow (Washington). H xvii, 134–138. W ii, 11–15. Original in Boston Public Library.	424
* March 24	Poe (Philadelphia) to P. D. Bernard (Richmond). H i, 178. Original in Virginia State Library.	425

March 24	J. R. Lowell (Boston) to Poe (Philadelphia). W II, 19–20. H XVII, 138–139.	426
* March 27	Poe (Philadelphia) to J. R. Lowell (Boston). W II, 20–23. Original in Harvard Library.	427
March 27	F. W. Thomas (Washington) to Poe (Philadelphia). W II, 17–18. H XVII, 140–141. Original in Boston Public Library.	428
ante March 31	Poe (Philadelphia) to Robert Tyler (Washington). Cited in Tyler to Poe, March 31, 1843.	429
March 31	Robert Tyler (Washington) to Poe (Philadelphia). W I, 321. Original in Boston Public Library.	430
April 17	J. R. Lowell (Boston) to Poe (Philadelphia). W II, 23–25. H XVII, 142–143.	431
* [*ca.* April]	Poe (Philadelphia) to William Mackenzie (Richmond). Original in Koester collection.	432
May 8	J. R. Lowell (Cambridge, Mass.) to Poe (Philadelphia). W II, 25–27. H XVII, 143–144.	433
May 13	Poe to William Poe. OCL 360 same as No. 434.	
ante May 15	Poe (Philadelphia) to William Poe (Baltimore). Cited in William Poe to Poe, June 15, 1843.	434
May 15	William Poe (Baltimore) to Poe (Philadelphia). Cited in William Poe to Poe, June 15, 1843.	435
May 16	J. R. Lowell (Boston) to Poe (Philadelphia). W II, 27–28. H XVII, 144–145.	436
early summer	T. H. Chivers (Oaky Grove, Ga.) to Poe (Philadelphia). Cited in Chivers to Poe, June 15, 1844.	437
[June 11	Poe (Philadelphia) to R. W. Griswold (Philadelphia). H XVII, 145. W II, 34. See No. 282.	438?]
June 15	William Poe (Baltimore) to Poe (Philadelphia). W II, 31–33. H XVII, 145–146. Original in Boston Public Library.	439
June 19	Robert Carter (Cambridge, Mass.) to Poe (Philadelphia). W II, 28–31. H XVII, 146–148.	440
ante June 20 (?)	Rosalie Poe (Richmond) to Poe (Philadelphia). Implied in Poe to Henry, June 20, 1843.	441

June 20	Poe to Fields. Erroneously stated as to James T. Fields, in H XVII, 149. See No. 443.	
* June 20	Poe (Philadelphia) to Lucy D. Henry (Red Mill, Va.). Original in Poe Shrine, Richmond.	442
* June 20	Poe (Philadelphia) to J. R. Lowell (Boston). H XVII, 149. W II, 33–34. Original in Koester collection.	443
June 20	Poe (Philadelphia) to John Tomlin (Jackson, Tenn.). Cited in Tomlin to Poe, July 2, 1843.	444
July 2	John Tomlin (Jackson, Tenn.) to Poe (Philadelphia). H XVII, 149–151. Original in Boston Public Library.	445
post July 2 (?)	Poe (Philadelphia) to John Tomlin (Jackson, Tenn.). Implied in Poe to Tomlin, Aug. 28, 1843.	446
Aug. 9	John Tomlin (Jackson, Tenn.) to Poe (Philadelphia). Original in Boston Public Library.	447
* Aug. 28	Poe (Philadelphia) to John Tomlin (Jackson, Tenn.). W II, 39–42.	448
Sept. 10	John Tomlin (Jackson, Tenn.) to Poe (Philadelphia). W II, 42. H XVII, 152. Original in Boston Public Library.	449
* Sept. 13	Poe (Philadelphia) to J. R. Lowell (Boston). W II, 44. Original in Harvard Library.	450
Sept. 25	T. E. Van Bibber (Avondale) to Poe (Philadelphia). Bangs sale, April 11, 1896, item 113, cited.	451
Sept. 28	Poe (Philadelphia) to L. M. Wilkins. American Art Association sale, Nov. 5, 1923, item 632, cited.	452
Oct. 1	A. M. Ide, Jr. (South Attleboro, Mass.) to Poe (Philadelphia). H XVII, 153–155. Original in Boston Public Library.	453
Oct. 13	J. R. Lowell (Cambridge, Mass.) to Poe (Philadelphia). Cited in Poe to Lowell, Oct. 19, 1843.	454
ante Oct. 19	Robert Carter (Boston) to Poe (Philadelphia). Cited in Poe to Lowell, Oct. 19, 1843.	455
Oct. 19	Poe (Philadelphia) to A. M. Ide, Jr. (South Attleboro, Mass.). Cited in Ide to Poe, Nov. 2, 1843.	456

* Oct. 19	Poe (Philadelphia) to J. R. Lowell (Cambridge, Mass.). W II, 44–47. Original in Harvard Library.	457
Oct.–March, 1844	Poe to Lowell. See No. 461. OCL 383 is a less satisfactory dating.	
Nov. 2	A. M. Ide, Jr. (South Attleboro, Mass.) to Poe (Philadelphia). H XVII, 156–157. Original in Boston Public Library.	458
Nov. 14	J. H. Hedges to Poe (Philadelphia). Cited in Poe to Hedges, Nov. 16, 1843.	459
* Nov. 16	Poe (Philadelphia) to J. H. Hedges. Henkels sale, Feb. 22, 1907, item 161, cited. Whitty (1917) 196.	460
Dec. 15	William Poe to Poe. Misdated in ABC II (Dec. 1932) 339; OCL 381. See No. 439.	
Dec. 23	Poe to Lowell. Misdated in ABC II (Nov. 1932) 292. See No. 407.	
Dec.–Jan., 1844 (?)	Poe (Philadelphia) to J. R. Lowell (Cambridge, Mass.). Implied in Lowell to Poe, March 6, 1844.	461

1844

January	J. R. Lowell (Cambridge) to Poe (?) (Philadelphia). Goodspeed's sale catalogue No. 237.	461a
* Jan. 13	Poe (Philadelphia) to J. B. Sutherland (Philadelphia). Original in Haverford College.	462
* [*ante* Jan. 31]	Poe (Philadelphia ?) to Mr. Clark (Philadelphia ?). [On a projected series of lectures in Baltimore.] Parke-Bernet Galleries sale, April 5–6, 1943, item 374. Original in Koester collection.	463
* [Jan. 31]	Poe (Baltimore) to Isaac Munroe (Baltimore). Copy of original in collection of John C. French.	464
* [Feb. 1]	Poe (Baltimore) to John P. Kennedy (Baltimore). Sotheby sale, June 2–3, 1924, item 321.	464a
ante Feb. 18 (?)	George Lippard (Philadelphia) to Poe (Philadelphia). Implied in Poe to Lippard, Feb. 18, 1844.	465
* Feb. 18	Poe (Philadelphia) to George Lippard (Philadelphia). Heartman and Canny 93–94.	466
Feb. 23	John Tomlin (Jackson, Tenn.) to Poe (Philadelphia). W II, 55–56. H XVII, 158. Original in Boston Public Library.	467

* March 1	Poe (Philadelphia) to J. C. Myers (Reading, Pa.). American Art Association sale, March 18–19, 1925, item 569 (F). Original in Koester collection.	468
March 5	Samuel Williams and William Graeff, Jr. (Reading, Pa.) to Poe (Philadelphia). Cited in Poe to Williams and Graeff, March 7, 1844.	469
March 6	J. R. Lowell (Cambridge, Mass.) to Poe (Philadelphia). W II, 56–59. H XVII, 158–160.	470
* March 7	Poe (Philadelphia) to Samuel Williams and William Graeff, Jr. (Reading, Pa.). P I, 858.	471
post March 7 (?)	Samuel Williams and William Graeff, Jr. (Reading, Pa.) to Poe (Philadelphia). Implied in Poe to Williams and Graeff, March 7, 1844, and by lecture delivered March 13.	472
March 10	Poe to Lowell. Misdated in P II, 863; OCL 389. See No. 476.	
* March 15	Poe (Philadelphia) to Cornelius Mathews (New York). P II, 865. Quinn, *Poe*, 402. Bixby 22–23 (F). Original in Huntington Library (HM 21864).	473
March 20–26	Poe to Horne. OCL 392 same as No. 475.	
March 22	A. M. Ide, Jr. (South Attleboro, Mass.) to Poe (Philadelphia). H XVII, 162–164. Original in Boston Public Library.	474
March late	Poe (Philadelphia) to R. H. Horne (London). Cited in Horne to Poe, April 16, 1844.	475
* March 30	Poe (Philadelphia) to J. R. Lowell (Cambridge, Mass.). W II, 60–63. Original in Harvard Library.	476
* April 7	Poe (New York) to Mrs. Maria Clemm (Philadelphia). W II, 65–68. Quinn, *Poe*, 406–407. Pratt 20 (F). Original in Pratt Library.	477
April 16	R. H. Horne (London) to Poe (Philadelphia: forwarded to New York). W II, 50–52. Original in Boston Public Library.	478
April 27	R. H. Horne (London) to Poe (Philadelphia: forwarded to New York, May 20). W II, 52–55. H XVII, 167–169. Original in Boston Public Library.	479

May 15	Chivers to Poe. Misdated in H XVII, 170–173; P II, 874; ABC II (Dec. 1932) 338. See No. 488.	
May 20	Poe to Lowell. Misdated in A II, 594. See No. 481.	
ca. May 23	J. R. Lowell (Cambridge, Mass.) to Poe (New York). Cited in Poe to Lowell, May 28, 1844.	480
* May 28	Poe (New York) to J. R. Lowell (Cambridge, Mass.). W II, 69–71. Original in Harvard Library.	481
* May 29	Poe (New York) to Mrs. S. J. Hale (Philadelphia). P II, 877. New York *Times*, Jan. 28, 1917.	482
May 30	Mrs. S. J. Hale (Philadelphia) to Poe (New York). Cited in Poe to Hale, May 31, 1844.	483
* May 31	Poe (New York) to Mrs. S. J. Hale (Philadelphia). New York *Times*, Jan. 28, 1917. Quinn, *Poe*, 417–418. Original in Huntington Library (HM 21875).	484
June 3	Poe (New York) to L. J. Cist (Cincinnati). Anderson Galleries sale, Jan. 16, 1923, item 215, cited.	485
June 3	Poe (New York) to ———. Henkels sale, May 8–10, 1895, item 289. [Perhaps same as preceding item.]	486
* [June 4]	Poe (New York) to Eli Bowen (Columbia, Pa.). J. E. Spannuth, *Poe's Doings of Gotham* (Pottsville, Pa.: 1929) 55	487
June 9	Poe to Keese. Misdated in OCL 405. See No. 544.	
June 14	Poe to Bowen. Misdated in OCL 406. See No. 487.	
June 15	T. H. Chivers (Oaky Grove, Ga.) to Poe (New York). H XVII, 170–173. Original in Boston Public Library.	488
June 27	J. R. Lowell (Cambridge, Mass.) to Poe (New York). W II, 87–89. H XVII, 180–182.	489
June	Poe to Anthon. See No. 505. H XVII, 175–180; W II, 72–79; P I, 545; Quinn, *Poe*, 426; OCL 410 are less satisfactory datings.	
June–Nov.	Poe to Anthon. See No. 506. OCL 411 is a less satisfactory dating.	

* July 2	Poe (New York) to J. R. Lowell (Cambridge, Mass.). W II, 90–95. Original in Harvard Library.	490
* July 10	Poe (New York) to T. H. Chivers (Oaky Grove, Ga.). *Century Magazine,* LXV (1903) 441–442. Original in Huntington Library (HM 24212).	491
Aug. 6	T. H. Chivers (Oaky Grove, Ga.) to Poe (New York). H XVII, 184–186. Original in Boston Public Library.	492
Aug. 8	Chivers to Poe. Misdated in ABC II (Dec. 1932) 338. See No. 492.	
* Aug. 18	Poe (New York) to J. R. Lowell (Cambridge, Mass.). W II, 96–98. Original in Harvard Library.	493
Aug. (?)	Swedenborgians of Philadelphia to Poe (New York). Cited in *Aristidean,* I (Oct. 1845) 317.	494
Sept. 2	F. W. Thomas (Washington) to Poe (New York). P II, 905. Original in Boston Public Library.	495
Sept. 2	Poe to Thomas. Misdated in Quinn, *Poe,* 430, but correctly dated 431. See No. 496.	
* Sept. 8	Poe (New York) to F. W. Thomas (Washington). H XVII, 187–188. W II, 98–100.	496
Sept. 24	T. H. Chivers (Oaky Grove, Ga.) to Poe (New York). H XVII, 188–190. Original in Boston Public Library.	497
Sept. 27	J. R. Lowell (Cambridge, Mass.) to Poe (New York). W II, 100. Original in New York Public Library.	498
Oct. 10	F. W. Thomas (Washington) to Poe (New York). P II, 905–906. Original in Boston Public Library.	499
Oct. 15	William Duane (Philadelphia) to Poe (New York). Cited in Poe to Duane, Oct. 28, 1844.	500
Oct. 20–24	Craig to Poe. OCL 422 same as No. 501.	
Oct. 21	Poe to Lowell. Misdated in ABC II (Nov. 1932) 292. See No. 504.	
ante Oct. 24	S. D. Craig (Quogue, N. Y.) to Poe (New York). Cited in Poe to Craig, Oct. 24, 1844.	501
* Oct. 24	Poe (New York) to S. D. Craig (Quogue, N. Y.). H XVII, 190. Copy in Boston Public Library.	502

Oct. 25	Poe to Craig. Misdated in ABC II (Dec. 1932) 338. See No. 502.	
* Oct. 28	Poe (New York) to William Duane (Philadelphia). W II, 366. Original in Pennsylvania Historical Society.	503
* Oct. 28	Poe (New York) to J. R. Lowell (Cambridge, Mass.). W II, 103–106. Original in Harvard Library.	504
* [*ante* Nov. 2]	Poe (New York) to Charles Anthon (New York). [Draft of a letter with cancellations and corrections.] H XVII, 180–182. Original in Huntington Library (HM 21870).	505
ante Nov. 2	Poe (New York) to Charles Anthon (New York). [Clean copy of draft, same date.] Established as sent, by Anthon to Poe, Nov. 2, 1844.	506
Nov. 2	Charles Anthon (New York) to Poe (New York). H XVII, 193. W II, 80–81. Original in Boston Public Library.	507
ante Nov. 12 (?)	Poe (New York) to N. P. Willis (New York). Implied in Willis to Poe, Nov. 12, 1844.	508
Nov. 12	N. P. Willis (New York) to Poe (New York). H XVII, 194. Gill 130 (F).	509
Dec. 10	F. W. Thomas (Washington) to Poe (New York). Original in Boston Public Library.	510
Dec. 12	J. R. Lowell (Cambridge, Mass.) to Poe (New York). W II, 106–108. H XVII, 194–195.	511
n. d.	Poe to Griswold. An unauthentic letter as printed in Griswold's Preface, xxii; H XVII, 169–170; OCL 432. See No. 534.	

1845

* [early]	Poe (New York) to George Graham (Philadelphia). *Graham's Magazine*, XXXVI (March 1850) 224–226. Quinn, *Poe*, 343.	512
* Jan. 4	Poe (New York) to George Bush (New York). Quinn, *Poe*, 420.	513
* Jan. 4	Poe (New York) to F. W. Thomas (Washington). Quinn, *Poe*, 435. Original in Huntington Library (HM 21866).	514
Jan. 5–May 3	F. W. Thomas (Washington) to Poe (New York). [2 letters.] Cited in Poe to Thomas, May 4, 1845.	515

Jan. 10	Poe to Griswold. An unauthentic letter as printed in Griswold's Preface, xxii; H xvII, 196; P II, 932; A II, 636; OCL 438.
Jan. 11	Griswold to Poe. An unauthentic letter as printed in Griswold's Preface, xxii; H xvII, 197; P II, 932–933; OCL 439. See No. 516.
Jan. 14	R. W. Griswold (New York) to Poe (New York). H xvII, 197–198. Quinn, *Poe*, 444. Original in Boston Public Library. 516
* Jan. 16	Poe (New York) to R. W. Griswold (New York). H xvII, 198. Quinn, *Poe*, 445. Original in Boston Public Library. 517
Jan. 25	Poe (New York) to R. H. Horne (London). Cited in Horne to Poe, May 17, 1845. 518
Jan. 27	Duane to Poe. OCL 443 same as No. 519.
ante Jan. 28	William Duane (Philadelphia) to Poe (New York). Cited in Poe to Duane, Jan. 28, 1845. 519
* Jan. 28	Poe (New York) to William Duane (Philadelphia). W II, 367. Original in Pennsylvania Historical Society. 520
* [Feb. 3]	Poe (New York) to J. A. Shea (New York). H I, 218. Original in Morgan Library. 521
ante Feb. 16	Poe (New York) to A. M. Ide, Jr. (South Attleboro, Mass.). Cited in Ide to Poe, Feb. 16, 1845. 522
Feb. 16	A. M. Ide, Jr. (South Attleboro, Mass.) to Poe (New York). Original in Boston Public Library. 523
* Feb. 24	Poe (New York) to R. W. Griswold (Philadelphia). H xvII, 201–202. Quinn, *Poe*, 446–448 (F). Original in Boston Public Library. 524
Feb. 24	Poe to Griswold. An unauthentic letter as printed in Griswold's Preface, xxii. See No. 524.
Feb. (?)	Poe (New York) to B. B. Minor (Richmond). P II, 950, cited. 525
February	Poe to Shea. See No. 521. H I, 218–219; Whitty 194; P II, 938–939; OCL 509 are less satisfactory datings.
[March 1] (Saturday morning)	W. M. Gillespie (New York) to Poe (New York). Original in Boston Public Library. 526
* March 8	Poe (New York) to Editor *Broadway Journal* (New York). Ingram 1, 292–293. 527

March 15	Mrs. M. E. Hewitt (New York) to Poe (New York). T. O. Mabbott, *A Christmas Book* (Hunter College, Dec. 1937), 116–117. Original in Boston Public Library.	528
* March 17	Poe (New York) to J. Hunt, Jr. (Ithaca, N. Y.). *Century Magazine*, LXV (Feb. 1903) 550. Quinn, *Poe*, 456. Original in Huntington Library (HM 24213).	529
March 19 (?)	Poe (New York) to Mrs. A. C. Mowatt (New York). Implied in Mowatt to Poe, March 20, 1845.	530
ca. March 20, Thursday evening	Mrs. A. C. Mowatt (New York) to Poe (New York). Original in Boston Public Library.	531
ante March 21	Poe (New York) to Mrs. M. E. Hewitt (New York). Cited in Hewitt to Poe, March 21, 1845.	532
March 21	Mrs. M. E. Hewitt (New York) to Poe (New York). T. O. Mabbott, *A Christmas Book* (Hunter College, Dec. 1937), 117–118. Original in Boston Public Library.	533
[March] Thursday Evening	Mowatt to Poe. See No. 531. H XVII, 207–208; P II, 1006; A II, 646; Quinn, *Poe*, 470 are less satisfactory datings.	
April 19	Poe to Griswold. An unauthentic letter as printed in Griswold's Preface, xxii. See No. 534.	
* April 19	Poe (New York) to R. W. Griswold (Philadelphia). H XVII, 202–203. Quinn, *Poe*, 449–450. Original in Boston Public Library.	534
* [May 4]	Poe (New York) to F. W. Thomas (Washington). H XVII, 203–205. W II, 133–135. Original in Boston Public Library.	535
May 12	F. W. Thomas (Washington) to Poe (New York). Original in Boston Public Library.	536
* May 14	Poe (New York) to F. W. Thomas (Washington). American Art Association sale, Dec. 16–17, 1929 (F). Original in Koester collection.	537
May 17	R. H. Horne (London) to Poe (New York). W II, 116–119. H XVII, 208–210. Original in Boston Public Library.	538
May 24	John Keese (New York) to Poe (New York). Cited in Poe to Keese, May 26, 1845.	539

* May 26	Poe (New York) to John Keese (New York). Original in Koester collection.	540
May 29	Mrs. M. E. Hewitt (New York) to Poe (New York). T. O. Mabbott, *A Christmas Book* (Hunter College, Dec. 1937), 118. Original in Boston Public Library.	541
ca. May–June	R. H. Stoddard (New York) to Poe (New York). R. H. Stoddard, *Recollections* (1903) 146.	542
June 1	A. M. Ide, Jr. (South Attleboro) to Poe (New York). Original in Boston Public Library.	543
* June 9	Poe (New York) to John Keese (New York). Original in Koester collection.	544
* [June 26] Thursday morning	Poe (New York) to E. A. Duyckinck (New York). W II, 156–157. Quinn, *Poe*, 493–494. Original in New York Public Library.	545
ante June 27	Poe (New York) to Mrs. A. C. Lynch (New York). Cited in Lynch to Poe, June 27, 1845.	546
[June 27] Friday morning	Mrs. A. C. Lynch (New York) to Poe (New York). H XVII, 258–259. P II, 1095. Original in Boston Public Library.	547
June	Poe to E. J. Thomas. See No. 548. Ingram II, 84; H XVII, 250–251; OCL 467 are less satisfactory datings.	
* *ante* July 5	Poe (New York) to E. J. Thomas (New York). Ingram II, 84. H XVII, 250–251.	548
July 5	E. J. Thomas (New York) to Poe (New York). Ingram II, 85. A II, 708.	549
July 10	F. W. Thomas (Washington) to Poe (New York). Original in Boston Public Library.	550
ca. July 15	T. W. Field (New York) to Poe (New York). Cited in Poe to Field, Aug. 9, 1845.	551
ca. July	Neilson Poe (Baltimore) to Poe (New York). Cited in Poe to Neilson Poe, Aug. 8, 1845.	552
* Aug. 8	Poe (New York) to Neilson Poe (Baltimore). W II, 373–374. Pratt 22. Original in Pratt Library.	553
* Aug. 9	Poe (New York) to T. W. Field (New York). P II, 1034. William E. Benjamin, *A Catalogue of Autograph Letters*, No. 30 (April 1890) cover (F). Original in Bradley Martin collection.	554

Aug. 9	Margaret Fuller (New York) to Poe (New York). P II, 1166–1167. Original in Boston Public Library.	555
ante Aug. 11	T. H. Chivers (Philadelphia) to Poe (New York). Cited in Chivers to Poe, Sept. 9, 1845.	556
Aug. 11	T. H. Chivers (Oaky Grove, Ga.) to Poe (New York). Cited in Poe to Chivers, Aug. 29, 1845.	557
* Aug. 11	Poe (New York) to T. H. Chivers (Oaky Grove, Ga.). W II, 153. Original in Huntington Library (HM 21863).	558
Aug. 14	Laughton Osborn (New York) to Poe (New York). Anderson Galleries sale, Dec. 7–8, 1909, part 2, item 1316.	559
* Aug. 15	Poe (New York) to Laughton Osborn (New York). Anderson Galleries sale, Dec. 7–8, 1909, part 2, item 1316.	560
Aug. 16	Laughton Osborn (New York) to Poe (New York). Bangs sale, April 11, 1896, item 75.	561
Aug. 24 or earlier	Chivers to Poe. [2 letters.] Misdated in OCL 477. See Nos. 556, 557.	
Aug. 25	T. H. Chivers (Oaky Grove, Ga.) to Poe (New York). Cited in Poe to Chivers, Aug. 29, 1845.	562
* Aug. 29	Poe (New York) to T. H. Chivers (Oaky Grove, Ga.). *Century Magazine*, LXV (1903) 545–546. Original in Huntington Library (HM 24214).	563
Sept. 9	T. H. Chivers (Oaky Grove, Ga.) to Poe (New York). H XVII, 210–215. Original in Boston Public Library.	564
* [Sept.] Wednesday 10	Poe (New York) to E. A. Duyckinck (New York). H XVII, 215–216. Quinn, *Poe*, 481. Original in New York Public Library.	565
Sept. 10	E. A. Duyckinck (New York) to Poe (New York). Cited in Poe to Duyckinck, Sept. 11, 1845.	566
* [Sept. 11] Thursday morning	Poe (New York) to E. A. Duyckinck (New York). T. O. Mabbott, *The Raven and Other Poems* (New York: Facsimile Text Society, 1942) vii.	567
* Sept. 28	Poe (New York) to R. W. Griswold (Philadelphia). T. O. Mabbott, *The Raven and*	

	Other Poems (New York: Facsimile Text Society, 1942) viii. Original in Boston Public Library.	568
Sept. 29	F. W. Thomas (Washington) to Poe (New York). Original in Boston Public Library.	569
Sept. 30	Chivers to Poe. Misdated in ABC II (Dec. 1932) 338; OCL 485. See No. 577.	
Sept.–Oct. (?)	Boston Lyceum Committee to Poe (New York). [2 letters.] Implied in P II, 1050–1051.	570
Sept.–Oct. (?)	Poe (New York) to Boston Lyceum Committee. Implied in P II, 1050–1051.	571
Oct. 1	Laughton Osborn (New York) to Poe (New York). Original in Mabbott collection.	572
ca. Oct. 20	Mrs. S. J. Hale (Philadelphia) to Poe (New York). Cited in Poe to Hale, Oct. 26, 1845.	573
* Oct. 26	Poe (New York) to R. W. Griswold (Philadelphia). H XVII, 216. Original in Boston Public Library.	574
* Oct. 26	Poe (New York) to Mrs. S. J. Hale (Philadelphia). P II, 1067. American Art Association sale, Nov. 13–14, 1935, item 300 (F). Original in Koester collection.	575
* Oct. 26	Poe (New York) to J. P. Kennedy (Baltimore). H XVII, 217. W II, 153–154. Original in Peabody Library.	576
Oct. 30	T. H. Chivers (Oaky Grove, Ga.) to Poe (New York). H XVII, 217–220. Original in Boston Public Library.	577
Oct. 31	Chivers to Poe. Misdated in OCL 490. See No. 577.	
October	Laughton Osborn (New York) to Poe (New York). Bangs sale, April 11, 1896, item 77.	578
ante Oct., late	Mrs. F. S. Osgood (New York) to Poe (New York). Cited in Poe to Osgood, late Oct., 1845.	579
* [Oct., late]	Poe (New York) to Mrs. F. S. Osgood (New York). *Literary Review,* March 5, 1921, p. 14. Original in University of Texas Library.	580
Nov. 1	Poe to Griswold. An unauthentic letter as printed in Griswold's Preface, xxii; H XVII, 220–221; P II, 1068–1069.	

Nov. 10	Mrs. M. E. Hewitt (New York) to Poe (New York). T. O. Mabbott, *A Christmas Book* (Hunter College, Dec. 1937), 119. Original in Boston Public Library.	581
Nov. 12	Laughton Osborn (New York) to Poe (New York). New York *Herald*, Nov. 6, 1921. Original in Mabbott collection.	582
* [Nov.] 13 Thursday morning	Poe (New York) to E. A. Duyckinck (New York). H XVII, 221–222. W II, 157–159. Original in New York Public Library.	583
Nov. 13	Poe to Duyckinck. Misdated in New York Public Library *Bulletin*, VI (Jan. 1902) 8; H XVII, 222–223; W II, 156–157; Quinn, *Poe*, 493–494; OCL 495. See No. 545.	
Nov. 14	Mrs. S. J. Hale (Philadelphia) to Poe (New York). Cited in Poe to Hale, Jan. 16, 1846.	584
* Nov. 15	Poe (New York) to T. H. Chivers (Oaky Grove, Ga.). Quinn, *Poe*, 490–491. *Century Magazine*, LXV (1903) 546–547. Original in Huntington Library (HM 24215).	585
Nov. 15	Poe to ——. Unidentified in ABC II (Nov. 1932) 292. See No. 585.	
* Nov. 30	Poe (New York) to George Poe, Jr. (Georgetown, D. C.). H XVII, 223–224. Pratt 23. Original in Pratt Library.	586
November	Poe (New York) to Charles Campbell (Petersburg). Anastatic circular in Morgan Library. See No. 588.	587
* November	Poe (New York) to George Watterston (Washington). *South in the Building of the Nation* (Richmond: The Southern Historical Publications Society, 1909) XII, 294 (F). Anastatic circular in Library of Congress.	588
November	Poe (New York) to William Green (Culpeper, C. H., Va.). Anastatic circular in Huntington Library. See No. 588.	589
November	Poe (New York) to ——. John W. Robertson, *Edgar A. Poe: A Psychopathic Study* (New York: Putnam, 1921) 324 (F). Anastatic circular. See No. 588.	590
Nov.–July, 1846	T. H. Chivers (Oaky Grove, Ga.) to Poe (New York). [At least 6 letters.] Cited in Poe to Chivers, July 22, 1846.	591

* Dec. 1	Poe (New York) to Fitz-Greene Halleck (New York). J. G. Wilson, *Life and Letters of Fitz-Greene Halleck* (New York: D. Appleton, 1869) 431. P II, 1071.	592
Dec. 1	J. P. Kennedy (Baltimore) to Poe (New York). W II, 154–155. H XVII, 224–225. Original in Boston Public Library.	593
* Dec. 10	Poe (New York) to E. A. Duyckinck (New York). Anderson Galleries sale, May 27, 1914, item 208.	594
ca. Dec. 15	Mrs. E. F. Ellet (New York) to Poe (New York). Original in Boston Public Library.	595
Dec. 16	R. H. Collyer (Boston) to Poe (New York). H XVII, 225–226.	596
Dec. 16	Mrs. E. F. Ellet (New York) to Poe (New York). Original in Boston Public Library.	597
Dec. 19	C. G. Percival (Utica, N. Y.) to Poe (New York). Bangs sale, April 11, 1896, item 113½, cited.	598
Dec. 21	G. W. Eveleth (Phillips, Maine) to Poe (New York). EP 172–174. Original in New York Public Library.	599
Dec. 22	Mrs. M. E. Hewitt (New York) to Poe (New York). T. O. Mabbott, *A Christmas Book* (Hunter College, Dec. 1937) 119. Original in Boston Public Library.	600
ca. 1845 (?)	Poe (New York) to N. P. Willis (New York). Implied in Willis to Poe, *ca.* 1845.	601
ca. 1845	N. P. Willis (New York) to Poe (New York). H XVII, 206. P II, 1028. Original in Boston Public Library.	602
* [1845]	Poe (New York) to [Evert A. Duyckinck] (New York). Anderson Galleries sale, January 17–18, 1928, item 369 [F].	602a
* [1845]	Poe (New York) to W. M. Gillespie (New York). Original in Longfellow House, Cambridge, Mass.	602b
n. d.	Poe to Osgood. See No. 580. *The Literary Review*, March 5, 1921, p. 14; P II, 1088; ABC II (Dec. 1932) 339; OCL 508 are less satisfactory datings.	
1845–1846 n. d.	Lynch to Poe. Misdated in H XVII, 258–259; P II, 1095. See No. 547.	
* [*ca.* 1845–1846]	Poe to ——. Original fragment in Alderman Library.	603

1846

Jan.–April 14	P. P. Cooke (Millwood, Va.) to Poe (New York). [3 letters.] Cited in Poe to Cooke, April 16, 1846.	604
* Jan. 3	Poe (New York) to C. G. Percival (Utica, N. Y.). W II, 374. Original in Valentine Museum.	605
Jan. 5	G. W. Eveleth (Phillips, Maine) to Poe (New York). EP 174. Original in New York Public Library.	606
* Jan. 8	Poe (New York) to E. A. Duyckinck (New York). H XVII, 227. Quinn, *Poe,* 496. Original in New York Public Library.	607
ante Jan. 10 (?)	R. Leighton, Jr., to Poe (New York). Implied in Poe to Leighton, Jan. 10, 1846.	608
* Jan. 10	Poe (New York) to Fitz-Greene Halleck (New York). Original in Koester collection.	609
Jan. 10	Poe (New York) to R. Leighton, Jr. American Art Association sale, Dec. 3, 1931.	610
* Jan. 10	Poe (New York) to C. Edwards Lester (New York). Original in Koester collection.	610a
* Jan. 16	Poe (New York) to Mrs. S. J. Hale (Philadelphia). P II, 1083. *New York Times,* Jan. 28, 1917. Original in Huntington Library (HM 24216).	611
* Jan. 30	Poe (New York) to [Duyckinck ?] [New York]. Original in Lilly collection.	612
Feb. 26	A. M. Ide, Jr. (South Attleboro, Mass.) to Poe (New York). Original in Boston Public Library.	613
March 17	Hawthorne to Poe. Misdated in ABC III (April 1933) 246. See No. 639.	
ante March 19	Poe (New York) to Charles Dickens (London). Implied in Dickens to Poe, March 19, 1846.	614
March 19	Charles Dickens (London) to Poe (New York). Original in Pennsylvania Historical Society.	615
ante April 3	Postmaster of Phillips, Maine, to Poe (New York). Cited in Eveleth to Poe, April 3, 1846.	616
April 3	G. W. Eveleth (Phillips, Maine) to Poe (New York). EP 174–175. Original in New York Public Library.	617

April 15 [14]   Mrs. M. E. Hewitt (New York) to Poe (New York). T. O. Mabbott, *A Christmas Book* (Hunter College, Dec. 1937), 120. Original in Boston Public Library.   618

April 15   Hewitt to Poe. Misdated in Quinn, *Poe*, 506. See No. 618.

ante April 16   Poe (New York) to William T. Porter (New York). Cited in Poe to Cooke, April 16, 1846.   619

ante April 16   William T. Porter (New York) to Poe (New York). Cited in Poe to Cooke, April 16, 1846.   620

* April 16   Poe (New York) to P. P. Cooke (Millwood, Va.). Original in Bradley Martin collection.   621

* April 16   Poe (New York) to G. W. Eveleth (Phillips, Maine). PE 6. Quinn, *Poe*, 521. H xvii, 230. American Art Association sale, May 2–3, 1934, part 1, item 214 (F). Original in Koester collection.   622

April 16 or later   Eveleth to Poe. Misdated in P ii, 1100; OCL 523. See No. 634.

April 25   Mary Neal to Poe (New York). Cited in Mary Neal to Frances S. Osgood, April 25, 1846 (see *Some Passages in the Correspondence of Rufus W. Griswold* [Cambridge, 1898] 203–204).   623

ante April 28 (?)   J. A. Maubey to Poe (Philadelphia: forwarded to New York). Implied in Poe to Maubey, April 28, 1846.   624

ante April 28   Vermont University Literary Societies to Poe (New York). Cited in Poe to Duyckinck, April 28, 1846.   625

ante April 28 (?)   Poe (New York) to Vermont University Literary Societies. Probable answer to Vermont University Literary Societies' letter to Poe, *ante* April 28, 1846.   626

ca. April 28   Poe (New York) to John Keese (New York). Cited in Poe to Duyckinck, April 28, 1846.   627

* April 28   Poe (New York) to E. A. Duyckinck (New York). H xvii, 230–232. Original in New York Public Library.   628

* April 28   Poe (New York) to J. A. Maubey. Anderson Galleries sale, March 14–15, 1921, item 332. Original in Koester collection.   629

April   Elizabeth Barrett (London) to Poe (New

York). W II, 163–165. H XVII, 229–230.
Original in New York Public Library. 630

April   Vermont University Literary Societies to Poe.
See No. 625. P II, 1100; OCL 528 are less
satisfactory datings.

ante May 25 (?)   T. Honland to Poe (New York). Implied in
Poe to Honland, May 25, 1846. 631

* May 25   Poe (New York) to T. Honland. A. H. Joline, *Meditations of an Autograph Collector*
(New York: Harper and Bros., 1902) 159.
Anderson Galleries sale, Dec. 15, 1914, item
834. 632

May (?)   Poe (New York) to L. A. Godey (Philadelphia). [More than one?] Implied in *Go-
dey's Lady's Book,* June 1846, p. 288. 633

June 9   G. W. Eveleth (Phillips, Maine) to Poe (New
York). P II, 1100. Cited in Poe to Eveleth,
Dec. 15, 1846. 634

* June 12   Poe (New York) to Mrs. Virginia Clemm Poe
(New York). H XVII, 232. W II, 217.
Copy in Alderman Library. 635

* June 15   Poe (New York) to J. M. Field (St. Louis).
P II, 1131–1132. L. Whiting, *Life of Kate
Field* (Boston: Little, Brown, 1899) 21–
22. Original in Huntington Library (HM
21872). 636

ante June 16 [?]   Dickinson College Literary Societies (Carlisle,
Pa.) to Poe (New York). Cited in Poe to
————, June 16, 1846. 637

* June 16 [?]   Poe (New York) to ————. Anderson Galleries sale, Dec. 15, 1914, item 832. [?] 638

June 16   Eveleth to Poe. Misdated in P II, 1189. See
No. 634.

June 17   Nathaniel Hawthorne (Salem, Mass.) to Poe
(New York). W II, 211–212. H XVII, 232–
233. Original in Bradley Martin collection. 639

* June 27   Poe (New York) to H. B. Hirst (Philadelphia). *Current Opinion,* LXX (1921) 823
(F). Original in Huntington Library (HM
21867). 640

ante June 29 (?)   Poe (New York) to Eliakim Littell (Boston).
Implied in Poe to Duyckinck, June 29,
1846. 641

ca. June 29 (?)   Eliakim Littell (Boston) to Poe (New York).
Implied in Poe to Duyckinck, June 29,
1846. 642

* [June] Monday 29	Poe (New York) to E. A. Duyckinck (New York). H xvii, 255. Original in New York Public Library.	643
ca. June 29 (?)	Poe (New York) to L. A. Godey (Philadelphia). Implied in Poe to Duyckinck, June 29, 1846, and in Poe to Godey, July 16, 1846.	644
June	Poe to Godey. [Several?] See No. 633. P ii, 1152 is a less satisfactory dating.	
July 4 or earlier	Poe to E. J. Thomas. Misdated in P ii, 1158; OCL 540. See No. 548.	
July 5	E. J. Thomas to Poe. Misdated in P ii, 1158–1159; OCL 541. See No. 549.	
July 9 or earlier	Poe to Godey. See No. 644. OCL 542 is a less satisfactory dating.	
July 14	Godey to Poe. See No. 645. OCL 543 is a less satisfactory dating.	
ante July 16 (?)	L. A. Godey (Philadelphia) to Poe (New York). Implied in Poe to Godey, July 16, 1846.	645
* July 16	Poe (New York) to L. A. Godey (Philadelphia). H xvii, 257–258. W ii, 191–193. Original in Boston Public Library.	646
* July 17	Poe (New York) to John Bisco (New York). Parke-Bernet Galleries sale, Jan. 15–16, 1941 (F).	647
July 17 (?)	L. A. Godey (Philadelphia) to Poe (New York). Implied in addressed envelope (no letter) of this date in the Boston Public Library.	648
July 20 or earlier	Poe to Simms. See No. 650. OCL 547 is a less satisfactory dating.	
July 20–23	Poe to Simms. See No. 651. OCL 548 is a less satisfactory dating.	
* July 22	Poe (New York) to T. H. Chivers (Oaky Grove, Ga.). *Century Magazine*, lxv (1903) 547. Quinn, *Poe*, 512–513. Original in Huntington Library (HM 24217).	649
ante July 23	Poe (Fordham) to W. G. Simms (New York). Cited in Simms to Poe, July 30, 1846.	650
ca. July 23	Poe (West Farms, N. Y.) to W. G. Simms (New York). Cited in Simms to Poe, July 30, 1846. ..	651
July 30	W. G. Simms (New York) to Poe (Fordham). W ii, 199–204. H xvii, 259–262. Original in Boston Public Library.	652

Aug. 4	P. P. Cooke (Millwood, Va.) to Poe (New York). H XVII, 262–264. W II, 204–207. Original in Boston Public Library.	653
* Aug. 9	Poe (New York) to P. P. Cooke (Millwood, Va.). H XVII, 265–268. W II, 207–211. Original in New York Public Library.	654
Aug. 14	F. W. Thomas (Washington) to Poe (New York). Original in New York Public Library.	655
Aug. 24	F. W. Thomas (Washington) to Poe (New York). Original in Boston Public Library.	656
Oct. 13	G. W. Eveleth (Phillips, Maine) to Poe (New York). EP 175–176. Original in New York Public Library.	657
Nov. 30	Arch Ramsay (Stonehaven, Scotland) to Poe (New York). H XVII, 268–269. Original in Boston Public Library.	658
Dec. 7 [?]	Poe (New York) to A. N. Howard. *American Literature,* XIII (Nov. 1941) 283 [?]	659
Dec. 10	Poe to Duyckinck. Misdated in OCL 567. See No. 594.	
* Dec. 15	Poe (New York) to G. W. Eveleth (Phillips, Maine). PE 7–12. Quinn, *Poe,* 521–524. Original in New York Public Library.	660
Dec. 20	Hewitt to Poe. Wrongly identified in ABC II (Dec. 1932) 339. This item probably confused with that from Hewitt to Mrs. Osgood (H XVII, 272).	
Dec. 21	Willis to Poe. Misdated in Stedman and Woodberry, *Works of Edgar Allan Poe* (Chicago: Stone and Kimball, 1894) I, 76; OCL 460. See No. 661.	
Dec. 23	N. P. Willis (New York) to Poe (New York). H XVII, 272. Stedman and Woodberry, *Works of Edgar Allan Poe* (Chicago: Stone and Kimball, 1894) I, 76. Original in Boston Public Library.	661
* Dec. 24	Poe (Fordham) to E. A. Duyckinck (New York). H XVII, 273. Original in New York Public Library.	662
* Dec. 24	Poe (New York) to W. D. Ticknor (Boston). A II, 725. Original in Library of Congress.	663
* Dec. 30	Poe (Fordham) to E. A. Duyckinck (New York). H XVII, 275–276. W II, 229–231. Original in New York Public Library.	664
* Dec. 30	Poe (New York) to Arch Ramsay (Stonehaven, Scotland). *Bookman,* XLIV (1916)	

20–21. John W. Robertson, *Commentary
on Edgar A. Poe,* II (San Francisco: Edwin
and Robert Grabhorn, 1934) 234 (F).   665

* Dec. 30   Poe (New York) to N. P. Willis (New
                   York). H XVII, 274–275. Ingram II, 100–
                   101.   666

Dec. 30   Willis to Poe. Misdated in P II, 1194. See No.
                   661.

Wednesday   Willis to Poe. Incompletely dated in H XVII,
                   272. See No. 661.

n. d.   Poe to Griswold. Wrongly identified as to
                   Griswold, in H XVII, 228. See No. 654.

                              1847

* Jan. 17   Poe (Fordham) to C. A. Bristed (New York).
                   Parke-Bernet Galleries sale, Dec. 4, 1945,
                   item 77. Original in Koester collection.   667

Jan. 19   G. W. Eveleth (Phillips, Maine) to Poe (New
                   York). EP 177–180. Original in New
                   York Public Library.   668

Jan. 28 or earlier   Shew to Poe. OCL 570 same as No. 669.
ante Jan. 29 (?)   Mrs. M. L. Shew (New York) to Poe (Ford-
                   ham). Implied in Poe to Shew, Jan. 29,
                   1847.   669

* Jan. 29   Poe (Fordham) to Mrs. M. L. Shew (New
                   York). W II, 223–224. Ingram II, 107
                   (F). Original in Huntington Library (HM
                   24221).   670

Feb. 2   Chivers to Poe. Misdated in ABC II (Dec.
                   1932) 338. See No. 673.

Feb. 3   Willis to Poe. OCL 572 same as No. 661.
* Feb. 16   Poe (New York) to G. W. Eveleth (Phillips,
                   Maine). PE 12–13. H XVII, 277–278. In-
                   gram I, 167. Original in New York Public
                   Library.   671

Feb. 20   Locke to Poe. Misdated in P II, 1214. See No.
                   675.

Feb. 20–21   Locke to Poe. OCL 575 same as No. 675.
* Feb. 21   Poe (New York) to Horace Greeley (New
                   York). P II, 1208–1209. W II, 426–427.
                   Quinn, *Poe,* 529–530. Original in Morgan
                   Library.   672

Feb. 21   T. H. Chivers (Washington, Ga.) to Poe
                   (New York). H XVII, 278–280. Original
                   in Boston Public Library.   673

Feb. 21	G. W. Eveleth (Phillips, Maine) to Poe (New York). EP 181–182. Original in New York Public Library.	674
Feb. 21	Mrs. J. E. Locke (Lowell) to Poe (New York). Cited in Poe to Locke, March 10, 1847.	675
Feb. 24	J. F. Reinman and J. H. Walker (Springfield, Ohio) to Poe (New York). Cited in Poe to Reinman and Walker, March 11, 1847.	676
February	Poe to Philosophian Society of Wittenberg College. Misdated in P II, 1220. See No. 680.	
* March 10	Poe (New York) to Mrs. J. E. Locke (Lowell). [Draft of letter of same date.] P II, 1215–1219 (F). H XVII, 280–282. Original draft in Boston Public Library.	677
March 10 (?)	Poe (New York) to Mrs. J. E. Locke (Lowell). [Clean copy of draft, mailed (?).]	678
* March 11	Poe (New York) to G. W. Eveleth (Phillips, Maine). PE 13–14. Copy in Alderman Library. Original in Koester collection.	679
* March 11	Poe (New York) to J. F. Reinman and J. H. Walker (Springfield, Ohio). Ingram II, 118. P II, 1220. Copy in Alderman Library.	680
April 4	T. H. Chivers (Washington, Ga.) to Poe (New York). H XVII, 282–284. Original in Boston Public Library.	681
April 14	Arch Ramsay (Stonehaven, Scotland) to Poe (New York). H XVII, 284–285. Original in Boston Public Library.	682
* [May] Sunday night	Poe (New York) to Mrs. M. L. Shew (New York). Ingram II, 153–154. H XVII, 297. Copy in Alderman Library.	683
ca. May (?)	Poe (New York) to Hiram Barney (New York). Cited in Mrs. Shew-Houghton to John Ingram, Jan. 23, 1875 (Ingram collection, University of Virginia).	684
ca. May	Mrs. M. L. Shew (New York) to Poe (New York). Cited in Poe to Shew, May 1847.	685
June	Poe (Fordham) to Professor C. P. Bronson (New York?). Dodd, Mead and Company sale No. 59, March 1901, item 269.	685a
July 27	G. W. Eveleth (Phillips, Maine) to Poe (New York). EP 182–184. Original in New York Public Library.	686

* Aug. 10	Poe (New York) to R. T. Conrad (Philadelphia). H I, 270–271. Quinn, *Poe*, 531–532. Original in Alderman Library.	687
* Aug. 31	Poe (New York) to R. T. Conrad (Philadelphia). P II, 1229. Kovach sale, Sept. 22, 1933 (F).	688
ante Nov. [?]	Poe (New York) to Mrs. S. A. Lewis (New York). Ingram II, 219.	689
ante Nov. 27	Mrs. S. A. Lewis (New York) to Poe (New York). Cited in Poe to Lewis, Nov. 27, 1847.	690
* Nov. 27	Poe (New York) to Mrs. S. A. Lewis (New York). H XVII, 286. Ingram II, 127–128. Original in Yale Library.	691
Nov. 29	Poe to Lewis. Misdated in ABC II (Nov. 1932) 291; OCL 593. See No. 691.	
November	N. P. Willis (New York) to Poe (New York). Cited in Poe to Willis, Dec. 8, 1847.	692
November	Poe to ———. Five pencilled lines on verso of *Stylus*. Misdated in OCL 594. See No. 694.	
Dec. 7 [?]	Poe to Collins or Mrs. Ellsworth. Printed in Richmond *Times-Dispatch*, April 15, 1935, p. 16. Very doubtful authenticity. [?]	
* Dec. 8	Poe (New York) to N. P. Willis (New York). P II, 1246–1247. W II, 233.	693
n. d.	Poe to ———. Undated and unidentified in H XVII, 285. See No. 700.	

1848

* Jan. 4	Poe (New York) to G. W. Eveleth (Phillips, Maine). PE 15–19. Ingram II, 132–134. Quinn, *Poe*, 536–537 (F). Original in Rosenbach collection.	694
Jan. 11	G. W. Eveleth (Phillips, Maine) to Poe (New York). EP 184–186. Original in New York Public Library.	695
* Jan. 17	Poe (New York) to H. D. Chapin (New York). H XVII, 290–291. Ingram II, 135.	696
* Jan. 17	Poe (New York) to L. A. Godey (Philadelphia). American Art Association sale, Nov. 23–24, 1937, item 353.	697
* Jan. 22	Poe (Fordham) to N. P. Willis (New York). H XVII, 291–292. Ingram II, 136–137.	698

Feb. 10	G. E. Isbell (Binghamton) to Poe (New York). Cited in Poe to Isbell, Feb. 29, 1848.	699
* Feb. 29	Poe (New York) to G. W. Eveleth (Phillips, Maine). PE 19–22. Ingram II, 139–141. Quinn, *Poe*, 557–559. Original in Morgan Library.	700
Feb. 29	Poe to Irbey. Wrongly identified in ABC II (Dec. 1932) 341. See No. 701.	
* Feb. 29	Poe (New York) to G. W. Isbell [called Irbey] (Binghamton). H I, 277–278. Heartman and Canny, 83–84. Original in Lilly collection.	701
February	Poe to Eveleth. Incompletely dated in W II, 441. See No. 700.	
March 9	G. W. Eveleth (Phillips, Maine) to Poe (New York). EP 186–188. P II, 1237–1238. Original in New York Public Library.	702
* March 30	Poe (New York) to Mrs. M. L. Shew (New York). Ingram II, 143.	703
ante May 3	H. B. Hirst (Philadelphia) to Poe (New York). Cited in Poe to Hirst, May 3, 1848.	704
* May 3	Poe (New York) to H. B. Hirst (Philadelphia). P II, 1266–1267. Original in Huntington Library (HM 21869).	705
May 9	Eveleth to Poe. Misdated in P II, 1237, 1262. See No. 702.	
May 15	J. H. Hopkins, Jr. (New York) to Poe (New York). Original in Boston Public Library.	706
ante May 19	Mrs. J. E. Locke (Lowell) to Poe (New York). [2 letters.] Cited in Poe to Locke, May 19, 1848.	707
* May 19	Poe (New York) to Mrs. J. E. Locke (Lowell). Original in Koester collection.	708
May 20–28	Blackwell to Poe. OCL 608 same as No. 709.	
ca. May 24	Anna Blackwell (Providence) to Poe (Fordham). Cited in Poe to Blackwell, June 14, 1848.	709
May	Poe to Blackwell. Misdated in P II, 1286–1287. See No. 712.	
* May	Poe (New York) to Charles H. Marshall (New York). Original in Koester collection.	710
May	Poe to Shew. See No. 683. Ingram II, 153–154; H XVII, 297; P II, 1268–1269 are less satisfactory datings.	

* June 7	Poe (Fordham) to C. A. Bristed (New York). American Art Association sale, Nov. 11–12, 1937, item 332 (F). Quinn, *Poe*, 566. Original in Koester collection.	711
June 10	Poe to Blackwell. Misdated in Ingram II, 165; H XVII, 296. See No. 712.	
* June 14	Poe (Fordham) to Anna Blackwell (Providence). Copy in Lilly collection, not original as Quinn says, *Poe*, 574 n.	712
* June 15	Poe (New York) to Bayard Taylor (New York). Whitty (1917) 270. W II, 374–375. Original in Koester collection.	713
June 19	Poe to Blackwell. Misdated in W II, 268–269. See No. 712.	
* June 21	Poe (New York) to Mrs. S. A. Lewis (New York). H XVII, 359–360.	714
June	Mrs. M. L. Shew (New York) to Poe (New York). Cited in Poe to Shew, June 1848.	715
* [June]	Poe (Fordham) to Mrs. M. L. Shew (New York). H XVII, 298–300. Quinn, *Poe*, 609–611. Copy in Alderman Library.	716
July 9	G. W. Eveleth (Phillips, Maine) to Poe (New York). EP 188–190. P II, 1233. Original in New York Public Library.	717
* July 13 [14]	Poe (Fordham) to T. H. Chivers (New York). *Century Magazine*, LXV (1903) 549. Quinn, *Poe*, 568. Original in Huntington Library (HM 24218).	718
* July 15	Poe (Fordham) to Mrs. Mary Osborne (Fordham). P II, 1289–1290. Washington (D. C.) *Post*, Jan. 17, 1909 (F). Original in Lilly collection.	719
* Sept. 5	Poe [pseud. Edward S. T. Grey] (New York) to Mrs. S. H. Whitman (Providence). P II, 1313. Quinn, *Poe*, 575. Original in Lilly collection.	720
Sept. 8	Poe to Whitman. Misdated in W II, 247; P II, 1313. See No. 720.	
* Sept. 20	Poe (Fordham) to C. F. Hoffman (New York). H XVII, 300–303. Ingram II, 149–152. Gill, 202–205.	721
Sept. 27–29	Mrs. S. H. Whitman (Providence) to Poe (Fordham). Cited in Poe to Whitman, Oct. 18, 1848.	722
* Oct. 1	Poe (Fordham) to Mrs. S. H. Whitman (Providence). LL 5–18. Quinn, *Poe*, 575–578. Original in Lilly collection.	723

ca. Oct. 10	Mrs. S. H. Whitman (Providence) to Poe (New York). Cited in Poe to Whitman, Oct. 18, 1848.	724
Oct. 15	Whitman to Poe. OCL 620 same as No. 724.	
ante Oct. 18	T. L. Dunnell (Providence) to Poe (New York). Cited in Poe to Dunnell, Oct. 18, 1848.	725
* Oct. 18	Poe (New York) to T. L. Dunnell (Providence). American Art Association sale, April 29, 1924, item 956.	726
* [Oct. 18]	Poe (New York) to Mrs. S. H. Whitman (Providence). LL 19–29. H xvii, 308–311, 316–317. Original in Lilly collection.	727
* October	Poe (Fordham) to Mrs. J. E. Locke (Lowell). Parke-Bernet Galleries sale, May 24, 1939 (F). Original in Koester collection.	728
* October	Poe (Fordham) to Mrs. A. L. Richmond (Lowell). American Art Association sale, April 24–25, 1935 (F). Original in Gimble collection.	729
ca. Nov. 1–2	Mrs. S. H. Whitman (Providence) to Poe (Lowell). Cited in Whitman to John Ingram, Oct. 25, 1875 (Ingram collection, Alderman Library).	730
Nov. 3	Whitman to Poe. OCL 625 same as No. 730.	
* *ca.* Nov. 3	Poe (Lowell) to Mrs. S. H. Whitman (Providence). Cited in Whitman to John Ingram, Oct. 25, 1875 (Ingram collection, Alderman Library). MS. fragment in Koester collection.	731
Nov. 4	Poe to Whitman. OCL 626 same as No. 731.	
ca. Nov. 5	Poe (Boston) to Mrs. A. L. Richmond (Lowell). Cited in Poe to Richmond, Nov. 16, 1848.	732
Nov. 6	Poe to Richmond. OCL 627 same as No. 732.	
* [Nov. 7]	Poe (Providence) to Mrs. S. H. Whitman (Providence). LL 30–31. H xvii, 311. Quinn, *Poe*, 579. Original in Lilly collection.	733
Nov. 7 (?)	Mrs. S. H. Whitman (Providence) to Poe (Providence). Varner 1, 325–326, cited. See also Quinn, *Poe*, 579. (This item may have been oral rather than written.)	734
Nov. 8	Poe (Providence) to Mrs. S. H. Whitman (Providence). Cited in Whitman to John Ingram, Oct. 25, 1875 (Ingram collection, Alderman Library).	735

* Nov. 14	Poe (New York) to Mrs. S. H. Whitman (Providence). LL 32–33. H xvii, 311–312. Copy in Alderman Library. 736
* Nov. 16	Poe (Fordham) to Mrs. A. L. Richmond (Lowell). Quinn, *Poe*, 589–592. Ingram ii, 193–194. Copy in Alderman Library. 737
Nov. 17	Mrs. S. H. Whitman (Providence) to Poe (New York). Cited in Poe to Whitman, Nov. 22, 1848. 738
ca. Nov. 18–20 (?)	Mrs. S. H. Whitman (Providence) to Poe (New York). Implied in Poe to Whitman, Nov. 24, 1848. 739
Nov. 20	Poe (New York) to Susan Archer Talley (Richmond). Cited in Talley to Poe, Nov. 29, 1848, and dated by Poe to Valentine, Nov. 20, 1848. 740
* Nov. 20	Poe (New York) to Edward Valentine (Richmond). H xvii, 197–198. Copy in Alderman Library. 741
Nov. 20	Poe to Whitman. Misdated in ABC ii (Dec. 1932) 341. See No. 747.
Nov. 20	Talley to Poe. Misdated in ABC ii (Dec. 1932) 339. See No. 749.
Nov. 22	Poe to Whitman. Ingram ii, 180–181; H xvii, 317–318; W ii, 290–291 print the Poe–Whitman letter of Nov. 26 under this date, and omit the Nov. 22 letter entirely.
* [Nov.] Wednesday morning — 22	Poe (New York) to Mrs. S. H. Whitman (Providence). LL 34–35. Original in Lilly collection. 742
* Nov. 23	Poe (Fordham) to Sarah Heywood (Westford, Mass.). H xvii, 319–320. Ingram ii, 195–196. Copy in Alderman Library. 743
ca. Nov. 23	T. L. Dunnell (Providence) to Poe (New York). Cited in Poe to Whitman, Nov. 26, 1848. 744
* [Nov.] Friday 24	Poe (Fordham) to Mrs. S. H. Whitman (Providence). LL 36–40. H xvii, 320–322. Original in Lilly collection. 745
Nov. 25	Poe to Whitman. Misdated in H xvii, 320–322. See No. 745.
ca. Nov. 25–26	Poe (New York) to T. L. Dunnell (Providence). Cited in Poe to Whitman, Nov. 26, 1848. 746
* [Nov.] Sunday evening — 26	Poe (New York) to Mrs. S. H. Whitman (Providence). LL 41–43. H xvii, 317–318. Original in Lilly collection. 747

Nov. 27	F. W. Thomas (Louisville, Ky.) to Poe (New York). Cited in Poe to Thomas, Feb. 14, 1849.	748
Nov. 29	Susan Archer Talley (Richmond) to Poe (New York). H xvii, 324. Original in Boston Public Library.	749
* Dec. 4	Poe (Fordham) to W. J. Pabodie (Providence). P ii, 1347. Facsimile in Ingram collection, Alderman Library.	750
Dec. 7	Poe (New York) to J. R. Thompson (Richmond). W ii, frontispiece & vii, cited.	751
Dec. 8	Poe to Willis. Misdated in H xvii, 324–325; P ii, 1246–1247. See No. 693.	
Dec. 14–15 (?)	Mrs. S. H. Whitman (Providence) to Poe (New York). Implied in Poe to Whitman, Dec. 16, 1848.	752
* [Dec. 16] Saturday 2 p.m.	Poe (New York) to Mrs. S. H. Whitman (Providence). LL 44. P ii, 1349. Caroline Ticknor, *Poe's Helen* (1916) 117 (F). Original in Lilly collection.	753
Dec. 17	Poe to Whitman. Wrong date, entered on MS. by Mrs. Whitman, reproduced in LL 44; Caroline Ticknor's *Poe's Helen* (1916) 117; P ii, 1349; ABC ii (Dec. 1932) 339. See No. 753.	
Dec. 18	E. H. N. Patterson (Oquawka, Ill.) to Poe (New York). Cited in Poe to Patterson, *ca.* April 30, 1849.	754
ante Dec. 20 (?)	T. L. Dunnell (Providence) to Poe (New York). Implied from Poe to Dunnell, *ca.* Nov. 25–26, 1848, and from delivery of lecture, Dec. 20, 1848.	755
ante Dec. 20 (?)	Poe (New York) to T. L. Dunnell (Providence). Implied from Poe to Dunnell, *ca.* Nov. 25–26, 1848, and from delivery of lecture, Dec. 20, 1848.	756
* [Dec. 23]	Poe (Providence) to Mrs. Maria Clemm (Fordham). LL 50. Quinn, *Poe,* 586. Original in Lilly collection.	757
* [Dec. 23]	Poe (Providence) to Dr. Crocker (Providence). LL 46. Quinn, *Poe,* 585. Original in Lilly collection.	758
* [December] Thursday morning — 28 December	Poe (Fordham) to Mrs. A. L. Richmond (Lowell). Ingram ii, 196–197. H xvii, 322.	759
	Poe to Crocker. Incompletely dated in ABC ii (Dec. 1932) 341. See No. 758.	

[Dec.] 28	Poe to Richmond. Incompletely dated in H XVII, 322. See No. 759.	
ca. 1848 late (?)	Mrs. S. A. Lewis (New York) to Poe (New York). Inferred from Poe to Lewis, *ca.* 1848 late.	760
* [*ca.* 1848 late]	Poe (New York) to Mrs. S. A. Lewis (New York). Whitty (1917) 210–211. Original in Alderman Library.	761
n. d.	Poe to Richmond. Misdated in H XVII, 318–319. See No. 763.	
n. d.	Poe to Whitman. Misdated in Ingram II, 186; H XVII, 323; W II, 292–293; P II, 1362–1364; Quinn, *Poe,* 586. See No. 769.	
n. d.	Mrs. J. E. Locke (Lowell) to Poe (?) (New York). Original (?) in Alderman Library.	762

1849

* [Jan. 11]	Poe (New York) to Mrs. A. L. Richmond (Lowell). H XVII, 318–319. W II, 291–292. Ingram II, 202.	763
* Jan. 13	Poe (New York) to J. R. Thompson (Richmond). P II, 1367–1368. Original in Huntington Library (HM 21874).	764
post Jan. 13 (?)	J. R. Thompson (Richmond) to Poe (New York). Inferred from Poe to Thompson, Jan. 13, and May 10, 1849.	765
Jan. 18	Poe to Thompson. Misdated in P II, 1367–1368. See No. 764.	
* Jan. 20	Poe (Fordham) to John Priestly (New York). Whitty (1911) lxxi.	766
ante Jan. 21	Mrs. A. L. Richmond (Lowell) to Poe (New York). Cited in Poe to Richmond, *ca.* Jan. 21, 1849.	767
* [*ca.* Jan. 21]	Poe (New York) to Mrs. A. L. Richmond (Lowell). H XVII, 327–329. Ingram II, 203–205. Quinn, *Poe,* 593–594.	768
* [*ca.* Jan. 21]	Poe (Fordham) to Mrs. S. H. Whitman (Providence). H XVII, 323. Quinn, *Poe,* 586–587. W II, 292–293. Copy in Alderman Library.	769
Jan. 23	Poe to Richmond. See No. 768. Ingram II, 203–205; H XVII, 327–329; P II, 1364–1367 are less satisfactory datings.	
Jan. 25	Poe to Richmond. See No. 768. Quinn, *Poe,* 593; OCL 663 are less satisfactory datings.	

Jan. 25   Poe to Whitman. See No. 769. Quinn, *Poe,* 586 is a less satisfactory dating.

Jan., late   Editor *Flag of Our Union* (Boston) to Poe (New York). Cited in Poe to Richmond, Feb. 8, 1849.   770

January   Poe to Whitman. See No. 769. LL 45; ABC II (Dec. 1932) 339; OCL 664 are less satisfactory datings.

Feb. 5   Poe (New York) to Frederick Gleason, Editor *Flag of Our Union* (Boston). Cited in Poe to Richmond, Feb. 8, 1849. Dodd Mead sale, March, 1897, item 76.   771

* [Feb.]   Poe (New York) to Mrs. A. L. Richmond
    Thursday 8   (Lowell). H XVII, 330–331. Ingram II, 205–207. W II, 417. Quinn, *Poe,* 594–595. Original fragment in Morgan Library.   772

* Feb. 14   Poe (Fordham) to F. W. Thomas (Washington ?). H XVII, 331–334. W II, 296–300. Original in Boston Public Library.   773

* Feb. 16   Poe (Fordham) to E. A. Duyckinck (New York). H XVII, 335. Original in New York Public Library.   774

Feb. 17   G. W. Eveleth (Brunswick, Maine) to Poe (New York). EP 190–191. Original in New York Public Library.   775

ante Feb. 18 (?)   Mrs. A. L. Richmond (Lowell) to Poe (New York). [Several?] Implied in Poe to Richmond, Feb. 18, 1849.   776

Feb. 18–19   Poe to Richmond. OCL 671 same as No. 777.
* Feb. 19 [18]   Poe (Fordham) to Mrs. A. L. Richmond (Lowell). H XVII, 335–338. Ingram II, 207–210. Quinn, *Poe,* 597–599. Copy in Alderman Library.   777

Feb. 29   Poe to Eveleth. Misdated in A II, 802. See No. 700.

Feb. 29   Poe to ——. Misdated and unidentified in H XVII, 338–341. See No. 700.

* March 1   Poe (New York) to Sarah Heywood (Westford, Mass.). Original in Lilly collection.   778

* March 8   Poe (Fordham) to E. A. Duyckinck (New York). H XVII, 341–342. W II, 301–302. Original in New York Public Library.   779

ante March 23 (?)   Mrs. A. L. Richmond (Lowell) to Poe (New York). Implied in Poe to Richmond, March 23, 1849.   780

* March 23	Poe (New York) to Mrs. A. L. Richmond (Lowell). H xvii, 342–344. Ingram ii, 210–212.	781
March 30	Poe to Shew. Misdated in H xvii, 344; A ii, 807. See No. 703.	
March	Poe to Griswold. Misdated in P ii, 1415; A ii, 807; OCL 674. See No. 796.	
March	Poe to Richmond. Misdated in A ii, 804–805. See No. 785.	
April 8	Poe to Patterson. See No. 786. A ii, 809–810 is a less satisfactory dating.	
* April 20	Poe (Fordham) to N. P. Willis (New York). H xvii, 351. Ingram ii, 212–213.	782
ca. April 26– May 21 (?)	Mrs. A. L. Richmond (Lowell) to Poe (New York). Implied in Poe to Richmond, April 28–May 23, 1849.	783
ante April 28– May 23	Mrs. J. E. Locke (Lowell) to Poe (New York). Cited in Poe to Richmond, April 28–May 23, 1849.	784
* [April 28–May 23]	Poe (New York) to Mrs. A. L. Richmond (Lowell). Ingram ii, 213–215. Quinn, *Poe,* 603–605.	785
* *ca.* April [30]	Poe (New York) to E. H. N. Patterson (Oquawka, Ill.). H xvii, 348–351. P ii, 1401–1403. SLP 11–13 (F).	786
April	Poe to Patterson. See No. 786. SLP 11–13; H xvii, 348–351; P ii, 1401–1403; Quinn, *Poe,* 612 are less satisfactory datings.	
May 7	Poe to Patterson. Misdated in A ii, 811, 815. See No. 794.	
May 7	E. H. N. Patterson (Oquawka, Ill.) to Poe (New York). H xvii, 352–355. SLP 15–21.	787
ante May 10 (?)	J. R. Thompson (Richmond) to Poe (New York). Implied in Poe to Thompson, May 10, 1849.	788
* May 10	Poe (New York) to J. R. Thompson (Richmond). P ii, 1403–1404. Original in Huntington Library (HM 21873).	789
ante May 17 (?)	Mrs. S. A. Lewis (New York) to Poe (New York). Implied in Poe to Lewis, May 17, 1849.	790
* May 17	Poe (Fordham) to Mrs. S. A. Lewis (New York). P ii, 1404. American Art Association sale, Feb. 28–March 1, 1935, item 344 (F). Original in Koester collection.	791

* May 18	Poe (Fordham) to G. P. Putnam (New York). Henkels sale, April 10, 1935, item 78. Original in Koester collection.	792
May 20	G. P. Putnam (New York) to Poe (New York). Cited on MS. of Poe to Putnam, May 18, 1849.	793
* May 23	Poe (New York) to E. H. N. Patterson (Oquawka, Ill.). H xvii, 356–357. SLP 21–23 (F).	794
May 27–June 7	Patterson to Poe. OCL 685 same as No. 797.	
ca. May 30– June 11	Poe (New York) to Mrs. A. L. Richmond (Lowell). Cited in Poe to Richmond, June 16, 1849.	795
* [May]	Poe (New York) to R. W. Griswold (New York). H xvii, 346–347. Quinn, *Poe,* 670. Original in Texas University Library.	796
May	Poe to Patterson. Incompletely dated in Quinn, *Poe,* 613. See No. 794.	
May	Poe to Richmond. See No. 785. W ii, 417 is a less satisfactory dating.	
ante June 7	E. H. N. Patterson (Oquawka, Ill.) to Poe (New York). Cited in Poe to Patterson, July 19, 1849.	797
June 7	Poe to Patterson. Wrongly identified in OCL 686. See No. 798.	
June 7	E. H. N. Patterson (Oquawka, Ill.) to Poe (New York). Cited in Poe to Patterson, July 19, 1849.	798
* June 9	Poe (Fordham) to J. R. Thompson (Richmond). Original in Morgan Library.	799
June 11	Poe to Thompson. Misdated in OCL 687. See No. 799.	
June 15 or earlier	Poe to Richmond. See No. 795. Ingram ii, 215; OCL 688 are less satisfactory datings.	
ante June 16	Poe (New York) to S. D. Patterson (Philadelphia). [As publisher of *Graham's Magazine.*] Cited in Poe to Richmond, June 16, 1849.	800
ante June 16	S. D. Patterson (Philadelphia) to Poe (New York). Cited in Poe to Richmond, June 16, 1849.	801
* June 16	Poe (Fordham) to Mrs. A. L. Richmond (Lowell). H xvii, 358–359. Quinn, *Poe,* 613–614. Original in Koester collection.	802
June 19	Poe to Shew. Misdated in Quinn, *Poe,* 609–611. See No. 716.	

June 21	Poe to Lewis. Misdated in Ingram II, 219; H XVII, 359–360; P II, 1411–1412. See No. 714.	
* June 26	Poe (New York) to G. W. Eveleth (Brunswick, Maine). PE 22–24. Ingram II, 217–219. H XVII, 360–362. Original in New York Public Library.	803
ante June 28	H. S. Root to Poe (New York). Cited in Poe to Root, June 28, 1849.	804
* June 28	Poe (New York) to R. W. Griswold (New York). H XVII, 362. Quinn, *Poe*, 612. Original in Boston Public Library.	805
* June 28	Poe (New York) to H. S. Root. Merwin-Clayton sale, May 13, 1912, item 965 A.	806
June 29	Poe to Griswold. Said to be Poe's request that Griswold edit Poe's works, in P II, 1408, 1557; A II, 812. Such a letter was probably never written.	
post June 30	Mrs. S. A. Lewis (New York) to Poe (Richmond). Cited in Poe to Lewis, Sept. 18, 1849.	807
June	Poe to Griswold. Misdated in W II, 417. See No. 796.	
June	Shew to Poe. OCL 695 same as No. 715.	
June–July	Griswold to Poe. Said to be Griswold's acceptance of editorship of Poe's works, in W II, 339; P II, 1409, 1484, 1559. Such a letter was probably never written.	
* July 7	Poe (New York [really Philadelphia]) to Mrs. Maria Clemm (New York). W II, 311–312. Quinn, *Poe*, 618.	808
* [July 7]	Poe (Philadelphia) to Mrs. S. A. Lewis (New York). Quinn, *Poe*, 633. Original in Koester collection.	809
* [July 14 Saturday] near Richmond	Poe (en route to Richmond) to Mrs. Maria Clemm (New York). W II, 313–314. Quinn, *Poe*, 619.	810
* [July 14] Richmond, Saturday night	Poe (Richmond) to Mrs. Maria Clemm (New York). W II, 314–315. Quinn, *Poe*, 620.	811
July 14–19	Mrs. Maria Clemm (Fordham ?) to Poe (Richmond). Cited in Poe to Clemm, July 19, 1849.	812
* July 19	Poe (Richmond) to Mrs. Maria Clemm (New York). W II, 315–317. A II, 820. Quinn, *Poe*, 620–621.	813

July 19	Poe (Richmond) to George Lippard (Philadelphia). Cited in Lippard to Griswold, Nov. 22, 1849 (MS. in Boston Public Library).	814
* July 19	Poe (Richmond) to E. H. N. Patterson (Oquawka, Ill.). H xvii, 363. SLP 24 (F).	815
July 23	Poe to Clemm. See No. 813. P ii, 1480 is a less satisfactory dating.	
Aug. 2–14 (?)	Poe (Richmond) to Mrs. Maria Clemm (New York). Inferred from Clemm to Mrs. Richmond, Aug. 4 and Sept. 3, 1849 (MSS. in Ingram collection, Alderman Library).	816
Aug. 4–14	Poe to Clemm. OCL 706 same as No. 816.	
* Aug. 7	Poe (Richmond) to E. H. N. Patterson (Oquawka, Ill.). H xvii, 363–364. SLP 24–26 (F).	817
Aug. 17 [?]	Poe (Richmond) to N. P. Willis (New York). Union Art Galleries sale, May 9, 1934 [?]	818
Aug. 21	E. H. N. Patterson (Oquawka, Ill.) to Poe (Richmond). H xvii, 365–366. SLP 26–28.	819
ante Aug. 28	T. H. Chivers (Washington, Ga.) to Poe (Richmond). Cited in Poe to Clemm, Aug. 28–29, 1849.	820
* [*ca.* Aug. 28–29]	Poe (Richmond) to Mrs. Maria Clemm (New York). H xvii, 368–370. Quinn, *Poe*, 625–626. Original in Boston Public Library.	821
Sept. 3	Chivers to Poe. OCL 710 same as No. 820.	
Sept. 5	Poe to Clemm. See No. 821. W ii, 326–329; Quinn, *Poe*, 571 n., 625–626 are less satisfactory datings.	
* [Sept. 10] Monday evening	Poe (Norfolk) to Susan V. C. Ingram (Norfolk). W ii, 331. Quinn, *Poe*, 534. Original in Morgan Library.	822
ca. Sept. 12–13	Poe (Norfolk) to Mrs. Maria Clemm (New York). Cited in Clemm to Mrs. Richmond, Sept. 15, 1849 (MS. in Ingram collection, Alderman Library).	823
Sept. 16	Clemm to Poe. OCL 714 same as No. 824.	
ante Sept. 18	Mrs. Maria Clemm (Fordham) to Poe (Richmond). [2 letters.] Cited in Poe to Clemm, Sept. 18, 1849.	824

ante Sept. 18	Mrs. S. A. Lewis (New York) to Poe (Richmond). Cited in Poe to Clemm, Sept. 18, 1849.	825
Sept. 18 or earlier	Poe to Clemm. OCL 716 same as No. 826.	
* Sept. 18	Poe (Richmond) to Mrs. Maria Clemm (New York). H XVII, 366–367. W II, 333–335. Quinn, *Poe*, 632–633. Pratt 24–25 (F). Original (part in Poe's hand) in Pratt Library.	826
Sept. 18 or earlier	Poe to Lewis. OCL 717 same as No. 827.	
* [Sept. 18]	Poe (Richmond) to Mrs. S. A. Lewis (New York). Quinn, *Poe*, 633. Original in Koester collection.	827
September	Poe to Clemm. See No. 821. H XVII, 368–370; P II, 1462–1464; OCL 711 are less satisfactory datings.	
September	Poe to Anna [Lewis]. See No. 809. Quinn, *Poe*, 633 is a less satisfactory dating.	
ante Oct. 7	G. W. Eveleth (Phillips, Maine) to Poe (Richmond). Cited in Clemm to Eveleth, May 20, 1850 (see Eveleth's transcripts in Ingram collection, Alderman Library).	828

1849

early	Poe to Griswold. OCL 719 same as No. 805.	
n. d.	Poe to Griswold. Incompletely dated in H XVII, 346–347. See No. 796.	
n. d.	Poe to Richmond. Incompletely dated in Ingram II, 213–215; P II, 1399–1400; Quinn, *Poe*, 603–605. See No. 785.	
n. d.	Poe to Mrs. A. L. Richmond. [Said to be Poe's last letter to Mrs. Richmond; but see No. 731.] Swann Galleries sale, Jan. 20, 1944.	
n. d.	Lewis to Poe. OCL 715 same as No. 825.	

LETTERS WITH NO DATE

——	Mrs. S. A. Lewis (New York ?) to Poe (New York ?). [Concerning *Politian*.] Anderson Galleries sale, March 19, 1917, cited.	829
——	Poe to ——. Bangs sale, Nov. 23, 1894, item 219.	830
Friday morning — 27	Lynch to Poe. Incompletely dated in ABC II (Dec. 1932) 339. See No. 547.	
Thursday morning	Mowatt to Poe. Misdated in ABC II (Dec. 1932) 339. See No. 531.	

Poe to Carter. OCL 720 same as No. 415.

Poe to Duyckinck. OCL 721 same as No. 567.

Poe to Graham. OCL 722 same as No. 512.

Poe to Griswold. OCL 723 same as No. 282. Undated in ABC II (Dec. 1932) 341.

Poe to Irving. OCL 724 same as No. 293.

Poe to Lewis. OCL 725 same as No. 761.

Poe to Mitchell. OCL 726 same as No. 231.

Poe to Osgood. OCL 727 same as No. 580. Undated in ABC II (Dec. 1932) 341.

Poe to Stoddard. Undated in ABC III (Apr. 1933) 246. See No. 257.

Poe to Thompson. OCL 728 same as No. 789.

Poe to ——. OCL 729 same as No. 830.

Poe to ——. Reference in P II, 1378–1379 without foundation.

Gillespie to Poe. Undated in ABC II (Dec. 1932) 339. See No. 526.

Lewis to Poe. OCL 731 same as No. 760.

Lewis to Poe. OCL 732 same as No. 829.

Longfellow to Poe. OCL 733 dropped.

Mitchell to Poe. OCL 734 same as No. 230.

Willis to Poe. Undated in ABC II (Dec. 1932) 340. See No. 602.

Willis to Poe. Undated in ABC II (Dec. 1932) 339. See No. 661.

INDEX TO CHECK LIST

(References are to numbers in the Check List)

INDEX OF CORRESPONDENTS

NOTE TO THE INDEX

[SEE ALSO INDEX OF CORRESPONDENTS]

The only topic indexed under Poe himself is "self-characterization," all other topics, such as Poe's health, have been indexed under "Health," etc. Works by Poe are indexed only under title; works of other authors are indexed under both author and title; titles of works are followed by identification of the author in parentheses. Tentative identification of people not definitely identified is supplied, with a question mark, in square brackets. When a subject is mentioned in text and footnotes on the same page, the footnote has not been separately indexed. No place names have been indexed, since the chronology in volume one shows where Poe was at any given time. Bibliographical matter has not been indexed.

CUE TITLES

BJ	Broadway Journal	P	Edgar Allan Poe
JA	John Allan	SLM	Southern Literary Messenger
MC	Maria Clemm	VP	Virginia Poe

INDEX TO THE LETTERS

313, 319, 329; *Crock of Gold,* 316; *Proverbial Philosophy,* 316

"Turkey-Hunter" (P. P. Cooke), 313

Two Lives (M. J. McIntosh), 375, 376n

Tyler, John: and P's government job, 170, 171, 172, 227; mentioned, 98, 215, 218, 219

Tyler, Robert: and *Penn,* 192, 193; and *Stylus,* 224, 227, 228n; and P's government appointment, 197, 198n, 199, 204, 210, 218, 219, 220, 262; "promising poem," 212; mentioned, 228; *Ahasuerus,* 192

Tyson, General J. W., 210

"Ulalume" (P): published, 353–54; and Willis, 436, 437n; mentioned, 357n, 408, 409n, 429, 433, 460

Union Magazine of Literature and Art (Post's), 365, 371, 437, 438n

United States Gazette (Philadelphia), 116, 125

United States Government: and General Poe's back pay, 92, 93; P tries for position in, 170–71, 172, 173n, 197, 198n, 199, 204, 210, 211, 212, 214–15, 216, 217, 262; hopes dashed, 218–19, 225; in Washington about, 227, 229

United States Magazine and Democratic Review: pay, 314; stops paying P, 437, 438n; mentioned, 211, 415, 416n

"Un no rompido" (Ponce de León), 18

"Unseen Spirits" (N. P. Willis), 246

Ups and Downs in the Life of a Distressed Gentleman (W. L. Stone), 101, 103n

Upshur, Judge Abel Parker: and *Stylus,* 224–25, 227, 228n; mentioned, 184, 185n

"Valdemar Case," *see* "Facts in the Case of M. Valdemar"

Valentine, Anne Moore, 5, 7, 17, 21, 30, 34, 37, 38, 39n

"Valley of Unrest" (P), 332

Vermont, University of, 316, 317n, 321

Verplanck, [Gulian C.?], 313, 316, 317n

Versification, 78, 86, 87

Vestiges of Creation (R. Chambers), 362–63, 364

Victorine, 129

Views Afoot (B. Taylor), 371

Virginia Star, 129

Virginia, University of: "disturbances" at, 4–5, 6; P's career at, 5n; building of, 6; "infamous conduct" at, 14; P's reasons for leaving, 39–41; mentioned, 17n, 42n, 359, 440, 441n

"Vision of Rubeta, The" (L. Osborn), 293–94, 295n

Voices of the Night (H. W. Longfellow), 159n

Voltaire, 379

"Voluminous History of the Little Longfellow War" (P), 284n

"Von Kempelen and His Discovery" (P), 433, 434n

Waif (H. W. Longfellow), 334

Wakondah (C. Mathews), 245n

Wallace, William Ross, 210

Walsh, Robert, 18, 19n, 20, 21n

Wandering Jew, The (E. Sue?), 305

Ward, Thomas, *see* Flaccus

Warwick, Corbin, 16, 17n

Washington, George: and General Poe, 92, 93n

Washington, The Life of George (J. Marshall), 61, 62n, 65–66

Webb, Colonel, 358

Weekly Messenger, Alexander's: and "House of Usher," 116; and P's cipher interest, 173n; mentioned, 117n, 125, 129n

Weekly Mirror, see New York Mirror

Weekly Universe, 360, 362n

Welby, Mrs. Amelia B. Coppuck, 211

Weld, Rev. Horatio Hastings, "Corrected Proofs," 179

West Point: P trying for cadet's appointment, 13–15, 25, 28, 29; recommended for, 16n, 17n, 21–22; expenses, 29–30; P at, 37–42; dismissal, 42n, 43, 44n; mentioned, 23n, 24n, 31, 33, 34n, 68, 69n, 105, 106n, 172, 359, 440, 441n

Western Quarterly Review, 458, 460n

Wetherald, Esther, 194

Wetmore, Prosper M., 316, 317n

Whelpley, James D., 417

Whig Review, see American Review